THE WOODWORKERS GUIDE
TO MAKING AND USING

JIGS, FIXTURES AND SETUPS

THE WOODWORKERS GUIDE TO MAKING AND USING

JIGS, FIXTURES AND SETUPS

HOW TO GET THE MOST FROM EVERY TOOL IN YOUR SHOP

David Schiff and Kenneth S. Burton, Jr.
Illustrations by Frank W. Rohrbach
Photography by Mitch Mandel

Rodale Press, Emmaus, Pennsylvania

Our Mission

We publish books that empower people's lives.

RODALE BOOKS

The authors and editors who compiled this book have tried to make all the contents as accurate and correct as possible. Plans, illustrations, photographs, and text have all been carefully checked and cross-checked. However, due to the variability of local conditions, construction materials, personal skills, and so on, Rodale Press does not assume any responsibility for any injuries suffered, or for damages or losses incurred, that result from the material presented herein. All instructions and plans should be carefully studied and clearly understood before beginning construction.

In many of the photographs in this book, safety guards have been removed from machines so that procedures may be seen more clearly. Readers are urged to use the safety guards that come with their machines wherever possible.

**Library of Congress
Cataloging-in-Publication Data**
Schiff, David.
    The woodworkers guide to making and using jigs, fixtures and setups : how to get the most from every tool in your shop / David Schiff and Kenneth S. Burton, Jr. ; illustrations by Frank W. Rohrbach ; photography by Mitch Mandel.
        p.   cm.
    Includes index.
    ISBN 0-87596-137-1   hardcover
    1. Woodworking tools.   2. Woodwork—Equipment and supplies—Design and construction.   I. Burton, Kenneth S.   II. Title.
TT186.S34   1992
684'.08'028—dc20   92-24185
                                CIP

Distributed in the book trade by St. Martin's Press

2 4 6 8 10 9 7 5 3 1   hardcover

Executive Editor: Margaret Lydic Balitas

Senior Editor: Jeff Day

Copy Editor: Susan G. Berg

Indexer: Richard Ruane

Editorial Assistance: Susan Nickol

Office Manager: Karen Earl-Braymer

Book Designer: Stan Green

Book Layout: Frank Milloni

**Photography and
    Illustration Direction:** Jerry O'Brien

Illustrator: Frank W. Rohrbach

Photographer: Mitch Mandel

If you have any questions or comments concerning this book, please write:
    Rodale Press
    Book Readers' Service
    33 East Minor Street
    Emmaus, PA 18098

■

To my father, Norman Schiff, an engineer
who would have appreciated the creative problem solving
described in these pages.

To my father, Kenneth S. Burton, Sr.,
who gave his 6-year-old son a set of real tools.

■

CONTENTS

THE MACHINES

Table Saw

Extra Hands

Assembly

Featherboard

Plywood Handling

Push Sticks

Roller Stand

Work Support

ACKNOWLEDGMENTS

We asked 14 of America's best woodworkers to contribute their favorite jig and fixture designs for this book. They responded with an avalanche of ideas and sketches. When we asked, they opened their shop doors and enthusiastically showed us how their jigs were made and how they are used. We knew gathering the information for this book would be an education. We never suspected it would be so much fun. Gentlemen, thank you. It was a pleasure working with you all.

In addition to the contributors who are listed below, we want to thank our editor, Jeff Day, who kept the book focused, concise, and accurate. Thank you to book designer Stan Green, who created a book that is attractive and easy to use. And thank you to photographer Mitch Mandel, who took the hundreds of photos in this book. Mitch is also a woodworker and contributed a few jigs of his own.

The Contributors

Glenn Bostock, designer and maker of cabinets and millwork, Rushland, Pennsylvania

Andrew Bukovsky, cabinetmaker, Barto, Pennsylvania

Ernie Conover, Conover Woodcraft Specialties, Parkman, Ohio

Michael Dunbar, author and Windsor chairmaker, Portsmouth, New Hampshire

Ben Erickson, Erickson Woodworks, Eutaw, Alabama

Nils Falk, Riverwood Studios, Frenchtown, New Jersey

Phil Gehret, prototyper, Rodale Design Center, Emmaus, Pennsylvania

Greg Glebe, Xylem Design, Phoenix, Arizona

Douglas Goodale, master carpenter, Frenchtown, New Jersey

Frederic L. Hanisch, woodworker, Quakertown, Pennsylvania

Fred Matlack, manager, Rodale Design Center, Emmaus, Pennsylvania

Andy Rae, woodworker, Princeton, New Jersey

Tim Steen, cabinetmaker, Doylestown, Pennsylvania

Jim Tolpin, INTERWOOD, Carlotta, California

HOW TO USE THIS BOOK

The *Woodworkers Guide to Making and Using Jigs, Fixtures and Setups* is designed to answer a key question that arises with every woodworking task you'll ever undertake: "How do I get the job done with the tools I have in my shop?"

The book is divided into four parts. The first part is called "Setups." This is the first place to look for the answer to your question. "Setups" describes all the major jobs that stationary woodworking machines can accomplish without jigs or fixtures—for example, cutting miters on the table saw or a decorative edge with a router.

"Setups" is worth a read even if you don't have a specific task in mind. It's a very useful overview of what your tools can do.

Before going further, we should note that the difference between a jig and a fixture is purely technical and has nothing to do with the organization of this book: A jig is secured to the workpiece and moves through the machine with it. A fixture is attached to the machine.

Some tasks can be accomplished on the machine alone but are easier if you take the time to make a jig or a fixture. For example, the "Table Saw" chapter in "Setups" will tell you how to cut tenons without a jig. But it also will refer you to the "Table Saw Tenoning Jig" in the second part of this book. If you have a few tenons to cut, you may not want to bother with the jig. If you cut a lot of tenons, you'll find that making the jig is well worth your time.

The second part of this book is called "The Tasks." Here you will find jigs and fixtures organized by the tasks they are designed to perform. Each of these tasks is listed in the Table of Contents.

One of the things that makes woodworking so interesting is that there usually are several ways to accomplish the same task. For example, if you look under "Panel Raising" in the Table of Contents, you'll find a jig and two fixtures listed: one for the jointer, one for the router, and one for the table saw. If you have a table saw but no router or jointer, it's obvious which method you'll choose. If, however, you are lucky enough to own two or three of these tools, you'll ask another question: "What's the *best* way to get the job done with the tools I have in my shop?" The answer to that question lies in the introductory text to each jig or fixture in this book. You'll discover that the router jig is easiest to build but requires a router table, the table saw jig can do the job quickest but leaves cuts that require more sanding, and the jointer fixture takes the most time to build but provides the cleanest results.

There are some jigs and fixtures you'll build without a specific task in mind—for example, a router table or an extension table for your drill press. You'll find these listed by machine in the Table of Contents. This third part of the book is called "The Machines."

The fourth part of the book is called "Extra Hands." These shop-built items aren't jigs, fixtures, or setups. But they are so important to safe and efficient work that we couldn't leave them out. Here you will find push sticks, a roller stand, shop horses, and other items designed to lend an extra hand when you need it and to protect the two hands with which you were born.

In making the jigs and fixtures in this book, keep in mind that jig making can be a very creative and spontaneous process. Most of the items in this book came into being because a woodworker faced a challenge and found a way to meet it. The way he chose to meet the challenge was affected by his own style and experience.

In this book, you'll find detailed instructions for making and using every jig and fixture. If the jig suits your needs exactly, follow the instructions exactly. However, after reading the instructions, you may say to yourself, "This jig would work better for me if I . . ." If that happens, great! Our book sparked an idea and you are about to design a jig that does precisely what *you* want it to do.

SETUPS

■ **BAND SAW** ■
DRILL PRESS
JOINTER
PLANER
RADIAL ARM SAW
ROUTER
■ **TABLE SAW** ■

BAND SAW

The band saw is not the most precise cutting tool, but it can make cuts other power saws can't. It can follow curves and resaw thick stock. It can even slice veneer from the face of a board. And although it is not as accurate as a table saw, it can cut to within 1/32 inch if set up properly.

SAWING

Match the blade on the saw to the type of cut you are making. If you cut a lot of curves, choose a narrow blade. If you are making straight cuts, use a wider blade. The extra width helps keep the cut going straight.

Before cutting, set the upper blade guard to within 1/4 inch of the workpiece. This keeps as much blade covered as possible and keeps the blade support close to the cut, where it will do the most good.

Keep your hands to either side of the cut. Never put them in a position where, should you slip, they would go into the blade. If you must make a cut that would bring your fingers close to the blade, push the workpiece with a piece of scrap wood as shown in Photo 1.

Make sure your workpiece is flat on the table or has some support. While a band saw won't kick wood back at you, it will slam unsupported work down on the table. This is especially true for round stock like dowels. Cut dowels with a V-block as shown in Photo 2. You can easily make a V-block on the table saw by tilting the blade over to a 45-degree angle.

Avoid backing the blade out of a cut. You can catch the back of the blade on the work and pull it off the wheels. If you must back out of a cut, watch the blade closely to be sure you're not pulling it forward. If you have a choice between backing out of a short cut or a long one, choose the short one.

Curved Cuts

The band saw really shines when it comes to cutting curves. Draw the curve on your stock and guide it through the saw. If the curve is very tight, make a series of relief cuts as shown in Photo 3. These cuts let the waste wood fall away from the cut, providing more room for the blade.

Sometimes you need to cut curves in a piece from two adjacent sides, such as when cutting out a cabriole leg. Lay out the cuts, then saw the first side as shown in Photo 4. Save the cutoffs as they fall away. When the

Photo 1   If you must make a cut that would bring your fingers close to the band saw blade, push the workpiece with a scrap of wood.

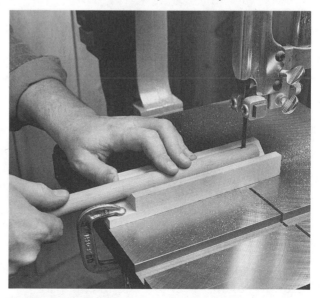

Photo 2   Use a V-block to support round stock such as dowels.

1

Photo 3 Make a series of relief cuts if you have to cut tight curves on the band saw.

Photo 4 To cut cabriole legs, lay out the cuts, then saw the first side. Save the cutoffs.

Photo 5 Tape the cabriole cutoffs back in place. Then cut the second side.

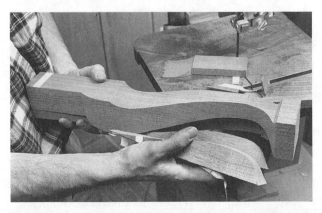

Photo 6 Peel away the tape and scrap, and you'll have the completed piece.

first side is cut out, tape the scraps back in place. Then cut the second side as shown in P*hoto* 5. Peel away all the tape and scrap, and you'll have the completed piece as shown in P*hoto* 6.

Straight Cuts

A band saw will make straight cuts, although not as accurately as a table saw. Lay out the cuts and guide the work through the saw. You'll notice with most saws that the cut will not be parallel to the sides of the table. It will go off at a slight angle to one side or the other. Rather than trying to force the saw to cut the way you think it should, follow the lead (as this slight angle is called). You'll get much straighter cuts this way.

You'll notice the blade leads the most when you try to saw pieces using a fence as a guide. Most band saws have a rip fence that can be attached to the table. If the blade leads the work away from the fence while you're trying to hold the work against it, your cut will not be accurate. You are better off carefully sawing freehand. Lead can also affect a crosscut made with a miter gauge. Generally speaking, however, if the cut is not very long, the results will be acceptable.

DRILL PRESS

While most of the machines in a wood shop are designed primarily to cut wood, the drill press is an exception. It performs admirably in a variety of materials, including metal. The ability to accurately drill metal can really expand the capabilities of your shop. In fact, you'll need to drill metal to build several of the jigs and fixtures in this book.

A drill press's main job is to bore holes. It can do this very precisely if set up correctly. This includes setting the spindle speed to match the material being drilled, choosing the right bit for the job, laying out the cut, and holding the work properly.

DRILLING WOOD

The drill press is one of the few stationary woodworking machines with variable speed control. Different materials require different cutting speeds. In general, the larger the bit and/or the harder the material, the slower the speed should be.

The speed you choose is less crucial for drilling wood than it is for drilling metal. Dense, light-colored woods such as cherry and maple burn easily and so require slower drilling speeds than oak or walnut. Softwood can be drilled at higher speeds. Forstner bits require slower speeds than twist bits. When in doubt, start with a slower speed.

Selecting a Drill Bit

Twist drills and brad point drills are the two most common types of bits in the shop. With one or the other you can handle most drilling tasks. Of the two types, the twist drill is the more common. It is what you will get if you ask a hardware store clerk for a drill bit.

While it is the most prevalent, and it will drill wood, the twist drill is not the best choice for woodworking. Twist drills are made for drilling metal. Brad point drills work much better in wood, for two reasons:

They have a center point that aligns the bit on the work, and they are ground so that the rim of the bit cuts the outline of the hole first. This produces a very clean hole with a minimum of tearout.

Laying Out

Lay out the holes that need to be drilled as shown on your plans. Most drawings, including those in this book, will give this location by dimensioning to the center of the hole. Mark the positions on your stock with a square and a sharp pencil. Start each hole with an awl to make it easier to align the piece on the drill press.

Holding the Work

Most often, you'll be drilling with the table of the drill press perpendicular to the spindle. The work will sit on the table or on the "Drill Press Auxiliary Table" described on page 227. You also can support the work on a piece of scrap. The auxiliary table or scrap will protect the drill press table and the bit in case you inadvertently drill too far. It will also help prevent tearout on the underside of the workpiece if you are making holes all the way through the stock.

The table on most drill presses tilts from side to side. There is usually a stop in the middle to lock the table perpendicular to the spindle. Check to be sure that the stop is accurate and that the table really is perpendicular. Do this with a piece of bent wire and a feeler gauge.

Bend the wire and mount it in the drill chuck as shown in *Photo* 7. Use a piece of wire that is stiff enough to retain its shape if it is inadvertently bumped. Coat hanger wire is a good choice. Lock the table in its horizontal position. Turn the spindle until the wire points to the right. Raise the table until it almost touches the wire. Lock the table at this height. Check the gap between the table and the wire with the feeler gauge as shown in *Photo* 7. Slowly rotate the spindle until the wire points to the left. Again check the gap with the feeler gauge. It should match the first measurement. If it doesn't, check your

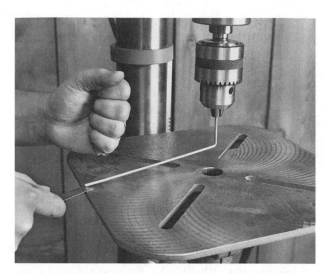

Photo 7 Use a feeler gauge to check the gap between the wire and the table at one side. Then turn the chuck to check that the other side of the table is in the same plane.

owner's manual for instructions on adjusting the table.

To tilt the table to a specific angle, mount a drill bit in the chuck. Set a sliding T-bevel to the necessary angle. As you tilt the table, check the angle with the bevel gauge as shown in P*hoto* 8.

For most holes in wood, you can hold

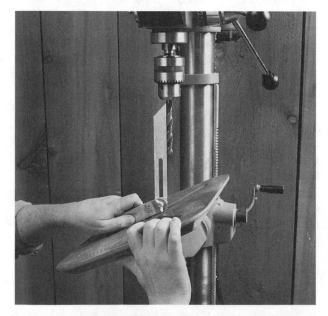

Photo 8 Set the sliding T-bevel to the angle you want to drill. Then use the gauge to set the angle of the drill press table.

the workpiece with your hand while drilling. Keep a firm grip on the piece and align it with the bit. Sometimes, however, you may want to clamp the workpiece down. You may be looking for extra precision, or you may be drilling a large hole in a small piece. Clamp the workpiece directly to the drill press table or hold it in a vise. You can even clamp small pieces in a hand screw and then hold on to that.

Making the Hole

Choose a drill bit whose diameter matches the hole you want. Mount it in the drill chuck. Tighten the chuck with the chuck key. If you are drilling to a specific depth, set the depth stop as described in your owner's manual.

Line up the drill bit with the center of the hole. Turn on the drill press. Make the cut by feeding the spinning bit into the work. If you are drilling a deep hole, drill a little, then back the bit out of the hole to clear the chips. Drill a little more and back out. Repeat until the hole is done. This prevents the chips from jamming in the bit. If they do, they will heat up and burn the bit, ruining it. The heat can also split your wood.

If you have a lot of similarly placed holes to drill, it may be worth building a jig to help locate them. One such jig is the "Drill Press Positioning Guide" detailed on page 234.

DRILLING METAL

Metal is harder than wood and so requires some extra considerations.

If you have to drill a large hole in metal, start the hole with a small-diameter bit. Next drill with an intermediate-diameter bit, then with the final-diameter bit. This lessens the stress on the large-diameter bit.

Selecting a Drilling Speed

Selecting the proper drilling speed is much more crucial for metal than for wood. Turning a small drill too slowly can easily break it, while turning a large drill too fast can overheat and ruin it. There are a number of books that have charts listing the speeds for different-size bits in different metals. One such book is the *Machinist's Practical Guide*, put out by the Morse Cutting Tools Division of Gulf and Western Manufacturing Co., P.O. Box F923, New Bedford, MA 02742.

If you do not have access to a chart, here is a formula for calculating the spindle speeds for different metals:

$$\frac{4 \times \text{desired cutting speed}}{\text{bit size numerator}} \times \text{bit size denominator} = \begin{array}{l}\text{rotations}\\\text{per minute}\\\text{(speed)}\end{array}$$

The cutting speed changes for different materials, depending on their hardness and composition. The cutting speeds (in rotations per minute, or RPM) for the metals a wood-worker is likely to use are:

cast iron	50
tool steel (annealed)	50
bronze	80
mild steel	100
aluminum	200
brass	200

For example: To drill a ¼-inch-diameter hole in a piece of mild steel, the spindle speed should be about 1600 RPM:

$$\frac{4 \times 100}{1} \times 4 = 1600$$

Set your drill press as close to this speed as possible without exceeding it.

Layout

Laying out holes in metal isn't quite as simple as it is in wood. Pencil lines don't show up on the hard surface. You can scratch the layout marks right into the metal's surface with an awl or a scriber. This can come back to haunt you, however, if you want to polish the surface later. Another way to make layouts on metal is with blue machinist's dye. Paint the dye on the surface you want to mark. When it dries, you can scribe your layout marks right on the surface without scratching the metal. The dye scratches away, leaving a bright line as shown in *Photo 9*.

Once you lay out the centers of the holes, you must dimple them, so that the drill bit has a place to start. To make the dimple, hold the punch on the center layout and strike it with a ball-peen hammer.

Photo 9   Paint machinist's dye on metal, so that your layout marks are easy to see.

Holding the Work

When drilling metal on a drill press, you must clamp it down. Metal catches very easily on drill bits and can instantly become a whirling finger slicer if it is not held securely. Small pieces can be held in a vise as shown in *Photo 10*. Larger pieces can be clamped directly to the table. If you are drilling a hole all the way through a piece, be sure to position the table so that the bit is over the hole in the center, so that you don't drill through the table.

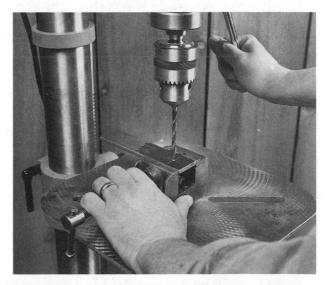

Photo 10   You must clamp metal when drilling it on the drill press. Small pieces can be held in a vise.

Tapping and Threading Metal

Threaded parts, such as nuts and bolts, make assembling things easy. Hardware stores have aisles devoted to nothing but threaded fasteners. But occasionally you'll need a threaded part that isn't available commercially. Or the threads in a hole will become stripped and you'll want to recut them. A tap and die set is the answer to these problems.

Taps and dies cut threads. Taps cut threads inside holes, and dies cut threads on the outside of rods. Together they make a formidable combination.

Tapping

To tap a hole, you must know what size bolt is going to go into the hole. If you have the bolt, the answer is right in your hand. Measure the diameter of the bolt and count the number of threads it has per inch. Then find a tap that matches this. If you are unsure about what size the bolt is, take it to a hardware store and search through their collection of nuts until you find one that fits. Nuts and bolts are specified by their diameters and threads per inch. For example, a bolt that has a diameter of ¼ inch and 20 threads per inch is specified as a ¼"-20 bolt. Note what size nut fits on your bolt. Then check another one, just to be sure some knucklehead didn't put the first one in the wrong container.

If you don't have a bolt to fit, you are free to decide what size threads to cut. Look at your available taps and the size of the piece you're tapping, then go from there. In general, larger-diameter bolts are stronger.

Lay out the location of the hole and center-punch it. Before drilling, look at the tap. It probably has the size of the tap drill stamped into its shank. A tap drill makes a hole somewhat smaller in diameter than the tap. This leaves some stock in which to cut the threads. (Instead of stamps, some tap and die sets come with a chart that will tell you the drill bit size to use.)

Most tap drills are usually number or letter drills. These bits drill holes sized in between the sizes the fractional drills make. You can either purchase the appropriate-size bit or consult a decimal equivalency chart. Often the number or letter drill specified will be very close in diameter to a fractional drill. A few thousandths one way or the other will not make much difference. Drill the hole on the drill press for greatest accuracy.

Clamp the piece to be tapped in a vise and mount the tap in a tap wrench. Put plenty of oil on the tap to lubricate it and to float away the cut metal. Regular motor oil works, or you can purchase a special tapping fluid. (Be careful, however: Some tapping fluids eat aluminum. Read the label carefully before you use the product.)

If you look closely at the tap, you'll see that the tap is slightly tapered and the first few threads are not fully formed. This is to help you start the tap straight. As the tap begins to cut, it makes partial thread forms. Then, as it advances into the hole, the full threads begin to cut, completing the thread forms.

As you turn the tap, apply downward pressure. Be sure to hold it straight up and down—if it veers to one side or the other, the threads will be crooked.

Once the tap is started, advance it about one-half turn, then turn it back

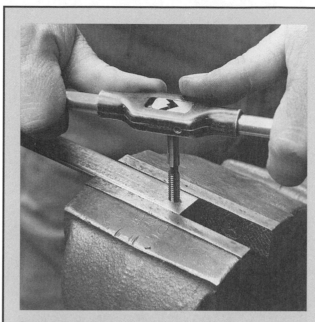

Apply downward pressure as you turn the tap. Be sure to hold the tap perpendicular to the workpiece.

Cut the external thread with a die. The die is mounted in a two-handled wrench called a diestock.

about one-quarter turn. Continue this sequence until the threads are complete. By advancing the tap and then backing it off, you clear the metal chips from the cut. If you don't do this, the threads you are cutting will be poorly formed. Worse yet, you break the tap, which is made from very brittle metal. Never force a cut. If a tap seems to jam, back it off a little, then resume the cut. If it is still jammed, back it all the way out of the hole. Clean off any chips, then resume cutting.

When tapping blind holes, periodically back the tap all the way out and shake the chips from inside the hole. Because of the partial threads at the beginning of the tap, the bottom threads of a blind hole will not be fully formed. Correct this with a bottoming tap, which has threads over its full length. Turn the tap into the threads you've cut with the regular tap. Always thread a blind hole with a regular tap, followed by a bottoming tap. A bottoming tap is too hard to control when threading the entire length of the hole.

Cutting External Threads

To cut external threads on a piece of rod, you'll need a die. Match the diameter of the rod you want to thread to the diameter of the hole or nut it must fit. If you need to match a specific thread, find a bolt that has that thread and measure it. Then get a die to match. Chamfer the end of the rod lightly with a grinder or file before cutting the threads.

Mount the die in a diestock, a two-handled wrench designed to hold dies. One side of the die has one or two partial threads to aid starting the die. Start threading from that side—it's usually labeled. Hold the rod upright in a vise. Hold the die on the rod. Turn the diestock clockwise. Keep a downward pressure on it until the die bites into the rod. Once the die starts cutting threads, back up the die about one-half turn for every one or two forward turns. This helps to clear the chips from the cut. Use plenty of oil to keep the die lubricated.

JOINTER

The jointer performs two key operations. It flattens and straightens boards—something the planer won't do. Unless you flatten your boards on the jointer before you run them through the planer, you're liable to be working with warped wood.

As an added bonus, some jointers can also cut rabbets. This is a nice feature but not a necessity. Rabbets are easy enough to cut with other tools.

SURFACING ON THE JOINTER

The first step in surfacing a board is to flatten one face. Cut the board roughly to length, but not less than 12 inches long. If you need shorter pieces, cut them to length after you surface them. Measure the board's width to see if your jointer is wide enough to flatten it in one pass. If not, cut the board down the middle lengthwise with a band saw. (Don't use the table saw with rough stock. Because rough stock isn't flat, it may kick back.)

Examine the board closely. Note any bow or cup. (See *Lumber Defects*.) Place the board on the infeed table with the concave side of the bow or cup down. Set the depth of cut to 1/16 inch. On most jointers, this adjustment is made with a hand wheel or lever under the infeed table. Move the fence to expose as little of the cutter head as possible. Turn on the jointer and feed the board across the machine. Use a push stick as shown in *Photo 11*. See "Jointer Push Stick," page 301, for plans.

If the board has a tendency to rock on the table, keep it balanced on the same

Photo 11 Always use a jointer push stick when surfacing the face of a board.

points as you run it across the machine. If you shift the balance points, you may never get the board flat, and you may even increase the warp.

If you are surfacing a rough-sawn board, keep passing the board across the machine until all the saw marks are gone. If you are flattening a board that has already been planed, it is harder to tell when to stop jointing. In this case, scribble all over the face you are jointing. Then joint until all the pencil lines are gone.

STRAIGHTENING AN EDGE

Once you have flattened one face of a board, you can square one edge to that face. Check to be sure the jointer's fence is square to the table. Sight down the edges of the board. Note any crook in the board's edge.

LUMBER DEFECTS

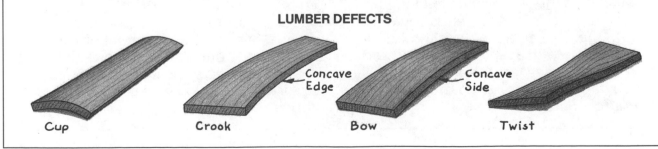

Cup   Crook   Bow   Twist

Concave Edge

Concave Side

Photo 12 To joint the edge of a board, place the board on the infeed table with the jointed face against the fence. Hold the board against the fence as you feed it across the machine.

(See *Lumber Defects.*) Place the board on the infeed table with the jointed face against the fence and the concave edge down. Hold the board against the fence and feed it across the machine as shown in P*hoto* 12. As the board moves over the jointer, reposition your hands so that you don't pass them over the cutters. Make more passes until the jointer knives have cut the full length and width of the board.

You could use the jointer to flatten and straighten the second face and edge, but these surfaces would not necessarily be parallel to the original face and edge. That's where the thickness planer comes in. Once you have jointed one face and one edge, pass the board through the thickness planer to make the other face flat and parallel to the jointed face. Then rip the board to width by running the jointed edge against the table saw rip fence. You can cut a cleaner edge with the jointer, so rip the board 1/16 inch wider than final width. Make one pass over the jointer to achieve final width.

MAKING RABBETS, TONGUES, AND TENONS

On jointers that can cut rabbets, the infeed table has an extension that wraps around the cutter head. As the infeed table is lowered, this extension drops down to expose one side of the knives. If you run a board across the machine with part of it riding on the extension, you'll cut a rabbet.

You can cut rabbets with the face of the board flat on the infeed extension as shown in P*hoto* 13 or with the board on edge as shown in P*hoto* 14. In general, it is easier to run narrow stock with its face on the extension. Once the board gets more than a

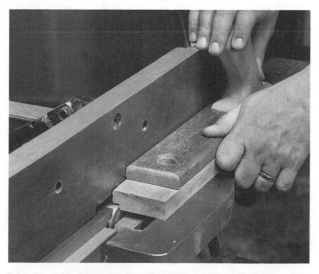

Photo 13 It is easier to rabbet narrow stock with its face on the infeed table extension.

Photo 14 Rabbet thicker stock by running the edge on the infeed table extension.

couple of inches wider than the infeed extension, it becomes easier to run the board on edge.

When running the board on its face, the jointer fence setting determines the rabbet width. The infeed table setting determines the rabbet depth. The opposite is true when you run the board on edge.

Lower the infeed table to about one-half the depth or width you need. Slide the fence close to the front edge of the jointer. Measure from the end of one jointer knife to the fence to set the rabbet's other dimension. Double-check this measurement against the other jointer knives. If one knife is shifted farther to the outside than the others, use that knife to make the setting. Lock the fence in place.

Run the stock across the machine. If you are rabbeting the face, use a push stick to keep your hands from harm as shown in *Photo 13*. Reset the depth of cut for the full depth or width of the rabbet. Run the stock again to complete the cut.

The rabbeting ledge is a great method of making tongues if you are milling tongue-and-groove stock. To do this, rabbet one edge

Photo 15 To make tongues on the jointer rabbeting ledge, rabbet one side, then turn the board over to rabbet the other side.

of the board, then flip the board over and rabbet the other side of the same edge as shown in *Photo 15*.

PLANER

The first thing to know about thickness planers is that they do *not* make boards flat. If you feed a warped board through a planer, it will come out thinner but still warped. What a thickness planer will do is make one side of a board parallel to another. So if a board is flat on one side, a planer will make the other side flat. And as the machine's name implies, it will also reduce the board's thickness.

PLANING TO THICKNESS

Joint one face of all the stock to be planed as described in "Surfacing on the Jointer," page 8. This provides a flat reference surface for the planer. Generally, the maximum depth of cut for a planer is $\frac{1}{16}$ inch, about one full revolution of the planer's crank. Check your owner's manual to be sure. Run the board through the planer with the jointed face down. Repeat this process until the top face is smooth. Now you have accomplished the flattening process—the faces of the board will be parallel. The next step is planing to the thickness you need.

Separate the stock to be planed into piles of similar thicknesses. For example, group all the boards that need to be planed to $\frac{3}{4}$ inch.

Find the thickest board in the first group. Set the planer's depth of cut to remove $\frac{1}{16}$ inch or less from this board. Turn on the planer and feed the stock through, this time with the jointed face up. Feed each piece in the group through before changing the setting. Some boards may not get planed at all the

Photo 16   The thickness planer makes one side of a board parallel to the other. It does not make boards flat.

first time you run them through. That's okay: Running each board through before changing the setting is the key to uniform final thickness.

Set the planer for a cut that is thinner by about $\frac{1}{16}$ inch. Run the stock again, this time with the original jointed face down. Continue this process, alternating board faces until the pieces are the necessary thickness. Alternating faces removes an equal amount of wood from each side of the board. This is important, because the board is likely to have a higher moisture content inside than at its surfaces. Removing equal amounts from each side results in final faces with equal moisture content. This will help prevent the board from warping after planing.

RADIAL ARM SAW

The radial arm saw is a product of the twentieth century. Other stationary power tools can be belt-driven—they were originally designed to be powered by water mills. But the radial arm saw's blade is bolted directly to the shaft of an electric motor. No other arrangement will work.

The radial arm saw was the invention of shop teacher Raymond DeWalt, and the early DeWalt saws are still some of the most accurate versions. In the do-it-yourself boom after the Second World War, the radial arm saw was king. But somehow, in the past few years, the radial arm saw has developed a reputation for being little more than a cantankerous cutoff machine. But it is capable of much more.

A radial arm saw can do almost everything a table saw can and a few things a table saw can't. If set up properly, a radial arm saw is capable of making incredibly accurate cuts.

Every radial arm saw operation is set up in reference to the table, so you can't make true cuts unless the table is flat. See the "Radial Arm Saw Table and Fence," page 267 for plans.

There are several other crucial adjustments in setting up a radial arm saw, all of which are covered in your owner's manual. These include making sure the table is parallel to the arm, adjusting the arm and blade pivot stops and the carriage, and aligning the blade.

USING THE SAW

A radial arm saw has two modes of operation. For crosscutting, the blade is set at an angle to the fence, the work is held stationary, and the blade is moved through the cut. For ripping, the blade is set parallel to the fence and the work is pushed through the cut.

Safety

Of the two modes, ripping is far more dangerous. However, any cut on the radial arm saw has the potential for disaster. To minimize the risk, wear safety glasses or goggles and hearing protection.

Know how the guards on the machine work and use them. And most importantly, keep your hands and arms out of line with the blade. Never reach across the blade to hold a piece or remove a scrap. Use a push stick for ripping narrow stock.

Crosscutting

Getting a true 90-degree cut is what crosscutting is all about. Set the arm in its 90-degree position. The guard should be in the horizontal position, and the anti-kickback fingers should be up, as shown in Photo 17. If you haven't made a kerf in the table yet, do so now. First adjust the height of the blade so that it is just above the table. Turn on the saw, then lower the blade 1/8 inch, cutting into the table. Draw the carriage forward, making a cut. Return the carriage to the rear of the arm. You now have a kerf as wide as a single saw blade in the table. As you use the saw, this kerf may widen. As it does, the quality of

Photo 17   For crosscutting, put the radial arm saw's guard in the horizontal position and the anti-kickback fingers up.

Photo 18   To cut a number of pieces to the same length, clamp a stop block to the fence to the left of the blade.

Photo 19   To make a miter that angles across the width of a board, swing the arm to the right and lock it at the necessary angle.

your cuts will decrease. Replace the table when this happens.

Loosen and position the fence so that the blade will make a fresh kerf in it. Make sure the fence is at least as tall as your workpiece, and lock it in place. Between the fresh kerf in the fence and the narrow kerf in the table, tearout should be eliminated.

Hold the work against the fence with your left hand as shown in P*hoto* 17. Grasp the handle with your right hand and pull the carriage forward, making the cut. Return the carriage to the rear of the arm before moving the workpiece.

If you need to cut a number of pieces to the same length, clamp a stop block to the fence at the needed distance from the left side of the blade as shown in P*hoto* 18. For convenience, you can make a self-clamping stop block such as the one described in "Radial Arm Saw Table and Fence," page 267. Always hold on to the piece that is against the stop block. Otherwise, the blade may catch it and throw it at you.

Mitering

The setup for mitering is similar to that for crosscutting. For best results, you should have a fresh kerf in the fence and a clean kerf

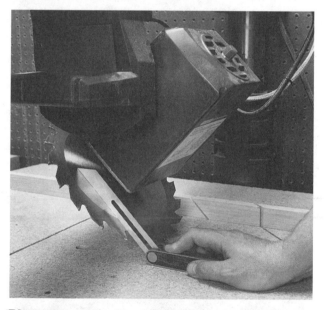

Photo 20   To make a beveled miter, leave the arm set at 90 degrees and tilt the blade. Use a triangle or a sliding T-bevel to set the angle.

in the table. To make a miter that angles across the width of the board, such as for a picture frame, swing the arm to the right and lock it at the necessary angle. (The left miter position is almost never used.) Hold the work against the fence with your left hand and pull the saw through the cut with your right. If you are mitering both ends of a piece, cut one end, then turn the piece around and cut the other end, as shown in P*hoto* 19. Again, you can use a stop block clamped to the left of the blade for duplicate cuts.

If you must make a beveled miter cut, such as for the corners of a box, leave the arm set at 90 degrees and tilt the blade. Use a sliding T-bevel to set the angle, as shown in P*hoto* 20. To make a compound miter cut, tilt the blade and angle the arm.

Ripping

Of all the operations you can do on the radial arm saw, ripping is the most nerve-racking. If you have a table saw, use it for ripping. If you must use the radial arm saw, be sure to use the guards that came with the machine.

All ripping is done with the blade turned parallel to the fence and the carriage locked in position along the arm. The fence should be whole, with no crosscut kerfs in it. You may want to make a fence just for ripping. The guard is tipped down to skim the infeed

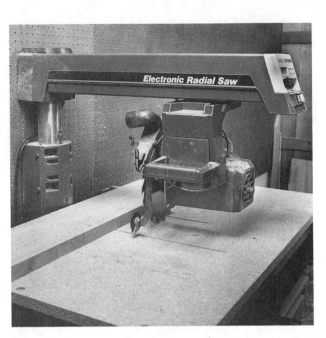

Photo 22 For in-ripping, turn the carriage so that the blade is between the motor and the fence.

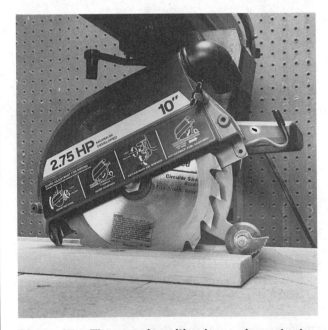

Photo 21 The guard position is very important when ripping on the radial arm saw. Tip the guard down to skim the infeed side of the workpiece. The anti-kickback fingers should hang down just below the surface of the stock.

side of the workpiece. The anti-kickback fingers hang down just below the stock's surface. (See P*hoto* 21.) These settings are critical. Failure to adjust the guards properly can cause the saw to kick back the workpiece with tremendous force.

There are two ripping positions: in-rip and out-rip. In-rip is for cuts less than about 12 inches wide, and out-rip is for wider cuts. With in-rip, you work from the right side of the saw. With out-rip, you work from the left.

For in-ripping, raise the blade above the table surface. Turn the carriage so that the blade is between the motor and the fence as shown in P*hoto* 22. Move the carriage along the arm until the blade is the proper distance from the fence, and lock the carriage in place. Turn on the saw and lower the blade into the table. Cut in about ⅛ inch. Turn off the saw. Set the guards as described.

Move the workpiece away from the blade and start the saw. Hold the work against the fence with your left hand and push it through the cut with your right as shown in P*hoto* 23. Keep your left hand well in front of the blade guard. Push the stock all the way past the blade with your right hand. You can hand feed stock down to 4 inches wide. For pieces

Photo 23 When in-ripping, hold the work against the fence with your left hand and push it through with your right.

Photo 24 For out-ripping, turn the carriage so that the motor is between the blade and the fence.

from 1 to 4 inches wide, use a push stick as you get near the end of the cut. Do not rip material less than 1 inch wide.

For out-ripping, turn the carriage around so that the motor is between the blade and

the fence as shown in P*hoto* 24. Again, raise the arm and slide the carriage to adjust the width of cut. Lock the carriage in place, turn on the saw, and lower it into the table ⅛ inch. This time, feed the work from left to right.

Photo 25 When out-ripping, hold the work against the fence with your right hand and feed it with your left.

Photo 26 When in-ripping stock narrower than about 3 inches, step to the left of the blade as you come to the end of the cut. Pull, rather than push, the work through the final part of the cut.

Adjust the guards as before. Hold the work against the fence with your right hand and push with your left, as shown in P*hoto* 25.

The most dangerous part of ripping is when the end of the board has cleared the guard but hasn't been cut yet, as shown in P*hoto* 26. For an out-rip, continue to hold the board firmly on the table as you complete the cut. You can do the same for an in-rip, being careful to keep your fingers well away from the blade. However, when in-ripping stock narrower than about 3 inches, you can't safely push the board through the end of the cut. Instead, as the cut comes to the end of an in-rip, step to the left of the blade, so that you can continue to hold the workpiece down on the table and against the fence. This will require you to pull, rather than push, the work through the final part of the cut.

Making Grooves and Dadoes

The radial arm saw is very handy for cutting dadoes and grooves with a dado cutter. Unlike the table saw, you can watch your layout lines during the cut.

Dado cutters for the radial arm saw are the same as for the table saw. For more information about dado cutters, see "Cutting Dadoes and Grooves," page 36. Mount the dado cutter on your saw and adjust it to the proper width. Set up for the cut as you would for a rip or a crosscut. This time, however, adjust the blade height to the proper measurement above the table. Make some test cuts in a scrap to be sure. Again, a fresh cut in the fence will help prevent tearout.

ROUTER

The electric router is arguably the most versatile woodworking tool in the shop. With the proper cutters and accessories, it can handle a long list of shaping, trimming, and joining tasks.

Originally, routers had fixed bases. With a fixed-base router, you must turn off the router before changing the depth of cut. Recently, however, plunge routers have entered the market. A plunge router will let you change the depth of cut safely and accurately while the tool is running. You can literally plunge a spinning bit into a piece of wood to start a cut. The ability to start cuts easily in the middle of a board makes plunge routers more versatile, particularly for hand-held applications. They don't work quite as well as fixed-base routers, however, when mounted upside down in router tables. The spring-loaded plunge mechanism makes setting the depth of cut more difficult. In spite of this, a plunge router is probably the tool to own if you're going to have only one router.

Speed Control

Most routers run at a single speed, about 20,000 revolutions per minute (RPM). Some routers, however, have variable speed control. With variable speed control, you set the speed of the router to match the cutter or the material being routed. Variable speed control not only makes your router run most efficiently, it also allows you to use some of the large-diameter bits available today. While the manufacturers claim some of these bits can run at 20,000 RPM, you'll get a better cut if you run them at about 10,000 to 12,000 RPM. Even at these lower speeds, some of these bits are quite intimidating.

Most large routers are available with built-in variable speed controls. If your router doesn't have speed controls, you can plug it into a small control sold separately.

Adjusting the Depth of Cut

Once you have selected a bit and put it in your router, there is only one adjustment

to make—the depth of cut. Depth of cut is determined by the distance the bit protrudes from the bottom of the router. It is controlled by moving the router up or down on its base.

Routers are not made to remove large amounts of wood at once. If you have a deep cut to make, you'll have to make it in several shallow passes. For most situations, cutting about ¼ inch deeper with each pass is a good plan. On a fixed-base router, turn off the router and set the final depth of cut before making the final pass. If you have several pieces to rout with the same setup, rout each piece before changing the depth setting. You'll save time, and your work will be more accurate. On a plunge router, you can set the final depth of cut first on the router's adjustable depth stop.

To set final depth for most bits, draw a line on the edge of a scrap marking the desired depth, as shown in *Photo* 27. Then set the scrap on the router. Adjust the bit until it matches the line on the scrap. Rout the scrap and measure the depth of the cut to test the setup.

To set the depth of cut on a router table, turn the scrap over and slide it up next to the bit.

Photo 27 With the router upside down, adjust the bit depth until it matches the depth mark on a piece of scrap.

Router Bits

A router is only as good as the bits you mount in it. In some cases, it may only be as good as *the way* you mount the bit. There's a transition between the shank and the flute that is wider than the shank. If the collet tightens around the transition, the collet may not hold it securely. When you insert a bit into the collet, let it touch the bottom, then pull it out about 1/16 inch.

Recent years have seen an explosion in the variety and sizes of bits available. Don't let the tool catalogs overwhelm you. There are only two categories of bits: decorative bits and utility bits. The two are not mutually exclusive, but they help to keep things straight.

Decorative bits have a profile that shapes the edge or surface of a board. Cutting ogees, corner rounds, chamfers, and raised panels are a few of the jobs you can accomplish with decorative bits.

Utility bits, on the other hand, generally have simpler profiles that cut joints in boards or cut boards to match a pattern. Examples include straight cutters, rabbeting bits, dovetail bits, and flush trimming bits.

Most decorative bits have pilots to guide the cut. Some utility bits, such as flush trimming and rabbeting bits, also have pilots.

Usually, the pilot is under the cutters. The pilot guides the bit as it cuts a profile on the top edge of the workpiece.

Unlike other piloted bits, a pattern cutting bit has its pilot mounted above the cutters. It is designed to follow a template secured above the workpiece. A pattern cutting bit is not limited to the edge of a workpiece. Flush trimming bits have the pilot below the bit and can also be used for pattern routing, as discussed in "Pattern Routing," page 28.

There are two types of pilots: solid

Examples of decorative bits include, from left: a roundover bit, a chamfering bit, a roman ogee bit, and a panel-raising bit.

Examples of utility bits include, from left: a rabbeting bit, a dovetail bit, a flush trimming bit, and a straight cutter.

and ball bearing. Solid pilots are built right into the end of bits and spin at the same speed as the bit. Avoid solid piloted bits. They're cheaper than ball bearing pilots, but you'll probably spend the savings on extra sandpaper. As one of these bits runs along the edge of a board, the friction from the spinning pilot can burn the wood unmercifully. Sanding away the resulting scorch mark can be considered penance for subjecting your materials to such abuse.

Ball bearing pilots are exactly what they sound like: a small ball bearing that is mounted directly to the router bit. They are usually attached to the end of a bit, but there are some bits that have a ball bearing mounted on the shank above the flutes. There are even bits that include a bearing between two sets of flutes.

The advantage of ball bearing bits is that the bearing surface doesn't spin with the bit. It rolls slowly along the edge of the board as you push the router through the cut. This eliminates burning.

When assembling a collection of bits, keep it simple. To start with, you'll probably want a selection of utility bits.

Buy straight bits of two or three different diameters, a flush trimming bit, and a couple of decorative bits—perhaps an ogee and a quarter-round. Add other bits to your collection as you need them.

Router bits are commonly available in two materials: high-speed steel (HSS), and carbide. HSS bits are made from a single piece of metal. They are cheaper than carbide bits, they cut well in softwood and hardwood, and you can sharpen them with regular sharpening stones. Unfortunately, they dull quickly under the stress and heat of routing.

Carbide-tipped bits are made from steel shanks with carbide cutting edges (flutes) brazed to the shank. They stay sharp up to 30 times longer than HSS bits—a real advantage when cutting plywood, particleboard, or other highly abrasive materials. Carbide bits are also available in more shapes than HSS bits. In general, carbide is a better buy for the bits you use all the time, whether you use them in solid wood or plywood. HSS is a better choice for the bits you need only once or twice a year.

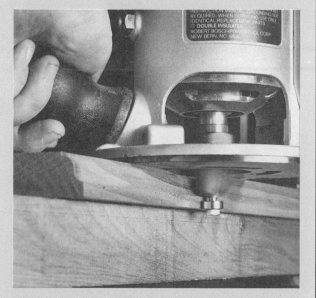

Ball bearing pilots use the edge of the workpiece to guide the bit.

HAND-HELD ROUTING

Most of the time, you will use a router in one of two ways: either held in your hands or mounted on a router table. If the workpiece is large, it is easier to clamp it down and move the router. If the workpiece is small, it is easier to move it and keep the router stationary.

No matter how you use the router, you must be able to guide it through the cut. While you can make some cuts freehand—like roughing out a hinge mortise—the cuts aren't very precise. With some sort of a guide, however, a router is a very accurate cutting tool. There are several guide options available. Some bits include their own guide, called a pilot. This pilot is usually located at the end of the bit. The pilot guides the router along the edge of a board.

Dadoes and Grooves

The pilot isn't the only way to guide a cut, however. Most router manufacturers make an accessory called an edge guide that attaches right to their router's base. This guide is perfect for routing dadoes and grooves with a hand-held router. If the dado or groove is beyond the reach of your edge guide, you can clamp a fence directly to the work and guide the router along it.

When routing with an edge guide, set the guide the required distance from the bit. To make a cut, run the guide along the edge of the board as shown in *Photo* 28. This arrangement makes it easy to make cuts parallel to the edge of a board.

When routing with a fence you've clamped to the stock, push the router through the cut with its base against the straightedge.

Before you begin, lay out the cut on the workpiece. Measure the distance from the edge of the router bit to the edge of the router base. Clamp the fence this distance from the layout line.

To simplify measuring, some woodworkers rout a sample groove template and use it to position the fence, as shown in *Photo* 29. Butt a piece of scrap against the fence and rout a groove. Mark the edge that was against the fence. Put the template over the layout lines for the actual groove. Position the fence against the marked edge, and clamp it in place. In this book, you'll find three jigs that make routing dadoes even easier.

Photo 28 Set the edge guide the required distance from the bit. Run the guide along the edge of the board to make the cut.

Photo 29 A sample groove template is an easy way to set a fence the proper distance from a dado layout line.

There is one trick to using a separate fence as a guide. Router bases aren't always centered on the router. As a result, the location of the groove may change, depending on which part of the base you run against the fence. A discrepancy of as little as 1/16 inch can throw off your cuts by as much 1/8 inch. To avoid this, pick one point on your router base and mark it with a dab of white paint. Always make your bit-to-base measurements to this point. Then as you rout, keep this point against the fence. This will help ensure your cuts are consistent.

The direction you push the router will also affect the quality of the cut. Feed the router so that the bit pushes the base against the fence or pulls the edge guide into the board's edge. This means if the router is between you and the fence, rout from left to right. If the fence is between you and the router, rout from right to left. With an edge guide, rout from right to left if the router is between you and the guide and from left to right if the guide is between you and the router.

Making Stopped Cuts with a Hand-Held Router

If the cut stops before the end of the board, be sure to mark this carefully and watch as you rout. Stop the cut when the bit touches the mark.

Cuts that stop and start away from the edges of a board are simple with a plunge router. If you must use a fixed-based router for a cut of this type, turn on the router and tip it into the cut as shown in P*hoto* 30. This tipping technique is particularly difficult if you are routing a groove that is the same width as your router bit. To make sure the bit tips in at exactly the right spot, use a fence that is tall enough to begin guiding the router base before the bit enters the workpiece.

Making Piloted Cuts

When cutting with a piloted bit, as with all router bits, it is better to make several shallow passes than one heavy one, so begin with a shallow cut.

Photo 30   If you must tip a fixed-base router into a cut, use a fence that is tall enough to begin guiding the router base before the bit enters the workpiece.

To start a piloted cut, hold the router with the bit hanging over the edge of the workpiece. Make sure the bit will not touch the work when it starts spinning. Turn on the router and let it come up to speed. When you are ready, ease the bit into the cut. Be sure to hold the router flat on top of the piece. If it tips, the bit will approach the stock at an angle, and the profile of the cut will change.

When the pilot makes contact with the edge of the workpiece, start routing along the edge. Move at a steady rate, about normal walking speed. If you move too slowly, the bit may scorch the wood. If you move too fast, you may overload both the router and bit and get a poor cut. Get used to listening to the sound and feel of the tool as it cuts. Soon you'll be able to recognize when the router is running best.

The direction of feed with a piloted bit is important. Because the bit is spinning, it can grab and pull itself along a cut. To avoid this, rout against the rotation of the bit. This means that if the router is between you and the edge it is cutting, you want to rout from left to right. If the work is between you and the router, rout from right to left.

TABLE-MOUNTED ROUTING

There are many times when it works better to hold the router stationary and run the work past it. One of the simplest and most versatile ways of doing this is to mount the router upside down under a table. The bits then stick up through a hole in the table surface. A router table can be as simple as a piece of plywood clamped over the edge of your bench or as elaborate as you care to make it. See "Router Table," page 271, for plans.

Edge Treatments

When shaping the edge of a board on a table-mounted router, you can use a fence, a piloted bit, or both to guide the stock. If you guide the cut with a fence, you'll need to notch the fence so that the bit can be partially buried as shown in *Photo* 31.

Make several test pieces, so that you can be sure the profile you're routing is the one you want. Mount the bit in the router. Set the depth of cut for a light pass.

If you are guiding the cut with a fence, position the fence to expose the portion of the bit that will do the cutting. If you are

Photo 32 To use the fence in conjunction with a piloted bit, align the fence and pilot with a straightedge.

using the fence in conjunction with a piloted bit, align the fence and pilot with a straightedge, as shown in *Photo* 32.

Rout a test piece. The direction of feed depends on the setup. If you are routing stock that is between you and the bit, rout from right to left as shown in *Photo* 33. (This rule applies whether you are using a fence or a piloted bit.) If you are routing inside a

Photo 31 To use the fence to guide a cut on the edge of a board, notch the fence, so that the bit can be partially buried.

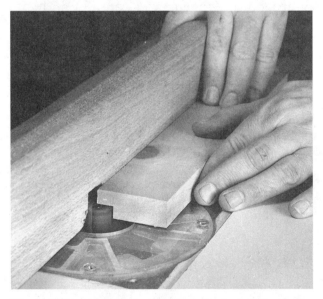

Photo 33 Rout from right to left when the stock is between you and the bit.

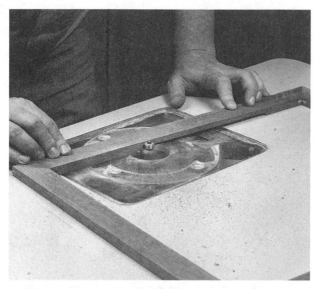

Photo 34 When routing inside a workpiece, rout from left to right.

workpiece, as when routing the inside of a frame, rout from left to right, as shown in P*hoto* 34. Keep raising the depth of cut and routing until the piece has the profile you want. When you're satisfied with the test profile, rout the actual stock.

Be careful when starting cuts with a piloted bit. The flutes can grab the stock out of your hands and fling it across the shop. Make very light passes and use a starting pin

to help ease the wood into the cut. A starting pin is simply a rod that sticks straight up from the table. To start a cut, hold the stock against the pin. Pivot it slowly into the bit as shown in P*hoto* 35.

Table-Routing Dadoes and Grooves

The router table is ideal for cutting dadoes and grooves. A groove is a U-shaped cut that runs *with* the grain. A dado is a groove that runs *across* the grain. While you usually make these cuts with straight router bits, sometimes you'll use bits with other profiles. A core box bit, for example, will produce a round-bottomed groove or dado.

Rout a dado or groove with a bit whose diameter matches the width of the cut you want to make. Set the depth of cut with a scrap as described in "Adjusting the Depth of Cut," page 17. As always, make deep cuts in several light passes.

To lay out a cut, mark the edge of the board that will run against the fence. Decide how far from that edge of the board the cut has to be and set the fence that far from the edge of the bit. Don't worry about setting the fence parallel to the table's edge. No matter what angle the fence forms with the table, it is still aligned with the bit. After clamping the

Photo 35 A starting pin provides a bearing surface before the workpiece contacts the pilot bearing.

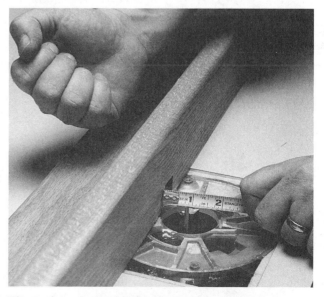

Photo 36 To make slight adjustments in the fence, loosen one clamp and tap the fence gently with your hand.

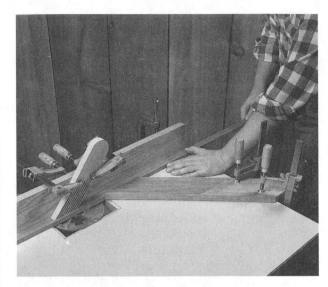

Photo 37 Support thin stock with two feather-boards—one to hold the stock against the table, the other to hold it against the fence.

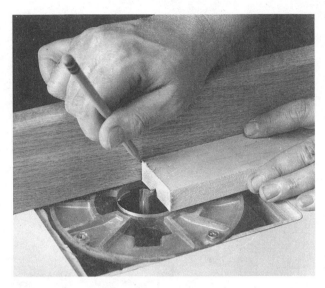

Photo 38 For a stopped cut, use the edge of the stock to mark the location of the right cutting edge of the bit on the fence.

fence down, double-check your setup. If you need to adjust the fence slightly, loosen one end and tap it over by hitting it gently with the side of your hand as shown in *Photo* 36. Run the stock from right to left, guiding the marked edge against the fence. If the stock is thin, use two featherboards as shown in *Photo* 37 to help steady the work. See "Feather-board," page 296, for plans.

If you don't have a large enough bit, you can reposition the fence to widen the cut. If you move the fence 1/8 inch or less, you can rout the entire depth in one pass. Move the fence any farther than that, and you will have to make several shallower passes. If you need to widen a groove by moving the fence closer to the cutter, feed the workpiece over the table from left to right.

Making Stopped Cuts on the Router Table

With a table-mounted router, cuts that stop before the end of a board present a slight problem. Since the bit is buried in the cut, you can't see where to start or stop routing. This is true even if you are cutting a slot all the way through the workpiece. Un-less the workpiece is less than 1/2 inch thick, you'll need to make the slot in several passes. You'll only see the bit on the last pass.

To overcome this problem, lay out the end of the cut and transfer this mark to the other side of the board, where you can see it during the cut. Set the router table fence, and then use the edge of the stock to mark the location of the right cutting edge of the router bit on the fence as shown in *Photo* 38. Rout from right to left until the mark on the workpiece aligns with the mark on the fence as shown in *Photo* 39. Turn off the router, wait for the bit to stop, and lift the workpiece from the bit.

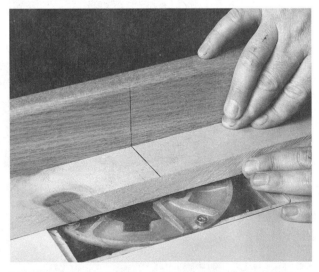

Photo 39 Rout from right to left until the mark on the workpiece aligns with the mark on the fence.

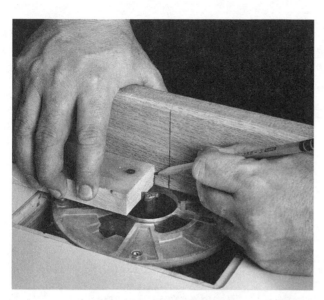

Photo 40 For a groove or slot that stops short of both ends of the board, mark the fence for the location of the right and left cutting edges of the bit.

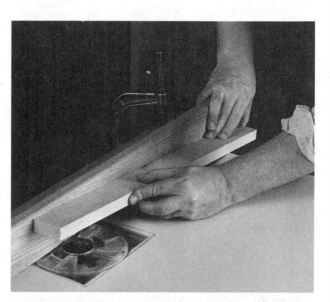

Photo 41 To start a groove or slot that stops short of both ends of the board, hold the right end of the workpiece on the table, with the left end in the air.

Routing a groove or slot that stops short of both ends of the board is a little more involved. For this operation, mark the location of the right and left cutting edges of the bit on the router fence as shown in Photo 40. On the workpiece, lay out where the cut is to start and stop and then transfer these marks

Photo 42 Align the stop layout on the left side of the workpiece with the left mark on the fence. Plunge the workpiece onto the bit. Rout until the right mark on the workpiece aligns with the right mark on the fence.

to the other side of the board. Turn on the router. Hold the right end of the workpiece on the table, against the fence, with the left end tilted in the air as shown in Photo 41. Align the stop layout on the left side of the workpiece with the left mark on the fence. Plunge the workpiece onto the bit as shown in Photo 42. Rout until the right mark on the workpiece aligns with the right mark on the fence.

This method of making stopped cuts works well for cutting dadoes, grooves, and slots as well as mortises. If you are routing a slot or a deep groove, you may want to begin by routing the ends of the groove full depth. Plunge the work onto the bit at each end of the cut. Then decrease the depth of cut and rout the area between the plunged cuts in small steps. This helps to keep the ends of the cut exact. Another way to accomplish this is with stops.

Using Stops

If you are routing stopped grooves in a number of pieces, consider clamping stops to the fence. Begin the cut against one stop, and guide the board across the bit until you hit the second stop. This will help you get consistent results.

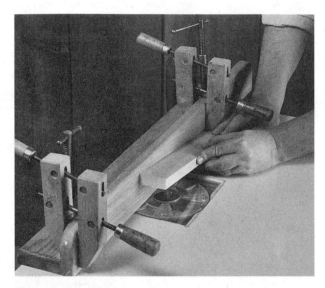

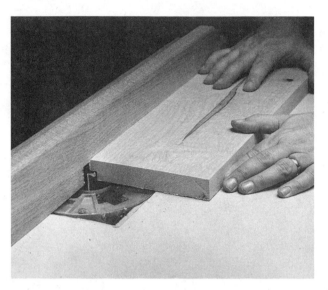

Photo 43 Using two stops ensures consistent results when you need to make a number of workpieces with grooves or slots that stop short of both ends.

Photo 44 To rout a rabbet with a straight bit, bury part of the bit in the fence.

The stop blocks can be pieces of scrap wood clamped to the router fence. Wooden hand screws clamped to the fence work well as stops, as shown in P*hoto* 43.

To determine where to place the stops, lay out the groove on the stock and the bit location on the fence exactly as already described; make one mark each on the workpiece and the fence for a groove that stops short of one end, two marks each for a groove that stops short of both ends. Then lower the bit below the table surface. Align the marks, put the stop against the end of the board, and clamp the stop to the fence. Align the other set of marks, if you made them, and clamp another stop in place.

Rabbets

You can rout rabbets on the router table with a standard rabbeting bit. If so, the procedure is similar to routing a rabbet with a hand-held router.

You can also rout a rabbet with a straight bit, guiding the cut against the fence. When you do this, the placement of the fence determines the width of the cut. To rout a rabbet that is narrower than the bit, bury part of the bit in the fence, as shown in P*hoto* 44. For general purposes, a ¾-inch-diameter bit works well for routing rabbets.

To bury the bit, first adjust it to the full depth of the rabbet. Clamp one end of the fence to the table. Then pivot the other end around so that the bit cuts into the fence. Cut in until the whole bit is covered. If you are cutting a rabbet deeper than ⅜ inch, make the cut in the fence in several shallower passes.

To set the width of the rabbet, measure from the fence to the outside of the bit as shown in P*hoto* 45. Clamp the fence in place.

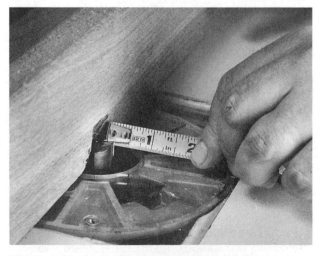

Photo 45 To set the width of the rabbet, measure from the fence to the outside of the bit.

Photo 46   A sliding dovetail joint has two parts: the dovetail itself, and the matching dovetail groove.

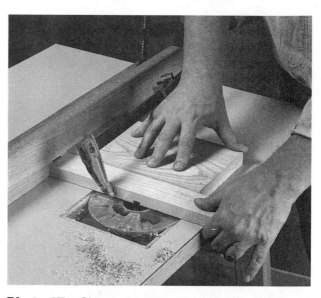

Photo 47   Clamp a square scrap to the workpiece to prevent chip-out at the end of the cut and to help keep the cut straight.

Once you have the fence positioned, set the depth of cut for a shallow pass. Put the stock between you and the fence, and run the stock from right to left. Increase the depth of cut and make another pass. Repeat until you've cut the rabbet to full depth.

Routing Sliding Dovetails

Sliding dovetails are used to form strong, interlocking joints. Most often, they are cut across the grain to hold drawer and cabinet parts together as shown in P*hoto* 46. They are called "sliding" dovetails because you have to slide the two parts together during assembly. Sometimes, however, sliding dovetails are used to join parts that actually will slide against each other in use. An example of this is the retractable legs on the "Drill Press Extension Table," described on page 229.

A sliding dovetail has two parts: the dovetail itself, and the matching dovetail groove. The dovetail groove is cut in the same way as a square groove. Instead of a straight bit, however, you rout the dovetail groove with a dovetail bit. The same bit is used to rout the dovetail.

Cut the dovetail groove first. Mount a dovetail bit in the table-mounted router. Unlike other operations, you must cut a

dovetail slot in one pass. Set the bit to its final depth of cut. Set the fence to position the cut on the workpiece. Run the stock against the rotation of the bit as shown in P*hoto* 47. (This will be from right to left if you are working with the stock between you and the fence.) Clamp a square scrap to the workpiece to prevent chip-out at the end of the cut and to help keep the cut straight. Make the groove ¼ inch deep for most applications.

If you have to cut a wide or deep dovetail groove, you can cut most of the waste with a straight bit. This eliminates stress on the dovetail bit and results in a cleaner cut. Cut the groove with a bit no wider than the narrowest part of the dovetail. Remove the bulk of the waste in several light passes. When the groove is almost deep and/or wide enough, switch to a dovetail bit. Set the bit for the finished depth and make the final cut. If the groove is wider than the bit, shift the fence to cut the two sides.

If you need to make a dovetail groove that stops short of the end of the board, use a stop block or layout lines as described in "Making Stopped Cuts on the Router Table," page 24. When you get to the end of the cut, turn off the router. Back the board out of the cut when the bit stops spinning.

Photo 48 Bury the bit in the fence and rout both sides of the dovetail. Again, a square scrap clamped to the workpiece prevents chip-out and adds support.

To make the dovetail to fit into the groove, leave the bit in the router table and don't change the height adjustment. This helps to ensure that the two parts of the joint fit together perfectly. Make several test pieces the same width and thickness as your good stock to test the setup.

Position the fence so that the bit is partially buried. Stand a test piece on end against the fence as shown in P*hoto* 48. Rout one side of the test piece, then the other. Check the fit in the dovetail groove. Unless you are making a moving sliding dovetail joint, the test piece should slide into the groove snugly, with no slop. If it is too tight, move the fence to expose a little more of the bit. If it is too loose, move the fence so less of the bit is exposed. Keep adjusting the fence and cutting test pieces until the joint fits perfectly. Then cut the good stock.

PATTERN ROUTING

When you are cutting several curves with the same profile, pattern routing will help ensure that they are identical. When pattern routing, you guide either the bit or the router against a pattern of the shape you want.

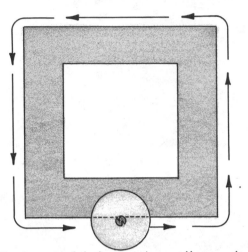

Rout counterclockwise when pattern routing the outside of a workpiece.

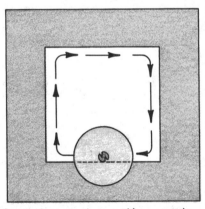

Rout clockwise when pattern routing inside a workpiece.

There are three methods of pattern routing. You can use a flush trimming bit, a pattern cutting bit, or a guide bushing. With any of these methods, you want the bit to pull the router toward the pattern. When you are routing around the outside edge of the workpiece, this means you must move the router counterclockwise. If you are routing within a workpiece, such as when making a mortise, you must rout clockwise. *Pattern Routing Direction* illustrates this.

Using Flush Trimming and Pattern Cutting Bits

The simplest form of pattern routing is with either a flush trimming bit or a pattern

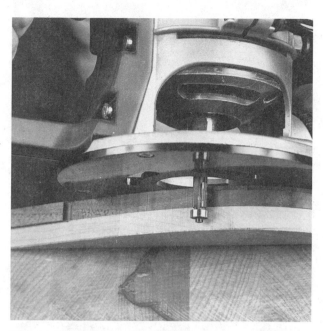

Photo 49 When pattern routing with a flush trimming bit, the pilot bearing rides on a template under the workpiece.

cutting bit. Both have pilot bearings whose diameter matches the diameter of the bit. On a flush trimming bit, the bearing is at the bottom of the bit. On a pattern cutting bit, the bearing is on the shank, right above the flutes.

Photo 50 A guide bushing is a short tube with a flange that fits into the router base.

When pattern routing with flush trimming bits, make a pattern the exact shape of the finished piece. In fact, the pattern could be an actual finished piece that you are duplicating. Attach the pattern to the underside of the workpiece with double-stick tape or clamps. Guide the bearing so that the bit rides along the pattern, as shown in P*hoto* 49. The flutes automatically cut the work to match. A pattern cutting bit works the same way, except you attach the pattern to the top of the workpiece. In both cases, you should cut the workpiece to within 1/16 inch of final size before routing. Also, be aware of what is under the workpiece as you rout. Don't cut into your workbench by mistake.

Using Guide Bushings

A guide bushing, sometimes called a template guide, is a short tube with a flange that fits into the router base as shown in P*hoto* 50. Guide bushings come in different diameters for different-size bits. A straight router bit sticks down through the center of the tube. As the tube rides along the template, the cutter routs the pattern. Commercial dovetail jigs, among others, use guide bushings to guide a cut.

With guide bushings, you can make your own patterns to rout mortises, cut pieces to shape, and more. Once you get used to the technique, the potential is tremendous. Guide bushings offer several advantages over the piloted pattern bits. Because they use regular router bits instead of flush trimming bits, you save money. Moreover, regular bits are available in many more shapes, and the depth of cut is easy to adjust. With flush trimming bits, the cut has to go all the way through the piece because of the location of the bearing. With pattern cutting bits, you can make shallow cuts, but the pattern must be very thick to stay in contact with the bearing. With guide bushings, however, the depth of cut can be whatever you want, regardless of the template thickness.

Setting up for pattern routing does take time. It probably is not worth the effort if you only have one or two pieces to shape. The reason that setting up takes so much time is that the bit and the bushing have different

Photo 51 When pattern routing with a guide bushing, the bushing rides against a template on top of the workpiece. The template must be offset by the difference between the bit and bushing diameters.

diameters. As a result, the template cannot be the same size as the finished piece. It must be offset as shown in *Photo* 51. The amount of offset depends on the difference between the diameter of the bushing and the diameter of the bit. Here is the formula for calculating the offset:

$$\frac{\text{bushing diameter} - \text{bit diameter}}{2} = \text{pattern offset}$$

For example, if you are using a ¾-inch-diameter bushing and a ⅜-inch-diameter bit, the pattern offset should be 3/16 inch. Remember, you have to add that offset to each guiding edge of your template. In this example, to rout a 1 × 3-inch mortise, you'd need a pattern slot that measures 1⅜ × 3⅜ inches.

Once you calculate the offset, make the pattern from ¼- to ½-inch-thick sheet material such as hardboard or high-quality plywood. Be sure to make the pattern big enough to support the router, and leave room to clamp the pattern in place. Carefully lay out the actual shape you want to cut. Do a good job: The accuracy of the pattern depends on it. Once you've drawn the line, measure over by the amount of the offset and draw a line parallel to the original line.

Position the pattern on your stock. If you are making the same inside cut in several pieces, you can attach fences to the underside of the pattern to help position it on the workpiece. The "Router Mortising Jig for Entry Doors," page 137, provides adjustable fences with interchangeable templates.

Clamp the pattern in position. Set the depth of cut, allowing for the thickness of the pattern.

If you are routing around the edge of the pattern and workpiece, just turn on the router and begin routing counterclockwise.

If you are routing inside the pattern and workpiece, such as for a mortise, you'll need to plunge the bit. With a plunger router, this is easy. Just position the router on the work and hold the guide bushing against the pattern. When you are ready, plunge the bit into the stock and guide the router clockwise around the pattern.

To rout an inside cut with a fixed-base router, you'll have to tip the tool into the cut with the motor running, as described in "Making Stopped Cuts with a Hand-Held Router," page 21. If the area you're going to rout is large enough, drill a hole whose diameter is larger than the router bit diameter. Start the cut by easing the bit into the hole. Make shallow passes until you have routed to the final depth.

TABLE SAW

At the center of most wood shops sits a table saw. Nearly every piece of wood that comes into a shop gets run through the table saw. Some pieces get cut once to rough size, while others see the saw again and again as they are cut precisely to size, then shaped and joined. In light of its potential, the table saw often is the first piece of stationary equipment a beginning woodworker buys.

There are many table saws on the market, from $100 discount-house specials to $15,000 computerized wonders. To be sure, more money buys more quality. However, spending a lot of money isn't the only way to get high-quality results. Even a low-end saw can be coaxed into sawing precisely—it just takes a little time.

The table saw is a remarkably versatile machine. Straight from the shipping crate, it is ready to crosscut and rip boards quickly and accurately. With a few jigs and accessories, it is capable of cutting complex joints and making decorative moldings. This book has a number of plans for things that will extend your table saw's capacity. But before you get too far into that, there are a few basic setups that are essential to table saw work.

MAKING THE BASIC CUTS

There are two basic cuts a table saw can make: rips and crosscuts. A rip is a cut with the grain. A crosscut is a cut across the grain. In general, rip cuts are guided past the saw blade with the rip fence, and crosscuts are guided with the miter gauge. There are some other cuts, such as miters and bevels, that are variations of the two basic cuts. All of these can be made with a table saw and its standard equipment.

Ripping

The setup for a rip cut is simple. Set the fence the needed distance from the blade and lock it in place. On most table saws, this is a matter of measuring from the blade to the fence. On most saw blades, the teeth alternate between angling toward and angling away from the fence. Choose a saw tooth that points toward the fence. Rotate this tooth to the infeed side of the saw. Measure from this point to the fence. Lock the fence in position.

Many rip fences won't automatically clamp down parallel to the blade, no matter how carefully you adjust them. If such a rip fence is part of your lot in life, rotate the same saw tooth to the outfeed side of the table and measure again. If the two measurements don't match, loosen the rip fence a bit and tap the outfeed side of the fence with your palm while measuring to check the alignment.

Before ripping, straighten the edge of the workpiece that you will run against the fence by running it over a jointer or jointing it with a hand plane.

Once the fence is set and you have a straight guide edge, you are ready to make the cut. You do not have to lay out the cut on the board. The fence will hold the board the appropriate distance from the blade. As long as the fence is set correctly, your cuts will be accurate. Some woodworkers like to set the fence for a cut that is $1/16$ inch wider than they need. They then run the sawed edge over the jointer to remove the saw marks and end up with a board that is the correct width.

To make a rip cut, hold the board against the fence. Stand to the left of the blade. Place your hands as shown in *Photo* 52. As you run the board past the blade, your right hand does all the pushing. Your left hand keeps the board against the fence. Never move your left hand beyond the front of the blade—this would push the kerf into the blade, causing kickback. When the trailing end of the board reaches your left hand, move your left hand away. Continue pushing the board through the cut with your right hand.

Beveling

Cutting a bevel along the length of a board is a variation on the ripping operation. Most saws have a gauge on their front panel that indicates the blade angle. This will give

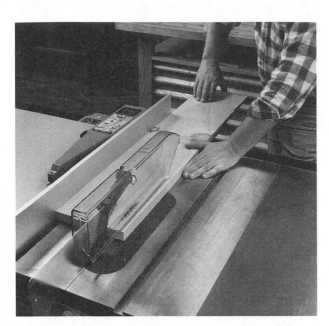

Photo 52 When ripping, your right hand does all the pushing. Your left hand keeps the board against the fence on the infeed side of the table.

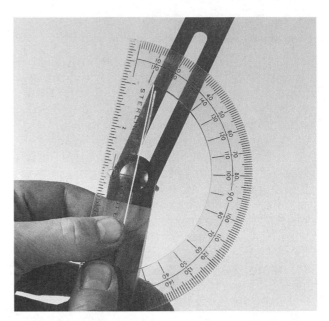

Photo 53 Use a protractor to set a bevel gauge to the bevel angle you want to cut.

you a rough idea of how far the blade is tilted, but don't count on this gauge to be accurate. Instead, use a protractor to set a sliding T-bevel gauge to the precise bevel angle as shown in *Photo* 53. Then crank the saw blade all the way up and tilt it until it

aligns with the bevel gauge as shown in *Photo* 54. Make sure the T-bevel is against the body of the saw blade, not resting on a tooth. Once the blade is set, lower it to a safe height to make the cut.

Cut bevels on wide boards the same way

Photo 54 Tilt the blade until it aligns with the sliding T-bevel gauge. Make sure the T-bevel is against the body of the saw, not resting on a tooth.

Photo 55 If your saw blade tilts to the right, bevel narrow stock with the fence to the left of the blade. Be sure to use a push stick.

you make wide rips. If you're ripping a narrow board, pay attention to the direction in which the blade tilts. If your saw is like most saws, the blade tilts to the right. If so, move the fence to the left side of the blade when making narrow cuts. If you try to make a beveled cut on a very narrow board with the fence to the right of the angled blade, the blade might cut into the fence. There is also a greater chance of kickback, since the board is stuck between the fence, the table, and the blade. Moving the fence to the left of the blade, as shown in *Photo* 55, eliminates these problems. If your blade tilts to the left, keep the fence on the right side of the blade for all bevel cuts. Use a push stick, such as the one described in "Table Saw Push Stick," page 304, if necessary.

Crosscutting

The setup for basic crosscutting also is quite simple. Slide the rip fence to the right as far as it will go, or remove it from the saw to get it out of the way. *Never* use the rip fence when crosscutting, except in the situation described later in "Making Multiple Crosscuts."

Place the miter gauge in a miter gauge slot. You can use either slot for crosscutting. For most operations, right-handed people find the left slot more convenient, while left-handed people prefer the right slot. Use an accurate try square to check that the miter gauge fence is square to the miter gauge bar as shown in *Photo* 56.

Lay out the cut with a square. Mark one face and one edge on your stock as shown in *Photo* 57. The line across the face of the board will allow you to monitor the cut as it progresses. Remember that the saw teeth alternate between tilting left and right. Select a tooth that leans toward the miter gauge and align it with your layout. Make sure that the blade is to the waste side of your layout line.

Place the board on the saw table and hold it against the miter gauge. If the board is fairly narrow, hold it against the miter gauge with both hands as shown in *Photo* 58. For wide boards, hold the board against the miter gauge with your left hand and push with your right as shown in *Photo* 59.

After making a number of crosscuts this way, you'll find the miter gauge that comes with most table saws is too short to provide enough support for a board longer than 20 inches or so. Trying to get accurate crosscuts with such a tool can be extremely

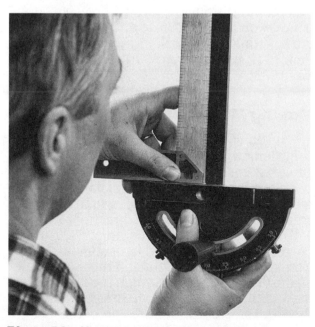

Photo 56 Use a try square to check that the miter gauge fence is square to the miter gauge bar.

Photo 57 Select a tooth that leans toward the miter gauge and align it to the waste side of your layout line.

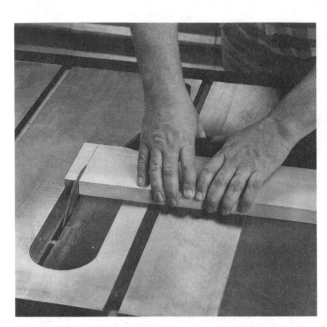

Photo 58 If the board is narrow, hold it against the miter gauge with both hands.

Photo 59 If the board is wide, hold it against the miter gauge with your left hand and push with your right.

frustrating. Before you throw the whole mess across the shop, there is a quick, easy solution. Screw an extension to the face of the miter gauge as shown in Photo 60.

The extension is merely a straight scrap of hardwood. It should extend just short of the blade to the right and at least to the edge

Photo 60 For additional support during crosscuts, screw an extension to the face of the miter gauge.

of the table to the left. This extension will provide much more support for the pieces you are crosscutting. After installing the miter gauge extension, if you still are not getting accurate crosscuts, glue a strip of sandpaper to the working face of the extension. This will prevent the wood from sliding or "creeping" along the fence as you cut it. For even more accurate and convenient crosscutting, see the plans for the "Crosscut Fence," page 278, or the "Crosscut Box," page 283.

Making Multiple Crosscuts

If you need to cut several pieces to the same length, clamp a stop block to the miter gauge extension.

Start by cutting one end of each workpiece square. Stack the pieces so that all the square ends face the same direction. This will help you keep things organized. On one piece, lay out the desired length, measuring from the square end. Position this piece against the miter gauge. Align the layout mark with the blade. Clamp the stop block to the extension at the square end of the workpiece as shown in Photo 61. The stop block has a small notch at the bottom of the

Photo 61   A miter gauge extension also provides a place to clamp a stop block for multiple crosscuts. A notch in the stop block prevents dust from causing inaccurate cuts.

Photo 62   A stop block on the rip fence lets you cut a single board into a number of pieces of the same length. Put the block against the saw, and measure between the stop and the blade.

working edge. This notch prevents dust from getting between the workpiece and the stop, which would make the cut inaccurate.

Make a test cut. Check the length of the test piece. If the length of the test piece is right, cut the rest of the pieces. Remember to

Photo 63   After locking the fence in position, move the stop block to the infeed side of fence. To prevent dangerous kickback, make sure the work-piece won't contact the block during the cut.

position them with the square end against the stop. If the test piece is not the right length, reposition the stop and try again.

If you want to cut a single board into a number of pieces of equal length, you can use a stop block in a slightly different way. Hold the stop block against the rip fence as shown in P*hoto* 62. Position the rip fence so that the distance between the stop block and the blade equals the workpiece length you need. Lock the fence in place. Move the stop block near the edge of the infeed side of the saw and clamp it in place.

Begin by cutting the end of the work-piece to square it. Slide the piece over until the square end touches the stop block as shown in P*hoto* 63. Make the cut. Turn off the saw and move the piece you just cut off away from the blade. Slide the board over against the stop and make another cut. Repeat until you have cut all the pieces you need. With this method, the workpiece is not in contact with the fence during the cut. Don't be tempted to eliminate the stop block and simply use the rip fence as a stop. The workpiece will jam between the fence and blade and will kick back at you with tremen-dous force.

Mitering

Miters are cuts made diagonally across the grain of a board. Simple miters can be cut two ways on the table saw. If you are cutting a miter across the width of a board, such as for a frame, angle the miter gauge in relation to the blade as shown in Photo 64. If you are mitering through the thickness of the board, such as for a box, leave the miter gauge set square and tilt the blade as shown in Photo 65.

For either mitering operation, set the angle with a protractor and a sliding T-bevel. If you will be tilting the blade, use the sliding T-bevel exactly as described in "Beveling," page 31. If you will be setting the miter gauge, put the body of the sliding T-bevel against the miter gauge and the blade of the sliding T-bevel against the saw blade as shown in Photo 66. Whether you are tilting the blade or setting the miter gauge, make sure the sliding T-bevel is against the body of the saw blade, not touching any saw teeth.

Once the angles are set, cut two test pieces. Guide the pieces past the blade with the miter gauge. Hold the miters together and check that they come together at the desired angle—usually 90 degrees. Adjust the saw if necessary.

Photo 64 **To cut a miter across the width of a board, angle the miter gauge in relation to the blade.**

Photo 65 **To cut a miter through the thickness of the board, leave the miter gauge square and tilt the blade.**

Cutting Dadoes and Grooves

A dado cutter is one of the first accessories many woodworkers buy for their table saws. It is a special blade or set of blades

Photo 66 **To set the miter gauge with a sliding T-bevel, put the body of the T-bevel against the miter gauge and the T-bevel's blade against the saw blade, not touching any teeth.**

that can cut a wide, square-bottomed groove in a board. Technically, the cut is called a groove if it runs with the grain and a dado if it runs across the grain.

There are two types of dado cutters: stacked cutters and wobble cutters. A stacked dado cutter consists of two outer blades and several inside chippers. The outer blades look like regular saw blades, but the chippers usually have only two teeth. Chippers come in several different thicknesses—$\frac{1}{16}$, $\frac{1}{8}$, and $\frac{1}{4}$ inch. By mounting different combinations of blades on the saw, you can adjust the stacked set to cut dadoes of different widths. Most stacked dado cutters can make cuts from $\frac{1}{4}$ to $\frac{13}{16}$ inch wide in increments of $\frac{1}{16}$ inch. In-between sizes can be set up by inserting metal or paper shims between the cutters. When setting up a stacked dado cutter, you must use both outside blades. Make sure all the teeth face forward before sawing.

Wobble dado cutters consist of a single blade set between two tapered washers. Turning the washers tilts the blade, allowing it to make a wider cut. Wobble dado cutters are infinitely adjustable between $\frac{1}{8}$ and $\frac{13}{16}$ inch.

Stacked dado cutters produce the cleanest cuts. They also produce a flat-bottomed groove. Wobble dado cutters make grooves with rounded bottoms. This is more pronounced on wider cuts. This may be a problem if you do exacting work with exposed dado joints.

Standard throat plate openings are not wide enough to accommodate a dado cutter. You can buy special throat plates, or you can make your own.

To make your own, start with a piece of hardwood or plywood that's the same thickness as your throat plate. Trace the standard throat plate onto your blank, marking for any screws that run through the throat plate. Cut the new throat plate to shape on the band saw or with a saber saw. If the throat plate that came with your saw fits into the opening without screws, you'll have to tap screw holes into the lip of the throat plate hole. Use one machine screw at the front of the lip and one at the rear. (See "Tapping and Threading Metal," page 6.) Countersink the screws in the

new throat plate. Crank the dado cutter below the table. Install the new throat plate. Turn on the saw and crank the blade up through the plate.

To use a dado cutter, turn the washers or add chippers as needed to achieve the necessary width. Put the cutter on the saw.

Raise or lower the saw arbor to set the depth of cut. Make a test cut and measure it. Make any necessary adjustments before cutting the actual stock.

Use the miter gauge to guide dado or groove cuts that run the entire width of the workpiece. Use the rip fence to guide cuts that run the entire length of the workpiece.

Dadoes or grooves that stop short of the width or length of a board require a little more preparation. Start by setting the height and width of the dado cutter as you would for any dado or groove cut. With the saw off, slide a drafting triangle along the rip fence until the triangle touches the infeed side of the blade. Draw a line across the table as shown in P*hoto* 67, marking where the saw starts to cut. If you will be using the rip fence for the cut, extend the line up the guiding edge of the fence. If you will guide the piece with the miter gauge, move the rip fence out of the way.

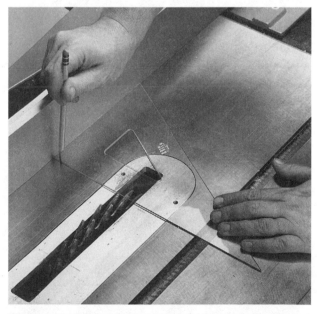

Photo 67 **To make stopped dadoes on the table saw, use a drafting triangle to mark the saw where the dado cutter starts to cut.**

Photo 68 Stop cutting the dado when the layout mark on the workpiece aligns with the mark on the saw.

Photo 69 To make multiple stopped dadoes with the rip fence, clamp a stop block to the outfeed side of the fence.

On the stock, lay out the end of the cut. Transfer this line to a surface that will be visible when you cut—up the edge of the piece for a miter gauge cut, across the top for a rip fence cut. Run the stock through the saw until the marks align as shown in Photo 68. Turn off the saw before you remove the workpiece from the saw. A groove or dado cut this way will be curved at the stopped end. You'll need to chop this curved section square with a chisel.

If you have a number of cuts to make that all stop the same distance from an edge, start by making the first one as described above. Turn off the saw and leave the workpiece in place over the blade. With the layout lines on the saw and workpiece aligned, clamp a stop block to the rip fence against the outfeed edge of the workpiece as shown in Photo 69. If you are using the miter gauge, clamp the stop directly to the table as shown in Photo 70.

If you don't have a dado cutter, you can use a regular saw blade to make dadoes and grooves. Set the blade at the necessary height. Lay out the shoulders of the dado or groove on the stock. For a groove that will be made with the rip fence, make a cut, then move the fence over ⅛ inch. Make the next

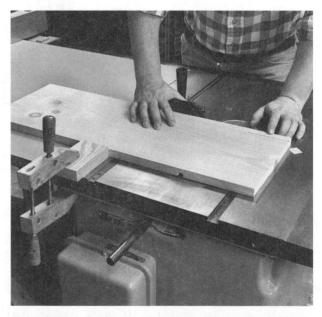

Photo 70 To make multiple stopped dadoes with the miter gauge, clamp the stop block to the table.

cut. Continue until the groove is wide enough. For a dado or groove that will be guided by the miter gauge, cut one shoulder, then shift the stock to cut the other shoulder. Then make repeated cuts to clean out the stock between the shoulders.

MAKING JOINTS

The table saw can make many different joints. Most of these joints require jigs to guide the work. There are plans for many of these jigs in "The Tasks," later in this book. However, two of the most important joinery cuts can be made on the table saw without jigs. They are rabbets and tenons.

Cutting Rabbets

A rabbet is an L-shaped cut in the edge of a board. There are two ways to make a rabbet on the table saw. The first is with a dado cutter. Set the dado cutter to about ¼ inch wider than than the rabbet you want. Lower the cutter below the saw table. Screw or clamp a wooden face to the rip fence. The wooden face, which protects the rip fence, should be at least ¾ inch wide. Position the fence so that the wooden face is over the cutter. Turn up the saw and raise the blade. Be sure that it will not cut the metal rip fence.

The dado cutter will make a semicircular cutout in the wooden face. Adjust the cutter

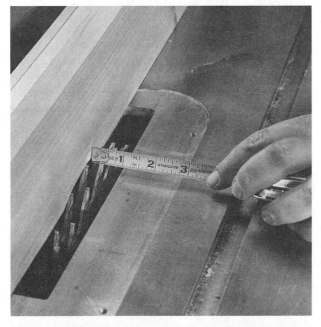

Photo 71 Rather than fussing to get the dado cutter set for an exact rabbet width, it's easier to bury the cutter partly under an auxiliary fence and then adjust the fence.

SAWING A RABBET IN TWO PASSES

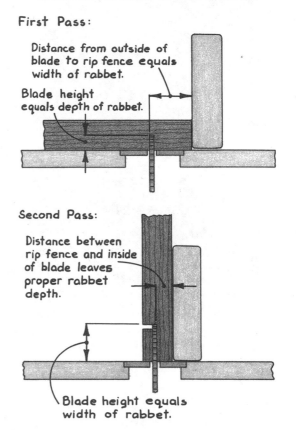

First Pass:

Distance from outside of blade to rip fence equals width of rabbet.

Blade height equals depth of rabbet.

Second Pass:

Distance between rip fence and inside of blade leaves proper rabbet depth.

Blade height equals width of rabbet.

to the cutting depth you need. Measure from the wooden face to the outside of the dado cutter to set the width of the rabbet as shown in *Photo* 71. Some of the cutter will remain under the face. Run the stock along the wooden face to cut the rabbet. An improvement on this wooden face is the "Plastic Laminate Fence or Auxiliary Fence for the Table Saw," page 169.

The other way to cut a rabbet is to make two cuts with a regular saw blade as shown in *Sawing a Rabbet in Two Passes*. Set up for the first cut by adjusting the height of the blade to match the depth of the rabbet. Measure from the outside of the blade to the fence to set the width of the rabbet. Run the stock across the saw. Then change the settings. Set the blade height to match the width of the rabbet. Using the depth of the kerf you made in the first pass as your guide, set the rip fence to leave the proper rabbet depth. Run the stock on edge across the saw to complete the rabbet.

Photo 72   Because there is no scrap to get caught, you can use the rip fence as a stop while guiding rabbet and tenon cuts with the miter gauge.

Photo 73   To make tenons with four shoulders, make the two face cuts first. Then change the cutter height, if necessary, and run the stock on edge over the blade.

Cutting Tenons

Make tenons by cutting rabbets across both sides of the end of a board. Set the dado cutter as wide as possible. Measure from the outside of the dado cutter to the fence to set the length of the tenon. (If the tenon length is equal to or less than the maximum width of your dado cutter, attach a wooden face to the rip fence, just as when cutting rabbets.) The height of the cutter controls the thickness of the tenon. Start with the dado cutter set slightly lower than you think it should be.

Always test your setup with a scrap piece the same thickness as the good stock. This is one of the few times you can use the rip fence as a stop—there is no scrap piece to get caught. Hold the test piece against the miter gauge and slide it to the right until it touches the rip fence as shown in P*hoto* 72. Turn on the saw and run the test piece over the cutter. If the tenon is longer than the dado cutter width, you will have to move the test piece to your left and make another, overlapping cut. Turn the board over and rabbet the other side. Check the thickness of the tenon. Raise

the cutter to make the tenon thinner, lower it to make the tenon thicker. Once the saw is set up, cut the good stock. To cut tenons with four shoulders, reset the cutter height, if necessary, and run the stock on edge over the blade as shown in P*hoto* 73.

For a faster method to cut cleaner tenons on the table saw, see the "Table Saw Tenoning Jig" on page 216.

CUTTING SHEET MATERIALS

Cutting plywood and other sheet stock on a table saw presents its own problems.

Size is the first problem. Most table saws are not big enough for a single person to safely cut 4 × 8-foot sheets. There are several solutions to this problem. You can build extensions for your saw that will support a full-size sheet as you cut it. You can enlist help. Or you can cut the sheets into more manageable pieces with a circular saw or saber saw.

Guiding plywood across the saw is almost always done with the rip fence. The factory edges on plywood are straight and square to one another and make good guide edges to run against the fence. If you cut the stock into smaller pieces first, try to leave a factory edge on each piece to run against the fence as you trim it to size.

While the factory edges are straight and true, they are not always presentable. By the time the stock reaches your shop, chances are the edges have been marred. For this reason, use the factory edges as a guide, but cut the pieces ¼ to ½ inch oversize. Then turn the pieces around and saw off the factory edges and their assorted scars.

Tearout is another problem with cabinet-grade plywood and other veneered sheet stock. This occurs when you cut across the grain of the outer veneer. When cutting on a table saw, tearout occurs on the face of the stock that is down on the table during the cut.

In solid wood, tearout is not a problem, because any slight tearout can be sanded away. But on veneered panels, it can be a disaster. There are three things you can do to prevent tearout. You can stretch a piece of masking tape along the length of the cut. The tape helps support the veneer as it is cut. Or before sawing, you can slice through the veneer with a sharp knife held firmly against a metal straightedge. This cuts the fibers cleanly before the saw has a chance to tear them. The third option is to make a zero-clearance throat plate for your saw. To do this, make a throat plate as described in "Cutting Dadoes and Grooves," page 36, raising your saw blade through the throat plate. This, too, will support the veneer and help prevent tearout.

THE
TASKS

■ **CIRCLE CUTTING** ■ **CLAMPING** ■

COVE MOLDING ■ **DADOES**

DENTIL MOLDING ■ **DOVETAILS, MOCK**

FINGER JOINTS ■ **FLUTING**

HINGE MORTISING ■ **HOLES**

IRREGULAR STOCK SAWING

JOINTING ■ **KERF BENDING**

MEASURING AND LAYOUT ■ **MITERS**

MORTISING ■ **MUNTINS** ■ **PANEL RAISING**

PLASTIC LAMINATE CUTTING

RABBETS ■ **RESAWING** ■ **SANDING**

SPLINE MITERS ■ **STAIR STRINGERS**

STRAIGHTEDGES ■ **TAPERING** ■ **TENONS**

■ **TRIMMING LAMINATED EDGES** ■

CIRCLE CUTTING ON THE BAND SAW

Design by Andy Rae

This band saw fixture is a reliable, safe, and accurate way to cut circles in wood. The cuts are very smooth, requiring little cleanup. The jig is adjustable for circle diameters from about 16½ inches up to about 80 inches.

One end of the fixture sits on the saw table. The other end is supported by an adjustable roller stand. As an alternative to the roller stand, you can make one of the adjustable sliding dovetail legs described in "Drill Press Extension Table," page 229.

To use the circle cutter, drill a small hole at least partway through the center of the stock you'll be cutting. The hole fits over a

tapered stud. Pivot the workpiece on the stud to cut the circle. The stud is on an adjustable slider. To change the diameter of the circle, change the distance between the stud and the saw blade.

MAKING THE JIG

1 Cut and assemble the base and cleats. Cut the base and cleats to the dimensions in the Materials List. Predrill and countersink the cleats for the drywall screws. Glue and screw the cleats to adjacent sides of the base as shown in the *Overall View.*

2 Make the saw blade slot. Turn on the band saw. Feed the fixture into the saw, with the cleat on the short side firmly pressed against the left side of the table. (See *Photo 1-1.*) Cut into the base until the other cleat stops against the front of the saw table. Turn off the saw and remove the fixture.

3 Make the slot. As shown in the *Slider and Slot Detail,* both the slider and the slot are rabbeted so that the top of the slider will be flush with the top and bottom of the base.

Lay out the slot so that its center aligns with the end of the saw kerf as shown in the *Overall View.* On the fixture shown here, the slot begins 6¼ inches from the saw blade. That's because the knob on the slider will bump into the side of the saw table when the slider is 6⅜ inches from the blade. (See *Determining Slot Length.*) If your table edge is a different distance from your blade, lay out your slot accordingly. Stop the layout line

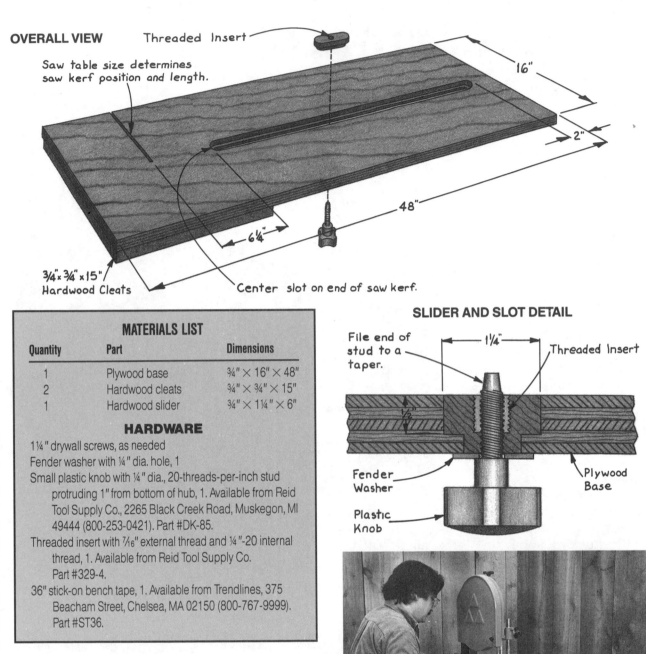

OVERALL VIEW

Threaded Insert

Saw table size determines saw kerf position and length.

16"

2"

48"

6¼"

¾"× ¾"× 15" Hardwood Cleats

Center slot on end of saw kerf.

MATERIALS LIST

Quantity	Part	Dimensions
1	Plywood base	¾" × 16" × 48"
2	Hardwood cleats	¾" × ¾" × 15"
1	Hardwood slider	¾" × 1¼" × 6"

HARDWARE

1¼" drywall screws, as needed

Fender washer with ¼" dia. hole, 1

Small plastic knob with ¼" dia., 20-threads-per-inch stud protruding 1" from bottom of hub, 1. Available from Reid Tool Supply Co., 2265 Black Creek Road, Muskegon, MI 49444 (800-253-0421). Part #DK-85.

Threaded insert with 7/16" external thread and ¼"-20 internal thread, 1. Available from Reid Tool Supply Co. Part #329-4.

36" stick-on bench tape, 1. Available from Trendlines, 375 Beacham Street, Chelsea, MA 02150 (800-767-9999). Part #ST36.

SLIDER AND SLOT DETAIL

File end of stud to a taper.

1¼"

Threaded Insert

½"

Fender Washer

Plastic Knob

Plywood Base

about 2 inches from the outboard end of the fixture.

Cut the slot with a ¾-inch straight bit in the router. Make the slot in three passes, each about ¼ inch deeper than the previous pass. Guide the router with a straightedge clamped along the plywood base, or use the "Router Dado Jig" described on page 65. Clamp the fixture to the bench with the cleats down. Put a scrap of ¾-inch-thick stock under the cleatless end to level the base and keep it off the bench as you rout.

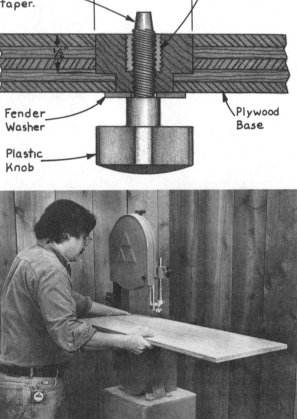

Photo 1-1 To make the kerf, feed the jig into the saw with the cleat at your left pressed firmly against the saw table. Feed until the other cleat stops against the table.

DETERMINING SLOT LENGTH

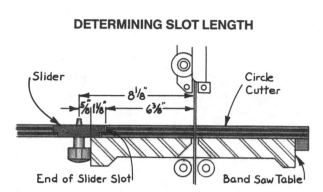

Lay out the slot so that the knob bumps into the band saw table when the slider is closest to the blade.

4 **Rabbet the slot.** Put a ¼-inch rabbeting bit in the router. Set the depth to ½ inch. Rout the inside of the slot.

5 **Make the slider.** The procedure is shown in *Making the Slider*. Start with a piece of ¾ × 1¼-inch hardwood that is at least 4 inches long. With a compass, lay out the ⅝-inch radius on each end of the blank. Cut these radii on the band saw and sand the cuts smooth. Put a ¼-inch piloted rabbeting bit in the router. Set the depth to ¼ inch. Rabbet the circumference of the slider as shown in *Photo 1-2*. Do this in two passes.

The knob for the jig shown in the photographs was made from an old plane knob and a machine bolt. The *Slider and Slot Detail* shows how to make the fixture with a knob you can buy. The knob comes with a stud attached. This simplifies construction.

MAKING THE SLIDER

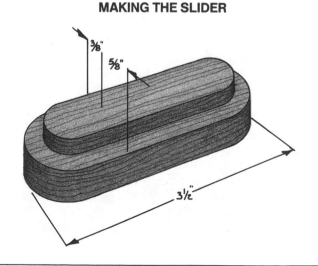

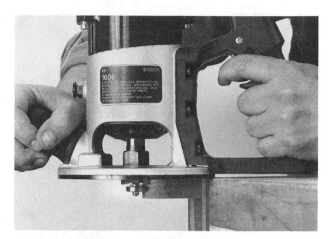

Photo 1-2 Clamp the slider in a bench vise and rabbet the circumference with a ¼-inch rabbeting bit set to ¼ inch deep.

Begin by drilling a ²³⁄₆₄-inch hole for the threaded insert in the center of the slider. Drill all the way through. Screw the insert all the way onto the knob. Then use the knob to screw the insert into the hole through the top of the slider. Remove the knob. Put the slider in the slot. Slip a washer over the knob, and install the knob through the bottom of the fixture.

USING THE JIG

Slide the circle cutter into the blade until both cleats are in contact with the table. Support the outboard side with a roller stand or sliding leg. Clamp one of the cleats to the side of the saw table.

Set the circle radius by measuring from the near side of the blade to the center of the stud. Tighten the knob.

Start with a square piece of stock whose width and length equal the diameter of the circle you wish to cut. Find the exact center of the piece. On this center, drill a ¼-inch-diameter hole into the side of the piece that won't be seen—the bottom of a tabletop, for example. Make the hole slightly deeper than ¼ inch.

Place the hole over the stud protruding from the slider. Push the workpiece against the blade, moving the slider along with it. Tighten the slider. Turn on the saw and slowly rotate the workpiece until you complete the circle.

ROUTER TRAMMEL

Design by Ken Burton

A router trammel essentially is a big compass with a router mounted on one end. It is used to rout perfect circles and circular arcs. There are many designs for this common jig. They all have a pivot point on one end and a router on the other end. The pivot holds the jig in place at the center of a circle while the router cuts the circumference. If you are in a hurry, you can make a trammel by removing your router's subbase and screwing the router to a piece of plywood. Drive a nail or screw into the other end of the plywood, and you are ready to rout.

The trammel shown here will take you longer to make, but it is much more convenient and accurate. It has a lightweight arm with a sturdy adjustable pivot, so you can set the jig to cut any size circle up to about 66 inches in diameter. You won't waste time scrounging around for a suitable plywood scrap the next time you want to rout a circle.

This jig was made to fit a big Elu plunge router. The Elu has a round base with a flat on one side. If your router base is rectangular, just cut the sides of the jig to match. If you have a completely round base, cut out the flat on the arm to match the base.

Although designed to work with a plunge router, the jig also works well with a fixed-base router.

MAKING THE JIG

1 Cut and rabbet the arm blank. Cut a blank for the arm to the dimensions in the Materials List. Do not cut the arm to shape yet. Cut the 1½-inch-wide rabbet on one end that will form a lap joint with the subbase. (See the *Overall View.*) To make this rabbet, mount a ¾-inch straight bit in a table-mounted router. Adjust the depth of cut to match the thickness of the plywood subbase. Set the fence to cut a ¼-inch-wide rabbet. Rout a rabbet across one end of the arm. Move the fence back from the bit about ¼ inch. Run the arm past the bit again to make the rabbet wider. Now set the fence a final time to increase the rabbet width to 1½ inches. When measuring, measure from the side of the bit farthest from the fence. For more information, see "Rabbets," page 26.

OVERALL VIEW

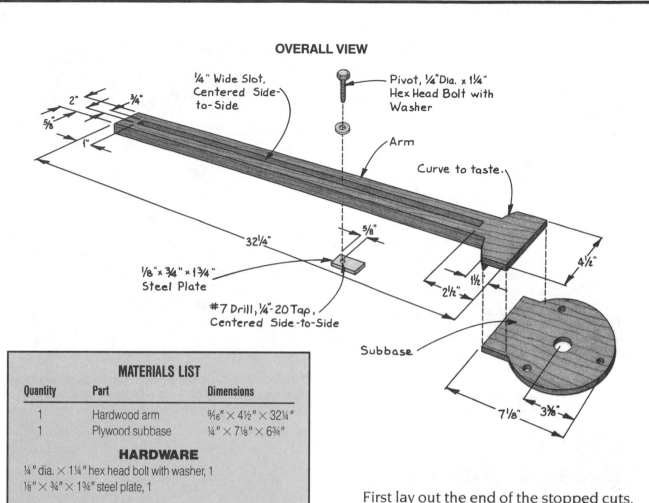

¼" Wide Slot, Centered Side-to-Side

Pivot, ¼"Dia. x 1¼" Hex Head Bolt with Washer

Arm

Curve to taste.

2"   ¾"
5/8"
1"

32¼"

5/8"

⅛" x ¾" x 1¾" Steel Plate

#7 Drill, ¼"-20 Tap, Centered Side-to-Side

4½"

2½"   1½"

Subbase

7⅛"   3⅜"

MATERIALS LIST		
Quantity	Part	Dimensions
1	Hardwood arm	9/16" × 4½" × 32¼"
1	Plywood subbase	¼" × 7⅛" × 6¾"

HARDWARE

¼" dia. × 1¼" hex head bolt with washer, 1
⅛" × ¾" × 1¾" steel plate, 1

2 Rout the adjustment slot in the arm.
Reset the depth of cut on the router table to slightly more than ⅛ inch. Adjust the router table fence so that the bit will cut right down the center of the arm. With the rabbeted surface facing down, rout a groove the full length of the arm.

Replace the ¾-inch bit with a ¼-inch straight bit. Do not move the fence. Rout a slot all the way through the arm. Stop the slot 2½ inches from the rabbeted end and 1 inch from the other end as shown in the *Overall View.* Make the cut in several shallow passes. For more information, see "Making Stopped Cuts on the Router Table," page 24.

3 Cut the arm to shape. The arm is shaped to make it less bulky and easier to manage. Shaping the arm involves making two stopped cuts on the table saw and then finishing them on the band saw.

First lay out the end of the stopped cuts. Draw a line across both faces of the arm, 3½ inches from the rabbeted end. This line is 1 inch before the curved section. You'll stop cutting when you see the blade reach this line. Because of the curve of the blade, the saw will cut slightly farther on the underside of the stock, but it won't cut into the curved section.

Set the rip fence on the table saw 1⅛ inches from the blade. Begin cutting the non-rabbeted end to the layout line. When the cut reaches the line, stop and turn off the saw. Hold the arm still until the blade stops, then back the arm out of the cut. Turn it over and repeat on the other side. With the band saw or saber saw, finish cutting the arm to the shape shown in the *Overall View.*

4 Make and attach the subbase. Cut the subbase to the shape and size shown in the *Overall View,* or adapt it by tracing the subbase of your own router. Cut the base on the band saw or with a saber saw.

At the center of the base, drill a 1-inch hole for the bit. Unscrew the base plate from your router and use it to lay out the mounting holes on the subbase. Drill and countersink these holes. Glue the subbase into the rabbet on the arm.

5 Make the pivot. The pivot consists of a hex head bolt and a threaded steel plate. The plate rides in the groove cut in the underside of the arm. It was made from a scrap of angle iron that was cut with a hacksaw and filed to shape, but any scrap of metal the right size will do. Drill the plate with a #7 drill as shown in the *Overall View.* Tap the hole with a ¼"-20 tap. For more information, see "Tapping and Threading Metal," page 6. Slip the washer onto the bolt and push the bolt through the slot in the jig. Thread on the plate from underneath.

USING THE JIG

In most cases, you'll want to rough-cut your circle on the band saw or with a saber saw. The "Extended Compass" on page 117 is a very accurate tool for laying out tabletops and other large circles. Make the rough cut about ⅛ inch beyond your finished circle, then trim the cut with the router trammel. You also can use the router trammel to do all of the cutting. This usually requires several passes, because you need to make the cuts in depth increments of about ¼ inch.

Whether trimming or doing all the cutting, you set the jig the same way. Mount your router on the jig. If you haven't rough-cut the piece, set the depth of cut to about ¼ inch. If you have rough-cut, set the depth to rout the full thickness of the edge. Turn the jig upside down. Loosen the pivot and slide it along the arm until the distance from the bit equals the radius of the circle you want. Measure from the center of the bolt to the nearest flute of the router bit as shown in P*hoto* 2-1. Tighten the bolt to lock the pivot in place.

Drill a ¼-inch-diameter hole at least ⅝ inch deep at the center of the circle you want to cut. Make the hole in the side that will be least visible in the finished workpiece. For example, drill the hole in the bottom of a

Photo 2-1 **Slide the pivot along the arm until the distance from the bit to the center of the bolt equals the radius you want.**

tabletop and then plug it after routing the circle.

Place the pivot in the hole. If you have a plunge router, turn it on and plunge into the cut. If the router base is fixed, lift the subbase off the work, but keep the pivot in the hole. Turn on the router and carefully lower the router into the work.

Rout the circle or semicircle counterclockwise as shown in P*hoto* 2-2. If you are making more than two revolutions with a plunge bit, retract the bit and turn the jig around clockwise twice. This prevents the cord from getting too twisted. If you are using a fixed-base router, you'll probably find it easier to untwist the cord by unplugging the router.

Cutting Big Holes

You can use the router trammel to make large circular cutouts, such as those in a countertop for a round sink. To do this, set the trammel and drill the pivot hole as described above. Now rout the stock in several passes as described above. But instead of cutting all the way through on the last

Photo 2-2   Drill a ¼-inch-diameter hole ⅝ inch deep at the center of the circle you are going to rout. Insert the pivot in the hole. Plunge the router into the cut. Rout the circle counterclockwise.

pass, leave about ¼ inch of material at the bottom of the cut. This is to prevent gouging the cutout as it separates from the circle.

Now follow the router path with a saber saw to separate the cutout from the circle. Stay at least ⅛ inch away from the cutout as you saw. Clean up the saw cut with a pattern cutting bit or a flush trimming bit in the router. A pattern cutting bit has a guide bearing over the cutter, so run the router on the same side you ran the trammel. A flush trimming bit has the bearing under the cutter, so you will have to flip the cutout to clean up the cut.

CLAMPING CAULS

Design by David Schiff

These clamping cauls are used to help glue up flat panels. In a perfect world, you wouldn't need them at all. You have planed and jointed all twists and bows from the pieces that will make your panel. You should be able to put glue on the edges, line the pieces up in a neat row, and clamp them together. Sometimes it works that way.

Other times, humidity changes play with your boards a bit after they leave the planer. You glue them up and discover that the faces are not all in the same plane. That's when you need clamp-

USING CURVED CAULS

Mark position of twisted board. Then saw a curve in the top caul with the mark as its lowest point.

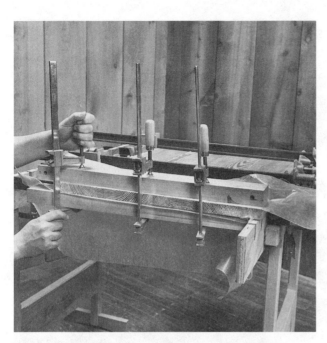

Photo 3-1   Place the cauls in pairs across the panel, one on top and one on bottom. Waxed paper under the cauls prevents gluing them to the panel.

Photo 3-2   To use the cauls on a bench, raise the glue-up on blocks to make room for the clamps.

ing cauls to persuade the maverick board or boards into line.

The cauls are stout pieces of hardwood that have been planed flat on at least one face. The dimensions of the cauls depend on the dimensions of the panel you are gluing up. As a rule of thumb, make the cauls approximately as long as the panel is wide. Make them about twice as thick and wide as the panel is thick. For example, a ¾ × 36 × 48-inch panel would require cauls that are about 1½ × 1½ × 36 inches.

Before putting the cauls in place, tighten clamps across the panel enough to bring glue joints together, but not too tight. Then place the cauls in pairs across the panel, one clamped on top of the panel and one directly below. This is most convenient to do if you use the "Clamp Racks" described on page 59. (See P*hoto* 3-1.) You can do it on the bench, too, if you raise the glue-up on blocks to make room for the clamps as shown in P*hoto* 3-2. Put waxed paper between cauls and workpieces to prevent gluing the two together.

The number of pairs you'll need depends on the length of the panel and how much persuading you must do to straighten it out. Usually, you'll need at least three pairs—one pair at each end and one in the middle. Check that the cauls are pulling the boards into the same plane. When the boards are in the same plane, tighten the rack clamps.

Sometimes on thick panels, you'll find that no matter how tightly you clamp the cauls, you still can't straighten out that one twisted board near the middle of the panel. That's because the cauls diffuse the clamping pressure across the face of the board. You can concentrate that pressure right where you need it by cutting a slight curve in one or more top cauls as shown in U*sing Curved Cauls*.

To do this, mark the top cauls where they pass over the twisted board. Then use a band saw or saber saw to cut a slight curve in the caul. Make the mark the lowest point on the curve. Use a belt sander to smooth the surface of the curve. This way, the caul won't dent the workpiece.

THREADED ROD CLAMPS

Design by Ben Erickson

These shop-made clamps are just the thing for gluing up bent laminations. Each clamp consists of two clamping blocks, two pieces of threaded rod, washers, and nuts. When you apply the clamps, one rod runs over the top of the glue-up and the other runs underneath, virtually ensuring even clamping pressure. What makes the clamps even more ideal is that they are very cheap and easy to make.

While these clamps were designed with bent laminations in mind, they work for other applications, too. The even clamping pressure is useful for edge-gluing panels or for gluing up frames.

Make the blocks from whatever scrap you have on hand. When you need to use the clamps for a different thickness, just make new blocks and reuse the hardware.

MAKING THE JIG

1 Cut the blocks to size. Cut the blocks to the width and thickness specified in the Materials List. Make the blocks 1¾ inches longer than the thickness of the form you are working with. The clamps shown have 3¼-inch-long blocks because they were designed to clamp parts on a form that is 1½ inches thick.

2 Drill the holes into the blocks. Drill the holes on a drill press. If you are making more than one or two clamps, set up a fence with a stop block to help position the holes. The center of each hole should be ⅝ inch from the end. The diameter of the holes should be ¹⁄₁₆ inch larger than the diameter of the threaded rod.

3 Cut the threaded rod. The threaded rods should be at least 3 inches longer than the span you are clamping. Don't make them too much longer, or you'll be trading convenience for versatility; you'll have longer rods on hand for future thicker glue-ups, but you'll spend more time threading nuts before this glue-up.

With a hacksaw, cut the threaded rod to the length desired. (Those pictured are 12 inches long.) Clean up the threads on the cut ends with a small triangular file.

4 Assemble the clamp. On each clamp, one block is locked in place by one set of washers and two sets of nuts. The other block is movable and has washers and nuts only on the outside. To assemble the clamp, first put

OVERALL VIEW

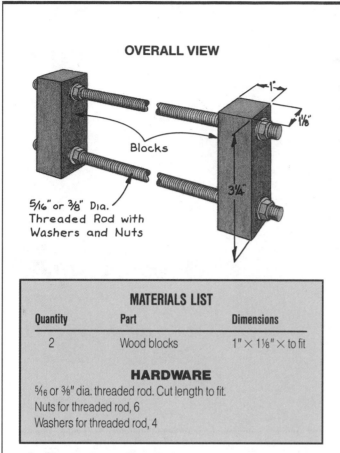

Blocks

5/16" or 3/8" Dia. Threaded Rod with Washers and Nuts

1"

1⅛"

3¼"

MATERIALS LIST		
Quantity	Part	Dimensions
2	Wood blocks	1" × 1⅛" × to fit

HARDWARE

5/16 or 3/8" dia. threaded rod. Cut length to fit.
Nuts for threaded rod, 6
Washers for threaded rod, 4

Photo 4-1 Make both edges of the form parallel to the curve, so that the clamps will exert even pressure perpendicular to the glue line.

a nut on one end of each rod. If you left your rods long, position these nuts to take up as much slack as possible on the fixed side. Slide the fixed block onto the rods. Put a washer over each rod then add another nut. Tighten these nuts. The clamp is now ready to use.

this process as shown in P*hoto* 4-2. Be sure that both sides of the clamp are tightened equally, so that the pressure will be distributed evenly over the work.

When gluing up a panel, tilt the clamping blocks to the right until the rods rest on the top and bottom of the panel. (See P*hoto* 4-2.) This will help keep the panel flat as you tighten the nuts.

USING THE JIG

When you are gluing up bent laminations, the clamps must exert even pressure perpendicular to the glue lines. To achieve this, make the edges of your clamping form parallel as shown in P*hoto* 4-1. Also, when you are ripping stock for your lamination, make a couple of extra strips. Use these strips as clamping pads between the clamps and the glue-up. The pads will distribute clamping pressure more evenly, and they will prevent the clamps from marring the stock.

To use the clamp, whether for lamination or other work, simply slide it over the workpiece and evenly tighten the nuts on the movable block. A deep socket on a ratchet drive or a variable speed drill will speed up

Photo 4-2 A deep socket on either a ratchet drive or a variable speed electric drill will make quick work of tightening the clamps.

MITER CLAMPING BLOCKS AND BOARD

Design by Fred Matlack

You've done it. With care and skill you've cut perfectly mitered frames. Now comes the next challenge—gluing them up.

Unlike other joints, miters need clamping pressure on both sides of each corner. One way to provide this pressure is to purchase special miter clamps. A cheaper way is to make the miter clamping blocks shown here. You can use these blocks with tape and clamps, as described in "Using the Jig." But the job will go more smoothly if you make the clamping board shown in the *Overall View*.

The board provides a flat surface for clamping. As shown in the *Overall View*, the corners of the frame are captured in blocks that have 90-degree notches. Two blocks are screwed to the board. The clamping action comes from driving wedges be-

tween cleats and the two remaining clamping blocks.

The dimensions in the Materials List are for boards and blocks used to glue up a 14 × 15-inch picture frame. However, the clamping board can be any scrap of ½-inch-thick plywood as long as it is at least 6 inches longer and wider than the frame you want to glue up. The blocks

can be plywood or solid wood as long as they are at least ¾ inch thick. If you intend to use the blocks without the clamping board, make them a little bigger to provide more surface for the clamps. The blocks shown in *Photo* 5-2 and *Photo* 5-3 were made from 2½ × 5½-inch scraps of plywood.

MAKING THE JIG

1 Make the clamping board. Cut the clamping board to the dimensions in the Materials List or at least 6 inches longer and wider than the frame you will glue up.

2 Make the clamping blocks and cleats. Cut the clamping blocks and cleats to the dimensions in the Materials List. Lay out the

notches in the clamping blocks as shown in the *Clamping Block Layout*. Cut the 90-degree notch on the band saw.

3 Make the wedges. Cut the wedge blanks to the dimensions in the Materials List. Lay out diagonal cuts as shown in the *Wedge Layout*. On the band saw, cut each wedge blank into two wedges. Guide the cut with a push stick.

OVERALL VIEW

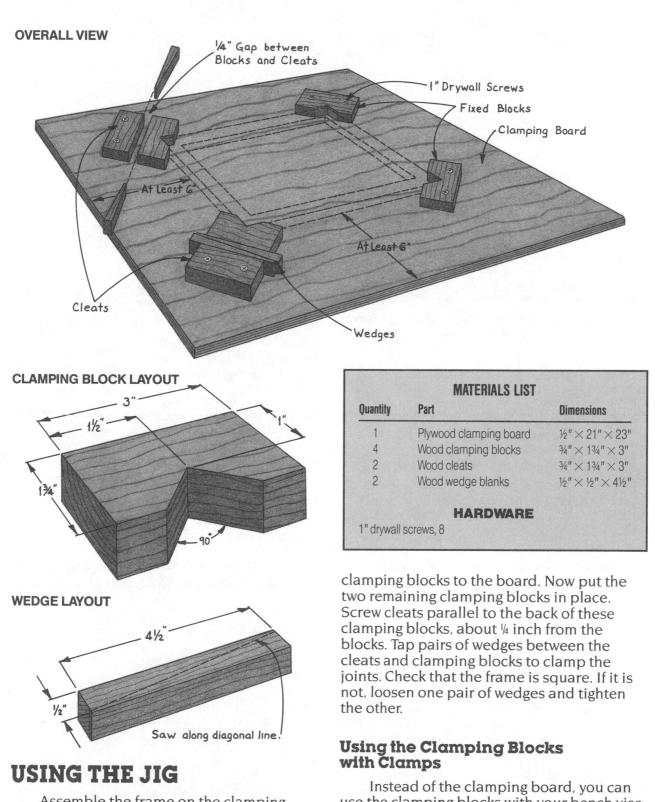

¼" Gap between Blocks and Cleats

1" Drywall Screws

Fixed Blocks

Clamping Board

At Least 6"

At Least 6"

Cleats

Wedges

CLAMPING BLOCK LAYOUT

3"

1½"

1"

1¾"

90°

WEDGE LAYOUT

4½"

½"

Saw along diagonal line.

MATERIALS LIST		
Quantity	Part	Dimensions
1	Plywood clamping board	½" × 21" × 23"
4	Wood clamping blocks	¾" × 1¾" × 3"
2	Wood cleats	¾" × 1¾" × 3"
2	Wood wedge blanks	½" × ½" × 4½"
HARDWARE		

1" drywall screws, 8

USING THE JIG

Assemble the frame on the clamping board. Place two clamping blocks in non-opposing corners as shown in the *Overall View.* Check that the frame is square. Screw these clamping blocks to the board. Now put the two remaining clamping blocks in place. Screw cleats parallel to the back of these clamping blocks, about ¼ inch from the blocks. Tap pairs of wedges between the cleats and clamping blocks to clamp the joints. Check that the frame is square. If it is not, loosen one pair of wedges and tighten the other.

Using the Clamping Blocks with Clamps

Instead of the clamping board, you can use the clamping blocks with your bench vise and dogs and one bar clamp. If you don't have a vise and dogs, you can use two bar clamps. Without the clamping board, you'll need

Photo 5-1 Hold the frame together with packing tape while you adjust the clamps.

another way to keep the miters from sliding around during clamping. One solution is to have a helper hold one diagonal in place while you clamp the other. Another solution is tape. The best tape for the job is plastic packing tape. This tape is wide and strong. Glue squeeze-out won't stick to it, and it leaves little or no residue. Best of all, packing tape stretches just enough. When you pull it around the joints, it provides enough pressure, so you know the joints won't slip while you are clamping.

Put glue on the joint faces, and wrap tape around each joint as shown in Photo 5-1. On a typical picture frame, the tape would cover the corner on the front and back of the frame as well as on the outside edges.

If you have a bench equipped with dogs, put the frame on the bench so that a diagonal stretches between a bench dog and a vise dog. Place a clamping block against the dogs at the two corners as shown in Photo 5-2. Tighten the vise just enough to hold the frame in place, but not enough to distort the frame. Now place a bar clamp across the other diagonal, with a clamping block at each corner. Gradually tighten the vise and the clamp, alternating half-turns of the vise and clamp screws. Check that the frame is square. If the frame is not square, you have more pressure across one diagonal than the

other. Loosen the clamp along the short diagonal and tighten the other.

If you don't have bench dogs, use two bar clamps. Put the clamping blocks around the taped frame. Put a clamp diagonally across the frame, laying the clamp on its side as shown in Photo 5-3. Place another clamp on top of the first and along the other diagonal. Gradually tighten the two clamps, alternating between clamps with each half-turn. Check that there are no gaps in the miter joints. Also check that the frame remains square and flat on the bench. If the frame is out of square, loosen the clamp along the short diagonal and tighten the other.

Photo 5-2 Clamp the frame between bench and vise dogs, then add a diagonal clamp. Check for square.

Photo 5-3 If you don't have bench dogs, clamp the frame between two bar clamps. Check for square once the clamps are set.

CLAMP RACKS

*Design by
Frederic L. Hanisch*

With these clamp racks, you can glue up panels on your sawhorses. Of course, you can do a fine job of gluing up panels right on your bench. Why, then, would you want to make these clamp racks?

There are several reasons. For one, the racks keep glue off your workbench. If you value your bench, you'd rather see glue drips land on the floor. Suspending your glue-up between horses also lets you get underneath the panel. You can watch how the boards are aligning and how the glue is squeezing out, from below as well as from above. Also, if you want to use cauls to straighten your glue-up, you'll have room to clamp the cauls across the top and bottom of the boards. Finally, the racks have slots, which prevent clamps from falling over during glue-up.

This jig clamps to the sides of the sawhorse cross-pieces. Make sure the cross-pieces on the horses you intend to use extend a couple of inches above the legs. If they don't, make this jig to fit between the legs. The racks will be especially convenient to use with the "Shop Horses" on page 309.

To make the racks, cut two pieces of ¾-inch-thick plywood to 4 × 48 inches. Put a dado head on your table saw, and cut a series of 1½-inch-deep notches on 3-inch centers. Make the notches as wide as your clamp bars are thick.

USING THE JIG

Clamp the racks to the horses. Space the horses so that you can fit the workpiece between them. When gluing, it's important that the tops of the racks are in the same plane: Misaligned racks yield twisted panels.

Place a 4-foot level across the racks as shown in *Photo* 6-1. Check that the racks are level with each other at both ends. Then drop the clamps into the appropriate slots.

Gluing Up

Now you are ready to glue up. Arrange the workpieces on the clamps, and put glue on the workpieces, as shown in *Photo* 6-2. Align the glue joints at the middle of the boards and tighten the middle clamp first. Then align the joints and tighten clamps to both sides of the middle. Continue working until you have aligned the ends of the boards and tightened the end clamps. You want

OVERALL VIEW

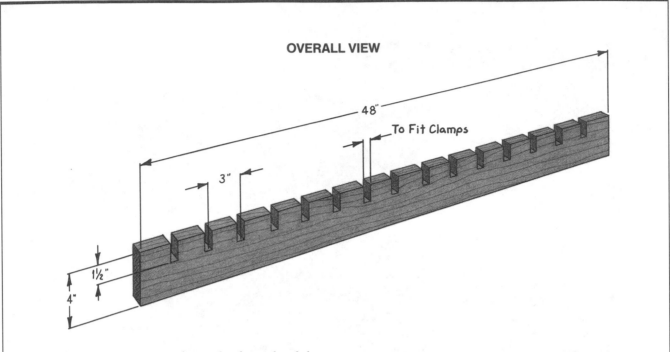

48"

To Fit Clamps

3"

1½"

4"

even glue squeeze-out along the length of the joints. As you proceed, check that the top and bottom faces of the workpieces remain flush and that the top surface remains flat.

Photo 6-1 Use a 4-foot level to make sure the racks are level with each other at both ends.

Photo 6-2 Stand the workpieces on the clamps to apply glue to the edges.

PARALLEL STRAIGHTEDGES

Design by Phil Gehret

The cleverest trick in this jig's bag is laying out cove molding cuts on the table saw. Once you build it, though, you'll grab it to lay out dadoes or any other parallel cuts. It's handy any time you need to draw parallel lines.

Like most versatile jigs, this one is very simple. It consists of two pairs of wooden straightedges held together with stove bolts and wing nuts. The long pair of straightedges acts as the guides, while the arms hold them in place. No matter how far apart the long straightedges are set, they will remain parallel to one another.

MAKING THE JIG

1 Cut the parts to size. Cut the parts to the dimensions in the Materials List. Choose a stable, straight-grained wood, so that the jig will remain straight and true. Round the ends of the arms as shown in the *Overall View*.

2 Drill the holes. The most important process in making this jig is drilling the holes for the bolts. For the jig to work properly, the holes on each arm must be the same distance apart. The holes on each straightedge must be the same distance from the guiding, or outside, edge. Two tricks to ensure success: First, tape or clamp each pair of parts together, face-to-face, before you drill; second, clamp a fence to your drill press table at the appropriate distance from the bit. This will place the holes an equal distance from one edge.

When you've taped the pieces together and set up the drill press, drill the holes in the end of each part. While you're at it, drill hanging holes near the ends of the long straightedge as shown in the *Overall View*.

If you don't have a drill press, drill only one set of holes after taping the pairs together. Then remove the tape and flip one arm or straightedge over so that the holes you just drilled act as guides for the remaining holes. Make sure the edges that were paired the first time the pieces were taped together are the edges that are paired the second time. Drill the remaining holes. Take care not to skew the holes.

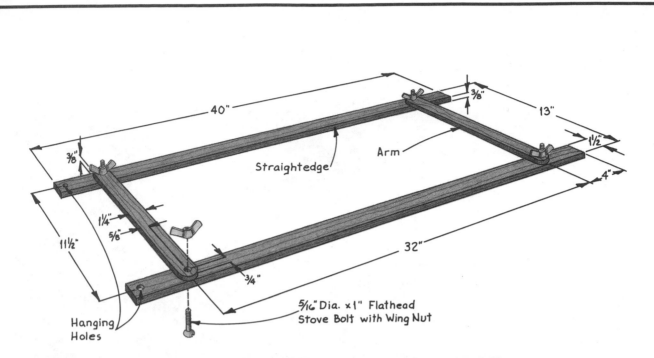

Straightedge

Arm

Hanging Holes

⁵⁄₁₆" Dia. ×1" Flathead Stove Bolt with Wing Nut

MATERIALS LIST		
Quantity	Part	Dimensions
2	Hardwood arms	⅜" × 1¼" × 13"
2	Hardwood straightedges	⅜" × 1½" × 40"

HARDWARE

⁵⁄₁₆" dia. × 1" flathead stove bolts with wing nuts, 4

Separate the pairs. Countersink the straightedges for the stove bolts.

3 Assemble the jig. Bolt the pieces together with the stove bolts and wing nuts. Spread the straightedges as wide as possible. Measure between them to make sure they are parallel. Double-check at several other settings. If the two straightedges don't remain parallel at all settings, remake the jig.

USING THE JIG

It's easy to see how to use this jig for laying out parallel lines. Just set the straightedges at the necessary distance apart. Use a square or T-bevel to hold the jig at the appropriate angle and lay out the lines as shown in P*hoto* 7-1.

Making Cove Molding

By running stock over the saw blade at an angle, you can cut a cove in it. The parallel straightedge helps you set the fence at the angle you need.

Raise the blade to the full depth of the cove. Set the distance between the jig's inside straightedges to the full width of the cove. Place the jig over the blade. Turn the jig

Photo 7-1   To lay out parallel lines, set the jig for the needed spacing. Use a square or T-bevel to position the jig at the appropriate angle.

Photo 7-2 Draw a reference line along the inside of the rear straightedge. Use this line to help position the fence for cove cutting.

Photo 7-3 Cut the cove in several passes, raising the saw blade about 1/16 inch each time.

clockwise until the inside of the rear straight-edge touches a tooth where the blade comes up out of the table. Hold the jig against this tooth and continue turning it until the inside of the front straightedge touches a tooth where the blade goes back into the table. Draw a line on the saw table along the inside of the rear straightedge as shown in P*hoto* 7-2. Remove the jig from the saw.

Now you will clamp a fence across the saw parallel to the line you just drew. The exact placement of the fence is determined by the position of the cove on the stock. Use the parallel straightedge jig to find the fence position. Let's say, for example, you are cutting a 2-inch-wide cove that starts 1/4 inch from the edge of the board. Set the distance between the inside straightedges to 2 1/4 inches. Set one straightedge along the line you drew on the saw table. Draw another line along the inside straightedge. Position the fence along this line and clamp it firmly to the table.

To cut the cove, lower the blade until only about 1/8 inch is showing above the table. Guide the workpiece along the fence past the blade as shown in P*hoto* 7-3. Raise the blade 1/16 inch and repeat. Continue until the cut is as deep as necessary. Scrape and sand away the saw marks.

Cutting Wide Dadoes

You can use this jig when you need to cut dadoes that are wider than the router bit you have available. Begin by laying out a dado. Measure from the edge of the router bit to the outside of the router base. Lay out this distance on either side of the dado. At these points, make lines across the piece parallel to the dado as shown in *Cutting Wide Dadoes*. Set the jig on the workpiece. Align the inside edges of the straightedges with the lines.

CUTTING WIDE DADOES

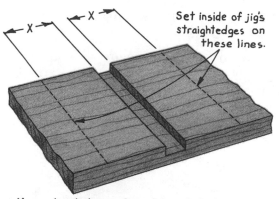

X equals distance from edge of router base to edge of router bit.

CUTTING EVENLY SPACED DADOES

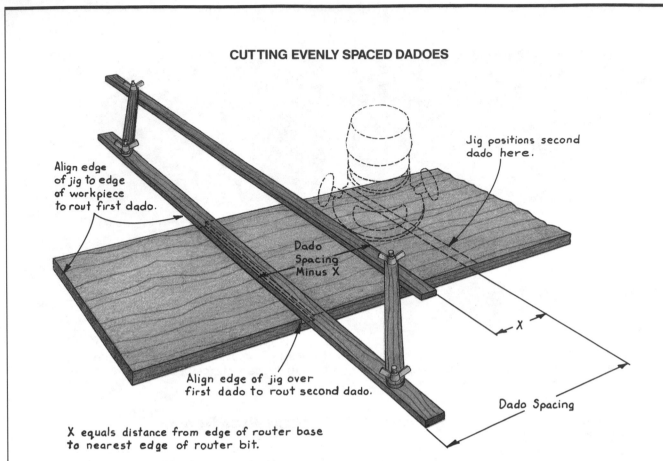

Align edge
of jig to edge
of workpiece
to rout first dado.

Jig positions second
dado here.

Dado
Spacing
Minus X

Align edge of jig over
first dado to rout second dado.

X

Dado Spacing

X equals distance from edge of router base
to nearest edge of router bit.

Clamp the jig in place. Rout the dado by guiding the router along the jig's straightedges. If the dado is more than twice the bit diameter, you'll be left with a strip in the middle of the dado. Clean this out by moving the router back and forth against the fences or by slicing it off with a chisel. If you have more than a few wide dadoes to rout, consider building the "Wide Dado Jig for the Router," page 72.

Making Evenly Spaced Parallel Cuts

You can also use the jig to guide a series of evenly spaced cuts—such as shelf dadoes in the sides of a bookcase. *Cutting Evenly Spaced Dadoes* shows how this is done. This time, you'll guide the router against the outside of the jig's straightedges.

To set the jig, measure from the edge of the router bit to the outside of the router base. Let's say the distance is 3 inches and you want the dadoes 12 inches apart on center. Subtract 3 from 12, and set the outside edges of the straightedges this distance apart—9 inches in this case. Tighten the wing nuts.

Align the outside edge of one of the jig's straightedges with the bottom of the workpiece. Clamp the jig in place. Guide the router against the outside of the other straightedge. The resulting dado will be 12 inches from the bottom of the workpiece.

Now align the outside of one straightedge over the first dado as shown in *Cutting Evenly Spaced Dadoes*. Clamp the jig in place and rout the second dado. The dadoes will be 12 inches apart on center. Continue this process until all the dadoes are routed.

ROUTER DADO JIG

Design by Mitch Mandel

With this jig, accurately positioning your router to cut dadoes is a snap. It's designed to lay out the cut from the centerline of a dado, so the jig works with any width of dado. In addition, the jig lets you stop dadoes quickly and easily, right where you want them. The jig is made from a piece of hardwood plywood.

MAKING THE JIG

1 Cut the plywood. Cut a piece of plywood to the dimensions in the Materials List.

2 Cut out the flap. Draw a line 4 inches from one end of the board as shown in the *Overall View*. Now set the table saw rip fence to make a cut 4 inches wide. Begin cutting at the end farthest from the line. Stop when the blade crosses the line. Now crosscut along the line

to remove the flap. You'll trim the flap to size later.

3 Bevel the guide surface. This is an important step that's easy to overlook. When you're using the jig, most of the chips and dust will be thrown behind the path of the router. Some of the chips, however, will be thrown ahead of the router. The debris gets trapped between the jig and the router, forcing the cut

OVERALL VIEW

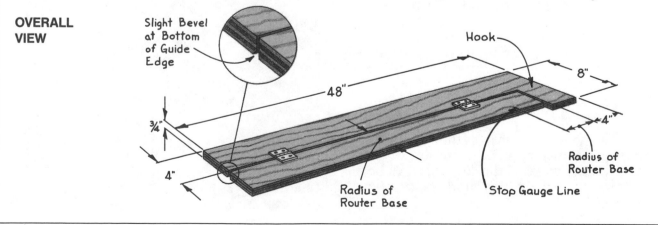

Slight Bevel at Bottom of Guide Edge

Hook

48"

8"

¾"

4"

4"

Radius of Router Base

Radius of Router Base

Stop Gauge Line

MATERIALS LIST		
Quantity	Part	Dimensions
1	Jig	¾" × 8" × 48"
HARDWARE		
2" butt hinges, 2		

Photo 8-1   Align the outside of the flap with the layout mark. Clamp the jig in position.

Photo 8-2   Flip up the flap and rout from left to right.

Photo 8-3   The hook will stop the router at the right spot.

out of alignment. To prevent this, give the debris someplace to go by slightly beveling the bottom of the guide edge with a block plane. Don't make the bevel as thick as the base of your router; you don't want the base to slip into the bevel during the cut.

4 **Measure your router and rip the flap.** The width of the flap equals the radius of your router base. Carefully measure the diameter of your router base and divide that number by 2 to get the radius. Rip the flap to that width. If the base is 6 inches in diameter, for example, set your rip fence precisely 3 inches from the blade and rip the flap. Draw a line this same distance from one end of the flap. When the jig is in use, this line will help you accurately position the jig for stopped dadoes. To make this a permanent accurate mark, cut it into the edge with a utility knife, then fill it in with a ballpoint pen.

5 **Attach the hinges.** Position two hinges along the guide edge of the jig, placing one about 12 inches from each end. Make sure that the hinges are square to the edge before screwing them in place. The hinge barrel will be proud of the guide edge, but it doesn't matter. The plywood is thick enough to allow the router base to slide under the hinge barrel. Put the flap in position, holding the ripped edge of the flap firmly against the guide edge of the jig as you screw the hinges to the flap.

USING THE JIG

The beauty of this jig is that it is simple to position. Just mark the centerline of the dado on the edges of the stock. If you'll be making stopped dadoes, mark the stopping points, too.

With the flap down and the jig hook on your right, align the outside of the flap with the layout marks as shown in P*hoto* 8-1. If you're routing a dado that stops on one end, align the stop gauge line with the stop mark on the work. If you are cutting through dadoes, make sure the router can complete the cut without bumping into the hook. Clamp the jig in position so that the clamps are out of the router's path.

Now flip up the flap and switch on the router. Place it firmly against the left side of the jig where the jig overhangs the work and begin your cut. For a stopped dado, the hook will stop the router at the right spot. You'll get a better, more easily controlled cut if you move the router from left to right as shown in P*hoto* 8-2 and P*hoto* 8-3. You'll also get better results if you rout deep dadoes in a series of passes. Adjust the depth of cut so that you're cutting no more than ⅛ inch deep with each pass.

ADJUSTABLE DADO JIG FOR THE ROUTER

Design by
Douglas Goodale

This jig lets you use a ½-inch-diameter straight bit to rout dadoes from ½ to 1½ inches wide. It works on boards up to 12 inches wide.

One advantage of this jig, of course, is that you don't need to buy a new bit for every dado width. That's not the only reason to build it, though. If you have ever tried to make snug dadoes in ¾-inch-thick plywood, you know that plywood is likely to be ¾ inches thick in name only. You'll get a snug fit if your dado is $^{11}/_{16}$ or maybe $^{23}/_{32}$ inch wide, but such bits aren't commonly available. Because this jig is infinitely adjustable, you can tailor dado width precisely to stock thickness. The jig also extends the usefulness of a light-duty router. You can cut wide dadoes in several passes rather than straining the router to cut the entire width at once.

The dimensions in the Materials List are for a router with a 6-inch-diameter base. If your router base is a different size, the dimensions are easy to adapt. Just make the base 5 inches wider than your router base width. Make the bottom cleats as long as the jig is wide.

MAKING THE JIG

1 Cut the base. Cut the plywood base to the dimensions in the Materials List if your router has a 6-inch-diameter base. If not, make the base 5 inches wider than your router base width. Be careful to make the base square.

2 Cut the cleats and fences. Rip plywood for the cleats and fences, and then crosscut the pieces to the dimensions in the Materials List. In case your router does not have a 6-inch-diameter base, remember to make the cleats as long as the jig is wide.

Glue and nail the cleats to the bottom of the jig as shown in the *Overall View.* Don't put any nails near the middle, where you will cut out for the bit slot. Make sure one side and both ends of both cleats are flush with the base.

3 Attach the fixed fence. Glue and nail the fixed fence to the top of the base as shown in the *Overall View.* Again, make sure one side and both ends of the fence are flush with the base.

OVERALL VIEW

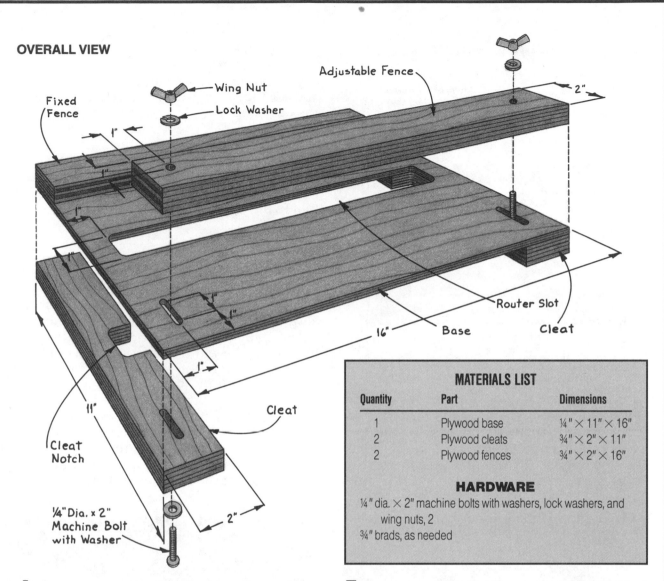

MATERIALS LIST		
Quantity	**Part**	**Dimensions**
1	Plywood base	¼" × 11" × 16"
2	Plywood cleats	¾" × 2" × 11"
2	Plywood fences	¾" × 2" × 16"

HARDWARE

¼" dia. × 2" machine bolts with washers, lock washers, and
   wing nuts, 2

¾" brads, as needed

4 Drill holes in the adjustable fence and base. Drill a ¼-inch-diameter hole in each end of the adjustable fence as shown in the *Overall View*. Place the fence on the base, with one side and both ends flush with the base. Now drill through the base and the cleat below.

   Move the adjustable fence 1 inch closer to the fixed fence. Make sure the adjustable fence is parallel to the fixed fence, then clamp it in position. Again, drill through the holes in the fixed fence, through the base and the cleat below. Remove the adjustable fence. With a straightedge and pencil, draw lines connecting the outside edges of the holes. Use a saber saw to carefully cut out the material between the lines, connecting the holes into slots.

5 Assemble the jig. Put the machine bolts in the slots through the bottom of the jig as shown in the *Overall View*. Place the adjustable fence on the bolts, then put the lock washers and wing nuts in place.

6 Cut the router slot. Position the adjustable fence so that it is flush with the outside edge of the jig. Tighten the wing nuts. Draw lines on the base 1 inch from the short edges, as shown in *Routing the Slot*. These lines mark the boundary of a slot you are about to rout. Put a ½-inch-diameter straight bit in the router. Set the cutting depth to ⅜ inch.

   Position the jig on the workbench so that the fixed fence is to your left. With a plunge router, plunge approximately in the middle of the base. If you don't have a plunge router,

ROUTING THE SLOT

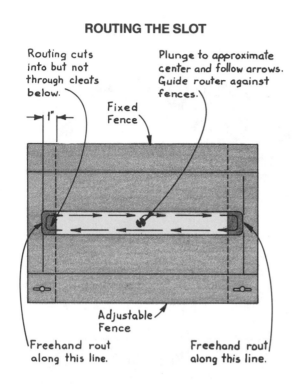

Routing cuts into but not through cleats below.

Plunge to approximate center and follow arrows. Guide router against fences.

Fixed Fence

1"

Adjustable Fence

Freehand rout along this line.

Freehand rout along this line.

hold the router off the base and turn it on. Place one edge of the router base on the jig base. Hold the router firmly and tilt the bit into the jig base. Now move the router to the left until it contacts the fixed fence. Continue

routing clockwise as shown in *Routing the Slot*. Do not rout across the boundary lines you drew. Routing the slot cuts into the cleats. You'll actually cut away the rest of the cleat in the next step.

7 Complete the cleat notches. With the saber saw, cut away the cleat exposed by routing the slot. Follow the profile of the slot as you work. These cleat notches are important to the operation of the jig.

USING THE JIG

With a 6-inch router base and a ½-inch straight bit, the width of the dado you cut will always be 5½ inches less than the distance between the two fences. For other router base sizes, the width of the dado will equal the distance between fences minus the router base width, minus the bit diameter.

When setting the adjustable fence, keep it parallel to the fixed fence. An easy way to do this is to make spacer blocks. Make the blocks 5½ inches wider than the dado you need and about 6 inches long. Then put the spacer against the fixed fence, butt the

Photo 9-1 Set the adjustable fence for the dado you want. Place the jig on the stock with the fixed fence to your left. Butt the cleat that's closest to you against the stock.

Photo 9-2 Place the bit in the cleat notch nearest you. Butt the router base against the fixed fence. Rout the length of the fixed fence.

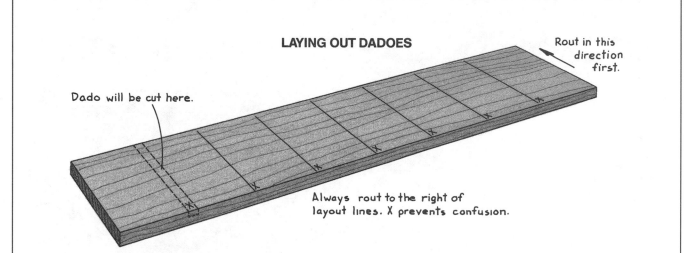

LAYING OUT DADOES

Rout in this direction first.

Dado will be cut here.

Always rout to the right of layout lines. X prevents confusion.

adjustable fence against the spacer, and tighten the wing nuts. Here are the widths of spacers that Goodale made to use with his jig and a ½-inch-diameter straight bit:

> 6 inches wide for ½-inch dadoes
> 6¼ inches wide for ¾-inch dadoes
> 6½ inches wide for 1-inch dadoes

No spacer block is necessary for 1½-inch dadoes, because it's easy to align the adjustable fence to the edge of the base.

Laying Out the Dadoes

Lay out the left side of each dado as shown in *Laying Out Dadoes*. Make an X on the right side to make sure you always rout on the correct side of the layout line.

Cutting the Dadoes

With this jig, most dadoes can be routed to full depth on the first pass. If the dado is deeper than about ½ inch, rout the depth in two or more passes. In any case, set the final bit depth to ¼ inch more than the dado depth you want to account for the thickness of the base. Rout all your dadoes with a ½-inch-diameter straight bit—the spacer sizes listed above depend on it.

First set the adjustable fence for the dado width you want. Then place the jig on the stock with the fixed fence to your left as shown in *Photo 9-1*. Butt the cleat that's closest to you against the edge of the stock.

Align the left side of the router slot with a dado layout line. Secure the jig to the workpiece with a clamp on the upper right side of the adjustable fence as shown in *Photo 9-2*. Make sure the clamp won't get in the way of the router. A spring clamp is ideal for this; it has a low profile and works quickly.

Place the router on the jig with the bit extending into the cleat notch nearest you. Butt the router base against the fixed fence. Turn on the router and rout along the length of the fixed fence as shown in *Photo 9-2*. Stop when the router bit leaves the workpiece and enters the other cleat notch. Then butt the router base against the adjustable fence and rout back toward you. Stop when the bit enters the first cleat notch.

If the dado you are making is wider than 1 inch, you will be left with a strip of material in the middle of your dado. In most cases, this strip can be removed with a freehand pass of the router. If you are not comfortable doing this, leave the middle strip until you have routed all the dadoes. Then reset the adjustable fence so that you can rout against it to remove the waste.

WIDE DADO JIG FOR THE ROUTER

Design by
Douglas Goodale

Many times you want to rout a dado wider than your widest bit. It's an easy problem to solve; all you need are four scraps of plywood and a dozen drywall screws.

The jig shown here cuts 1⅛-inch-wide dadoes in 11¼-inch-wide stock. It requires a ½-inch-diameter straight bit in a router with a 6-inch-diameter base. That's the only job it will do.

You can easily build this jig, however, to fit any router and to cut any width dado with any straight bit. One thing to consider: Make the jig from plywood that is no thicker than the stock you'll dado.

MAKING THE JIG

1 Cut the plywood to size. Douglas Goodale made the jig shown here with plywood 3 inches wide. The width is arbitrary. Goodale happened to have some 3-inch-wide plywood on hand. Use any width between about 2 and 4 inches. Rip stock for the four pieces.

To determine the length of the fences, add the combined width of the cleats to the width of the stock you'll dado. For example, if the stock is 11¼ inches wide and each cleat is 3 inches wide, cut the fences 17¼ inches long.

To determine the length of the cleats, subtract the diameter of the router bit you'll use from the width of the dado you want to make. To this figure, add the combined width

of the fences and the diameter of the router base. Cut the cleats to this length.

2 Assemble the jig. In use, the jig should fit snugly over the workpiece. The easiest way to achieve this is to assemble the jig directly on a piece of the stock you will dado.

First lay the stock on the bench and draw a square line across it, a few inches from one end. Next place one cleat on each side of the stock so that one end of each cleat is even with the line as shown in *Photo* 10-1. Shim the cleats so that they are flush with the top of the workpiece.

Put glue on one fence where it will overlap the cleats. Then place the fence over the workpiece along the square line as shown in *Photo* 10-2. Check that it is square to

OVERALL VIEW

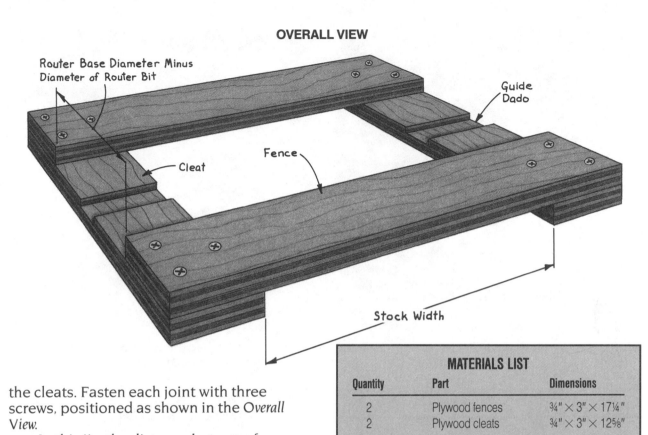

Router Base Diameter Minus
Diameter of Router Bit

Guide
Dado

Cleat

Fence

Stock Width

the cleats. Fasten each joint with three screws, positioned as shown in the *Overall View.*

In this jig, the distance between fences determines the width of the dado. If lengths and widths of all four parts are exact, the edges of the parts will be flush at all four

MATERIALS LIST		
Quantity	Part	Dimensions
2	Plywood fences	¾" × 3" × 17¼"
2	Plywood cleats	¾" × 3" × 12⅝"

HARDWARE

1¼" drywall screws, 12

Photo 10-1 Align one end of each cleat with a square line across the stock.

Photo 10-2 Place a fence over the workpiece along the square line. Check that the fence is square to the cleats.

Photo 10-3 Make guide dadoes in the cleats by guiding the router against the fences.

Photo 10-4 Place the jig on the workpiece with the guide dado aligned to the dado layout line.

Photo 10-5 Start routing away from you, guiding the router against the fence to your left.

Photo 10-6 Rout back toward you, guiding the router against the fence to your right.

corners. But it is better not to rely on that. Instead, subtract the diameter of the router bit from the width of the dado. To this amount, add the diameter of the router base to get the distance between the fences. Draw square lines across the cleats this distance from the fence you have already assembled.

Put glue on the other fence and screw it to the cleats.

3 Cut the guide dadoes. Clamp one cleat to the bench. Select the bit you'll use for dadoing and put it in the router. Set the bit depth to the dado depth you want. Guiding the router against one fence and then the other, rout a guide dado in one cleat as shown in P*hoto* 10-3. Repeat the process to make guide dadoes in both cleats.

USING THE JIG

Laying Out the Dadoes and Aligning the Jig

Lay out one shoulder of each dado. Make an X on the waste side of each layout line. Place the jig on the workpiece with the guide dado aligned as shown in P*hoto* 10-4. The jig can be clamped to the workpiece, but this shouldn't be necessary, since the jig was made for a snug fit.

Routing the Dado

Turn on the router. Put the base on the front cleat and bring it into contact with the fence to your left as shown in P*hoto* 10-5. Push the router slowly and steadily away from you until it leaves the workpiece and is resting on the back cleat. Bring the base into contact with the fence on your right and rout back toward you as shown in P*hoto* 10-6 until the router base rests on the front cleat again.

Depending on router bit diameter and dado width, there may be a strip of waste left in the middle of the dado. Remove this strip with a freehand pass of the router. If you are not comfortable using the router freehand, remove the strip with a chisel.

INCREMENTAL INDEXING

Design by Fred Matlack

You'll reach for this table saw jig any time you need to cut regularly spaced kerfs. It's the jig you'll need to cut finger joints, grids, dentil molding, and kerfs for bending. All of these operations involve making a cut, then moving the workpiece a specified distance to make the next cut.

The incremental indexing jig makes it easy to move the stock that specific distance. The jig consists of a miter gauge extension fence with an adjustable reference pin. You set the pin a given distance from the blade and make the first cut. For the next cut, you shift the work so that the fresh kerf is over the reference pin. The process is repeated until all the cuts are made.

If you have ever tried to cut finger joints with a fixed

pin jig, you'll really appreciate the adjustable pin on this jig. To make the finger joint (also called a box joint), the spaces between kerfs must be precisely as wide as the kerfs. The slightest error accumulates and ruins the joint. The adjustable pin on this joint lets you make minute adjustments on trial pieces

until you get the jig set precisely.

The jig shown is designed to cut ⅛-inch-wide saw kerfs at any spacing. For wider kerfs, you'll need to cut wider reference slots and to make a thicker reference pin. Cut the slots as wide as the desired kerf. Cut the pin to fit into the slots.

MAKING THE JIG

1 Cut the fences to size. Cut the fences to the dimensions in the Materials List. Round-over the back corners of the fixed fence as shown in the *Overall View.*

2 Cut the screw slots. The adjustable fence is attached to the fixed fence with ¼-inch-diameter × 2-inch machine screws, washers, and wing nuts. The screws pass through slots

in the adjustable fence, allowing you to move the adjustable fence.

As shown in the *Overall View,* the slot is stepped to house the bolt head. Cut these slots with a table-mounted router. (See "Making Stopped Cuts on the Router Table," page 24.) Cut the wider slot first with a ⅝-inch straight bit. The bolt heads fit into this slot. To cut it, clamp the fence ¹¹⁄₁₆ inch from the bit. Set the depth of cut for ⅛ inch. Cut the

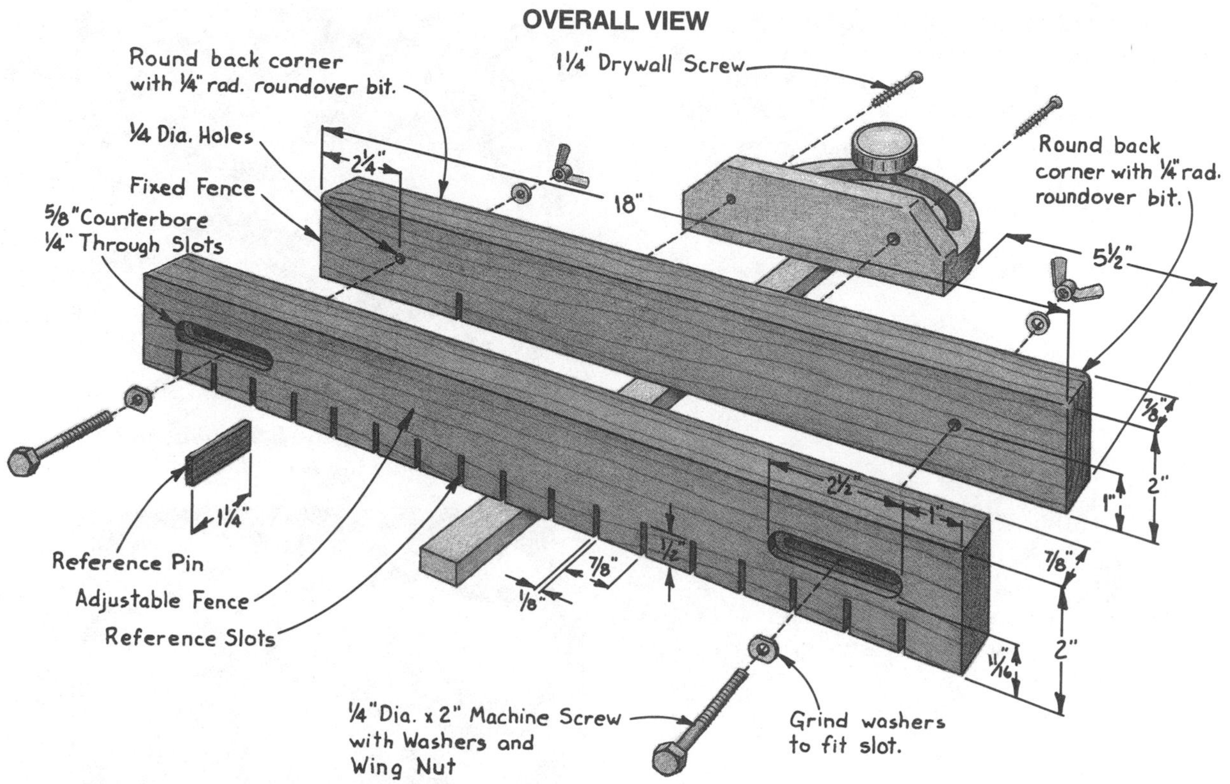
OVERALL VIEW
Round back corner with ¼" rad. roundover bit.
1¼" Drywall Screw
¼ Dia. Holes
Fixed Fence
⅝"Counterbore ¼" Through Slots
2¼"
18"
Round back corner with ¼" rad. roundover bit.
5½"
⅞"
2"
1"
2½"
1"
1¼"
Reference Pin
Adjustable Fence
Reference Slots
⅞"
½"
⅛"
⅞"
2"
11/16"
¼"Dia. x 2" Machine Screw with Washers and Wing Nut
Grind washers to fit slot.

MATERIALS LIST

Quantity	Part	Dimensions
1	Fixed fence	⅞" × 2" × 18"
1	Adjustable fence	⅞" × 2" × 18"
1	Reference pin	⅛" × ½" × 1¼"

HARDWARE

1¼" drywall screws, 2

¼" dia. × 2" machine screws with washers and wing nuts, 2

slots shown in the *Overall View.* Then raise the bit to ¼ inch and repeat, cutting the slots to their final depth.

Replace the ⅝-inch bit with a ¼-inch straight bit, but don't move the fence. Cut the ¼-inch slots all the way through the piece. Make the slots in several passes to avoid stressing the bit.

3 Cut the reference slots. As shown in the *Overall View,* the kerfs in the adjustable fence are ⅞ inch apart. Cut the reference slots on the table saw. To space them evenly, you will need to make a temporary indexing fence—a sort of "Which came first, the chicken or the egg?" situation.

Make the temporary fence by attaching a 2 × 18-inch scrap to the miter gauge so that at least 6 inches of it extends beyond the blade. Set the blade height to ½ inch. Square the miter gauge to the blade and cut through the scrap.

Cut a reference pin to fit snugly into the slot. Loosen the clamps and slide the scrap to the right until the pin is ⅞ inch from the right side of the blade. Clamp the adjustable fence against the scrap so that one end butts against the reference pin. Cut the first reference slot. Move the adjustable fence to the right until the slot you just cut slips over the pin. Make the next cut, then move the fence again. Repeat until there are slots all along the fence.

4 Assemble the jig. Lay out and drill the bolt holes through the fixed fence as shown in the *Overall View.* Bolt the adjustable fence to the fixed fence. You will have to grind or file the washers to fit into the slots. Center the jig on the miter gauge and screw it in place with 1¼-inch drywall screws.

5 **Make the reference pin.** Cut the reference pin to the dimensions in the Materials List. You could also salvage the one from the temporary indexing jig you made earlier. If you are making a fresh pin, make several extra pins while you're at it, so you'll have some on hand. Fit the pin carefully to the reference slots.

USING THE JIG

The jig works essentially the same way the temporary fence did when cutting reference slots. Position the reference pin at the needed distance from the blade as shown in *Photo* 11-1. For example, if you want to cut kerfs that are 2 inches apart, set the pin 2 inches from the blade. Make the first cut.

Put the first kerf over the reference pin and make the second cut as shown in *Photo* 11-2. Repeat to create as many evenly spaced kerfs as needed.

With time, you'll adjust this jig for a variety of cuts. Each new setting probably will cut a new kerf in the adjustable fence. In time, you may chew up a couple of inches of the adjustable fence. When you can no longer find a slot that will work for the spacing you need, it's time to make a new adjustable fence.

Cutting Finger Joints

Even with the best of jigs, setting up to cut finger joints can be tricky. Test your setup on scrap wood. When satisfied with the fit, cut the joint in good stock.

The jig shown here cuts ⅛-inch-thick finger joints. Make the width of the stock a multiple of ⅛, so that the spacing works out evenly. Set the depth of cut to slightly more than the thickness of the stock.

Position the pin ⅛ inch from the blade. Butt the first test piece against the pin. Run the piece across the blade. Move it over so that the kerf you just cut straddles the pin. Make another cut. Continue cutting and moving until you have cut fingers across the end of the board.

Position the second test piece on the jig.

Photo 11-1 Set up the first cut by butting the workpiece against the reference pin.

Photo 11-2 Set up the second cut by placing the first cut over the reference pin.

Photo 11-3 Start making the finger joint in the second board by aligning the board's edge with the edge of the kerf in the jig.

Photo 11-4 Clamp one end of the board to the bench and lift the other end until the kerf closes about halfway.

Photo 11-5 Measure the gap between the bench and the underside of the board at the radius mark. This measurement equals the kerf spacing.

Align the right edge of the piece with the right edge of the saw kerf in the jig as shown in Photo 11-3. Cut fingers across the end of this board. Check the fit. If the fingers are too tight, move the pin toward the blade. If they are too loose, move the pin away. Once you've made the adjustment, recut both pieces. Keep testing until you have test pieces that fit perfectly. Then make your finger joints.

Kerf Bending

Kerf bending is a technique that allows you to bend a thick board without steaming or laminating it. Make a series of kerfs across the width of the board, each about two-thirds to three-quarters the thickness of the stock. The kerfed piece will bend like the top on a rolltop desk. If the kerfs are all the same depth and evenly spaced, the piece will bend smoothly. Even spacing is where the indexing jig comes in.

The exact depth of the kerf depends on the species of wood and how much you intend to bend it. Woods with long, coarse grain, such as oak and ash, bend better than woods with short, fine grain, such as mahogany. As a result, mahogany needs to be kerfed more deeply than oak to make the same bend. You'll have to experiment with different kerf depths to find out what works.

The more you want to bend the wood, the closer the kerf spacing will need to be. Here is how to determine the spacing:

Cut several test pieces that are the same thickness and species as the good stock. Make the pieces at least 2 inches wide. Cut a kerf 4 inches from one end of a test piece. Clamp the 4-inch section to the bench, with the kerf facing up. Determine the radius of the desired curve, and make a mark that distance from the kerf.

Bend the piece up until the kerf closes about halfway as shown in Photo 11-4. Measure the gap between the bench and the underside of the board at the radius mark as shown in Photo 11-5. The kerfs should be this distance apart.

Set the indexing jig reference pin one kerf space from the table saw blade. Use the jig as described to cut evenly spaced kerfs across the test piece. Bend the test piece to the radius you want. If it makes the bend without cracking or splintering, cut the good stock. If it does crack or splinter, raise the height of the blade slightly and/or move the pin closer to the blade. Then cut another test piece.

MOCK DOVETAILS AND SPLINE MITERS WITH THE ROUTER

Design by Nils Falk

A spline miter is a slot cut in an already assembled miter joint and reinforced with a piece of wood called the spline. The mock dovetail is really just a spline miter joint with flare: The slots and splines are dovetail-shaped.

This jig uses the router to make both spline miter and mock dovetail joints. With a straight bit, you cut a spline miter. Substitute a dovetail bit, and you're routing mock dovetails.

In solid stock or plywood, spline miters give a mitered box contemporary appearance and strength.

The obvious advantage of mock dovetails is that once you set up a jig, you can make them much faster than hand cutting real dovetails. Another advantage is that they let you make mitered plywood boxes look like traditional hardwood boxes. The miters hide the plies at the corners, and the mock dovetails give the piece a handmade look. Unlike real dovetails, however, mock dovetails look exactly the same on both faces of a corner.

Incidentally, if you are making spline miters in

Photo 12-1 The box at left is joined with mock dovetails, which flare at both sides of the joint. Real dovetails, in the lid and box at top, flare at only one side of the joint. Below the real dovetails is an example of a spline miter joint.

narrow stock, such as a picture frame, you'll get better results with the jig described in "Spline Miters on the Table Saw," page 185.

OVERALL VIEW

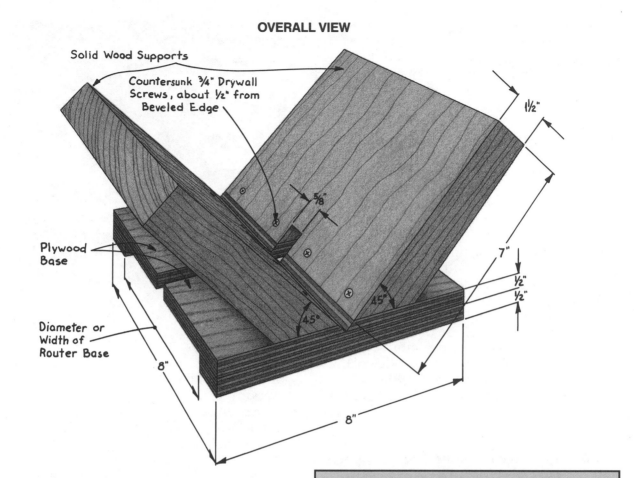

Solid Wood Supports

Countersunk ¾" Drywall Screws, about ½" from Beveled Edge

1½"

5⁄8"

Plywood Base

7"

½"
½"

Diameter or Width of Router Base

45°

45°

8"

8"

MAKING THE JIG

1 Cut and groove the base. Cut the base to the dimensions in the Materials List. Mark the center of one edge as shown in *Cutting the V-Groove*. Raise the blade on your table saw to ⅜ inch. Then tilt the blade 45 degrees. Position the base so that the top of the blade touches the centerline as shown. Move the table saw rip fence up against the base.

MATERIALS LIST		
Quantity	Part	Dimensions
1	Plywood base	½" × 8" × 8"
2	Plywood guides	½" × to fit × 8"
2	Solid wood supports	1½" × 8" × 7"

HARDWARE

¾" drywall screws, as needed

CUTTING THE V-GROOVE

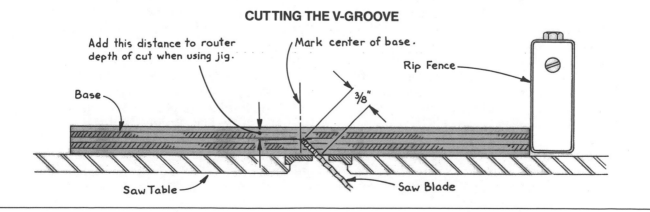

Add this distance to router depth of cut when using jig.

Mark center of base.

Rip Fence

⅜"

Base

Saw Table

Saw Blade

Check that the fence is square to the table and lock it in place. Make one pass over the blade, then turn the base around and make a second pass, completing the V-shaped groove.

2 Cut and attach the guides. The width of the guides depends on the diameter or width of your router base. Subtract the diameter or width of the router base from the width of the jig base. Divide the results by 2. For example, many router bases are 6 inches in diameter. The jig base is 8 inches wide. Eight minus 6 equals 2. Divide 2 by 2, and you'll find that each guide should be 1 inch wide. Cut the guides to width and length.

Clamp the guides to the base and check the fit of your router. It should move easily, with no play between the router base and the guides. Adjust the position of the guides, if necessary, and retighten the clamps. (As long as the guides are parallel to the edge of the jig, they don't need to be flush.) When positioning is perfect, drive the drywall screws through the guides and into the base. Remove the clamps.

3 Cut and attach the solid wood supports. You can use any straight piece of solid wood to make the supports. Two-by lumber is about 1½ inches thick, so one alternative would be to rip a piece of 2 × 10 to width and then cut it into two pieces, each a little more than 7 inches long. Once you've cut the stock, cut a 45-degree bevel on one end of each piece.

Drill and countersink pilot holes in the supports for four drywall screws. Make the holes about ½ inch from the beveled edge as shown in the *Overall View.* Keep the screw holes about 1 inch away from the center of the support, so that the router bit won't hit a screw when you cut through the jig in the next step. Put glue on the beveled edge of one of the supports. Align the support with the groove as shown in the *Overall View.* Drive the screws. Align and attach the other support the same way.

4 Cut the router bit slot. This slot runs the entire length of the jig base. Center it between, and parallel to, the guides. The cut you make

Photo 12-2 Secure the jig between the bench vise and dog to rout the router bit slot.

for the slot will also notch the bottom of the supports.

Secure the jig between the bench vise and dog as shown in *Photo* 12-2. Put a ⅝- or ¾-inch straight bit in the router. Make three passes over the jig base, each about ¼ inch deeper than the previous cut. Set the bit depth to ⅞ inch and make a fourth pass.

USING THE JIG

The jig can be used with any dovetail bit or straight bit. If, in the future, you want to use it with a bit that's wider than the slot you cut in the base, just widen the slot with the wider bit.

To set the depth of the router bit, add the depth of the spline groove to the distance between the bottom of the V-groove and the guiding surface of the base. This distance should be ¼ inch, but measure it, in case your jig came out a little differently.

Lay out the centerline of each spline or mock dovetail on one side of each corner of the assembled workpiece. Put the jig in place as shown in *Photo* 12-3. Judging by eye, position the jig so that a layout line is centered in the slot. Clamp the jig in place. Rout the groove as shown in *Photo* 12-4.

Photo 12-3 Place the jig over the corner of the assembled workpiece. Judging by eye, center the slot in the jig over the groove layout line on the workpiece.

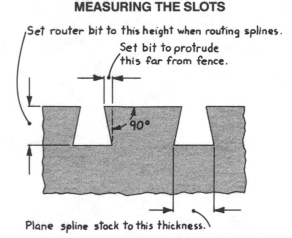

MEASURING THE SLOTS

Set router bit to this height when routing splines.

Set bit to protrude this far from fence.

90°

Plane spline stock to this thickness.

Photo 12-4 Clamp the jig in place and rout the groove.

Making Mock Dovetail Splines

The most accurate way to make dovetail splines is to rout them on a piece of over-sized stock and then cut away the waste. The slot and spline will automatically match, if you make them with the same bit.

First set the router bit height to equal the depth of the spline slot as shown in *Measuring the Slots*. Then bury the bit in a wooden fence. If your fence doesn't already

have a cutout to allow it to go over a bit, clamp one end of the fence to the table, turn on the router, and swing the other end toward the cutter, cutting a notch in the fence.

Measuring the Slots shows how to determine how much of the bit should protrude from the fence.

For safety, the stock you use to make the splines should be at least 1½ inches wide. Plane the stock to a thickness equal to the widest part of the slot.

Run both sides of the stock over the dovetail bit as shown in *Photo 12-5*.

Photo 12-5 Make the dovetail splines from stock that is at least 1½ inches wide. Run both sides of the stock over a dovetail bit to create the dovetail shape.

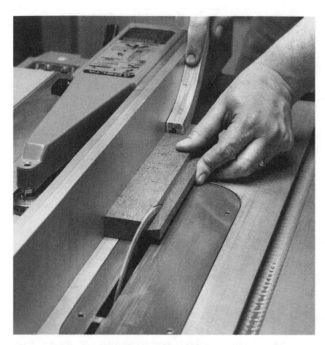

Photo 12-6 Set the table saw fence to rip the spline stock from the wider piece.

The dovetail spline is now on the edge of a wider board; you need to cut off the waste. With the waste side of the stock against the table saw rip fence, set the fence to cut the spline off of the stock at the shoulder left by the dovetail bit. (See Photo 12-6.) Measure the length of the slot at the bottom and then cut the splines about ¼ inch longer.

Making Spline Miters

Spline miters are much simpler: You mill the splines to fit the slots. If you have slots ¾ inch deep × ½ inch wide, for example, plane the spline stock to ¾ inch thick and rip it to ½ inch wide. Measure the length of the slot at the bottom and cut the splines about ¼ inch longer.

Inserting the Spline

Put glue in the slots and slip the splines into place. Let the glue dry overnight, then pare the splines flush with a sharp chisel.

FLUTING TURNINGS WITH THE LATHE AND ROUTER

Design by Ben Erickson

This fixture combines the lathe and router to cut flutes in columns or other turnings. The lathe acts as a clamp and indexing mechanism, while the router cuts the flutes. The fixture provides a track that guides the router above the turning. The fluting fixture shown here can handle turnings up to 6 inches in diameter. It will fit on a lathe designed to handle turnings up to 12 inches in diameter. You can alter the height and length of the fixture to fit your work and your lathe.

The fixture consists of an open-top plywood box that attaches to the lathe bed. An auxiliary router base runs along rabbeted tracks at the top of the box. The tracks can be adjusted to follow tapers.

The router uses a core box bit to cut the flutes. A plunge router works best, particularly if the flutes stop before the ends of the turning. You can make stopped cuts with a fixed-base router by carefully tipping the router into the cut.

The jig requires a lathe with an indexing head.

MAKING THE JIG

1 Cut the parts to size. Cut the parts to the dimensions in the Materials List. Make the sides, bottom, and ribs from plywood. Make the mounting blocks, hold-downs, tracks, and locater strip from a hardwood such as oak. To determine the width of the locater strip, measure between the ways on your lathe. The strip should fit snugly between them.

Cut the ribs to the shape shown in the *Side View.*

2 Cut the adjustment slots. Each router track is screwed to three mounting blocks. The mounting blocks are bolted to the fixture through vertical slots cut in the sides as shown in the *Overall View.* These slots allow the track to be adjusted up and down to follow the contours of the turning. Two additional slots help you align the track.

OVERALL VIEW

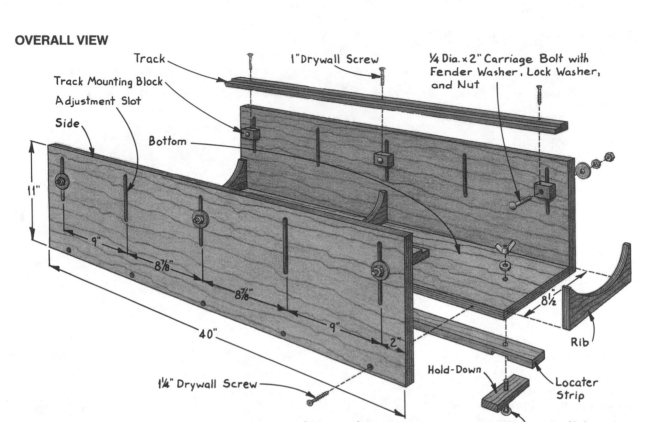

SIDE VIEW

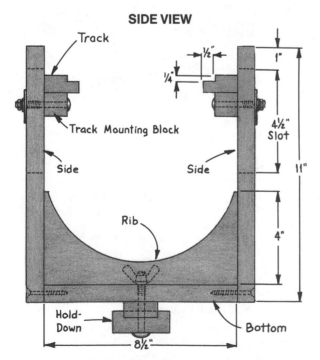

Photo 13-1 Clamp the sides together on the bench to rout slots all the way through one side and partway through the other. Remove the top piece and complete the slots through the bottom piece.

Lay out the tops of the slots 1 inch from the tops of the sides as shown in the *Overall View.* Make each slot 4¼ inches long.

Cut the slots with a ¼-inch straight bit in the router. It is important that the slots be located in the same positions on each piece. To ensure this, tack the two sides together on the bench, making sure all edges are aligned.

MATERIALS LIST

Quantity	Part	Dimensions
2	Plywood sides	¾" × 11" × 40"
1	Plywood bottom	¾" × 8½" × 40"
3	Plywood ribs	¾" × 4" × 8½"
6–10	Hardwood mounting blocks	1" × 1¼" × 2"
2	Hardwood hold-downs	1" × 1¼" × 2½"
2	Hardwood tracks	¾" × 1½" × 40"
1	Hardwood locater strip	Thickness and width to fit × 40"

HARDWARE

Drywall screws, ½" longer than locater strip thickness, as needed

1¼" drywall screws, as needed

1" drywall screws, as needed

⅜" dia. × 2½" carriage bolts with washers and wing nuts, 2

¼" dia. × 2" carriage bolts with fender washers, lock washers, and nuts, 6

¼" × 6½" × 6½" acrylic plastic for router base, 1

Guide the router with a straightedge clamped across the sides as shown in P*hoto* 13-1. Rout the slots in a series of passes, each slightly deeper than the previous pass. Set the bit depth to about 1 inch for the last pass, so that you rout completely through the side on the top and make a ¼-inch groove in the side on the bottom. Remove the top piece and use the groove to align the router to complete the remaining slot.

3 Assemble the box. Attach the sides to the bottom with glue and 1¼-inch drywall screws, as shown in the *Overall View*. Check to see that the sides are parallel to each other.

4 Notch and attach the locater strip. The locater strip must be ¼ inch thicker than the lathe ways. Cut the locater strip to fit snugly between the ways. The strip has a notch 3 inches from each end. As you tighten the wing nuts, the hold-down fits into this notch, clamping the fixture in place.

Lay out the notch 3 inches from each end of the locater strip. To lay out the depth of the notch, put the strip between the ways. Make sure the top of the strip is flush with

the top of the ways. Duck under the lathe and draw a line marking where the bottom of the ways meets the edge of the locater strip. With a dado blade on the saw, cut the notches to extend ¹⁄₁₆ inch beyond this line.

Predrill the locater strip for drywall screws. Screw the locater strip to the exact center of the bottom of the fixture, using screws that are about ½ inch longer than the locater strip is thick. Place the fixture on the lathe, and check to be sure that the fixture is centered and that the sides are parallel to the lathe's axis. Make any adjustments necessary. Then remove the strip, apply glue, and screw it back on. Leave the fixture on the lathe bed while the glue dries.

5 Rabbet the track. Rabbet the track pieces as shown in the *Side View*. Rout the rabbets on the router table for the smoothest possible track.

6 Mount the track. Drill a ¼-inch-diameter hole into the center of each mounting block. Bolt the blocks to the inside of the fixture through the adjustment slots with ¼-inch-diameter × 2-inch carriage bolts. Place a fender washer and lock washer on each bolt before fastening it with a nut, as shown in the *Overall View*. Fasten the tracks to the mounting blocks with 1-inch drywall screws, as shown in the *Overall View*.

The screws allow removal of the tracks without disturbing the fixture's adjustment. This comes in handy when the track gets in the way of inserting and removing large-diameter turnings.

7 Attach the hold-downs. Turn the fixture upside down and place the hold-downs in their notches. Drill a ⅜-inch-diameter hole through each hold-down and through the bottom of the fixture. Put ⅜-inch-diameter × 2½-inch carriage bolts through the hold-downs and through the fixture. Secure them with washers and wing nuts inside the fixture.

8 Make the router base. Cut a piece of acrylic plastic to the dimensions in the Materials List. Remove the base plate from your router. Use it as a template to mark the mounting holes for the router on the acrylic.

Be sure to center the router carefully on the new base. Drill and counterbore the mounting holes. Then drill or cut out a 1½-inch-diameter hole in the center for the bit. Screw the new base to the router.

USING THE JIG

Set the fixture on the lathe with the hold-down blocks turned parallel to the

ADJUSTING THE TRACKS

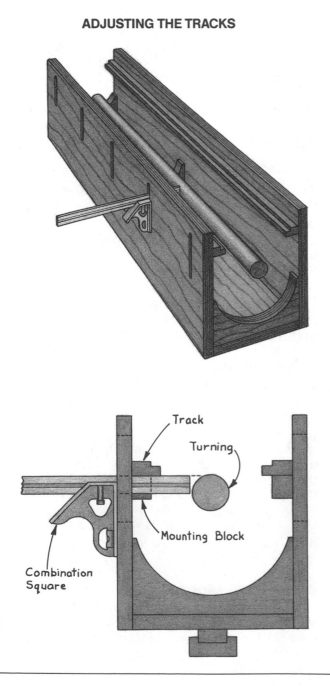

locater strip. When the fixture is seated, rotate the hold-downs 90 degrees. Tighten the wing nuts inside the fixture to lock it in place. Place the turning between centers on the lathe. Be sure to mount the turning in the end-grain holes you created when turning it, so that it is centered accurately.

Adjusting the Tracks

Adjust the height of both tracks to follow the contour of the turning. First tighten the mounting blocks until they are just snug. Begin adjustment of the tracks by sticking a combination square through the empty slot closest to the left end of the fixture. Slide the square under the tracks as shown in _Adjusting the Tracks._ Sight through the slot to bring the top of the square level with the top of the turning, as shown in P_hoto_ 13-2. Make sure the track is touching the square, and tighten the left mounting block. Repeat this process at the other end of the fixture. Use the same procedure to adjust the other track.

Mount a core box bit in the router. The diameter of the bit should equal the width of the turning flute at its widest point. (Core box bits are available in diameters from ⅛ to 1½ inches.) To check and fine-tune the track

Photo 13-2 Slide a combination square in the slots under the tracks. Sight through the slot to bring the top of the square level with the top of the turning.

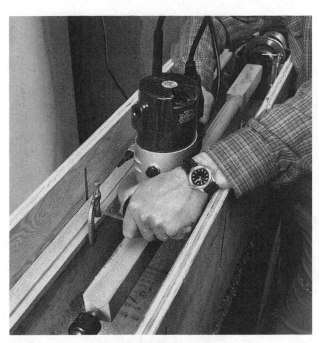

Photo 13-3 Use C-clamps as stops when cutting flutes that stop short of the column ends.

position, adjust the bit's cutting depth so that the bottom of the bit touches the turning at one end. Without turning on the router, move it slowly along the track. If the bit starts to dig into the turning, or if you see a gap, adjust the tracks accordingly.

Cutting the Flutes

Engage the lathe indexing head to lock the turning in position. To prevent tearout and gouges, cut each flute in several light passes rather than in one heavy one. Turn on the router, lower it into the stock, and guide the router along the fixture. At the end of the flute, turn off the router and increase the depth of cut. Repeat until you've reached the final depth.

If you are cutting stopped flutes, mark where the flutes end on the turning. Lower the cutter into the turning. Slide the router along the track, routing to the mark. When you've cut the flute to final depth, turn off the router and put a small C-clamp on the track against the router base as shown in P*hoto* 13-3. The clamp will act as a stop for the rest of the flutes. If the flutes stop at both ends, attach a clamp at both ends. Once you've cut the flute, disengage the indexing head, rotate the turning, and engage the indexing head again for the next cut. Sand away burn marks and smooth the flutes with a strip of sandpaper wrapped around the proper-diameter dowel. You can cut your sanding time significantly by scraping the flutes first with the "Flute Scraper" described on page 90.

Cutting Tapered Turnings

Tapered turnings present a special challenge in fluting operations. The fillet, or flat part between the flutes, usually stays the same width or narrows only slightly as the turning diameter shrinks at the top. Meanwhile, the flute narrows significantly. As a result, the bit must cut less deeply as it progresses along the turning. This means that the track cannot exactly follow the taper of the turning. If it did, the flutes would converge at the top of the column. On your first column, set the tracks as explained on the opposite page. Cut several shallow flutes to get an idea of how the fillets will work out, and then adjust the track height as needed.

If you are working with classical forms, keep in mind that an Ionic column usually has 24 semicircular flutes. Each fillet is one-third the width of the flute. A Doric column usually has 20 elliptical flutes with no fillets in between.

FLUTE SCRAPER

Design by Glenn Bostock

If you were to open the toolbox of an old-time craftsman, you would find a wealth of scraper planes similar to this one. You would find not only flute scrapers but also a host of unique scraper planes used to create original moldings and decorative profiles. Once you have made this simple flute scraper, you might try your hand at making your own original profile scrapers.

The flute scraper can be used for two purposes. First, if you have ever routed flutes along the edge of a cylindrical bedpost or table leg, you know that the router bit often burns the wood. The flute scraper is designed to run along the inside of the flute to remove burn marks. In the process, it leaves the bottom of the flute smooth and straight.

Second, the flute scraper can be used to produce flutes on flat stiles, square table legs, and square bedposts. With the help of a straight-edge, it can make flutes quickly and easily.

The blade on this scraper fits flutes that have a ⅜-inch diameter. Grind the cutting edge to fit the flutes you are making.

MAKING THE JIG

1 Mill the body stock to size. Make the body of the flute scraper from a tough hardwood such as cherry, maple, or oak. Joint, plane, cut, and rip the body stock to the dimensions in the Materials List.

2 Cut the throat. The blade and wedge fit into a wedge-shaped slot, called the throat, shown in the *Side View* and *Top View*.

First adjust the table saw blade to cut a ⅝-inch-deep kerf. Cut a slot 1⅝ inch from the front of the plane. Guide the cut against the rip fence, with a miter gauge set at 90 degrees.

Next reset the miter gauge to 84 degrees as shown in P*hoto* 14-1. Adjust the table saw fence to cut the opposite edge of the slot, leaving a slot approximately ⁷⁄₁₆ inch wide at the top of the plane. Clean out the waste between the edges of the slot with a couple of more passes of the table saw blade.

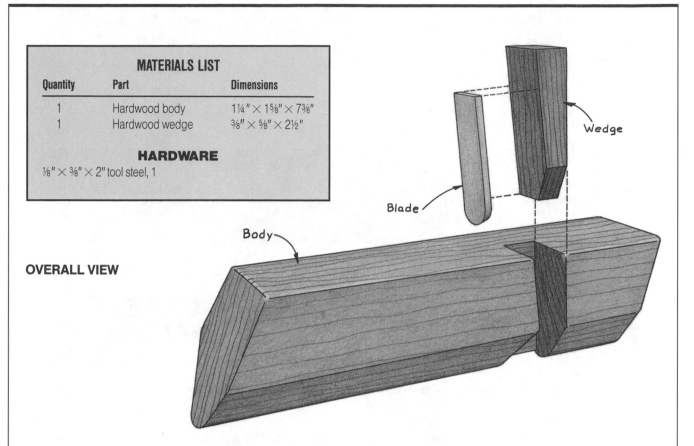

MATERIALS LIST		
Quantity	Part	Dimensions
1	Hardwood body	1¼" × 1⅝" × 7⅜"
1	Hardwood wedge	⅜" × ⅝" × 2½"

HARDWARE

⅛" × ⅜" × 2" tool steel, 1

OVERALL VIEW

3 Shape the ends of the body stock. The shape of the body stock ends is simply aesthetic and will not affect the performance of the scraper plane.

Photo 14-1   To make the throat, cut the second kerf with the miter gauge set to 84 degrees.

Cut a 70-degree angle on the front of the plane with the table saw.

Next cut a curve at the back of the body similar to that shown in the *Side View.* Cut the curve on the band saw, and sand the cut smooth.

4 Cut and grind the blade to shape. The thickness of the tool steel you use is not important. The ⅜-inch width specified will be most handy for grinding a ⅜-inch-diameter round for the scraping edge. (See the *Cross Section.*) If you have a piece of tool steel that's a little wider, grind a taper in it before you grind the round.

Start with a piece of steel that is several inches longer than specified in the Materials List. This will make it easier to hold while grinding. It also will give you some leverage later when you break the blade to length. If you don't have a piece of tool steel, you can make the blade from a file. If you use a file, start by grinding the teeth off both sides.

Tape a piece of 220-grit sandpaper to the surface of your table saw and carefully slide the back of the blade blank over it until

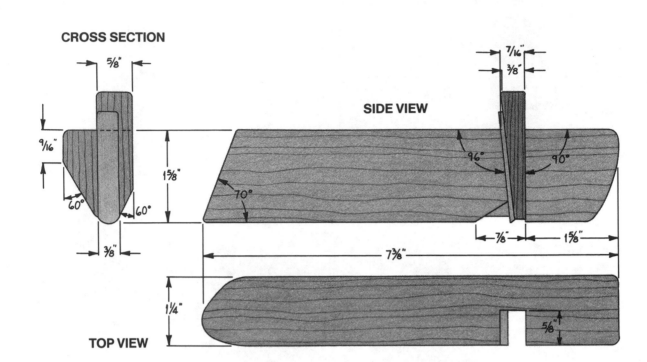

CROSS SECTION

SIDE VIEW

TOP VIEW

you have completely removed all grinding or milling scratches from both sides. You don't need to sand the full length of your blank, just about 2 inches. Be sure to keep the blank perfectly flat as you remove these marks, or you will round-over the blade edges.

Next polish the front and back of your blank with an 800- to 1200-grit polishing stone until it has a gray sheen. Shine the front of the scraper blade with a 6000- to 8000-grit stone.

When you have polished the front of the scraper blade to a mirrorlike shine, draw a 3⁄8-inch-diameter cutting edge on it. Grind to your layout lines. Dip the steel frequently in water, so that you don't lose the temper of the steel.

When you've ground the radius, grind a 75-degree bevel along the curved cutting edge toward the back of the blade as shown in the *Side View.* Polish the beveled edge on the coarse and fine polishing stones, and remove the grinding burrs from the edge by running the flat front of the scraper blade over the fine-grit stone.

When you've polished the blade, make a pencil mark on both sides, 1⅝ inches from the working end. On the edge of your grinding wheel, grind a notch on both sides. Leave at least ⅛ inch of material between the

notches, so that there is no chance the piece will break off while grinding.

Place the working end of the blade in the vise, with the notches at the top of the vise. Wrap the protruding waste end in a rag to protect your hands and to catch any shrapnel. Put eyeglasses on everybody in the shop, and snap off the waste. Round off the broken end of the blade on the grinder, so that it won't cut your hand.

5 Shape the bottom of the body. As shown in the *Cross Section,* the bottom of the body is shaped to match the profile of the scraper blade. First cut the large 60-degree bevel on the table saw. Tilt the blade to 60 degrees, and position the fence so that the blade is tilting away from it. Adjust the fence to produce the bevel shown in the *Cross Section* and guide the body through the blade with a push stick as shown in *Photo* 14-2.

Next finish shaping the bottom of the body with a stationary belt sander or a portable belt sander turned upside down in a vise. First shape the smaller, 60-degree bevel. Then rotate the body from side to side against the sander to shape the bottom. (See *Photo* 14-3.) Keep the length of the bottom straight by avoiding undue pressure at the front or back of the body. Continually compare the shape of the scraper blade to the

6 Cut the waste notch. As you use the scraper, waste will build up in front of the blade. For the jig to scrape properly, you must provide a spot for the waste to go. Chisel a waste notch in front of the throat as shown in the *Side View*. Cut the notch at approximately 35 degrees.

7 Make the wedge. Make the wedge from hardwood, with the grain running the length of the wedge. For safety, begin by crosscutting a piece of wood 2½ inches long and at least 4 inches wide. Set the table saw miter gauge to 84 degrees. Mark the beginning of the cut. Then use the miter gauge to guide the cut as you rip the wedge from the stock. (See *Photo* 14-4.)

Photo 14-2   Cut the large, 60-degree bevel on the table saw, guiding the body over the blade with a push stick.

bottom of the body as you sand. The shaping is complete when the bottom of the body perfectly matches the shape of the scraper blade.

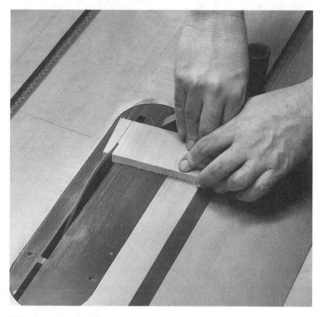

Photo 14-4   Set the miter gauge to 84 degrees to cut the wedge. Make sure the grain runs in the same direction as the cut.

Check the fit of the wedge with the scraper blade in the throat. If necessary, adjust the miter gauge and cut another wedge. Round-over the sharp edges at the top of the wedge with sandpaper, and shape the bottom of the wedge to match the shape of the body.

Photo 14-3   Use a belt sander to shape the bottom of the scraper to match the profile of the cutter.

8 Install the blade. Position the scraper blade in the throat, and slide in the wedge behind it. Adjust the blade so that it extends a scant $\frac{1}{64}$ inch beyond the bottom of the body. Flip the body upside down and press down the top of the wedge on a hard surface to set it firmly behind the blade. To remove the blade, simply pull the top of the wedge sideways out of the throat.

USING THE JIG

To smooth irregularities and remove burn marks from routed flutes, place the jig at the beginning of the flute and push it

forward along the flute as needed. When the waste notch becomes clogged, tap the body lightly on a hard surface to remove the waste.

When creating new flutes in a stile or table leg, draw layout lines along the length of the stock to represent the flutes. Clamp a straightedge to the stock and adjust it so that when the flute scraper slides against it, the scraper is over the layout lines. Pass the flute scraper over the stock several times to create the flute. Remove the waste from the flute scraper as necessary.

Photo 14-5   Guide the scraper along routed flutes to remove burn marks.

Photo 14-6   A straightedge guides the scraper as it is used to cut new flutes.

HINGE MORTISING WITH THE ROUTER

Design by Ken Burton

Mortising hinges into a door or cabinet can be nerve-racking. It normally is one of the last steps in a project, so a slip can ruin several hours of work. This jig puts a router to the task and makes cutting hinge mortises easy and fast.

The jig adjusts to rout mortises for almost any size hinge. Clamp it directly to the workpiece and feed the router clockwise around the guides to cut the mortise.

The jig works either with a straight bit and a guide bushing or with a pattern cutting bit.

MAKING THE JIG

1 **Make the back guide.** Select a durable close-grained wood such as maple, cherry, or birch for the hardwood parts. Joint the stock flat. Cut the back guide to the dimensions in the Materials List. Plane the back guide to exactly ¾ inch thick.

On the router table, cut the dado shown in the *Overall View*. The mounting bracket travels back and forth in this dado, allowing you to position the jig properly. Make the dado ⁵⁄₁₆ inch deep, so that the ¼-inch-thick track won't touch the bottom. If your router table doesn't have a miter gauge groove, guide the cut with a rectangular piece of plywood, as shown in *Photo* 15-1.

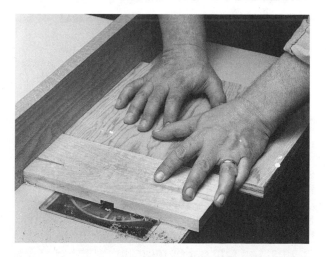

Photo 15-1 Use a rectangular piece of plywood to back up the back guide as you rout the dado.

OVERALL VIEW

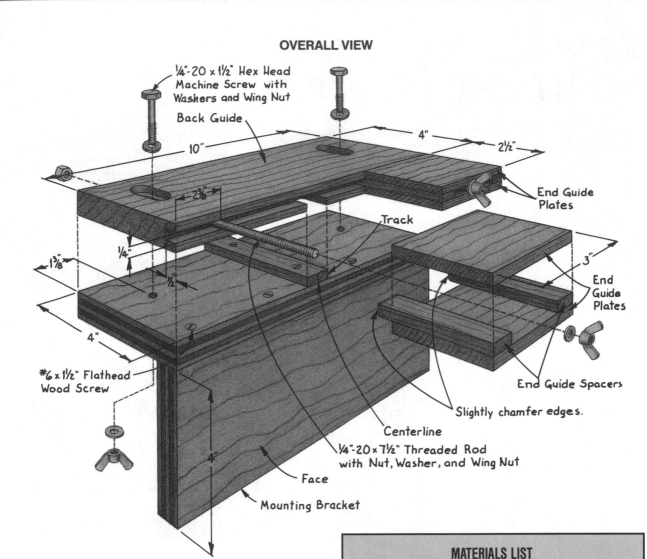

¼"-20 x 1½" Hex Head Machine Screw with Washers and Wing Nut

Back Guide

10"

4"

2½"

2⅜"

¼"

1⅜"

½"

4"

4"

#6 x 1½" Flathead Wood Screw

End Guide Plates

Track

3"

End Guide Plates

End Guide Spacers

Slightly chamfer edges.

Centerline

¼"-20 x 7½" Threaded Rod with Nut, Washer, and Wing Nut

Face

Mounting Bracket

Cut a ½-inch-deep × ¼-inch-wide groove along the exact center of one edge as shown in the *Overall View*. The end guides will slide back and forth in this groove.

2 Rout the slots. On the table-mounted router, rout through slots in the back guide for the ¼"-20 × 1½-inch hex head machine screws. The *Groove Detail* shows the position of these slots. Cut the slots in three passes to avoid overloading the bit. Without moving the router table fence, put a ¾-inch straight bit in the router. Rout the counterbores against the fence. For more information, see "Making Stopped Cuts on the Router Table," page 24.

MATERIALS LIST

Quantity	Part	Dimensions
1	Hardwood back guide	¾" × 4" × 10"
4	Hardwood end guide spacers	¼" × ½" × 3"
4	Hardwood end guide plates	¼" × 2½" × 3"
1	Hardwood mounting bracket track	¼" × ¾" × 4"
1	Plywood mounting bracket top	¾" × 4" × 10"
1	Plywood mounting bracket face	¾" × 4" × 10"

HARDWARE

#6 × 1½" flathead wood screws, 4
#6 × ¾" flathead wood screws, 2
¼"-20 × 1½" hex head machine screws with washers and wing nuts, 2
¼" dia. × 7½" threaded rods with washers, nuts, and wing nuts, 2

GROOVE DETAIL

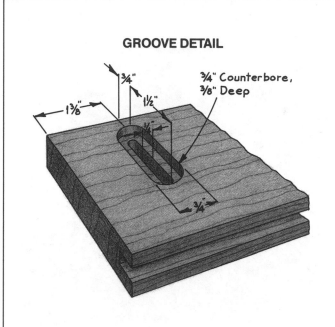

Photo 15-2 Tighten the nuts so that they are horizontal and won't interfere with the router base.

3 Drill the back guide. Mark the centers of the holes for the threaded rods shown in the *Overall View.* Drill these holes on the drill press. Make sure the holes are parallel to the faces of the guide. If the bit seems to drift out of line, or if it is not long enough, drill the holes halfway through, then flip the board and drill from the other side.

4 Make the end guides. Plane stock for the spacers, plates, and track to ¼ inch thick. The "Planer Board for Thin Stock" on page 253 is useful for planing thin stock such as this. Plane the stock until it fits snugly into the back guide groove. Cut the spacers and plates to the dimensions in the Materials List. Glue up the end guides as shown in the *Overall View.*

Note that the spacers extend ½ inch beyond the plates. This is so that the spacers can travel in the back guide slot. When the glue dries, test fit the end guides in the slot. They should fit snugly against the back guide, with their faces flush. If the faces aren't flush, use a scraper to make them so. Lightly chamfer the corners of the spacers that go into the groove. Also chamfer the edges of the spacers that fit into the groove. (See the *Overall View.*) Do this with two or three strokes of a block plane on each edge.

Slide the threaded rods through the back guide. Leave enough rod protruding

from the back (ungrooved) side of the back guide to thread on a nut. Before you do this, put a few drops of epoxy glue around the rods to keep the nuts in place. Let the epoxy set. Slide the end guides onto the rods and lock them in place with washers and wing nuts. Turn the rods so that the wing nuts are horizontal when they are tight as shown in *Photo* 15-2. This way, the nuts won't protrude above the top of the guide edge, where they would get in the way of the router base.

5 Make the bracket. Make the top and face from cabinet-grade plywood. Cut these parts to the dimensions in the Materials List. Screw them together as shown in the *Overall View,* using #6 × 1½-inch flathead wood screws. Cut the track to the dimensions in the Materials List, checking that it fits snugly into the dado in the back guide. Drill and countersink ³⁄₁₆-inch-diameter holes through the track as shown. The holes are slightly larger than the screw diameter. This allows you to adjust the position of the track if necessary. Position the track on the bracket as shown and screw it in place using #6 × ¾-inch flathead wood screws. Make sure it is square to the edge of the mount.

6 Assemble the jig. Slide the back guide onto the track. Check to be sure its front edge is parallel to the edge of the bracket. Adjust the track if necessary. Move the guide until its front edge is about ⅛ inch behind the edge of the bracket. Drill holes for the machine screws down through the mount. Locate the holes at the front of the slots in the guide. Screw the guide to the mount. Mark a centerline on the end of the track for alignment.

USING THE JIG

If you want your hinges to be within 5 inches of the top and bottom of the door, make the hinge mortises in the face-frame stiles before you assemble the frame. In an assembled frame, the jig would bump into the rails, preventing you from routing within 5 inches of the face-frame corners. Later, after the face frames are assembled to the cabinet, you can fit the doors and align the door hinge mortises to the face-frame mortises.

Laying Out the Hinge Mortises

Lay out a mortise on one workpiece. You'll use this layout to adjust the jig. Once the jig is set up, you need only lay out the centerline of subsequent identical mortises.

If you will be using a template bit (a straight bit with a shank-mounted bearing), lay out the actual perimeter of the hinge. If you will be using a guide bushing, offset the layout lines to allow for the distance between the outside of the bushing and the cutting edges of the bit. (See "Using Guide Bushings," page 29.)

Setting the Jig

Most stiles will be narrower than the 4-inch-wide clamping block. In this case, clamp the jig in your bench vise. Then clamp the stile to the clamping block as shown in Photo 15-3. If you are mortising a door, or a stile that is wider than 4 inches, clamp the workpiece in the vise as shown in Photo 15-4.

Photo 15-3 When mortising a stile that is less than 4 inches wide, clamp the jig's clamping block in the bench vise. Clamp the stile to the jig.

Then clamp the jig to the workpiece. For parts that are 4 inches wide or close to that width, clamp the part and the jig in the vise together. Once the jig and work are clamped in position, align the guides with the layout lines and tighten the wing nuts.

Photo 15-4 When mortising a door, clamp the door in the bench vise. Clamp the jig to the door.

Setting the Router Bit

The bit size you use depends on the size of the hinge. For most cabinet work, a ⅜-inch-diameter bit is appropriate. Put the bit in the router and attach the guide bushing if necessary. Set the router on the jig. Tape the hinge leaf to the end guide to gauge the router bit depth as shown in *Photo* 15-5.

Routing the Mortises

Remove the workpiece from the jig and replace it with a piece of scrap. Move the router clockwise around the jig to rout a sample mortise. In a wide mortise, the router may leave a strip of wood. If so, keep the router base on the guides, but ease the bit away from the guide edges. Move the router along the strip to rout away the waste.

Finish the mortise by squaring the corners with a sharp chisel. Check that the hinge fits neatly in the mortise and is flush at the surface. Make any necessary adjustments, and rout another sample if necessary.

Mark the mortise centerline across the edge of each workpiece. Align this centerline with the centerline on the jig as shown in *Photo* 15-6. Rout the mortises as before.

Photo 15-5 Tape the hinge to the end guide to gauge the router bit depth.

Photo 15-6 Once the jig is adjusted, align its centerline with the hinge centerline on each workpiece.

BORING HOLES FOR EUROPEAN-STYLE HINGES

Design by Andy Bukovsky

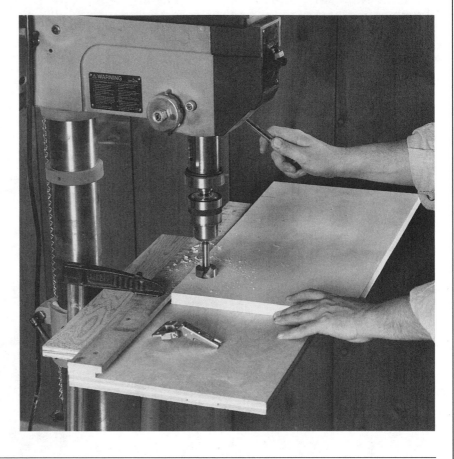

European-style hinges were designed to eliminate the exacting work required to fit traditional butt hinges. They slip into a hole bored to accept the hinge body. They allow some adjustment of the doors once they are hung. They are totally concealed within the cabinet when the doors are closed.

This fixture is an auxiliary table for the drill press, designed to make installing European-style hinges even easier. It features a large table to help balance the doors on the machine and a fence to align the holes for the hinges.

MAKING THE JIG

1 Make the table. The table shown here is made from cabinet-grade particleboard. Cabinet-grade plywood will work as well. Cut the table to the dimensions in the Materials List.

2 Make the fence. Cut a piece of hardwood to the dimensions in the Materials List. True the board on the jointer. Cut a ⅜ × ⅜-inch rabbet on one edge of the board. This will help keep chips from interfering with the jig's operation.

3 Attach the fence to the table. Screw the fence to the table with drywall screws as shown in the *Overall View.* Mark a centerline on the top of the fence and continue it across the table. This will help you to align the jig on the drill press.

USING THE JIG

Place the jig on the drill press with the centerline aligned with the center of the drill bit. Slide the jig back and forth along this line until the distance from the edge of the bit to the fence equals the setback—the distance from the edge of the door to the hinge. Clamp the jig in place.

Determine where the hinges go on each

OVERALL VIEW

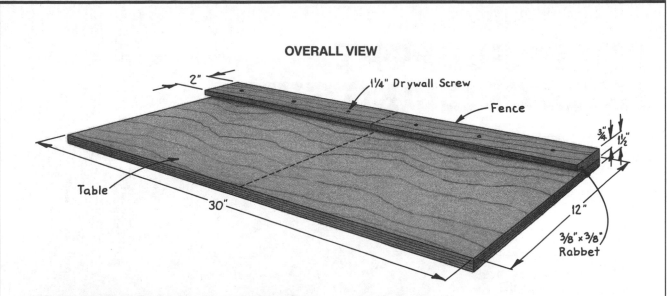

2"

1¼" Drywall Screw

Fence

Table

30"

¾"

1½"

12"

⅜" × ⅜" Rabbet

MATERIALS LIST		
Quantity	Part	Dimensions
1	Particleboard table	¾" × 12" × 30"
1	Hardwood fence	¾" × 2" × 30"

HARDWARE

1¼" drywall screws, as needed

door, and draw a centerline on the doors for each hinge. Determine how deep the holes should be and set the depth stop appropriately. Drill the holes by aligning the centerlines on the door with the centerline on the jig as shown in the photo.

SHELF SUPPORT HOLE DRILLING GUIDE

Design by Ben Erickson

I t's virtually impossible to accurately position holes for shelf supports without some kind of drilling guide. If the opposing holes don't correspond exactly, the shelves rock on their supports.

The jig for this purpose can be as simple as a length of plywood with holes drilled into it. Some woodworkers use pegboard, so that they don't have to lay out the holes. This kind of drilling guide will work fine for one or two bookcases. But after you drill through the guide a couple of times, the holes become larger and, as a result, inaccurate.

The drilling guide shown here is made to last. Its holes, drilled on 1½-inch centers, are reinforced with bronze bushings that keep them accurate. The bushings are available at well-stocked hardware stores. The guide is 1⅛ inches thick, providing plenty of guiding depth to help keep the drill bit perpendicular to the workpiece. It's made in two parts to increase its versatility. A short section fits into base cabinets, while the longer section is for upper shelves.

The two pieces fit together with dowels, so you can drill holes in bookcases up to 8 feet tall. A simple wooden stop on your hand drill controls the depth of the support holes.

Because the bronze bushings are softer than steel drill bits, the guide holes eventually will become inaccurate. When this happens, just knock out the old bush-

ings by tapping in new ones, and the jig is as good as new. The bushings specified in the Materials List have an inside diameter of ¼ inch, so they will work with shelf supports that have ¼-inch-diameter pins. If you use pins of a different size, you'll need to find bushings that have the same inside diameter.

OVERALL VIEW

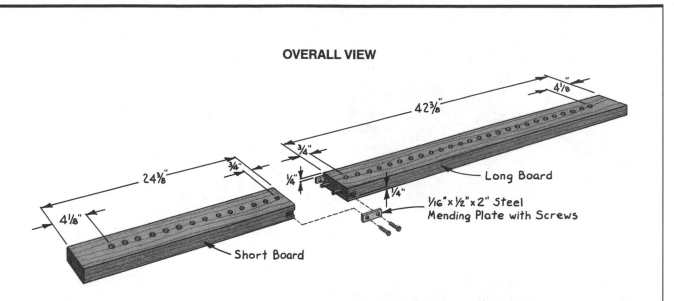

24³⁄₈"

4¹⁄₈"

³⁄₄"

¹⁄₄"

Short Board

42³⁄₈"

³⁄₄"

4¹⁄₈"

¹⁄₄"

Long Board

¹⁄₁₆" × ¹⁄₂" × 2" Steel
Mending Plate with Screws

MAKING THE JIG

1 Prepare the boards. Select a stable hardwood such as maple for the long and short boards. Plane, joint, and cut these pieces to the dimensions in the Materials List.

2 Make the dowel joint. Use a doweling jig to drill holes for two ³⁄₈-inch-diameter dowels in one end of each board. Put glue in the holes in one board (it doesn't matter which) and insert the dowels. When the glue dries, assemble the jig. Trace the outline of the mending plates across the joint on both sides of the jig. For a better joint, offset their positions as shown in the *Overall View.* Disassemble the jig and chisel mortises for the plates so that they will be slightly below the surface.

3 Drill the guide holes. Chuck a ³⁄₈-inch drill bit in the drill press and drill a hole in scrap stock. Test fit the bushing in the hole to be sure it is a tight friction fit. If it is not, try another drill bit. Assemble the two jig boards. Screw the mending plates in place. Draw a line across the short board, 4¹⁄₈ inches from the bottom. Now draw a line every 1¹⁄₂ inches along the length of the jig. Draw the last line 4¹⁄₈ inches from the top of the long board. If you have measured and cut everything correctly, there will be 14 lines across the

MATERIALS LIST

Quantity	Part	Dimensions
1	Hardwood long board	1¹⁄₈" × 3¹⁄₂" × 42³⁄₈"
1	Hardwood short board	1¹⁄₈" × 3¹⁄₂" × 24³⁄₈"
1	Hardwood drill stop	³⁄₄" × ³⁄₄" × to fit
2	Plywood shims	³⁄₈" × 1" × 2"

HARDWARE

³⁄₈" dia. × 2" dowels, 2
¹⁄₁₆" × ¹⁄₂" × 2" steel mending plates with screws, 2
¹⁄₄" inner diameter × ³⁄₈" outer diameter × 1" bronze bushings, 40

short board and 26 lines across the long board. The joint between the boards will be equidistant between two lines.

Position a fence on the drill press to center the holes on the layout lines. Clamp a backup board to the press table to prevent tearout on the bottom of the jig. Drill the holes completely through the jig board.

4 Insert the bushings. Hammer or press the bushings into the holes. Use another bushing or a ³⁄₈-inch-diameter dowel to set the bushings ¹⁄₁₆ inch below the surface as shown in the *Guide Hole Cutaway.* Put a ¹⁄₂-inch-diameter bit in the drill press. Countersink all the holes ¹⁄₁₆ inch. This will make it easier to insert the drill bit and also will provide a space for chips when the drill bit stop comes down on the workpiece.

GUIDE HOLE CUTAWAY

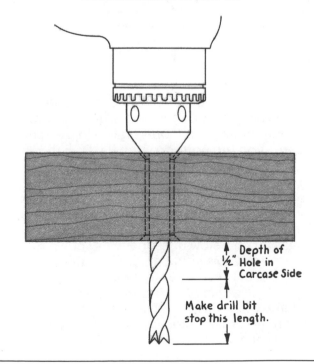

¼" I.D. x ⅜"O.D. x 1"
Bronze Bushing

½" Dia. Countersink

5 **Round the jig board edges.** Round all edges of the jig boards with sandpaper or a ⅛-inch-radius roundover bit on the router. This makes the jig more pleasant to handle and ensures that it will fit tightly in carcase corners.

6 **Make the drill stop.** To prevent tearout around the edges of the shelf support holes, select a drill bit that has a brad point center and cutting spurs on the sides. The bit diameter must match the diameter of the holes you want to drill—¼ inch for most shelf supports.

MEASURING STOP DEPTH

Depth of
½" Hole in
Carcase Side

Make drill bit
stop this length.

For most supports, you will want to drill ½-inch-deep holes. To make all the holes the right depth, make a simple wooden drill stop. M*easuring Stop Depth* shows how to determine how long to make the stop. Put a bit in your portable power drill. Make sure the bit hits the bottom of the chuck and then tighten the chuck. Insert the drill bit through the jig. Measure how much of the bit's length protrudes from the jig. Subtract ½ inch from this to get the stop length.

Cut a piece of hardwood to ¾ inch × ¾ inch × the stop length. Draw diagonals across one end of the bit to mark the center. Chuck a ¼-inch-diameter bit in the drill press. Drill through the length of the stop.

Now chuck a ½-inch-diameter bit in the drill press and drill ¹⁄₁₆-inch-deep countersinks on both ends of the stop.

USING THE JIG

Put the ¼-inch-diameter bit back in the portable drill, making sure it hits the bottom of the chuck before tightening. Put the jig on a piece of scrap, slip the stop over the drill, and make a test hole to see if the depth is right. If the stop tends to slip off the bit between holes, tape it to the drill chuck.

Aligning the Jig

Use the jig board that is appropriate for the job, or both boards joined together for long jobs. Always orient the jig with the same end down for all the sets of holes.

It is easiest to drill the shelf support holes before you put the back on the carcase. Butt one end of the jig against the bottom of the carcase, making sure there are no chips or other debris under the bottom of the jig. Align the jig with the front or back edge of the carcase, and clamp it in place at top and bottom as shown in P*hoto* 17-1.

If the back is on the carcase, place the jig against the back and wedge a stick from the jig to the inside of the face frame as shown in P*hoto* 17-2. If there is no face frame, wedge the stick between the jig and a block clamped near the front of the carcase. Be sure there

Photo 17-1 It's easiest to drill shelf support holes before you put the back on a carcase. Just clamp the drilling guide in position.

are no chips under the bottom of the jig that would throw off the alignment of the holes, and butt the jig against the bottom of the carcase every time.

Drilling the Holes

Once the jig is secured, you can drill the holes with the carcase upright or lying on its side.

If you are drilling shelf support holes on both sides of a ¾-inch shelf divider, you may want to offset the holes horizontally. Shelf supports are sometimes too long to install back-to-back. To offset the holes, place ⅜-inch-thick shims between the jig and the back of the shelf divider as well as between the jig and the front of the shelf divider. Use one shim near the top of the jig and one shim near the bottom. Make the shims from scraps of ⅜-inch-thick plywood that are about 1 inch wide and 2 inches long.

Photo 17-2 If the back already is installed on the carcase, drill rear shelf support holes by wedging the drilling guide in place with a stick.

FLATTENING A LOG ON THE BAND SAW

Design By
Frederic L. Hanisch

A band saw is great for sawing small logs into lumber. Before you can start slicing logs into boards, however, you need to create a flat surface on the log. The flat surface will rest on the table during resawing.

One way to create this surface is on the jointer. This involves passing a heavy log over the machine several times, just to get through the bark. If you've tried this method, you know that bark chips tend to clog jointer cutters. With the simple jig shown here, you can create a smooth, flat surface with one clean, safe pass through the band saw blade. You'll find the jig useful for creating a flat on any odd-shaped piece that can be clamped or screwed to the jig.

The jig has just two pieces: the base and the fastening fence. The base

can be plywood or a solid board. The fastening fence is solid construction lumber. The log is held in place by screws that pass through the fence. The base provides a flat bearing surface as you

move the log through the blade. The jig shown here is used with an old 36-inch band saw with a big table. If you have a smaller band saw, you may want to make the jig shorter and narrower.

MAKING THE JIG

1 Cut the parts. Cut the base and the fence to the dimensions in the Materials List.

2 Assemble the jig. The fence is attached off-center on the base to make the jig more versatile. If you need to saw a log smaller than about 6 inches in diameter, turn the jig

around and support the work on the narrow side.

Draw a line 2½ inches from one long edge of the base. Place the fence on this line, and center it along the length of the jig. Screw it in place with 1½-inch drywall screws spaced about 6 inches apart. Attach the fence with screws only, so that if necessary,

OVERALL VIEW

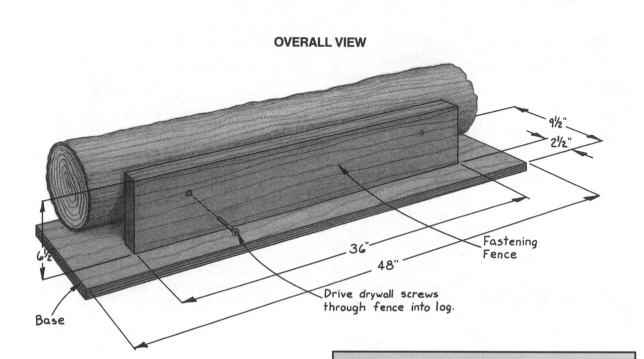

9½"

2½"

Fastening
Fence

36"

48"

6½

Drive drywall screws
through fence into log.

Base

you can change the position of the fence. For
example, if you saw logs with a diameter
greater than about 10½ inches, the jig will
work better if you move the fence flush to the
right edge of the base.

MATERIALS LIST		
Quantity	Part	Dimensions
1	Plywood or wood base	¾" × 9½" × 48"
1	Wood fastening fence	1½" × 6½" × 36"

HARDWARE

1½" drywall screws, as needed

USING THE JIG

Attach the log by driving two screws
through the fence into the log. The length of
the screws depends on what you are cutting;
you'll want to get at least ½ inch of screw into
solid wood. If the log has no bark, 1¼-inch
drywall screws will do. If the bark is thick, you
might need 2-inch screws. Drill holes for
these screws as you need them.

If your band saw tracks very well and the
log is straight-grained, you can run the jig
against a fence. Screw the log to the jig and
place the jig on the table. Position the jig in
front of the blade so that the flat area is as
wide as you need. Put the fence against the
jig base and clamp it loosely to the table.
Move the jig out of the way and adjust the
fence so it is parallel to the side of the saw
table. Clamp the fence in place. Run the
base of the jig against the fence to make
the cut.

Using the Jig with the Resawing Guide

Often you may find that using a fence on
the saw table doesn't work. This is because
band saw blades usually twist left or right
when cutting thick material, especially if the
grain is wild. If you try to move straight
through the blade without compensating for
this twist, the blade will bind. Instead of a
fence, use the "Band Saw Resawing Guide"
described on page 177. This guide keeps the
blade a set distance from the right edge of
the jig but allows you to steer the jig to
compensate for the blade's twist.

Keep in mind that the first cut to make a
flat doesn't need to be absolutely straight. It
just needs to be straight enough to create a
stable surface. With a little practice, you may
find that you can make the cut without the
resawing guide.

Making a Second Flat

Now the log has a flat surface to ride on the band saw table. If the log has bark that is rough or irregular, or if the diameter of the log varies along its length, you may want to make a second flat perpendicular to the first. To do this, place the first cut facedown on the jig. Screw the log to the jig and make your second cut. Now you have one flat to ride on the table and another flat to guide along the resawing guide or fence.

Photo 18-1 If the log has bark that is rough or irregular, or if the diameter of the log varies along its length, you may want to make a second flat perpendicular to the first.

SHORT RIPPING BOARD FOR THE TABLE SAW

Design by Fred Matlack

The short ripping board is used when a board doesn't have an edge straight enough to run along the rip fence. When trimming small pieces, it's handier than the "Long Ripping Board for the Table Saw," page 112. And unlike the long version, you won't have to make holes in your workpiece. However, you can't use the short board for stock that is any longer than the length of your table saw miter gauge slots.

The jig consists of a base, a stop, and a runner. You place the runner in the miter gauge slot, place the workpiece on the base against the stop, and run an edge of the board over the blade. The jig travels in the miter gauge slot, creating a straight cut.

MAKING THE JIG

1 Cut the base and stop to size. On most table saws, the two miter slots are not equidistant from the blade. The jig will be sized to work with one slot, so pick the one you prefer now. (Think of which slot you like to use when doing cutoff work with the miter gauge.) Measure the distance between the blade and the slot. Add 1 inch and cut the base to this width. Measure the length of your table saw slots. Make the base this long.

Cut the stop to 1½ inches wide and as long as the base width.

2 Make the runner. Make the runner from a straight piece of durable hardwood such as maple or oak. Cut it to the same width and length as the table saw slot. Make it ⅛ inch thinner than the slot, so that it can't hit the slot bottom.

3 Assemble the jig. Drill and countersink the runner about every 6 inches for #6 × ⅝-inch flathead wood screws. Mark a centerline on one edge of the board as shown in the *Overall View.* Apply glue to the runner, and center it roughly on the centerline. Check to

OVERALL VIEW

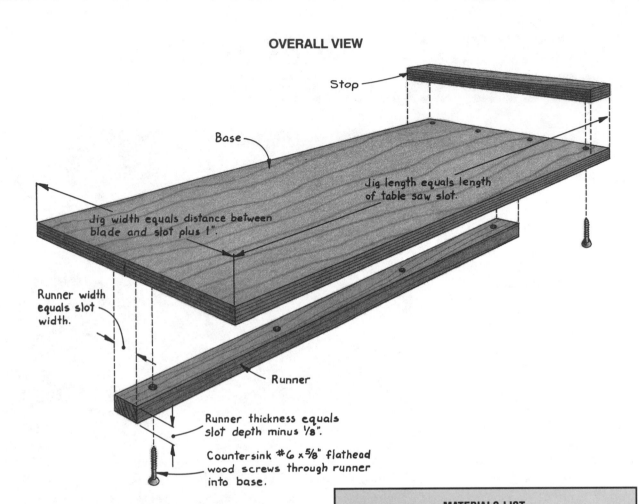

Stop

Base

Jig length equals length of table saw slot.

Jig width equals distance between blade and slot plus 1".

Runner width equals slot width.

Runner

Runner thickness equals slot depth minus ⅛".

Countersink #6 x ⅝" flathead wood screws through runner into base.

make sure that the runner is square to the ends of the base. When the glue dries, screw the runner to the bottom of the base.

Put glue on the stop. Position it on one end of the base as shown in the *Overall View*. Turn the jig over. Drill and countersink through the base and into the top for four #6 × ¾-inch flathead wood screws. Make sure no screws are within 1 inch of the edges. Drive the screws.

Wipe all glue squeeze-out from the jig with a wet cloth or sponge.

4 Trim the jig. When the glue dries, try running the jig in the slot. If it is too tight, wrap a piece of sandpaper around a block and sand one runner edge. If the jig moves easily enough but drags at one point, it means the runner is slightly bowed. Push the jig back and forth over that point a few times. Then remove the jig. The bowed section will be shiny or show signs of wear. Sand the

MATERIALS LIST

Quantity	Part	Dimensions
1	Plywood base	½" × width and length to fit
1	Plywood stop	½" × 1½" × to fit
1	Hardwood runner	To fit

HARDWARE

#6 × ¾" flathead wood screws, as needed
#6 × ⅝" flathead wood screws, 4

bowed section until the jig travels in the slot. When you are satisfied with how the runner is working, wax it.

Raise the table saw blade high enough to cut through the base and the stop. Turn on the saw, put the jig in your preferred slot, and run it through the blade as shown in *Photo 19-1*. Turn the jig around and trim the other edge in the same way. Now, when you align a workpiece on the base, you'll know that the cut will be exactly at the edge of the jig.

Photo 19-1 Trim the jig after attaching the runner. That way, when you align workpieces on the base, you'll know that the cut will be exactly at the edge of the jig.

USING THE JIG

To use this jig safely, the workpiece must be no longer than the jig. If it is longer, use the "Long Ripping Board for the Table Saw," page 112.

One end of the workpiece must be straight enough to butt against the stop. If it doesn't have a straight end, cut one with a radial arm saw, circular saw, or hand saw. The cut doesn't have to be perfect, just straight enough that the workpiece can't rock when butted against the stop.

You'll feed the jig over the saw so that the stopped end comes through last. Align the workpiece on the jig with enough stock overhanging to make a continuous straight cut.

Raise the blade high enough to cut through the workpiece. Turn on the saw. Place the runner in the slot. Keep one hand on the stop, pressing the jig firmly on the table throughout the cut. Keep the other hand on the workpiece, pressing it firmly on the jig.

LONG RIPPING BOARD FOR THE TABLE SAW

Design by Jeff Day

The long ripping board is used to rip a straight edge along the length of a board that has two irregular edges. The jig consists of a long piece of ½-inch-thick plywood with straight, parallel long sides. Any grade of plywood will do.

You can make the ripping board up to 96 inches long—the length of a full sheet of plywood. Make it about 18 inches wide to handle most board widths you are likely to encounter. For workpieces that are no longer than the length of your table saw slots, you may want to make the

OVERALL VIEW

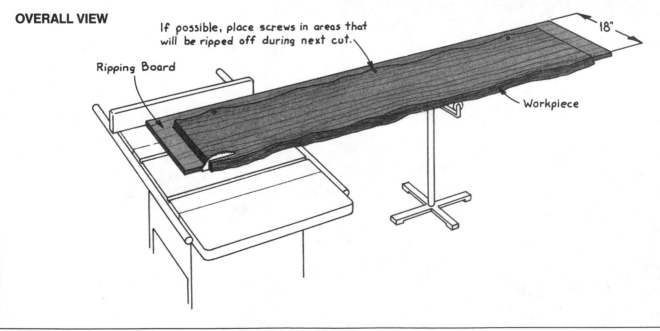

If possible, place screws in areas that will be ripped off during next cut.

Ripping Board

Workpiece

18"

"Short Ripping Board for the Table Saw," page 109.

To ensure that the long edges of the ripping board are parallel and straight, start with a length of plywood that is at least 18½ inches wide. Set the table saw rip fence to 18¼ inches and rip off one edge. Reset the fence to 18 inches and rip the other edge.

Joint and plane the faces of the stock before using the jig. When you have two smooth, flat surfaces, put the workpiece on the jig. Align the edges so that the irregular edge of the stock overhangs the jig along its entire length. Then screw the other edge of the workpiece to the ripping board as shown in the *Overall View.* Try to place the screws in areas that will be removed when you rip the second edge straight.

Set the rip fence 18 inches from the blade. Set the blade high enough to cut through the workpiece. If you don't have an extended outfeed table, set up an outfeed roller stand. (See the "Adjustable Roller Stand," page 305.) Turn on the saw and make the rip with the edge of the ripping board against the rip fence. Remove the board from the jig. Reset the rip fence and guide the newly cut edge against it.

ADJUSTABLE SHOOTING BOARD

Design by
Michael Dunbar

Machines are great for making the edges of a board square or for beveling them accurately. By tilting the blade on your table saw or the fence on your jointer, you can get exactly the angle you need. But you can't always get the surface you need. Machines leave machine marks. Only the continuous slicing action of a hand plane will leave a perfectly smooth surface. This is particularly important if the edge is to be a gluing surface.

Hand planing the edge of a board can be tricky if you are using a plane alone; you'll get the edge smooth, but you may lose the accuracy of the angle. Woodworkers have long used simple shooting boards to joint edges at a perfect right angle to the face of a board. The adjustable shooting board is much more versatile. It supports the workpiece on an adjustable table that lets you plane edges square or bevel them at any angle.

MAKING THE JIG

1 Make the parts. Cut the parts for the shooting board to the dimensions given in the Materials List. On the table saw, bevel the outside edge of the table at 45 degrees. This will keep the table's lower corner from interfering with the plane when the table is elevated. Then run the table through the table saw again to create a ⅛-inch-wide flat as shown in the *Overall View*.

2 Install the T-nuts. Drill four ⁵⁄₁₆-inch-diameter holes through the table as shown in the *Overall View*. Counterbore these holes from underneath with a ¾-inch Forstner bit. Insert the T-nuts and hammer them home.

3 Assemble the jig. Place the hinges as shown in the *Overall View*. Mortise them into

OVERALL VIEW

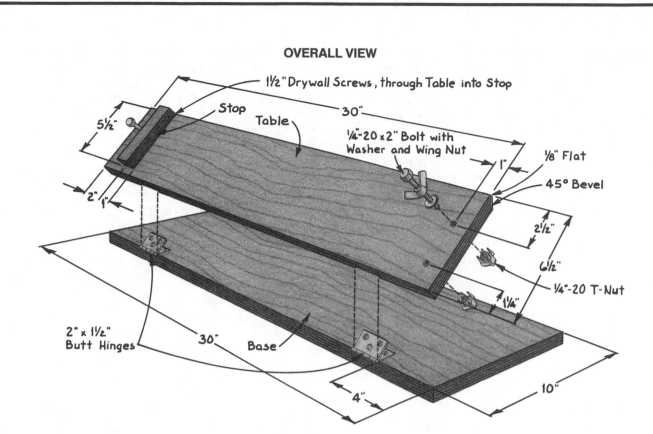

1½" Drywall Screws, through Table into Stop

Stop

Table

30"

5½"

¼"-20 x 2" Bolt with Washer and Wing Nut

⅛" Flat

45° Bevel

1"

2"

1"

2½"

6½"

¼"-20 T-Nut

1¼"

2" x 1½" Butt Hinges

30"

Base

4"

10"

MATERIALS LIST		
Quantity	Part	Dimensions
1	Plywood table	¾" × 6½" × 30"
1	Plywood base	¾" × 10" × 30"
1	Plywood stop	¾" × 1" × 5½"
As needed	Plywood shims	¾" × 3" × 30"

HARDWARE

1½" drywall screws, 3
¼"-20 × 2" hex head bolts with washers and wing nuts, 2
¼"-20 T-nuts, 4
2" × 1½" butt hinges with screws, 2

Thread a wing nut upside down onto each bolt as shown in the *Overall View*. Add a washer over the wing nut. If you are using the shooting board to joint an edge square to the face of the board, you won't need the adjust-

Photo 21-1 To set the shooting board for steeper angles, align the bevel gauge to a try square.

the table and the base, then fasten them with screws. Glue and screw the stop to the table as shown. Use three drywall screws through the bottom of the table into the stop.

USING THE JIG

First use the table saw or power jointer to cut the edge of the workpiece to the angle you want.

ment bolts. For edges beveled at less than 23 degrees, thread the bolts into the holes farthest from the hinges. Use the other pair of holes for larger bevels. Set a protractor or sliding T-bevel to the exact angle you want. Then use the T-bevel to adjust the bolts to adjust the table to match. Turn the bolts until you get the right angle. Then tighten down the wing nuts to secure the bolts. For steeper angles, align the bevel gauge to a try square as shown in *Photo* 21-1. Check the angle at both ends of the jig. Place the board to be planed on the table, with one end against the stop. Tip a hand plane on its side and run it along the base to plane, or "shoot," the edge of the board. One or two passes are all that is required to remove most machine marks.

If the bevel is very steep, the plane may not be wide enough to shoot the edge as it rides along the base. In this case, screw one or more shims to the base to bring the plane up to the required height.

The adjustment of the plane you use is critical. The sole must be at right angles to the sides. Make sure the blade is razor sharp and not skewed. You might want to keep a plane specifically tuned for use with the shooting board.

EXTENDED COMPASS

Design by Glenn Bostock

his shop-made compass draws circles up to 62 inches in diameter. It's the perfect tool for laying out round tabletops.

The compass is designed to be easy to use and easy to make. The compass pivot point is a drywall screw with its threads filed off. The point is affixed to the bottom of a block that slides along an arm. The block clamps in place with a common window sash lock.

The arm and the middle section of the sliding block you see here are made from mahogany because it is durable, lightweight, and stable. The top and bottom of the block are made from cabinet-grade plywood.

The length of this compass is purely arbitrary. Make the arm whatever length suits your work.

MAKING THE JIG

1 Make the arm. Select a piece of stock with straight grain and cut it to the dimensions in the Materials List. Drill a ¼-inch-diameter hole in one end for the pencil, as shown in the *Overall View.*

Next lay out the slot in the pencil end of the arm. Make a mark across the piece, 2½ inches from the end. Set the table saw rip fence to cut through the pencil hole. Cut into the end of the piece until the blade reaches the mark. While the cut will be longer at the bottom, it doesn't matter.

Now cut the dovetail shape into the arm. First tilt the blade 12 degrees off square. Set the rip fence so that the blade tilts away from it and the blade and fence are ⅝ inch apart when measured along the surface of the saw table. Rip both sides of the stock to give the arm its dovetail shape. Save a cutoff.

Drill and countersink a hole for the 1-inch drywall screw that locks the pencil in place. Locate the hole as shown in the *Overall View.* Drill the hole about 1¼ inches deep, not all the way through the arm.

2 Make the sliding block. Cut two 3-inch-long pieces from the arm cutoff. These will form the sliding block sides.

Cut the bottom cap to the dimensions in the Materials List. Drill and countersink a hole for a 1¼-inch drywall screw in the

OVERALL VIEW

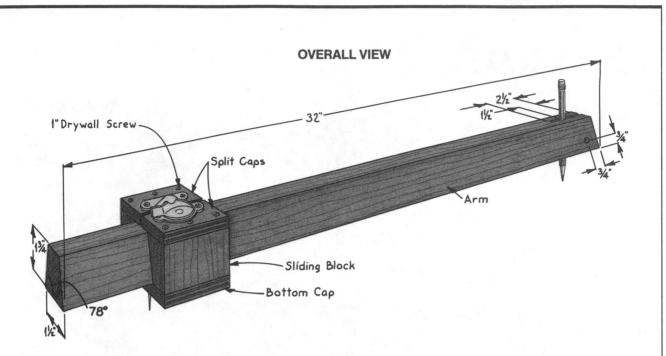

1" Drywall Screw

Split Caps

32"

2½"

1½"

¾"

¾"

Arm

1¾"

Sliding Block

Bottom Cap

78°

1½"

bottom cap. Position the hole as shown in the *Sliding Block Detail*. Drive the screw into the hole. File the threads off the screw to complete the compass point.

Position the bottom cap on the blocks, making sure all outside edges are flush as

SLIDING BLOCK DETAIL

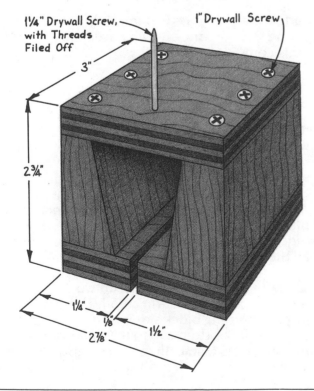

1¼" Drywall Screw, with Threads Filed Off

1" Drywall Screw

3"

2¾"

1¼"

⅛"

1½"

2⅞"

MATERIALS LIST		
Quantity	Part	Dimensions
1	Hardwood arm blank	1¾" × 3" × 32"
2	Hardwood sliding block sides	Make from arm cutoffs
1	Plywood bottom cap	½" × 2⅞" × 3"
1	Plywood split cap	½" × 1½" × 3"
1	Plywood split cap	½" × 1¼" × 3"

HARDWARE

1¼" drywall screw, 1
1" drywall screws, 13
Window sash lock, 1
Pencil, 1

shown in the *Sliding Block Detail*. Drill and countersink for six 1-inch drywall screws, positioned roughly as shown. Screw the cap in place.

Cut the split caps to the dimensions in the Materials List. Drill, countersink, and screw one to each side block as shown.

3 Install the sash lock. Several sash lock styles are available. Any will work as long as the two parts are pulled closer together when you close the lever. Screw the levered part of the lock to the wider split cap. Put the sliding block over the arm.

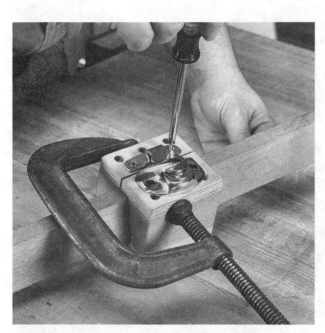

Photo 22-1 To properly position the sash lock, put a C-clamp across the block near the top. Tighten the clamp just until you can't slide the block.

To properly position the other side of the sash lock, put a C-clamp across the block near the top as shown in P*hoto* 22-1. Tighten the clamp just until you can't slide the block, but don't cinch down hard. With the sash lock lever in the closed position, put the sash

hook on the other split cap. Bring the two lock pieces together, as they will be in the locked position. Screw the hook to the block and remove the clamp.

4 **Install the pencil.** The compass is most convenient to use with a mechanical pencil because you don't have to remove the pencil to sharpen the point. Also, a mechanical pencil provides a consistent line width. A wooden pencil line gets wider as the point dulls. Either type of pencil will fit into the compass.

The pivot point protrudes about 1¼ inches from the arm. Insert the pencil into the compass until it extends an equal amount. This keeps the arm level during use. Tighten the screw to lock the pencil in position.

USING THE JIG

You can use the compass for full-scale layout on paper or templates or directly on the stock. Open the sash lock. Slide the block along the arm until the distance between the pivot point and the pencil point equals the radius of the circle you want to draw. Place the pivot point on the center of the circle. Rotate the compass to draw the circle.

INSIDE MEASURING STICKS

Design by Jim Tolpin

Making inside measurements with a tape measure or folding rule is always a hit-or-miss proposition. With a tape, you have to bend it into place or rely on the length of the case for an accurate reading. The sliding extensions on folding rules are awkward to use. You can never be sure the extension didn't move before you got a chance to read it. Then you have to add. Neither method is very accurate.

Old-time finish carpenters and cabinetmakers knew that the most accurate way to take an inside measurement was to skip the numbers. Instead, they made themselves an inside measuring stick such as the one shown here. It locks positively, providing dead-on accuracy. It's perfect for measuring inside cabinets or for determining the length of header jambs and stops in doorways and windows.

The sticks are bound together by two easily made brass keepers. A brass round-head bolt threaded through one of the keepers locks the sticks to take the measurement. The ends of the sticks are pointed, so you can tell exactly from where you are measuring.

You can make your sticks any length you like. The tool shown here is a good length for most cabinet and finish carpentry work. It will fit into spaces from about 24 to 36 inches wide.

In addition to inside measurements, the sticks are handy for checking whether a cabinet is square. Simply use it to check the diagonal measurements. If they're not equal, your cabinet is not square.

MAKING THE JIG

1 Cut the sticks to size. Make the sticks from a stable, straight-grained hardwood. Hard maple or birch would be a good choice. If you want to make the tool into something a bit more special, consider using bird's-eye maple or one of the dark tropical woods.

Cut the sticks to the dimensions in the Materials List. Miter one end of each stick at a 45-degree angle as shown in the *Overall*

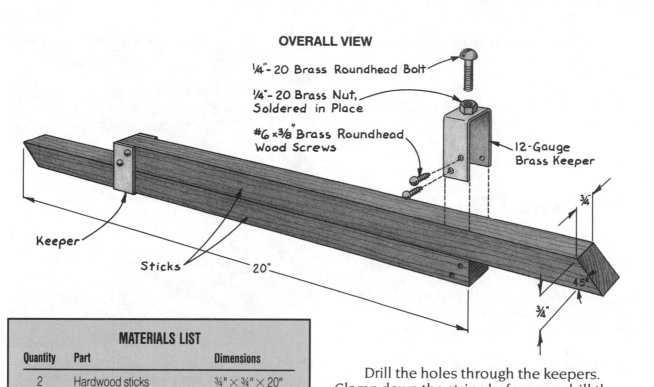

OVERALL VIEW

¼"-20 Brass Roundhead Bolt

¼"-20 Brass Nut, Soldered in Place

#6 × ⅜" Brass Roundhead Wood Screws

12-Gauge Brass Keeper

Keeper

Sticks

20"

¾

¾"

45°

MATERIALS LIST

Quantity	Part	Dimensions
2	Hardwood sticks	¾" × ¾" × 20"

HARDWARE

#6 × ⅜" brass roundhead wood screws, 8
¼"-20 × ¾" brass roundhead bolt, 1
¼"-20 brass nut, 1
¾" × 3¾" 12-gauge sheet brass, 2

View. Sand the sticks. Sand a flat of about ¹⁄₃₂ inch on the pointed ends, but be careful to keep them crisp. Apply a lacquer or varnish finish.

2 Make the keepers. The keepers are made from thin sheets of brass, which is easily worked with woodworking tools. Cut each keeper to the size in the Materials List. Make the cuts with a hacksaw or on the band saw using a ¼-inch-wide, 32-teeth-per-inch blade. Clean up any rough edges with a file.

Once the keepers are cut to size, lay out four ⅛-inch-diameter screw holes in each as shown in the *Keeper Detail.* Lay out the ⁵⁄₁₆-inch-diameter nut hole in only one keeper. Mark the center of each hole by punching a small dimple into the stock with a center punch or small-diameter nail set. The dimple will keep the bit from wandering as you start the cut.

Drill the holes through the keepers. Clamp down the strips before you drill them; sheet metal is notorious for becoming a whirling finger processor on the drill press. File away any blurs remaining around the holes.

Solder a ¼-inch brass nut above the nut hole. Before you do, sand the strips and the nut with 220-grit sandpaper. This will give them an attractive brushed apprearance and prepare them for soldering. Apply flux to the joining surfaces. Center the nut over the holes in the strips. Solder the nut in place. Regular plumbing solder will work, but silver solder is better. Heat the pieces until they are hot enough to melt the solder. Touch the solder to the joint, and let it flow into the joint. Let the joint cool slowly in the air. When it is cool to the touch, sand away the

KEEPER DETAIL

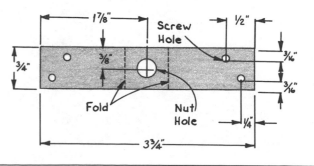

1⅞"

½"

Screw Hole

¾"

⅜"

³⁄₁₆"

³⁄₁₆"

Fold

Nut Hole

¼"

3¾"

oxidation from soldering. Bend the keepers to the shape shown, using one of the sticks as a form.

3 Attach the keepers. Screw a keeper to the unpointed end of each stick as shown in the *Overall View.* Slide the two sticks together and thread the bolt through the nut.

USING THE JIG

To use this measurement tool, loosen the bolt and slide the sticks apart until the tips touch the points you want to measure between. Tighten the bolt to keep the measurement. You can then either measure from tip to tip with a tape measure or transfer the distance directly to your stock.

Checking for Square

To check a cabinet or any other rectangular form for square, extend the sticks diagonally across the inside as shown in *Photo* 23-1. Lock the sticks in place once one tip is in each corner. Slide the jig out and check it against the other diagonal. The two measurements will be equal if the cabinet is square.

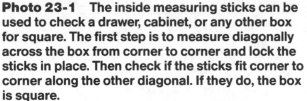

Photo 23-1 The inside measuring sticks can be used to check a drawer, cabinet, or any other box for square. The first step is to measure diagonally across the box from corner to corner and lock the sticks in place. Then check if the sticks fit corner to corner along the other diagonal. If they do, the box is square.

MITER SHOOTING BOARD

Design by Michael Dunbar

Mitering is fussy work. More often than not, you need to trim off just a sliver to get a perfect fit. You might do an acceptable job with a fine-cutting blade on a power saw or with careful work on a belt sander. But no power tool can match the crisp cut of a well-honed plane guided by an old-fashioned miter shooting board.

In addition to providing a superior cut, the miter shooting board is safer and more accurate. It's also inexpensive and easy to take along on the job. On top of it all, the miter shooting board is quite easy to make.

As shown in the *Overall View,* the miter shooting board has only three parts: a base, a ledge, and a stop. The base must be stable and perfectly flat, so make it from cabinet-grade plywood. Select a piece with a smooth face veneer such as birch or maple. While plywood is perfect for the base, make the ledge and stop from solid wood, so that you can joint the edges square. Any species will do as long as the wood is clear and straight-grained.

The shooting board shown here is a large version designed with trim carpentry in mind. If you need to miter only small pieces, you could make your shooting board smaller and narrower.

MAKING THE JIG

1 Cut the base and ledge. Cut the base and ledge to the dimensions in the Materials List. Joint the edges of the ledge perfectly square.

2 Make the waste groove. Dust and chips can gather in the corner formed by the base and ledge. They can lift the plane out of square during shooting. To prevent this, make a groove in the base where the debris can settle. Mark an end of the base 5½ inches from one side as shown in the *Overall View.* Crank the table saw blade to 45 degrees. Set the blade height at about ¼ inch. Set the rip fence so that the blade will cut through the center of the 5½-inch line. Run the base over the blade with one long edge against the fence. Turn the base end for end to run the other edge against the fence to complete the groove.

OVERALL VIEW

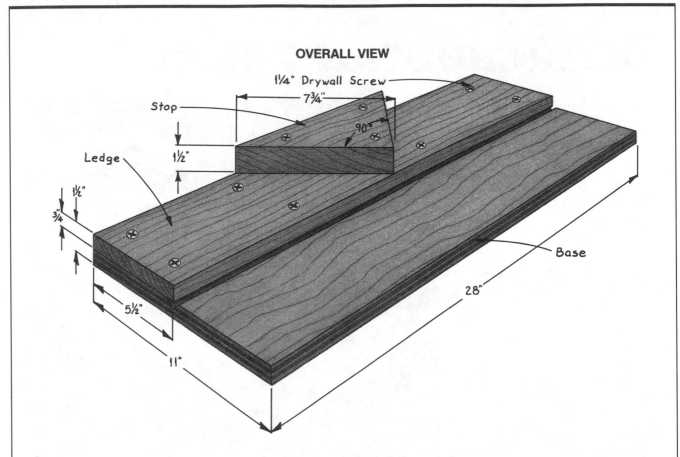

3 **Attach the ledge to the base.** Align the ledge on the base. Drill and countersink holes around the perimeter of the ledge for 1¼-inch drywall screws as shown in the *Overall View.* Insert the screws.

4 **Make the stop.** The stop is a perfect 90-degree triangle. Start with a piece of hardwood that is at least 20 inches long. Rip and joint it to 7¾ inches wide. Check that your table saw miter gauge is square to the blade. Also check that the blade is exactly 90 degrees to the table. Put the jointed edge of the stock against the miter gauge and cut the piece square. From this square end, measure 7¾ inches along the board. Strike a 45-degree line from this point to the opposing edge of the piece, forming a right triangle. Set the table saw miter gauge to 45 degrees. Make the cut, guiding what will be the scrap with the miter gauge. The cutoff is the stop.

5 **Attach the stop.** Drill and countersink three holes around the edges of the stop for 2¼-inch drywall screws, as shown in the *Overall View.* Drill one hole at each corner.

MATERIALS LIST		
Quantity	Part	Dimensions
1	Plywood base	¾" × 11" × 28"
1	Wood ledge	¾" × 5½" × 28"
1	Wood stop	1½" × 7¾" × 7¾"

HARDWARE

2¼" drywall screws, as needed
1¼" drywall screws, as needed

Mark the working edge of the ledge at the halfway point. Place the 90-degree corner of the stop at this mark, and put in a screw. Make the screw tight enough that the stop pivots with effort.

Set a 45-degree square on the edge of the ledge, and rotate the stop until its edge presses against the square. Check that the other side also forms a perfect 45-degree angle. Drive and tighten all the screws that hold the stop to the ledge. Apply a coat of paste wax to the base, so that the plane slides more easily.

USING THE JIG

The miter shooting board is for trimming flat miters for picture frames or door casings. This trimming work is called "shooting." When trimmed in this way with a plane, a surface is said to be "shot."

Preparing the Plane

You'll need to reserve one plane, or at least one plane blade, for shooting. That's because the cutting edge must be straight. Blades used for general planing should have slightly curved edges, so that the corners don't dig into the work. To check if the edge is straight, hold a square against it as shown in *Photo* 24-1. Check if light comes through between the blade and the square. Grind the blade until the square contacts the entire cutting edge. When you are done grinding, hone the blade razor sharp. A sharp plane is especially important for shooting miters because the plane must slice across end grain.

The type of plane you use depends on the size of your board. A jack plane works well with the large board shown here. You may find a smooth plane more comfortable, or for very fine work, you may want to use a block plane. Check that the side of the plane is perfectly square to the sole. If it is not, you can't shoot square. If necessary, you can have a machine shop grind your plane body. While you are at it, check that the sole is flat and the sides are parallel.

Shooting the Miters

At last, the fun part. Grip the shooting board either between bench dogs or in the side vise. Cut your miters on the table saw, radial arm saw, or miter box, whichever you prefer. Then place the workpiece firmly against the stop. Allow the end of the miter to project just a hair's breadth over the ledge so that as the plane passes, it slices off a paper-thin shaving. Hold the workpiece in place with one hand. Place the plane's toe (the area of the sole in front of the mouth) against the work, and give the tool a firm, uninterrupted push with the other hand. (See *Photo* 24-2.) Only one or two passes should be necessary to create a perfect miter with a glassy-smooth surface.

Photo 24-1 Use a square to check that the cutting edge of the plane blade is straight.

Photo 24-2 Allow the end of the miter to project slightly over the ledge. Hold the workpiece with one hand. Place the plane's toe against the work and give the tool a firm push with the other hand.

MICRO MITER BOX

Design by Ben Erickson

This miniature miter box is perfect for cutting cockbeads and other tiny moldings. It's tailor-made to hold small moldings securely. Because it's designed for a fine, 26-teeth-per-inch-blade backsaw, the cuts are smooth, crisp, and precise. At heart, the jig is simply a piece of solid hardwood stock with a groove cut into it. A hardwood stop clamps into the groove, so that you can cut several pieces exactly the same length.

The dimensions given work well for most small moldings. However, since the box is easy to make, consider making several boxes, tailoring each to a specific job. One saw that works well with this jig is the Micro Saw

(catalog #05.64.26) from Highland Hardware, 1045 North Highland Avenue NE, Atlanta, GA 30306. It will work well with any fine-toothed western or Japanese saw.

MAKING THE JIG

1 Prepare the stock. Make the jig from a stable, seasoned hardwood such as maple. Quarter-sawn stock is less likely to warp, although it's not strictly necessary. Joint one face and one edge of the stock. Plane to thickness and width. The stock must be straight for an accurate box.

2 Cut the groove. Rout a ¾-inch-wide groove in the blank in a series of passes, each slightly deeper than the one before. See "Table-Routing Dadoes and Grooves," page 23. The groove shown here is ¾ inch deep.

Make the groove shallower if the saw you plan to use won't cut that deep.

3 Cut guide kerfs. A miter box usually has three kerfs in it to guide the saw. One kerf guides the saw for a left-hand 45-degree miter. Another guides the 90-degree cut. A third kerf guides a right-hand 45-degree miter. Lay out a line for each kerf.

Because these cuts must be precise, guide them against your combination square. To prevent damage to the saw's teeth and the square's edge, place a scrap of veneer or plastic laminate under the square as shown in *Photo* 25-1. Clamp the square to the top of

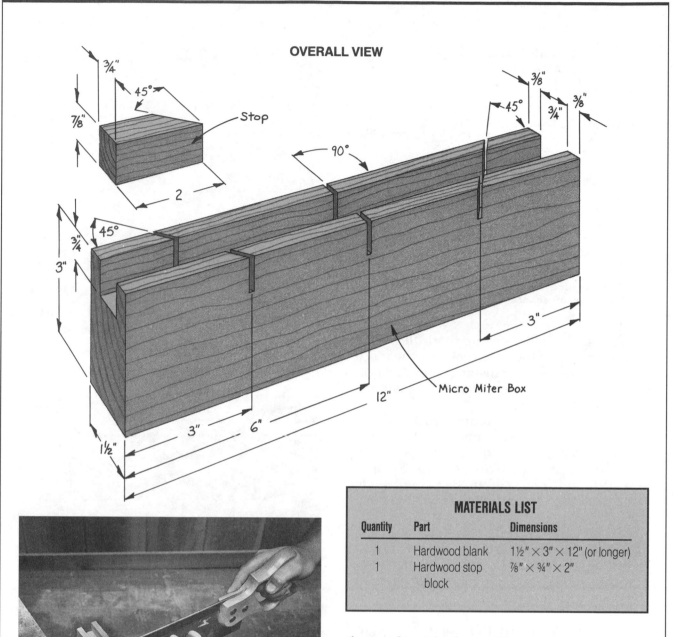

OVERALL VIEW

Stop

Micro Miter Box

MATERIALS LIST

Quantity	Part	Dimensions
1	Hardwood blank	1½" × 3" × 12" (or longer)
1	Hardwood stop block	⅞" × ¾" × 2"

Photo 25-1 Guide the saw with a miter gauge when cutting the kerfs in the miter box. Protect the teeth of the saw with a piece of plastic laminate under the square.

the jig along the layout lines. Press the saw blade against the square's edge. Cut down about ¼ inch. Don't cut the entire depth of the groove yet.

Remove the saw from the kerf, and lay out the rest of the cut with a knife and a 90-degree square. Keep the saw in the kerf you've cut and tilt it slightly toward you. Cut down the side of the box nearest you, following the line carefully. Tilt the saw forward to cut the other side.

If you don't have an accurate miter square, substitute a framing square as shown in *Laying Out Kerfs with a Framing Square*. Set the framing square across the miter box so that

**LAYING OUT KERFS WITH
A FRAMING SQUARE**

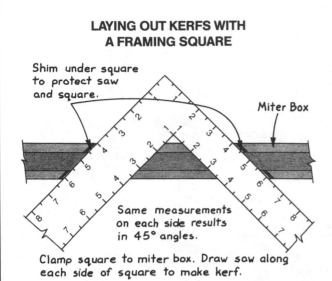

Shim under square to protect saw and square.

Miter Box

Same measurements on each side results in 45° angles.

Clamp square to miter box. Draw saw along each side of square to make kerf.

Photo 25-2   Square or miter one end of the stock.

Photo 25-3   The stop block has a mitered end and a square end. Clamp it into the miter box to make multiple cuts of exactly the same length.

the inch scale on the square reads the same on each blade of the square. Use either both outside scales or both inside scales, but not one of each. Clamp the square to the miter box and cut the kerf.

A saw with teeth that are only slightly set makes a narrower, more precise cut. If your saw has too much set, hold a sharpening stone flat against the blade. Draw the stone across the side of the teeth. Be careful not to remove all the set, or the blade will bind in the cut.

4 **Cut the box to length.** Cut the miter box to the length desired. To accommodate the stop, make the box 5 or 6 inches longer than the parts you'll cut with it.

5 **Make the stop.** Size the stop to fit snugly into the miter box groove and to protrude slightly from the top of the box. Cut one end of the stop square, for use with square cuts, and the other end at a 45-degree angle, to use with miter cuts.

USING THE JIG

Clamp the box in a bench vise and place the stock in the groove. Push the stock against the side farthest from you if your saw

cuts on the push stroke, as do all western and some Japanese saws. Push the stock against the side nearest you if you are using a Japanese saw that cuts on the pull stroke. Square or miter one end of the stock. Then measure and cut the other end. If several cuts the same length are to be made, clamp the stop in the box before making the second cut and push the stock firmly against it.

MITERING ON THE RADIAL ARM SAW

Design by Ben Erickson

Making miter joints is a challenge no matter how you go about it. The angles have to be cut just right, or the joint won't fit well. This radial arm saw jig takes the hassle out of making perfect miters. The two fences are mounted at exactly 90 degrees to each other and at 45 degrees to the path of the saw.

To cut a miter joint, put the first workpiece against one fence and make a cut. Then put the other workpiece against the second fence. Because the two fences set at a 90-degree angle to each other, the jig is self-correcting: You'll get a perfect joint, even if the saw path is slightly off square.

MAKING THE JIG

1 Cut the parts to size. Cut the parts to the dimensions in the Materials List. Use cabinet-grade plywood for the base and a stable hardwood such as mahogany for the fences. Joint and plane the fences straight and true. Make sure the edges of the base are straight and that the piece is square. (To check a large panel for square, measure across the diagonals. If the diagonals are equal, the piece is square.)

2 Position the fences. This is the most important step. The layout must be done carefully to ensure an accurate jig. Make sure the measuring tools you are using are square and accurate. To lay out the fences, draw a centerline on the jig base as shown in *Laying Out the Fence*. Make sure the line is square to the long edges of the base. Make two marks along this line: one 3 inches from the edge, the other 14 inches from the same edge. Draw a line through the 14-inch mark parallel to the long edges of the base.

To locate the fences, align the point of a framing square on the 3-inch mark. Adjust the angle of the square until the 14-inch line crosses the square at the same point on each leg. (The measurement should be the same

OVERALL VIEW

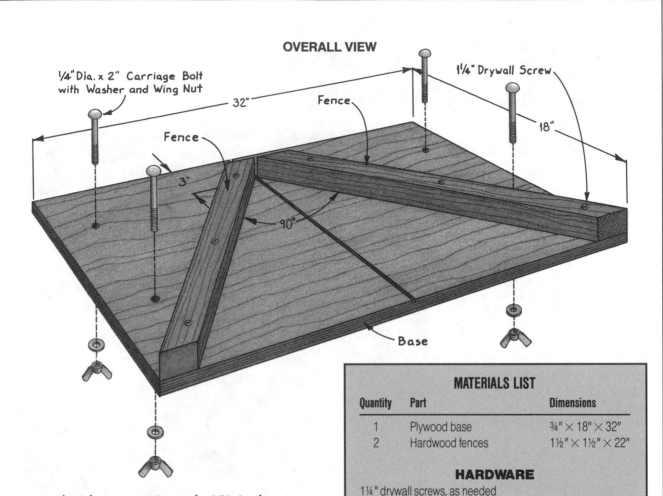

¼" Dia. x 2" Carriage Bolt with Washer and Wing Nut

1¼" Drywall Screw

Fence

Fence

32"

18"

3"

90°

Base

MATERIALS LIST

Quantity	Part	Dimensions
1	Plywood base	¾" × 18" × 32"
2	Hardwood fences	1½" × 1½" × 22"

HARDWARE

1¼" drywall screws, as needed
¼" dia. × 2" carriage bolts with washers and wing nuts, 4

on each side, approximately 15½ inches.) This guarantees that each leg of the framing square is angled 45 degrees from the edge of the base. Draw a line along each outside edge of the square.

3 Attach the fences. Cut the ends of the fences to 45-degree angles as shown in *Laying Out the Fence.* Put glue on the bottom of the

LAYING OUT THE FENCE

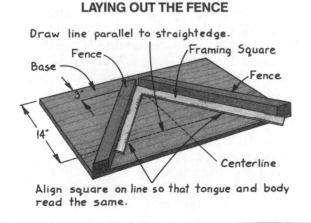

Draw line parallel to straightedge.

Fence

Framing Square

Base

Fence

3"

14"

Centerline

Align square on line so that tongue and body read the same.

the fences, and position their inside edges along the layout lines. Clamp the fences in place. Make sure the fences meet at the 3-inch mark, with little or no gap between them.

Drill and countersink holes through the bottom of the base into the fences for drywall screws. Remove the clamps.

USING THE JIG

Raise the blade on the saw until it clears the jig base. Make sure the base is tight against the saw fence. Position the jig so that the blade will cut exactly through the center-line as shown in *Photo* 26-1. Clamp the jig in place along the front edge. You may also want to screw it to the saw table along the back, near the saw fence. Pull the blade

Photo 26-1 Position the jig so that the blade will cut exactly through the centerline.

Photo 26-2 Check the angles between the fences and the kerf with a drafting triangle. The two angles should be equal. The jig is self-correcting, however, so a slight variation is not a problem.

forward until it touches the wooden strips, and check again that it will cut through the middle of the centerline.

Return the blade to its home position. Lower it slightly, so that it will cut a shallow kerf in the jig base. Turn on the saw and draw the blade across the jig. Return the blade home and turn off the machine. When the blade quits spinning, check the angles between the fences and the kerf with a 45-degree drafting triangle as shown in Photo 26-2.

The angles should be identical, but because the jig is self-correcting, a small variation is no problem. If one angle is 44½ degrees, the other is automatically 45½ degrees. If the angles are off by more than 1 degree or so, loosen the clamps and insert shims between the jig and the saw fence to compensate. Once the jig is positioned, clamp it to the table. Turn on the saw and cut across the fences again. Check the new kerf path with the drafting triangle.

When the angle is correct, drill holes and bolt it to the saw table. This will allow the jig to be realigned instantly the next time you need it.

Cut the pieces to be joined to their finished length using a stop on the radial arm saw fence. Place the stock against one of the jig's fences. Align the corner of the workpiece to the end of the fence as shown in *Aligning the Workpiece for the Cut*. Firmly hold the stock down and against the fence as you make the cut. Do not let the piece creep along the fence into the blade. Pull the saw all the way through the cut and slide the mitered piece out of the way. Be careful when pushing the saw back; the little cutoff blocks can be thrown quite easily. Cut the other half of the same miter joint against the opposite fence.

ALIGNING THE WORKPIECE FOR THE CUT

Align corner of workpiece to end of fence.

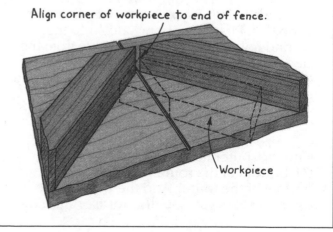

Workpiece

SMALL PARTS MORTISING JIG FOR THE PLUNGE ROUTER

Design by Andy Rae

There are countless jigs that help you turn your plunge router into a mortiser. This one is simple, and once you've made it, you'll never again have to measure to position a mortise. The router travels against a fence on the jig; a spacer properly positions the stock, so that the mortise is where you want it. Changing the thickness of the stock you mortise? Change the spacer.

The jig can handle stock up to 6 inches wide. It uses your bench-vise-and-dog system to secure the work during routing. This makes it very convenient to clamp

and unclamp stock as you mortise. It also supports the work on your bench, the most stable work surface in your shop.

MAKING THE JIG

1 Make the base and fence. Your jig must be custom-built to fit your router and your workbench. *Determining Dimensions* shows how to do this. First put a bench dog into the second hole in the bench. Measure from the clamping face of the dog to the inner face of the vise. Add ½ inch to this measurement and make that the width of your base. The jig shown here is 10½ inches wide. Cut the base to width and 17 inches long.

Size the fence so that it won't interfere with the router handles. First measure from the bottom of the router handles to the bottom of the router. Add the width of the thinnest stock you usually mortise. Make the

fence ¼ inch narrower than this and 17 inches long.

Attach the base to the fence with glue and ¾-inch drywall screws. Countersink the screws, so that the base sits flat. Drill a hole into one end of the base, so that you can hang the jig on the wall.

2 Make a spacer. The spacers are specific to the mortise you are routing, so make them as the need arises. When mortising, the router rides on both the spacer and the workpiece, as shown in *Determining Dimensions*. Make the spacer as thick as the width of the stock you are mortising. (See *Determining Dimensions*.)

DETERMINING DIMENSIONS

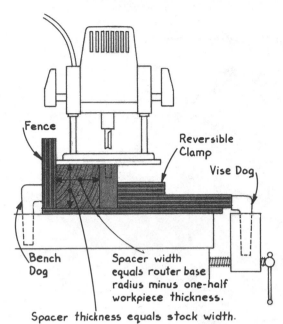

Fence

Reversible Clamp

Vise Dog

Bench Dog

Spacer width equals router base radius minus one-half workpiece thickness.

Spacer thickness equals stock width.

To figure out the spacer width for a centered mortise, begin with the radius of your router base. Subtract half the thickness of the piece you're mortising, and make the spacer that wide. (A 6-inch router base has a 3-inch radius. If the stock is 1 inch thick, the spacer should be 2½ inches wide.) It's tough to get the width exactly right on the first try, so begin by making the spacer about ⅛ inch wider than necessary. Rout a test mortise in scrap stock of the right width. Now measure from the edge of the scrap to the edge of the mortise to find exactly how much to trim the block. Saw or plane the block to exact width.

For an off-center mortise, put the bit in the router and measure from a cutting edge to the outside edge of the router base. (See *Sizing a Spacer Block for an Offset Mortise.*) Make the spacer width equal to this measurement minus the distance between the outside face of the workpiece and the side of the mortise.

Drill a hanging hole in one end of the block.

3 Make the reversible clamp. The reversible clamp is simply two scraps of plywood screwed together. When mortising stock narrower than 1½ inches, put the ¾-inch face against the workpiece. For wider stock, flip the clamp around and put the 1½-inch face against the workpiece. If your workpiece is 3½ inches or more wide, add another ¾-inch-thick piece of plywood to the bottom of the clamp.

To make the clamp, start with a piece of plywood about 10 inches long and about 6 inches wide. To determine the length of the bottom piece, put the jig against the bench dog, and put the spacer block in the jig. With the vise closed, measure from the spacer block to the clamping face of the vise dog. Cut the plywood to this length.

The width of the clamp's top piece isn't important. Just be sure it won't get in the way of the router base. Screw the two pieces together with 1¼-inch drywall screws.

4 Make extension fences, if needed. If you mortise stock that is wider than your fence height, you'll need an extension fence or fences to guide the router base. (See the *Overall View.*) Make the extension fences in ¾-inch height increments to make the jig as versatile as possible. Cut as many extensions as you need to the dimensions given in the

SIZING A SPACER BLOCK FOR AN OFFSET MORTISE

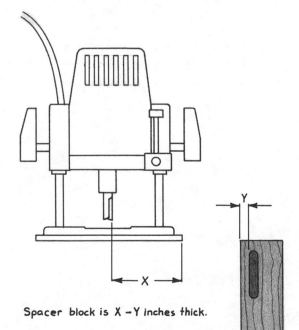

Y

X

Spacer block is X − Y inches thick.

OVERALL VIEW

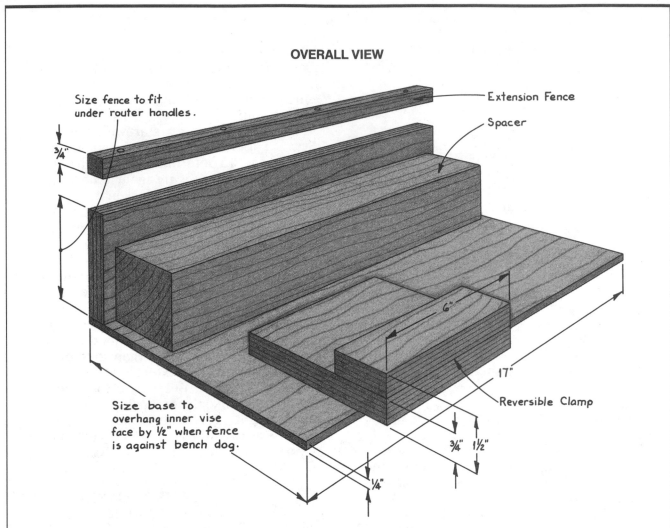

Size fence to fit under router handles.

Extension Fence

Spacer

¾"

Size base to overhang inner vise face by ½" when fence is against bench dog.

6"

17"

Reversible Clamp

¾" 1½"

¼"

MATERIALS LIST		
Quantity	**Part**	**Dimensions**
1	MDF base*	¼" × to fit × 17"
1	Plywood fence	¾" × to fit × 17"
1	Hardwood spacer	Thickness and width to fit × 17"
1	Plywood clamp bottom	¾" × 6" × to fit
1	Plywood clamp top	¾" × to fit × 6"
As needed	Hardwood fence extensions	¾" × ¾" × 17"

*Medium-density fiberboard

HARDWARE

1½" drywall screws, as needed
1¼" drywall screws, as needed
¾" drywall screws, as needed

Materials List. Attach the first extension fence to the main fence with four countersunk 1½-inch drywall screws. Stack additional fences by screwing into the fence below, making sure to position screws so that they don't hit screw heads below. When attaching fences, be sure the guiding face is flush with the face below. Mark the stacking order on the fences.

USING THE JIG

If you are routing mortises in both ends of pieces such as door stiles, select the surface that will face out and mark it in pencil. In many designs, the mortises are offset rather than centered. In this case, draw an arrow on the surface you'll mortise. Draw the arrow so that it points to the outside

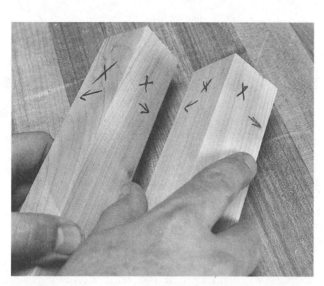

Photo 27-1 The mortises on these table legs are offset. The arrows show which part of the leg can be seen in a room setting. To rout mortises like this, make sure the arrow is against the jig's spacer block.

surface of the workpiece—the one that will be exposed in the finished piece. Photo 27-1 shows a typical pair of table legs that is marked for mortising.

Laying Out the Mortise

When you are routing mortises, make sure the outside face of the workpiece is

LAYING OUT A MORTISE

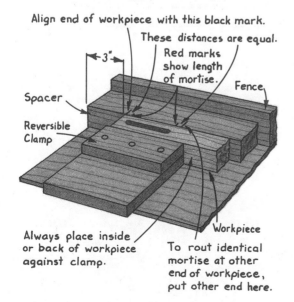

Align end of workpiece with this black mark.

These distances are equal.

Red marks show length of mortise.

Fence

3"

Spacer

Reversible Clamp

Always place inside or back of workpiece against clamp.

Workpiece

To rout identical mortise at other end of workpiece, put other end here.

against the spacer block. If you put the inside face against the spacer when routing an offset, the mortise will be offset toward the wrong side. When routing centered mortises, putting the outside face against the spacer assures the joints will be flush on the outside, even if the stock thickness varies.

The spacer width positions the mortise, but you'll still have to lay out the mortise length. Save time by marking the layout on the spacer block. As shown in *Laying Out a Mortise*, this requires four marks. First make a black mark about 3 inches from the end of the spacer that will be closest to you when you rout the mortise. This mark will be used to align one end of the stock. Now make red marks showing where the mortise is to begin and end. Make another black alignment mark as shown in *Laying Out a Mortise*. This mark will be used to align the other end of a frame member or the adjacent side of a table leg as described below.

Selecting a Sequence

Setting up a standard sequence is the key to getting all your mortises in the right place. Let's say you are routing centered mortises in both ends of a stile. Place a stile in the jig as shown in *Laying Out a Mortise* and tighten the vise. Rout the mortise. Loosen the vise and slide the stile toward you until the other end is aligned with the other black mark. Tighten the vise and rout the second mortise.

Let's say you are routing one of the table legs shown in Photo 27-1. Each of these legs will get two offset mortises. Put the leg in the jig so that one arrow faces the spacer. Rout a mortise, then put the leg in the jig so that the other arrow is pointing toward the spacer.

Routing a Mortise

Spiral-fluted straight bits are the easiest to use for routing mortises. The flutes pull up the waste wood like a drill bit. Most cabinetmakers like to rout a hole at the beginning and end of the mortise before removing the waste in between. This assures the ends of the mortise will be square.

To begin routing, align the end of your

ROUTING A MORTISE

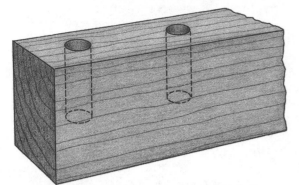

1. Plunge both ends of the mortise to full depth.

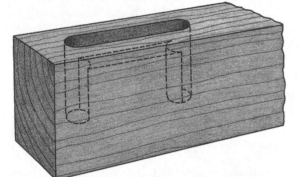

2. Set router bit depth to ½". Rout the full length of the mortise.

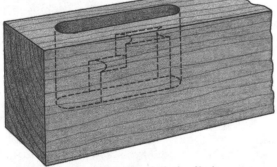

3. Rout mortise to full depth in ½" increments.

workpiece with the black mark. Tighten the vise. Set your plunge router to the full mortise depth. With the router off, align the bit with one of the red marks that indicates the end of the mortise. Turn on the router and plunge. Pull up the bit, then turn off the router. (It won't hurt if you've routed about 1/16 inch past the line. It won't compromise strength as long as the joint is snug from side to side. In fact, you may find the slop very handy when you tap parts into alignment during assembly.)

Now position the bit at the other end of the mortise. Plunge down and pull up.

Set the router stops so that you can plunge about ½ inch deep. Starting from the closest end of the mortise, rout away from you until you meet the hole you routed on the other end. Repeat this process, routing about ½ inch deeper with each pass until you reach full mortise depth.

The mortise will be rounded at the ends. Either round-over the tenon to match or square off the end of the mortise with a chisel.

ROUTER MORTISING JIG FOR ENTRY DOORS

Design by Fred Matlack and Jim Tolpin

his jig fits onto the edge of a door stile to act as a template and support for routing mortises. It's designed for large doors, such as entry doors that are too awkward to fit into the "Small Parts Mortising Jig for the Plunge Router," page 132. Use the jig for stiles that are at least 1 inch thick. Thinner stiles, such as those for cabinet doors, are too flimsy to support the jig shown here.

This jig uses a straight router bit with a template guide bushing. The bushing is guided by a slot cut into the middle of the jig's interchangeable template. You'll want to make a template for each mortise size you use.

This jig works best with a plunge router. If you use a fixed-base router, or if you are routing mortises more than about 1½ inches deep, you'll have to drill part of the mortise before routing.

MAKING THE JIG

1 Make the sides. Cut the side pieces to the dimensions in the Materials List.

2 Drill the stop bolt holes. When you put a stile in the jig and butt it against the stop bolt, the mortise is properly positioned in relation to the end of the stile. It isn't important exactly where the bolt passes through the sides of the jig, because you lay out each template from the bolt. Center the stop bolt holes approximately across the width of the sides and about 5½ inches from one end. It is important that the holes be in the same place in both sides. To ensure this, stack the sides together with all edges flush and drill a ¼-inch-diameter hole through both at the same time.

3 Make the braces. Cut four hardwood braces to the dimensions in the Materials List. Cut out the notches to the dimensions shown in the *Overall View.*

4 Drill the bolt holes in the braces. Lay out the bolt holes on the braces as shown in the

OVERALL VIEW

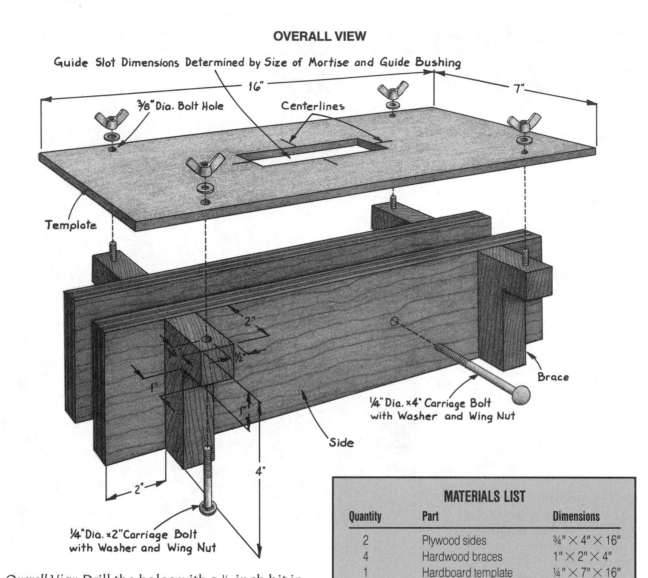

Guide Slot Dimensions Determined by Size of Mortise and Guide Bushing

16"

7"

⅜"Dia. Bolt Hole

Centerlines

Template

2"

½"

1"

1"

¼" Dia. ×4" Carriage Bolt with Washer and Wing Nut

Brace

Side

2"

4"

¼"Dia. ×2"Carriage Bolt with Washer and Wing Nut

MATERIALS LIST		
Quantity	Part	Dimensions
2	Plywood sides	¾" × 4" × 16"
4	Hardwood braces	1" × 2" × 4"
1	Hardboard template	¼" × 7" × 16"

HARDWARE

¼" dia. × 4" carriage bolt with washer and wing nut, 1
¼" dia. × 2" carriage bolts with washers and wing nuts, 4

Overall View. Drill the holes with a ¼-inch bit in a hand drill.

5 Glue the braces to the sides. Draw lines across the sides 2 inches from each end to mark the brace positions. Glue the braces in place, making sure the braces are square to the sides.

6 Make the templates. Each size mortise requires a different template. Cut as many templates as necessary to the dimensions in the Materials List.

7 Drill bolt holes in the templates. Put a template blank on the bench with the good side down. Strike a centerline along the length of the blank as shown in *Drilling Bolt*

Holes in the Template. Put a scrap of plywood or a couple of blocks under the template, so that you don't drill into your bench.

Put the stop bolt through the sides. Place the sides on the template. Align the ends of the sides with the ends of the template.

Use one of the stiles you will mortise to help align the bolt holes. Mark the center of the stile on the end grain as shown in *Drilling Bolt Holes in the Template.* Put the stile in the jig.

DRILLING BOLT HOLES IN THE TEMPLATE

Mark centerline of stile thickness and align with template centerline.

Mark holes in template through brace holes.

Butt stile against stop bolt.

Mark where end of stile meets bottom of template.

Mark centerline of template.

Butt the end of the stile against the stop bolt, and close the sides against the stile. Check that the jig sides are square to the ends of the template.

Mark where the end of the stile meets the bottom of the template. Lay out the bolt holes in the template by putting a #12 screw through the brace holes and hitting the screw with a hammer. Drill the holes with a ⅜-inch-diameter bit. The oversize holes will provide a little leeway in case you need to use this template later with stock of a slightly different thickness.

8 Lay out and rout a guide slot in each template. In the previous step, you marked the centerline of the templates. You also marked where the end of the stile meets each template. The *Template Slot Layout* shows how to use these lines to lay out the position of the mortise on each template.

First mark where the mortise will start. Do this by measuring from the stile end mark as shown in the *Template Slot Layout*.

Because of the way guide bushings work, the slot must be larger than the final mortise. To find out how much larger, subtract the diameter of the router bit from the outside diameter of the guide bushing, and divide by 2. This amount is called the offset. Measure this distance from the line at the beginning of the mortise, and make a mark as shown in

the *Template Slot Layout*. This marks the beginning of the guide slot.

To determine the size of the template slot, double the offset and add this amount to the width and length of your mortise. Lay out the slot from the offset mark you just made, centering it on the centerline. For more information on offsets, see "Using Guide Bushings," page 29.

Rout the guide slots as described in "Making Stopped Cuts on the Router Table," page 24. Mark the centerlines of the guide slot on the top face of the template as shown in the *Overall View.*

TEMPLATE SLOT LAYOUT

Template Slot Length

First Offset Mark

Template Slot Width

Mortise starts here.

Distance between End of Stile and Beginning of Mortise

Template Centerline

Stile End Mark

USING THE JIG

There are two ways to use this mortising jig. If the mortises are no deeper than the cutting length of your router bit, and if you have a plunge router, you can use the jig and router to do the whole job. For deeper mortises, you'll also need to use a drill press or portable drill and a chisel. If you're using a fixed-base router, drill out the waste on the drill press, regardless of the mortise depth.

Lay out the center of the mortise on one stile. Draw perpendicular lines through the center of the mortise as shown in *Photo* 28-1. Make these layout lines equal to the thickness of the door and about 1 inch longer than the mortise. Place the jig on the stile. Align the layout lines on the stile with the centerlines on the jig as shown in *Photo* 28-2.

Photo 28-1 Draw perpendicular lines through the center of the mortise on one stile.

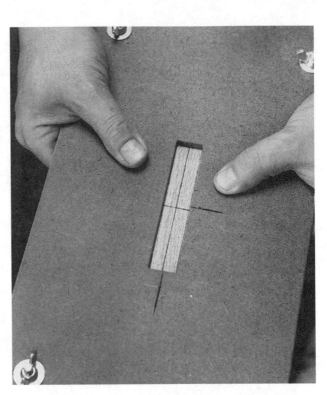

Photo 28-2 Align the layout lines on the stile with the centerlines on the jig.

Photo 28-3 If you drill out waste with a hand drill, wrap a piece of tape around the bit as a depth guide.

Adjust the jig accordingly and tighten the wing nuts.

Drilling Out Mortises

If the mortises are deep, or if you are using a fixed-base router, the first step in mortising is to drill out most of the waste from your mortises. Begin by laying out all the mortises on the stiles. It's easiest and most accurate to drill out the waste on the drill press. Careful work with a portable electric drill will do a fine job, too. Drill out the waste with a brad point bit or Forstner bit. A spade bit is not accurate enough for precise work.

Drill to the depth of the mortise and to within $1/16$ inch of your layout lines. If you are using a hand drill, wrap a piece of tape around the bit as a depth guide, as shown in *P*hoto 28-3.

Routing Mortises

Set your router to cut about $1/4$ inch deep. Clamp a stile firmly to your bench. Position

Photo 28-4 If you are unable to rout to the final mortise depth, hold the flat of a chisel against the mortise walls and cut down to the final depth.

the jig on the stile and clamp it in place to make sure it won't shift while you are routing. Begin by routing counterclockwise around the perimeter of the mortise. Then move the router back and forth to clean out the middle of the mortise. Repeat this process in ¼-inch depth increments until you reach the bottom of the mortise.

Finishing with the Chisel

Remove the jig. If you were unable to rout to final mortise depth, hold the flat of a chisel against the mortise walls and cut down to the final depth, as shown in *Photo* 28-4. The corners of the mortise will be rounded. You can either square these corners with the chisel or round the edges of the tenons to fit.

MORTISING MACHINE

Design by Greg Glebe

If you have lots of mortises in your future, this shop-made machine is for you. Slip the workpiece on the machine, secure the on-board clamp, push the work into the router bit, and pull the lever. It won't take much longer to make a mortise than it just took you to read about it.

The mortising machine looks complex, but it really is quite simple to assemble. An organized woodworker could do it in a few hours. You can buy a machine like this for about $600. As of this writing, the shop-made version will cost about $150; not a bad return on your time. Still, if you make mortises only occasionally, you can accomplish the job efficiently enough with the simpler, cheaper "Small Parts Mortising Jig for the Plunge Router" on page 132.

The mortising machine shown here employs a router and two sliding tables to make the cuts. One table

holds the work and moves it in and out in relation to the cutter, controlling mortise depth. The other table holds the router and moves from side to side, controlling mortise width.

The tables slide on drill rod runners captured in pillow blocks. These allow very smooth, accurate travel. Adjustable stops on the drill rods let you set up your cuts precisely.

The lever and the router brackets are aluminum. Aluminum works easily with common tools and yet is tough enough to stand up to hard use. The hand grip shown came from a Schwinn bicycle, though any other grip could be used. Plastic tassle is optional.

MAKING THE JIG

1 Cut the parts to size. Cut the wood and plywood parts to the dimensions in the Materials List. Use a cabinet-grade plywood and durable hardwood such as oak or maple. Glue together two pieces of plywood for each table. Make sure the face veneer grain runs the same way on the pieces before you glue them. Glue up the router mounts from several thinner pieces of hardwood.

2 Mount the pillow blocks on the router table. The exact placement of the pillow

OVERALL VIEW

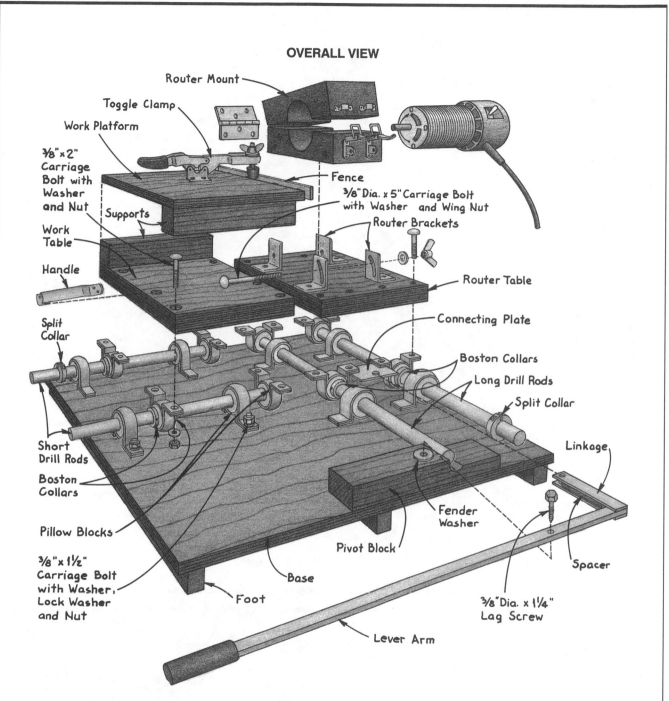

blocks is not critical. What is critical is that the drill rods remain parallel to each other. The easiest way to do this is to make spacers to hold the drill rods in position while you bolt the pillow blocks in place.

Start by attaching the pillow blocks to the router table. Make two spacers from ¾-inch-thick plywood as shown in *Spacer Detail 1.* To ensure that their holes are exactly the same distance apart, stack the spacers and

drill them at the same time. Slide them onto the long drill rods, followed on either side by a Boston collar, a pillow block, and another Boston collar. (Boston collars have a single set screw that bears right on the shaft.)

Position the whole assembly on the underside of the router table, with one block at each corner and the drill rods parallel to the *long* sides of the table. Hold the blocks in place with the Boston collars as shown

MATERIALS LIST

Quantity	Part	Dimensions
2	Plywood router table blanks	¾" × 9" × 11"
2	Plywood work table blanks	¾" × 9" × 11"
2	Hardwood router mounts	2½" × 3¾" × 8"
1	Plywood base	¾" × 19⅝" × 24"
1	Plywood work platform	¾" × 9½" × 11"
2	Hardwood supports	1" × 1¾" × 9"
1	Hardwood pivot block	1½" × 2⅛" × 10"
3	Hardwood feet	1" × 1¼" × 19½"

HARDWARE

#10 × 2½" flathead wood screws, 4
#10 × 1½" flathead wood screws, 6
#10 × 1" roundhead wood screws, 4
1½" drywall screws, as needed
⅜" dia. × 1¼" lag screw with fender washer, 1
⅜" dia. × 1" hex head bolt with lock washer, 3 flat washers, and nut, 1
¼" dia. × 1" hex head bolt with lock washer and nut, 1
⅜" dia. × 5" carriage bolts with washers and wing nuts, 2

HARDWARE—Continued

½" dia. × 2" carriage bolts with washers and nuts, 4
⅜" dia. × 2" carriage bolts with washers, lock washers, and nuts, 16
⅜" dia. × 1½" carriage bolts with washers, lock washers, and nuts, 16
¼" nuts, 4
3½" × 3½" hinge with screws, 1
Tool box catches with screws, 2
Handle, 1
Hand grip, 1
⅜" × ¾" × 24" aluminum for lever arm, 1
⅜" × ¾" × 4" aluminum for linkage, 1
⅛" × 1" × 11" aluminum for fence, 1
⅛" × 1" × 6" aluminum for linkage, 2
⅛" × 2½" × 3" aluminum for connecting plate, 1
¾" self-aligning, bronze-bushing pillow blocks, 16
¾" dia. × 18" drill rod, 2
¾" dia. × 14" drill rod, 2
¾" Boston collars, 8
2" × 3" × 1½" long, ¼" thick aluminum angle iron for brackets, 4
Toggle clamp, 1
¾" split collars, 2

---

in Photo 29-1. Mark the centers of the bolt holes on the table. Set the pillow block assembly aside, then drill the ⅜-inch-diameter bolt holes on the drill press. Bolt the pillow blocks in place with ⅜-inch-diameter × 2-inch carriage bolts, washers, lock washers, and nuts.

SPACER DETAIL 1

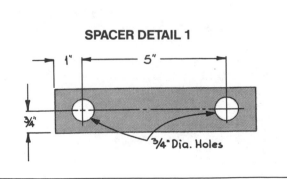

1" 5" ¾" ¾" Dia. Holes

Photo 29-1 Plywood spacers keep the rods parallel and properly spaced while you mark the router table for the pillow block bolt holes.

BASE LAYOUT

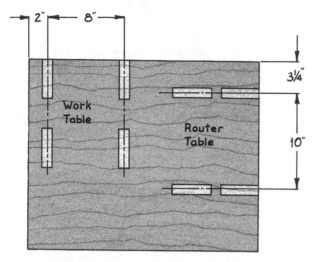

5 Make the router mount. Clamp the two router mount blocks together, face-to-face. Make sure the edges are flush. Measure the diameter of your router motor. Lay out the hole for the router on the blocks. Center the circle on the seam between the two pieces. Unclamp the pieces and cut the semicircles on the band saw. Carefully file and sand the curves to fit your router. When the mount is closed, you want it to hold the router securely but not so tightly that it crushes the motor casing.

Once the cutouts fit properly, clamp the two blocks together again. Screw the hinge to one end and the catches to the other.

6 Drill and shape the router mount. Lay out the pivot and lock holes on the lower part of the mount as shown in the *Router Mount Detail*. Drill the holes on the drill press with a ⅜-inch bit. Round the lower corner on the hinged end as shown. Make the cut on the band saw and sand it smooth.

3 Mount the base pillow blocks. Once you've attached the blocks to the router table, attach the corresponding blocks to the plywood base. Remove the collars and slide the rods out of the first set of pillow blocks. Slide the spacers, collars, and a second set of pillow blocks on the rods as before. Position this new set of blocks on the base as shown in the *Base Layout*. Align the drill rods so that they're parallel to the *short* side of the base. Bolt the blocks in place as before, using ⅜-inch-diameter × 1½-inch carriage bolts, washers, lock washers, and nuts.

4 Mount pillow blocks on the work table. Repeat the process to locate the blocks for the work table. This time, however, use the spacers shown in *Spacer Detail 2*. Align the rods parallel to the *short* side of the table and the *long* side of the base. Countersink the bolt heads beneath the surface of the table.

ROUTER MOUNT DETAIL

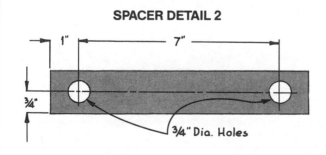

SPACER DETAIL 2

7 Drill the router brackets. The brackets hold the router mount to the router table. Drill a ½-inch-diameter mounting hole in the short side of each bracket as shown in the *Bracket Layout*. Then drill a ⅜-inch-diameter pivot hole in the long side of two of the brackets as shown.

BRACKET LAYOUT

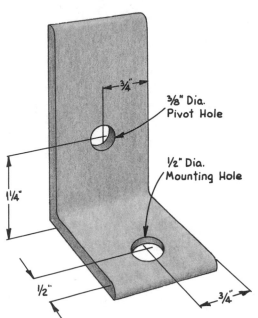

- ¾"
- ⅜" Dia. Pivot Hole
- ½" Dia. Mounting Hole
- 1¼"
- ½"
- ¾"

The placement of these pivot holes is critical, because they must align for the jig to work properly. Make sure the holes are equidistant from the bottom of the brackets. The best way to control the placement of the holes is to use a fence on the drill press. One such fence is described in "Boring Holes for European-Style Hinges," page 100. Clamp the fence the necessary distance from the bit. Then clamp the pieces against the fence as you drill them. Clamping the work adds accuracy and safety to the operation. For more information, see "Drilling Metal," page 4. After you drill the pivot holes, file one of them square to fit the carriage bolt head.

8 Cut the curved slots. The remaining two brackets have curved slots. These slots allow you to raise and lower the router to position the mortise. Lay out a slot on one bracket as shown in the *Slot Layout*. Use a large compass to draw the arcs. (For a large compass you can make, see "Extended Compass," page 117.) Align the bottom of the bracket with the edge of your bench. Locate the compass pivot point with respect to that edge as shown. Mark both the outside and inside curves.

It is important that the curved slots be identical, mirror images of each other. You can ensure this by drilling them together. To do this, clamp the two brackets together against a piece of plywood as shown in *Drilling the Curved Slots*. First cut a scrap of plywood ¾ × 2 × 3 inches. Drill holes into the plywood to match the ½-inch holes in the brackets. Bolt the upper bracket to the plywood as shown.

Cut a block of solid wood that fits under the bracket assembly, as shown in *Drilling the Curved Slots*. Position the block under the bracket as shown and drill a hole to match the one in the bracket. Bolt the block to the bracket.

Make the curved slots by drilling a series of holes into the brackets. Clamp the wood block to the drill press when you drill through both brackets for the curved slots. Remove

SLOT LAYOUT

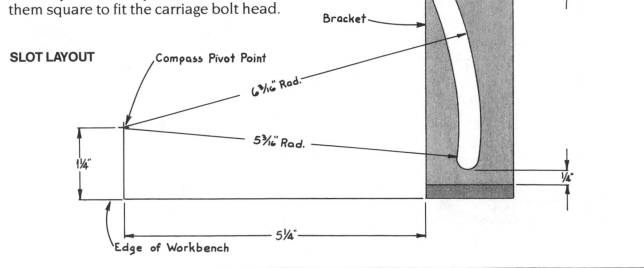

- Compass Pivot Point
- Bracket
- 6³⁄₁₆" Rad.
- 5³⁄₁₆" Rad.
- ¼"
- ¼"
- 1¼"
- 5¼"
- Edge of Workbench

DRILLING THE CURVED SLOTS

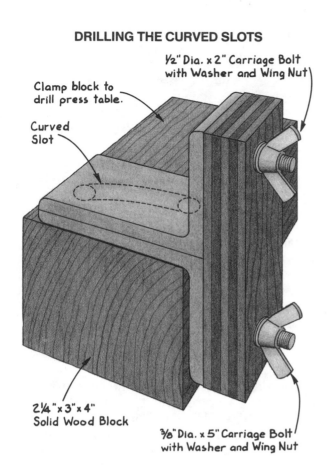

½" Dia. x 2" Carriage Bolt with Washer and Wing Nut

Clamp block to drill press table.

Curved Slot

2¼" x 3" x 4" Solid Wood Block

⅜" Dia. x 5" Carriage Bolt with Washer and Wing Nut

the wood block, and bolt both brackets to the plywood. Clean up both slots with files.

9 Install the brackets. Bolt the brackets to the router mount with ⅜-inch-diameter × 5-inch carriage bolts, washers, and wing nuts. Center the mount across the length of the router table, positioning the brackets as shown in the *Overall View*. Mark the centers of the mounting holes on the router table. Drill ½-inch-diameter mounting holes through the router table. Bolt the mount in place with ½-inch-diameter × 2-inch carriage bolts, washers, and nuts.

10 Make the work platform. The work platform and the work table form an assembly, as shown in the *Overall View*. Screw supports to both ends of the work table with #10 × 2½-inch flathead wood screws. Position the work platform on the supports so that its one edge overhangs the supports by ½ inch and its other edge is flush with the supports. Screw the work platform to the supports with #10 × 1½-inch flathead wood screws.

11 Drill and attach the fence. Lay out the four slots in the metal fence as shown in the *Fence Detail*. Drill each slot on the drill press by making three holes with a 3/16-inch bit. Clean up these slots with a small file.

Lay out a line along the center of the overhanging edge of the work platform. Drill through the fence into the line for four #10 × 1" roundhead wood screws. Slip the screws through the holes in the fence. Put ¼-inch nuts over the screws. Screw the fence to the platform. As shown in P*hoto* 29-2, the nuts create a gap between the platform and the fence. This gap prevents dust from accumulating against the fence as you work. The slots in the fence let you adjust the fence to accommodate different workpiece thicknesses.

12 Make the connecting plate. The connecting plate is a piece of aluminum that connects the router table to the control lever. It is attached to the router table with the same bolts that hold two of the pillow blocks.

Remove the router mount and pillow blocks from the table. Position the plate under the router table, and clamp the plate and table in position on the drill press as shown in P*hoto* 29-3. Place a scrap of aluminum under the other side of the router table to keep it level. Drill holes down through the

FENCE DETAIL

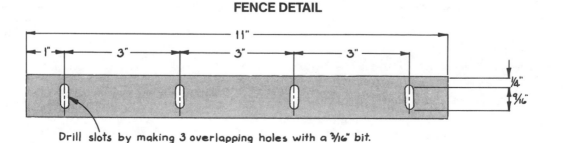

11"

1"   3"   3"   3"

¼"

3/16"

Drill slots by making 3 overlapping holes with a 3/16" bit.

Photo 29-2 Create a gap between the table and the fence by slipping ¼-inch nuts on the screws that join the two. The gap keeps dust from accumulating around the fence.

plate using the holes in the router table as a guide. Unclamp the plate and drill a ⅜-inch hole through it for the lever. The exact location of the hole is not critical. Position it roughly as shown in the *Overall View.*

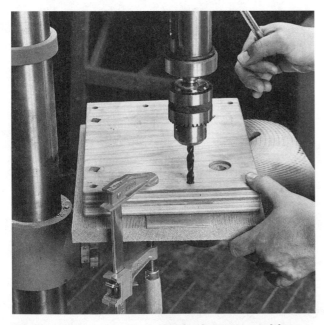

Photo 29-3 Use the holes in the router table as guides to drill holes in the connecting plate.

Reassemble the router table with the connecting plate in place. Put the pillow blocks on first, followed by the plate. There's no need for a washer between the nut and the connecting plate.

13 Install the tables. Install the work table and router table on the base as shown in the *Overall View.* Lock the drill rods in place with Boston collars, positioned as shown. On the router table, position a Boston collar on either side of the pillow blocks nearest the lever. On the work table, position a Boston collar on either side of the blocks farthest from the router, as shown in the *Overall View.*

Move the rods until they are flush with the pillow blocks at the fence end of the work table and with the pillow blocks at the end opposite the connecting plate on the router table. Tighten the collars to lock the rods in place.

14 Make the pivot block. The lever arm mounts on a wooden pivot block as shown in the *Overall View.* Clamp the blank securely to the drill press and drill a 1-inch-diameter hole as shown in the *Pivot Block Detail.* Note that the hole extends beyond the face of the blank. Cut the rest of the shape on the band saw. Drill the hole on the top of the block as shown. Position the block on the base so that the drill rod runs in the curved, cut-out area as shown in the *Overall View.* Screw the block in place from underneath using 1½-inch drywall screws.

PIVOT BLOCK DETAIL

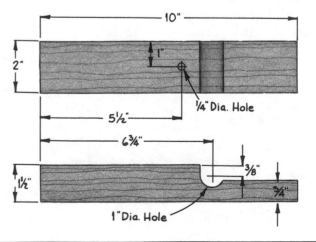

CONTROL LEVER DETAIL

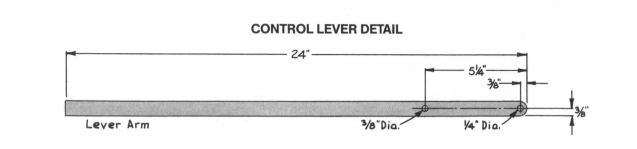

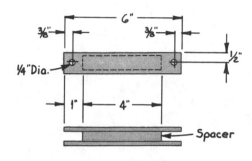

— Spacer

15 **Make the control lever.** The control lever is made from aluminum bar stock. The linkage is made from three separate pieces, two ⅛-inch-thick pieces on the outside with a ⅜-inch-thick spacer in between.

Make the linkage as shown in the *Control Lever Detail*. In the mortiser shown here, the three pieces are welded together. If you don't weld, join the pieces with epoxy. When the epoxy hardens, drill the holes on each end of the linkage with a drill press. Also drill the holes in the lever arm. File the end of the lever round, as shown. Attach the lever arm to the linkage with a ¼-inch-diameter × 1-inch hex head bolt, lock washer, and nut.

Attach the linkage to the connecting plate with a ⅜-inch-diameter × 1-inch hex head bolt, lock washer, and nut. Use several washers between the connecting plate and linkage to get the spacing right. Move the lever arm until the remaining hole is centered over the hole in the pivot block. Place a fender washer between the two and attach the lever arm to the block with a ⅜-inch-diameter × 1¼-inch lag screw. Slip the handle grip on the end of the arm.

16 **Finish the jig.** Glue the three feet to the underside of the base as shown in the *Overall View*. Attach the toggle clamp and the handle to the work table as shown. Sand the entire jig, rounding all rough corners. Move the tables back and forth to be sure they slide smoothly. Slip a split collar on one drill rod for each table. (Split collars cost a bit more than Boston collars but won't mar the shafts—an important consideration, since you'll reposition this set of collars often.) Tighten them so that they won't fall off. Get ready to cut some mortises.

USING THE JIG

As you work with the mortiser, the lever will be to your right and the work table and platform will be to your left. The right-hand router stop is built into the jig. The left stop is controlled with the split collar on the router table drill rod. The depth of cut is controlled by the split collar on the work table drill rod.

Lay out the mortise on your stock. If you are cutting a number of duplicate mortises, lay out only the first one. You can then attach stop blocks to the work platform to use as references for the subsequent cuts.

Select a straight router bit whose diameter equals the width of the mortise you want to rout. Spiral-fluted straight bits work great for mortising. Mount the bit in the router. Clamp the workpiece roughly in position on the table. Slide the work table forward until the workpiece barely touches the bit. Then loosen the wing nuts that lock the router mount to the brackets. Adjust the bit height to match the mortise as shown in *Photo* 29-4.

Move the router table all the way to the right, against the fixed stop. Unclamp the workpiece from the table, and position it with the right-hand layout mark in line with the right edge of the bit as shown in *Photo* 29-5. Clamp the workpiece in place. Move the

Photo 29-4 To adjust the mortise height, position the bit so that the flutes point up and down. Loosen the wing nuts that lock the router mount to the brackets. Adjust the bit height to match the mortise layout on the workpiece.

router to the left until the left edge of the bit lines up with the left-hand layout mark. Loosen the split collar and slide it over to stop the router's travel at this point. Run the router back and forth a time or two to double-check your setup.

Push the work table forward until the workpiece is in contact with the bit. Check the depth of cut by measuring the distance between the split collar and the pillow block as shown in P*hoto* 29-6. Move the collar as needed to set the depth of cut.

To cut a mortise, check to be sure that the workpiece is clamped securely in position. Back the work table away from the bit. Start the router, and move it to the extreme right position. Then advance the work into the bit. Plunge in about ⅛ inch and move the router to the left. When it hits the stop, return it to the right position. Plunge the work in another ⅛ inch, and cut from right to left. Continue until the mortise is cut to full depth. As you cut from right to left, the bit pushes the work against the table. A cut from

Photo 29-5 To set the mortise length, move the router table against the fixed stop. Position the bit flutes horizontally. Align the right-hand mark on the workpiece with the right edge of the bit. Clamp the workpiece. Move the router until the bit's left edge touches the left-hand layout line. Adjust the split collar stop.

Photo 29-6 To set the mortise depth, push the work table forward until the workpiece touches the bit. The distance between the work table split collar and the pillow block will equal the cutting depth.

Photo 29-7 The mortising machine is great for loose tenon joinery. Make mortises in both pieces and make loose tenons to fit between.

left to right tends to pull the work up off the table and results in a ragged cut.

Cutting mortises with a router bit results in mortises with rounded ends. To accommodate this, you can square the ends of the mortises with a chisel after they are cut. Or you can round the corners of the tenons to fit.

Another option is to make loose tenons. Instead of cutting the tenon as an integral part of a piece, cut a mortise into the end grain of what would ordinarily be the tenoned stock. Then make a separate tenon to fit into the mortise as shown in *Photo* 29-7. The resulting joint is every bit as strong as its traditional counterpart and has several advantages. You save wood, because you don't have to cut parts oversize to allow for the tenon. Angled joinery becomes much easier, because the shoulders are cut in one pass. And you save time, because there is only one setup to make on the mortiser.

ROUTING MUNTIN MORTISES

Design by Andy Rae

The wooden grids you often see on glass windows and doors are made from pieces called muntins. In the old days, making large panes of glass was difficult, and the muntins provided a framework to hold small panes of glass. These days, the muntin framework is usually applied over a single, large pane of glass.

This jig routs a mortise in a door to hold the muntin. As shown in *Muntin Installation*, it's designed for the type of muntin that overlays a single pane of glass. This jig uses a template guide bushing with a straight router bit to make little pocket mortises to hold the muntin. The dimensions given are for a jig that will work on stiles or

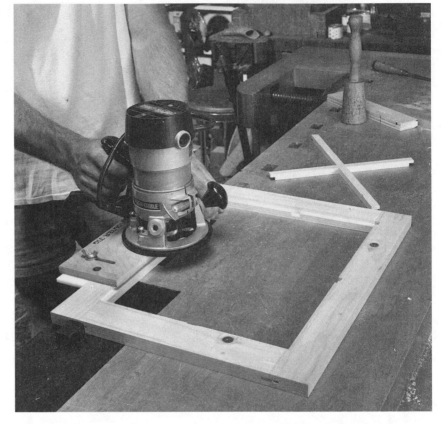

rails up to 2½ inches wide. For wider frame members, just make the template wider and increase the length of the slots.

MAKING THE JIG

1 Make the template. Cut a piece of plywood to the dimensions in the Materials List. Rout two ¼-inch-wide slots for the carriage bolts as explained in "Making Stopped Cuts on the Router Table," page 24. Position the slots as shown in the *Overall View*.

2 Notch the template. This jig is designed for use with a ¼-inch-diameter straight bit and a ⅜-inch-outer-diameter (O.D.) guide bushing. A guide bushing is a small cylinder of steel that fits into the base of a router. The cylinder protrudes slightly beyond the base and surrounds the router bit. The cylinder rubs against the notch in the template and

guides the cut when you rout a muntin mortise. The size of the notch determines the width and length of the mortise.

Lay out a notch in the jig that is ⅛ inch wider and ¹⁄₁₆ inch longer than the muntin mortise you need. The notch must be larger than the muntin because of the way guide bushings work. Because the bushing surrounds the router bit, the path cut by the bit is slightly offset from the path traveled by the bushing.

Lay out the notch on the edge of the template as shown in the *Overall View*. Cut the notch on the band saw or jigsaw, being careful to keep the cuts straight and square.

Clamp the template along the edge of a

OVERALL VIEW

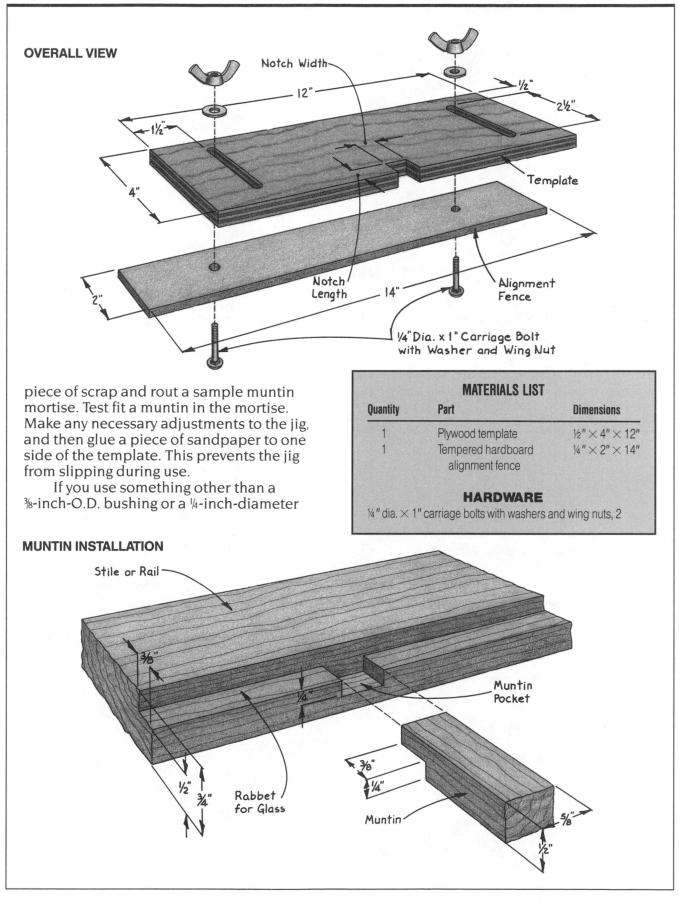

Notch Width

12"

1½"

½"

2½"

1½"

4"

Template

2"

Notch
Length

14"

Alignment
Fence

¼"Dia. x 1" Carriage Bolt
with Washer and Wing Nut

piece of scrap and rout a sample muntin mortise. Test fit a muntin in the mortise. Make any necessary adjustments to the jig, and then glue a piece of sandpaper to one side of the template. This prevents the jig from slipping during use.

If you use something other than a ⅜-inch-O.D. bushing or a ¼-inch-diameter

MATERIALS LIST		
Quantity	Part	Dimensions
1	Plywood template	½" × 4" × 12"
1	Tempered hardboard alignment fence	¼" × 2" × 14"

HARDWARE

¼" dia. × 1" carriage bolts with washers and wing nuts, 2

MUNTIN INSTALLATION

Stile or Rail

⅜"

¼"

Muntin
Pocket

½"

¾"

Rabbet
for Glass

⅜"

¼"

Muntin

⅝"

½"

Photo 30-1 Check the router bit depth against the pocket depth mark on a rail or stile.

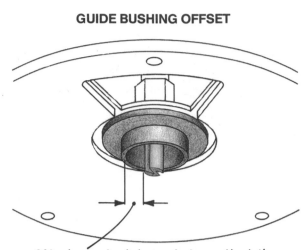

GUIDE BUSHING OFFSET

Offset equals distance between the bit's cutting edge and the inside diameter of the guide bushing.

router bit, *Guide Bushing Offset* helps you calculate the proper size notch. Add the offset to the length of the mortise to get the length of the notch. Add twice the offset to the mortise width to get the notch width.

3 Make the alignment fence. The alignment fence can be made from hardboard or plexiglass. Cut it to the dimensions in the Materials List. Position the fence under the template and mark holes for the carriage bolts. Drill the holes with a ¼-inch-diameter bit.

4 Assemble the jig. Put a carriage bolt through each hole in the alignment fence. Place the template on the fence and over the bolts, with the sandpapered side down. Put a washer and wing nut over each bolt.

USING THE JIG

Set the router bit depth to the desired mortise depth plus the thickness of the template. For a ¼-inch-deep mortise with a ½-inch template, set the bit depth at ¾ inch. To make sure you have set the depth accurately, mark the mortise depth directly on a rail or stile and check the bit against the mark as shown in *Photo* 30-1.

Rout the muntin mortises after you have made the door and the muntin frame. Position the muntin frame on the door. With a sharp pencil, scribe where the rabbets in the door need to be mortised for the muntins.

Remove the muntin frame. Place the jig on the door frame so that the notched edge is flush with the inside of the door frame. Move the alignment fence against the outside edge of the door and tighten the wing nuts. Sighting by eye through the notch, position the jig so that the scribe lines are centered within the notch.

Photo 30-2 Lay the muntins over the door frame and use a sharp pencil to scribe the pocket locations onto the rabbets.

It's a good idea to clamp the jig down the first couple of times until you get a feel for using it. Once you get the hang of it, you'll discover the sandpaper you glued to the template provides enough friction to hold the jig in place. To avoid tearout, rout one side of the notch, pull the router out, and rout the other side of the notch. Then rout out the waste in the middle.

When the mortises are routed, square their corners with a chisel. If you are working in softwood, you can often skip this step; the muntins will squeeze into the corners for a tight fit. Put a dab of glue in the pocket mortises. Assemble the muntin to the door frame.

If you like, you can rout a small chamfer into the front edges of the muntins and the inside front edges of the door frame. You'll have to finish the corners of the chamfers with a chisel.

Photo 30-3   Square the corners of the muntin pockets with a chisel.

RAISING PANELS ON THE JOINTER

Design by Ben Erickson

The jointer probably isn't the first tool you think of when it comes to raising panels. But short of a panel-raising cutter on the shaper, the jointer may be the most efficient way to get the job done. The jig holds the panel at an angle to the table, trimming a bevel into the panel with each pass.

Admittedly, the jointer fixture shown here requires several passes to cut each panel bevel. The table saw jig described in "Raising Panels on the Table Saw," page 165, cuts a bevel in one pass. But the table saw panels require a fair bit of scraping and sanding to remove saw marks and burns. The jointer, on the other hand, leaves you with faint ripples that sand away easily.

Once you've built this fixture to raise panels, don't overlook another handy feature. This jig enables you to joint the face of stock that

is wider than your jointer table.

This jig was designed to fit a Powermatic 8-inch jointer. The dimensions may vary if you have a different machine. For example, the large notch in the side of the table accommodates the shape of the Powermatic's infeed table. On many

jointers, the notch won't be necessary.

You also may need to devise a different way of attaching the jig to your jointer if you cannot clamp to the side of the jointer table. It may be possible to drill holes into the castings and bolt the jig in place.

MAKING THE JIG

1 **Cut the parts to size.** Cut all the plywood parts from cabinet-grade plywood. Don't make the clamp blocks yet.

2 **Make the table.** If your outfeed table protrudes to wrap around the side of the cutter head, notch the jig table to fit around it. The dimensions in the *Overall View* are for the Powermatic 8-inch jointer.

OVERALL VIEW

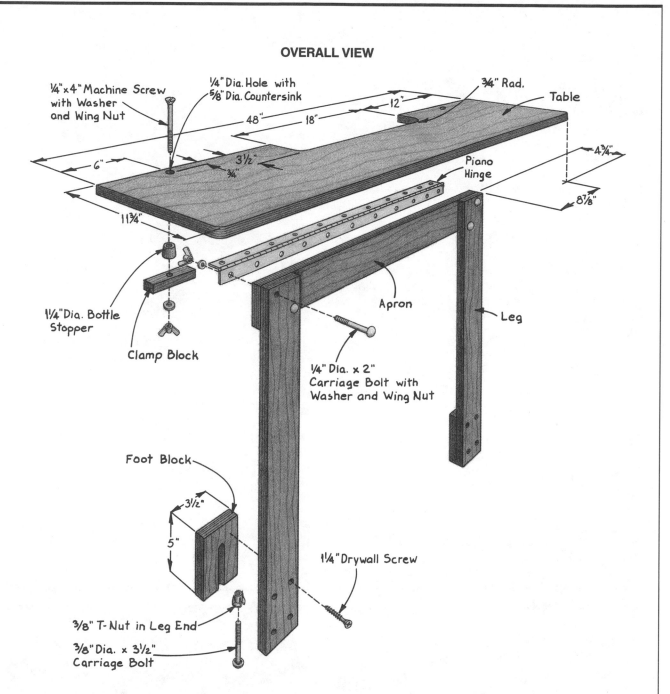

¼"x4" Machine Screw with Washer and Wing Nut

¼" Dia. Hole with ⅝" Dia. Countersink

¾" Rad.

Table

48"

18"

12"

6"

3½"

¾"

Piano Hinge

4¾"

8⅛"

11¾"

Apron

Leg

1¼" Dia. Bottle Stopper

Clamp Block

¼" Dia. x 2" Carriage Bolt with Washer and Wing Nut

Foot Block

3½"

5"

1¼" Drywall Screw

⅜" T-Nut in Leg End

⅜" Dia. x 3½" Carriage Bolt

3 **Attach the apron.** Screw the piano hinge along one side of the apron. Screw the other hinge leaf to the bottom of the table as shown in the *Overall View.*

4 **Make the legs.** Attach the foot blocks to the legs using glue and 1¼-inch drywall screws. After the glue dries, drill a 3-inch-deep clearance hole into the bottom of each leg for the T-nut. Center the holes on the seam

between the leg and the foot block. Tap the T-nuts into place and thread in the ⅜-inch-diameter × 3½-inch carriage bolts.

5 **Attach the legs.** Locate one leg at each end of the apron and clamp them in place. Drill two ¼-inch-diameter holes through each end. Bolt the legs in place with the ¼-inch-diameter × 2-inch carriage bolts, washers, and wing nuts.

MATERIALS LIST

Quantity	Part	Dimensions
1	Plywood table	¾" × 11¾" × 48"
1	Plywood apron	¾" × 3½" × 30"
2	Plywood foot blocks	¾" × 3½" × 5"
2	Plywood legs	¾" × 3½" × 29¾"
2	Hardwood clamp blocks	1⅜" × 1½" × 4"

HARDWARE

1¼" drywall screws, 8
¼" × 4" flathead machine screws with washers and wing nuts, 2
⅜" dia. × 3½" carriage bolts, 2
¼" dia. × 2" carriage bolts with washers and wing nuts, 4
⅜" T-nuts, 2
1½" × 30" piano hinge with screws, 1
1¼" dia. bottle stoppers, 2

CLAMP BLOCK DETAIL

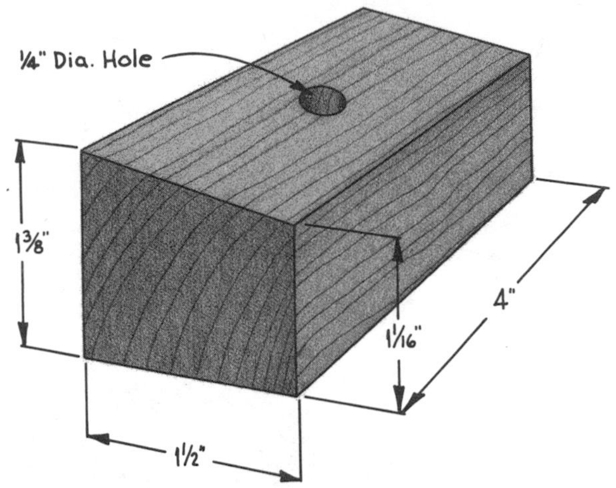

¼" Dia. Hole
1⅜"
1½"
1¹/₁₆"
4"

6 Make the clamp blocks. Make the clamp blocks from a dense hardwood such as maple. Cut a piece to the width and thickness in the Materials List, but leave it at least three times as long as specified. This way, you'll have a longer piece to run through the machines. Lay out and drill the ¼-inch-diameter holes into each block as shown in the *Clamp Block Detail*.

Tilt the blade on the table saw and cut the bevel on one side of the clamp block as shown in the *Clamp Block Detail*. Run the sawed face over the jointer to clean up the saw marks. Cut the blocks to the length specified.

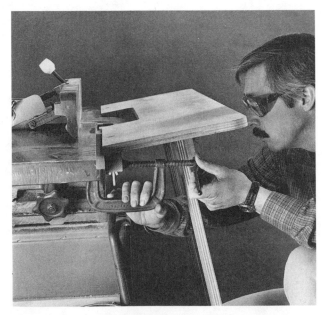

Photo 31-1 Align the edge of the jig table parallel to, and slightly below, the surface of the jointer.

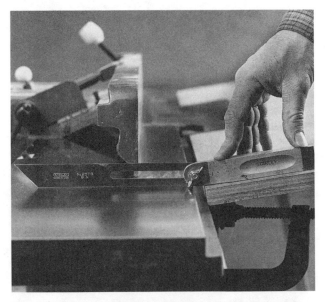

Photo 31-2 Use the sliding bevel gauge to set the angle of the jig table in relation to the jointer. Change the angle by raising or lowering the adjustable foot bolts.

7 **Attach the clamp blocks.** Countersink the holes in the blocks. If the bottle stoppers are not predrilled, drill a ¼-inch-diameter hole through both. Slip the machine screws down through the table. Slide on the bottle stoppers, the clamp blocks, and the washers and nuts.

USING THE JIG

Before you make the panels, make the stiles and rails and cut the panel grooves in these frame members. You'll need the parts to test the panel fit.

Attaching and Aligning the Table

Clamp the jig to the jointer. Adjust the alignment of the table by tightening or loosening the clamp block machine screws. Set the edge of the jig table so that it's parallel to the outfeed table and slightly below it, as shown in P*hoto* 31-1.

The amount of drop from the jointer outfeed table to the jig table determines the depth of the shoulder on the panel. The shoulder is the step between the bevel and the field. Typically, this shoulder is about ¹⁄₁₆ to ⅛ inch; therefore, the jig table should be about ¹⁄₁₆ inch or ⅛ inch lower than the outfeed table.

Lay out the raised panel bevel on the edge of a panel as described in "Laying Out the Bevels," page 167.

Setting the Bevel Angle

First set a sliding bevel gauge to the bevel angle you laid out on the panel, as shown in S*etting the* B*evel* G*auge.* Then use the

SETTING THE BEVEL GAUGE

Lay out bevel on the edge of a panel. Set sliding bevel gauge to the angle.

bevel gauge to adjust the angle of the table as shown in P*hoto* 31-2. Set the table angle by adjusting the bolts in the feet.

Setting the Bevel Width

Set the bevel width with the jointer fence. The bevel width will equal the distance between the fence and the edge of the jointer table. (See P*hoto* 31-3.) If your bevel comes to a fine edge, clamp a piece of wood to the fence to prevent the panels from sliding underneath it.

Set the jointer depth of cut for about ⅛ inch. The depth of cut governs how many passes it will take to finish a bevel, but it doesn't affect the depth of the bevel. The jointer won't cut once the panel's field is riding on the fixture table. If you have trouble with tearout on a panel, decrease the depth of cut and/or slow the feed rate.

Raising the Panels

Once you get the jig set up, make a trial cut in a test piece. For safety, use scrap that is at least 6 inches wider than the bevel and at least 12 inches long. It will probably take

Photo 31-3 **Adjust the width of the bevel by moving the jointer fence.**

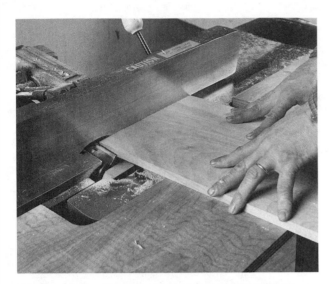

Photo 31-4 **Bevel across the grain first. That way, any chip-out at the end of the cut will be removed when you bevel with the grain.**

three passes to make the bevel. Check the test piece in the frame groove. If you need to adjust the fit, you have several options: You can change the angle of the table; you can change the width of the bevel; or you can change the depth of the shoulder. Any of these things, or a combination of them, will alter the thickness of the panel at the edge and thus the panel's fit in the groove.

When the test piece fits perfectly, you are ready to raise all your panels. Cut them with the good side down. Cut across the end grain first, as shown in *Photo 31-4*, so that chip-out near the board edges is eliminated by subsequent cuts. Occasionally test a panel against the groove to be sure the jig is holding its adjustment.

One disadvantage of this jig is that it leaves the shoulder slightly undercut. If you like, you can clean it up with a quick pass of a rabbet plane.

Flattening Cupped Boards

You can also use this fixture to flatten cupped boards that are wider than your jointer. This method won't work, however, if the board is twisted as well as cupped.

Start with the fixture table level with the jointer's infeed table. Feed the board with the concave side down as shown in *Flattening Cupped Boards*. The fixture table will support the uncut part of the board, while the outfeed table supports the cut part.

Turn the board end for end. Reset the fixture table level with the outfeed table. Joint the board. This time, the jig will support the cut part as the uncut part is jointed. Repeat this process until the cutters cut across the entire face of the board. At this point, the board is flat, and you can run it through the planer.

FLATTENING CUPPED BOARDS

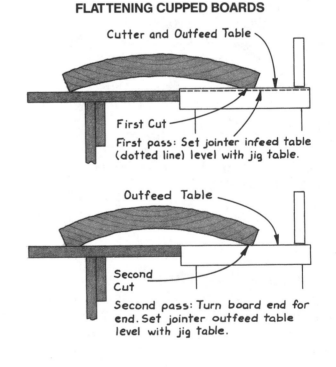

RAISING PANELS ON THE ROUTER TABLE

Design by Glenn Bostock

Without this jig, raising panels on the router table requires an expensive bit that may be more than 3 inches wide. These wide bits require a powerful router to drive them. They also require a big hole in your router table, which usually means making a special insert. And all that spinning steel protruding from your router table is a scary sight.

The panel-raising jig shown here lets you raise a panel with an inexpensive mortising bit and a 1- or 1½-horsepower router. The entire 1¼-inch diameter of the bit is used to cut the raised panel bevel. The tongue is cut in a separate operation.

The jig has just three parts: a base, a lipped fence, and a runner. The base has a hole that you position over the hole in your router table. The edge of the panel rides on a lip in the fence. The runner holds the panel at

the proper angle as it runs over the bit.

The jig shown in the *Overall View* is set up to raise the bevel and shoulder on a ⅝-inch-thick panel with a tongue that is ¼ inch thick × ⅜ inch wide. The shoulder will be ³⁄₃₂ inch high. The bevel is 1¼ inches wide, the same width as the router bit. In "Using the Jig," you will

learn how to change the position of the runner to accommodate different bevel widths.

When building the jig, keep in mind that the fence must be clamped to the router table. On some tables, you will have to make the fence and base wider, so that the clamp can reach.

MAKING THE JIG

1 Cut the parts. Cut the parts to the dimensions in the Materials List. You can use any wood for the fence and runner, as long as it is straight.

2 Rabbet the fence. Rout a ⅜-inch-deep × ¼-inch-wide rabbet in the fence.

3 Drill a hole in the base. Drill a 1⅝-inch-diameter hole in the base, positioning it as shown in the *Overall View.*

OVERALL VIEW

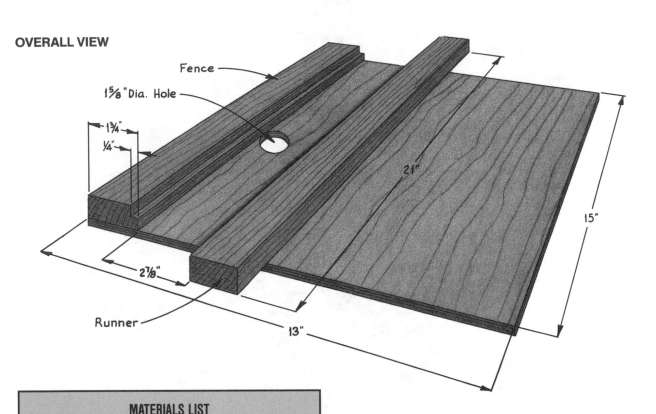

Fence

1⅝ "Dia. Hole

1¾"

¼"

21"

15"

2⅞"

Runner

13"

MATERIALS LIST		
Quantity	Part	Dimensions
1	Wood fence	¾" × 1¾" × 15"
1	Wood runner	¾" × 1½" × 21"
1	Plywood base	¼" × 13" × 15"

HARDWARE

#6 × ¾" flathead wood screws, 4
Freud #16-106 (¼-inch shank) or #16-108 (½-inch shank)
    router bit, 1

4 Assemble the jig. Drill and countersink pilot holes in the base for two screws that attach the fence. Glue and screw the fence to the base. Draw a line across the base to lay out the position of the runner. Screw the runner in place, making sure it is square to the edge of the base.

USING THE JIG

Make your frames before you make the panels, so that you can size the panels to fit. After you raise the panels, you can joint the panel edges, if necessary, to fit the frames.

Rabbeting the Panels

After cutting the panels to size, rabbet all four edges of one side as shown in Photo 32-1. To make a ¼-inch-thick tongue in a ⅝-inch-thick panel, use a ⅜-inch rabbeting bit set ⅜ inch above the router table.

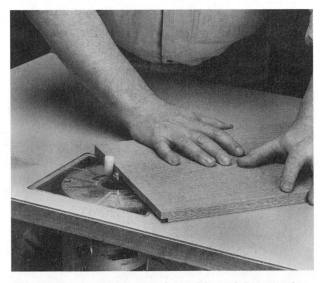

Photo 32-1   Rabbet all four sides of the panel to form the tongues that will fit into the frame grooves.

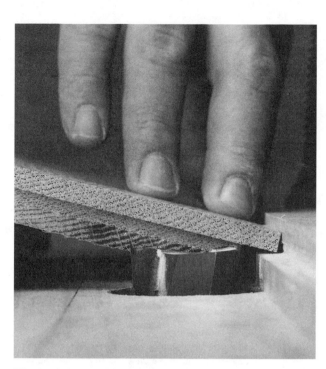

Photo 32-2 To set the bit and jig, align the top corner of one cutter to the inside corner of the panel rabbet.

Photo 32-3 Trim undercut shoulders with a rabbet plane.

Setting the Bit Height

Put the bit in the router and mount the router under the table. Place the jig on the table with its hole over the router bit. To set the bit height, put a rabbeted edge of the panel on and against the fence lip. Raise the bit and adjust the jig position until the top corner of one cutter meets the inside corner of the panel rabbet. (See P*hoto* 32-2.) Clamp the jig to the table.

Raising the Panel

Raise the end-grain bevels first. This way, any tearout will be removed when you rout bevels that travel along the grain. Turn on the router. Firmly hold the panel against the fence rabbet and down on the runner. Move the panel slowly and steadily over the bit.

Trimming the Shoulders

The shoulders will be slightly undercut. This can result in slight shadows on your panels. Trim the shoulder with a rabbet plane as shown in P*hoto* 32-3.

Setting Up the Jig for Different Bevels

Setting Up the Jig provides four steps for setting up the jig for different panel thicknesses or bevel widths. This is done by making a full-scale layout on paper.

First lay out the panel thickness and then the tongue thickness and width as shown in Step 1. Then lay out the panel height and the bevel. The bevel can be at any angle, but it must be the same width as the router bit. The bit in the Materials List cuts a 1¼-inch-wide path, but bits of other diameters are also available.

Now draw the two reference lines shown in Step 2. Draw the first line between the top of the tongue and the top of the shoulder. Then draw a perpendicular line that intersects the bottom of the tongue as shown.

Use these reference lines to draw the fence, as shown in Step 3. Make the height of

SETTING UP THE JIG

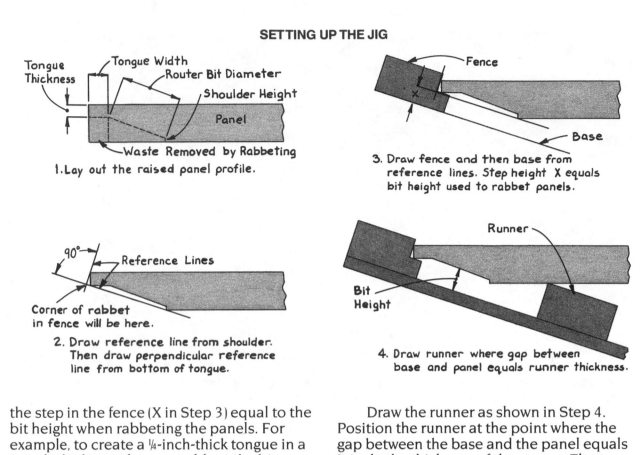

1. Lay out the raised panel profile.

2. Draw reference line from shoulder. Then draw perpendicular reference line from bottom of tongue.

3. Draw fence and then base from reference lines. Step height X equals bit height used to rabbet panels.

4. Draw runner where gap between base and panel equals runner thickness.

the step in the fence (X in Step 3) equal to the bit height when rabbeting the panels. For example, to create a ¼-inch-thick tongue in a ⅝-inch-thick panel, you would set the bit height at ⅜ inch. For a ¼-inch-thick tongue in a ¾-inch-thick panel, you would need a ½-inch bit height.

Draw the base under the fence as shown in Step 3.

Draw the runner as shown in Step 4. Position the runner at the point where the gap between the base and the panel equals ¾ inch, the thickness of the runner. The completed layout shows you the distance you need between the runner and the fence. It also shows the bit height you will need to raise the panel.

RAISING PANELS ON THE TABLE SAW

Design by Mitch Mandel

To raise a panel on a table saw, you usually stand it on edge and cut a bevel on it. It's a risky business at best. The panel wobbles, damaging the wood and often injuring the operator.

This panel-raising jig solves the problem. You slip the jig over the saw's rip fence, clamp the panel to it, and guide the jig along the fence to raise the panel. The jig ensures a smooth, accurate cut that requires little cleanup. More importantly, the jig makes the job much safer. Not only does it eliminate the possibility of twisting and binding that can result in injury, but it also keeps your hands well away from the high, unguarded saw blade.

MAKING THE JIG

1 Cut the jig panels. The large panel is sized to give you plenty of surface for clamping the panel. Cut it to 12 × 20 inches; cut the smaller panel to 8 × 20 inches.

2 Scribe for the first dado. The crosspieces fit into dadoes cut in each panel. To lay out the first dado, lock the fence in position. Put the large panel against the fence, and draw the height of the fence on the panel with a pencil. If there are nuts on the top of your fence, make sure the crosspiece will clear them.

3 Dado the panels. Set up the saw to cut dadoes ⅜ inch deep × ¾ inch wide, as explained in "Cutting Dadoes and Grooves," page 36. You'll cut three dadoes in each panel as shown in the *Overall View.* Cut the first dado on the large panel above the line you scribed from the fence. Cut a matching dado on the small panel.

The exact locations of the remaining dadoes are not important, as long as they are the same on each panel. Set up the saw to cut the middle dado about 2 inches above the lowest dado, and cut the dado on both panels. Reset the saw and cut the top dado about 1 inch above the middle dado.

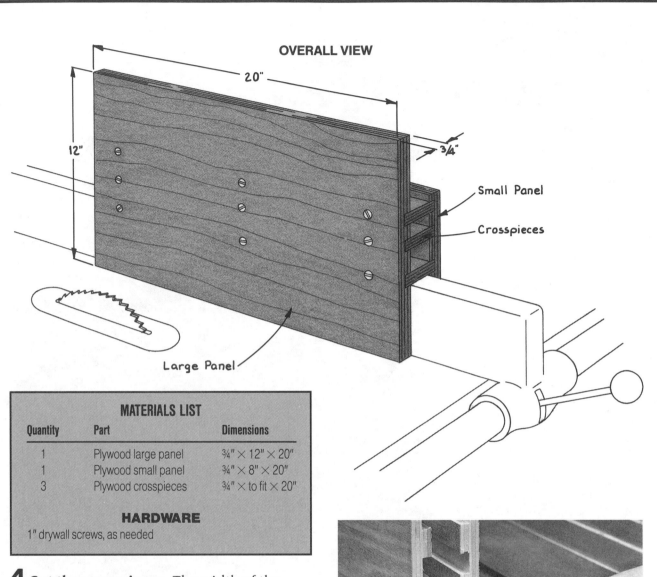

OVERALL VIEW

20"

12"

3/4"

Small Panel

Crosspieces

Large Panel

MATERIALS LIST

Quantity	Part	Dimensions
1	Plywood large panel	3/4" × 12" × 20"
1	Plywood small panel	3/4" × 8" × 20"
3	Plywood crosspieces	3/4" × to fit × 20"

HARDWARE

1" drywall screws, as needed

4 Cut the crosspieces. The width of the crosspieces is crucial. Make them too narrow, and the jig will bind as it travels along the fence. Make them too wide, and the jig will wobble. To determine the exact width, clamp the panels lightly on opposite sides of the fence. Set inside calipers to the distance from the bottom of one dado to the bottom of the other as shown in P*hoto* 33-1. Use the calipers to set the table saw rip fence. Rip the crosspieces to this width. Cut them to length. If you don't have calipers, you can use a compass.

5 Assemble the jig. Put the crosspieces in the dadoes. Countersink and drill through the panel into the crosspieces for 1-inch drywall screws. Screw the crosspieces to the panels.

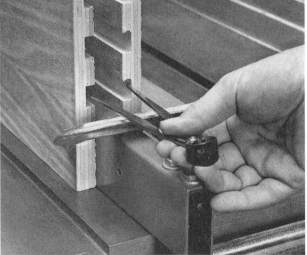

Photo 33-1   To determine the exact width of the crosspieces, clamp the jig panels loosely against opposite sides of the rip fence. Set inside calipers to the distance between the bottom of the dadoes. Use the calipers to set the rip fence for cutting the crosspieces.

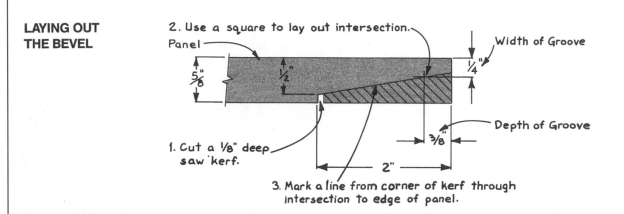

LAYING OUT THE BEVEL

2. Use a square to lay out intersection.
Panel
Width of Groove
¼"
5⁄8"
½"
Depth of Groove
1. Cut a ⅛" deep saw kerf.
3⁄8"
2"
3. Mark a line from corner of kerf through intersection to edge of panel.

USING THE JIG

Before you raise a panel, you should always make the frame that will hold it. Measure the frame, and then cut a panel blank to fit.

A raised panel has several parts: the bevel at the edge of the board; the flat central plane, called the field; and a small step between the two, called the shoulder. You'll cut the shoulder first.

Cutting the Shoulder

Let's say you want to raise a panel that's ⅝ inch thick and fits into ¼-inch grooves. Mill the panel blank to size and thickness, and then determine the height and location of the panel shoulders. Distances of 1½ to 2 inches from the edge of the panel are common.

Set the rip fence to position the shoulder. The panel shown in *Laying Out the Bevel* has a shoulder 2 inches from the edge. Set the fence 1⅞ inches from the blade—the thickness of the blade will place the shoulder 2 inches from the edge.

Set the saw blade to the height of the shoulder—⅛ inch in the panel shown. Lay the panel flat on the saw, and guide it against the rip fence to cut all four shoulders.

Laying Out the Bevels

The slope of the bevel determines how the panel fits into the groove that holds it. The sample panel fits into a groove that is ⅜ inch deep × ¼ inch wide. To fit the groove properly, the panel should be ¼ inch thick when measured ⅜ inch from its edge.

To determine the proper bevel, first lay

Photo 33-2 Cut four kerfs to define the shoulders of the raised panel.

Photo 33-3 Check the bevel layout against one of the frame pieces.

out the point at which the panel and groove meet as shown in *Laying Out the Bevel*. Draw a line connecting this point with the shoulder as shown to determine the proper bevel.

To check your layout, hold the edge of one of the frame pieces against the panel edge as shown in *Photo 33-3*.

Setting the Table Saw

Set a sliding T-bevel gauge to the angle of the bevel you just drew, and set the saw blade to the angle of the bevel gauge. With the saw turned off, put the panel on edge. Raise the blade until it reaches, but does not touch, the shoulder line.

Put the panel-raising jig on the fence. To position the jig, first measure the thickness of the panel at the shoulder—½ inch on the sample panel. Set the fence so that the face of the jig is this distance from the blade.

Cutting the Bevels

Clamp the panel to the jig. To eliminate tearout, clamp it so that you'll be cutting end grain first. Double-check your settings by sighting along the blade at your layout lines. Make sure the fence is locked in place. Make the first cut.

Turn off the saw, rotate the panel 90 degrees, and repeat the process until you

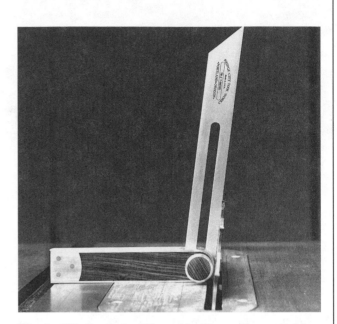

Photo 33-4 Set a T-bevel to the angle you laid out on the panel edge. Then use the T-bevel to transfer this angle to the saw blade.

have beveled three sides. There's no need to use a clamping pad to protect the panel during the first three cuts. The panel areas dented by the clamps will be cut away. But for the fourth cut, you have to clamp to a beveled surface. To protect this surface, put the third cutoff between the panel and the clamps before beveling the fourth edge.

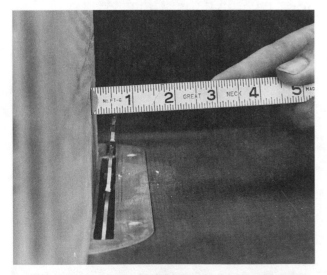

Photo 33-5 Measure the thickness of the panel at the shoulder. Set the saw blade this distance from the fence.

Photo 33-6 Put the jig and panel in place on the saw. Sight along the blade to check that the blade aligns with your layout.

PLASTIC LAMINATE FENCE OR AUXILIARY FENCE FOR THE TABLE SAW

Design by Andy Rae

This is a simple box that fits snugly over your rip fence. Make the box alone, and you have an auxiliary fence. Add two small pieces of plastic, and the fence is perfect for cutting plastic laminates, like Formica. (See *Photo* 34-1.)

As shown in *Photo* 34-2, the auxiliary fence is useful when you need to position a blade against or partially under the fence. It protects the rip fence when cutting rabbets or moldings.

By adding Plexiglas and the plastic laminate shown in the *Overall View*, the fence is perfect for cutting plastic laminate. Laminates are so thin that they tend to slip under a standard rip fence, ruining the cut and endangering the operator. At the same time, laminates are so lightweight that the blade lifts them, risking kickback.

The fence shown here is sized to fit over a Biesmeyer rip fence. The Materials List gives dimensions for this fence. If you have a different fence, you'll need to change the dimensions to fit. For some fences, you may have to change the front panel to accommodate the clamping lever or knob. If the lever or

Photo 34-1 One version of this fixture is designed for cutting plastic laminate. **Photo 34-2** The other version is for when you need to bury the blade in the fence.

knob really poses a problem, or if you just want to simplify construction, don't make the entire fence. Simply fasten a piece of plywood or solid stock to the standard rip fence to make an auxiliary fence. For laminate work, fasten the laminate strip and the Plexiglas to a piece of plywood as described. Clamp or screw this fence to your standard rip fence.

OVERALL VIEW

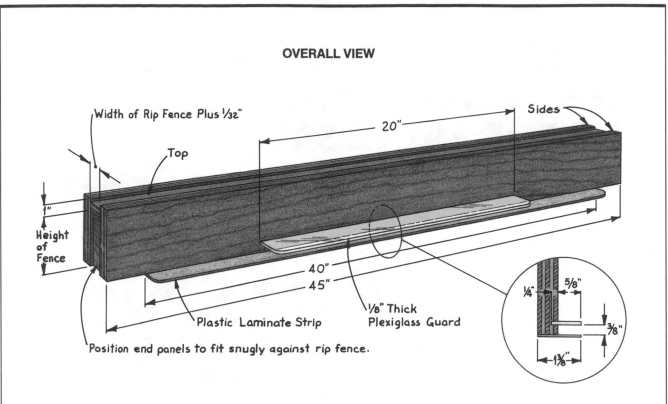

Width of Rip Fence Plus 1/32"

Top

Sides

20"

1"

Height
of
Fence

40"

45"

Plastic Laminate Strip

1/8" Thick
Plexiglass Guard

1/4"   5/8"

3/8"

1 3/8"

Position end panels to fit snugly against rip fence.

MATERIALS LIST

Quantity	Part	Dimensions
2	Plywood sides	3/4" × 4 1/2" × 45"
1	Plywood top	3/4" × 4 1/32" × 45"
2	Plywood ends	3/4" × 4 1/32" × 3 1/2"

HARDWARE

4d finishing nails, as needed
1/8" × 7/8" × 20" clear Plexiglas or Lexan, 1
1 3/8" × 40" plastic laminate, 1

MAKING THE JIG

1 Cut the plywood parts. The *Overall View* shows how to size this fixture to fit your rip fence. The dimensions in the Materials List are for a Biesmeyer rip fence. First lock the rip fence to the saw table. Measure from the table to the top of the fence and add 1 inch. This gives you the width of the side pieces. Rip the sides to width, and cut them to the length in the Materials List.

The top in the Materials List is designed

for a 4-inch-wide rip fence. To fit the auxiliary fence to your saw, measure the width of your rip fence and add 1/32 inch. This gives you the width of the auxiliary fence top and ends. Make the auxiliary fence ends as high as the existing rip fence. Rip a piece of plywood to width. Make it long enough to make the 45-inch-long top plus the two end pieces. Then crosscut to make the end pieces.

Making the Plastic Laminate Fence

2 Install the guard. If you are making the fence for plastic laminate work, the fence has a guard that holds the laminate as you cut it. The guard, made from clear plastic, fits into a 1/8-inch-wide stopped groove in the working side of the fence. On the fence shown, the kerf is about 20 inches long, because a 20-inch length of Plexiglas was on hand. Any length within a few inches of that would work fine. Lexan is an even tougher material than Plexiglas and would also work. The important thing is to use clear plastic, so that you can watch the cut.

Center the groove on the fence as shown in the *Overall View.* Cut the groove 1/4 inch deep, using a standard ⅛-inch-wide blade in the table saw. For more on cutting stopped grooves, see "Cutting Dadoes and Grooves," page 36.

Cut the Lexan or Plexiglas to ⅞ inch wide and glue it into the slot with epoxy.

3 **Install the bottom strip.** The bottom strip is for plastic laminate work only and is designed to keep the laminate from slipping under the fence. You won't need this strip if you are making a simple auxiliary fence. Cut a piece of plastic laminate to the dimensions in the Materials List. Fasten this strip to the bottom of the working side with contact cement as shown in the *Overall View.*

4 **Assemble the fence.** Lock the rip fence in place on the saw, and place a side of the auxiliary fence against it. Mark the height of the rip fence on the auxiliary fence. Glue and nail the auxiliary fence top to the sides along this line.

Put the fixture back on the rip fence and position the jig ends against the rip fence. You want a snug fit, but not so tight that it is hard to get the fixture on and off the fence. Mark the location, and glue and nail the ends in place.

USING THE AUXILIARY FENCE

You'll probably find 100 uses for the auxiliary fence. The three most common are rabbeting, using molding heads, and cutting tenons. In each, you'll often bury part of the blade inside the fence, leaving only part of the blade exposed. Always make sure that the buried section is no more than ⅝ inch wide; otherwise, the blade might cut into the standard rip fence.

Rabbeting with the Auxiliary Fence

When rabbeting on the table saw, you put the dado cutter right up against the rip fence. The auxiliary fence is designed to protect the saw's rip fence from damage. It also makes it easy to adjust the width of the rabbet.

Set the dado cutter a bit wider than you need—say, ⅝ inch for a ½-inch-wide rabbet. Set the fence so that ⅛ inch of the cutter is underneath the fence. Then turn on the saw and raise the cutter about 1 inch, cutting a semicircle into the bottom of the fence as shown in *Photo* 34-2. Now turn off the saw and lower the blade to the height you want. With the board flat on the saw table, make a test cut, guiding the board along the rip fence. Check the width of the resulting rabbet. To fine-tune the width, just move the fence.

You'll find the fence particularly useful if you're making a cabinet or case with shelves that dado into the sides and a top that rabbets in place. Let's say you are making a bookcase with shelves and a top, all of which are the same width. The shelves are dadoed in place. The top is rabbeted. Set your cutter to dado the sides. When you've cut the dadoes, put the auxiliary fence in place. Move the fence over until the cutter grazes the auxiliary fence. The rabbet you cut with this setup will be exactly the same size as the dadoes.

When rabbeting a board along its length, the rip fence alone is enough to guide the cut. When rabbeting the end of a workpiece, the procedure is more like a crosscut. Guide the workpiece with the miter gauge, butting the end of the board to be rabbetted against the auxiliary fence. In this case, the fence becomes a stop gauge.

Using a Molding Head

If you have a molding head for your table saw, the auxiliary fence can greatly increase the versatility of your cutters. For example, you may have a molding head that cuts three beads. You can use it to cut a single bead by burying two of the beads in the auxiliary fence. Measure first to make sure that the width of the two beads is less than the thickness of the auxiliary fence sides. Then install the cutters and lower them to just below the saw table. Position the rip fence so that the auxiliary fence covers two beads. Turn on the saw and raise the cutters to about 1 inch. This will cut a semicircle from the bottom of the auxiliary fence as shown in *Photo* 34-2. Now lower the cutter to the bead depth you want. Make a test cut. Make any necessary adjustments, and then cut the bead.

Making Tenons with the Auxiliary Fence

The rabbeting fence is perfect for cutting tenons. Cut a rabbet on one face of the board, as described on page 171. Then cut a rabbet on the opposite face. The result is a tenon. Rabbet the remaining two sides and you have a tenon with four shoulders. For tenons that are longer than the width of the dado blade, cut all four surfaces and then reset the fence. Cut all four surfaces again to lengthen the tenon.

USING THE PLASTIC LAMINATE FENCE

Place the jig over the rip fence and adjust the fence for the width to be cut. If you use the scale on the rip fence, remember to allow for the thickness of the laminate fence when setting the fence.

Turn on the saw. Lay the plastic laminate on the jig's bottom strip. Most likely, you'll be trimming a small piece of laminate off a large piece. If this is the case, begin the cut as shown in *Photo* 34-1. Holding the laminate as shown gives you the best control over the cut. As you get near the end of the cut, lower your left hand. This will take pressure off the left side of the blade, preventing the laminate from binding at the end of the cut. The eraser end of a pencil makes a good push stick when ripping narrow bands of laminate.

CHISEL RABBET PLANE

*Design by
Frederic L. Hanisch*

Most woodworkers don't cut rabbets with a rabbet plane these days. It's an expensive tool you may not need very often. But when you need to plane the bottom of a rabbet or groove, no other tool does the job. For example, some table saw dado cutters make cuts that are uneven at the bottom. A rabbet plane cleans them up quickly and accurately. Rabbet planes are perfect for cleaning up tenon shoulders or tuning up wooden drawer guides.

You can make this rabbet plane in an hour or two from three scraps of wood and a chisel. There's no modification to the chisel, so you can easily remove it when you need it for chiseling jobs. Even if you already own a rabbet plane, you may want to make a couple more:

Because you can make this jig to fit any width chisel, you can make a plane to fit where your store-bought plane may not.

The dimensions in the Materials List are for a ½-inch chisel. "Making the Jig" explains how to adapt the dimensions to any chisel.

MAKING THE JIG

1 Prepare the stock. Use your best scraps to make the plane. The wood must be dry, stable, straight, and clear. Hard maple is perfect. Plane the body ¹⁄₆₄ inch thicker than the chisel width, and then cut it 9 inches long. (You'll cut the wood down to finished size in the course of making the plane.) Use a hand plane and a shooting board to shoot the sole perfectly straight and flat. For more information, see "Adjustable Shooting Board," page 114.

Prepare two pieces of stock for the cheeks, leaving each a couple of inches longer than final length.

2 Lay out and cut the hole. Mark the point 4⅛ inches from the front of the body and ⁷⁄₁₆ inch from the sole as shown in the *Pattern*. Drill a 1-inch-diameter hole that has this point as its center. The perimeter of the drill will extend slightly beyond the bottom of the sole, as shown.

For a smooth cut, drill the hole with a Forstner bit.

OVERALL VIEW

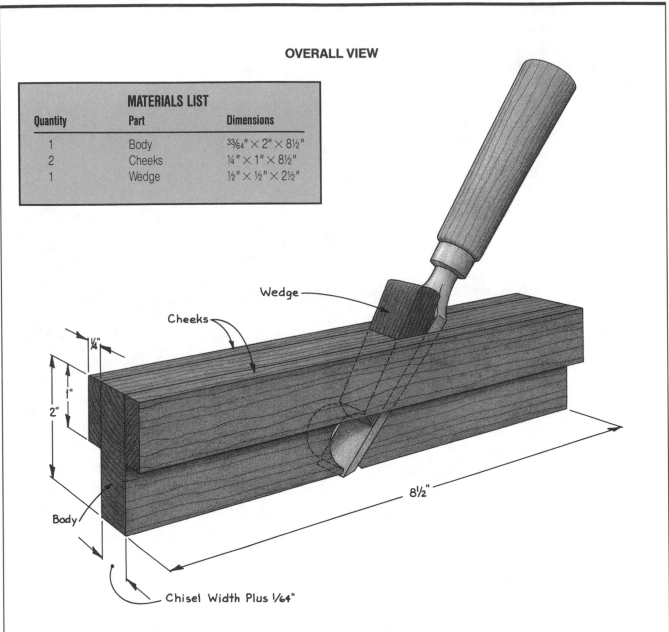

MATERIALS LIST		
Quantity	Part	Dimensions
1	Body	$^{33}/_{64}$" $\times$ 2" $\times$ 8½"
2	Cheeks	¼" $\times$ 1" $\times$ 8½"
1	Wedge	½" $\times$ ½" $\times$ 2½"

Wedge

Cheeks

¼"

2"

1"

8½"

Body

Chisel Width Plus 1/64"

3 **Lay out and make the wedge slot.** The *Pattern* shows two cuts that create the slot for the wedge. The rear cut determines the plane's cutting angle. An angle of 50 degrees is good for planing hardwood. A 45-degree angle is better for softwoods. For end-grain work, an angle of about 40 degrees works best. If your chisel blade is the same thickness along its entire length, lay out the rear cut to the desired cutting angle. If your chisel tapers from top to bottom, subtract 2 degrees from the angle of the rear cut.

To determine the angle of the front cut, add 10 degrees to the angle of the rear cut.

PATTERN

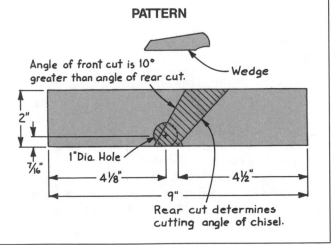

Angle of front cut is 10° greater than angle of rear cut.

Wedge

2"

7/16"

1"Dia. Hole

4⅛"

4½"

9"

Rear cut determines cutting angle of chisel.

Make the rear cut first, cutting the body in two. Trim the sharp bottom edge of the rear piece with a belt sander or block plane to the profile shown in the *Pattern*. Make the front cut so that it runs from the top of the plane to the hole. Don't continue the cut through the circle to the sole.

4 Make the wedge. The wood for the wedge must have grain that runs the length of the wedge: The cutout from the wedge slot won't do. Lay out the width of the wedge from the chisel; like the chisel, the wedge must be 1/64 inch narrower than the body, so that it can slide in and out. Cut the wedge to the shape shown in the *Pattern*.

5 Fit the wedge. Assemble the body, wedge, and chisel against a block as shown in *Photo 35-1*. Test fit and shave the wedge until it contacts the chisel along the length of its blade. Trim the bottom of the front piece to create a gap of about 1/32 inch between the tip of the chisel blade and the sole. This is the mouth of the plane—it gives the shavings a place to go as they come off the work.

6 Assemble the plane. Reassemble the body, wedge, and chisel against the block.

Clamp the body pieces to the block as shown in *Photo 35-2*. Check that the chisel and wedge fit properly between the clamped body pieces and make any necessary adjustments. Put glue on the cheeks and clamp them across the body. Leave the strips long at front and back. When the glue dries, unclamp the plane and cut the strips flush with the front and back. Slightly round all edges with sandpaper.

USING THE JIG

As with any wooden plane, adjusting this plane is a matter of tapping and trying until you get the shaving you are after. Begin by putting the chisel in place so that it barely protrudes beyond the sole. If you'll be using the plane to trim a rabbet, make sure that the side of the chisel is flush with the side of the plane that will ride against the rabbet's shoulder. Put in the wedge and tap it lightly with a wooden mallet until it is snug. Don't jam the wedge in too tightly; you could distort the shape of the plane.

Now turn the plane upside down and hold it to the light as shown in *Photo 35-3*. Sight along the sole and tilt the plane until

Photo 35-1 Clamp the body, wedge, and chisel together against a straight block. Test fit and shave the wedge until it contacts the chisel along the length of the blade.

Photo 35-2 When the body pieces are clamped in the proper position against the block, glue and clamp the cheeks to the body.

Photo 35-3 To adjust the plane, sight along the sole and tilt the plane until light reflects off the chisel's bevel. You want to see a thin, constant band of light glinting off the bevel.

Photo 35-4 If the plane is cutting too deeply, tap the back of the plane to push the chisel up slightly.

the light reflects off the chisel's bevel. You want to see a very thin band of light glinting off the bevel. The thickness of the band should be a constant, indicating that the blade is protruding equally along its length. If necessary, move the chisel handle from side to side to adjust the band. If you can't see any reflection, it's time to hone your chisel.

Try the plane. If the cut is too shallow, tap lightly on the chisel handle to increase the depth of cut. If the plane chatters or gouges, it's cutting too deeply. To remedy

this, tap the back end of the plane as shown in *Photo* 35-4. This pushes the chisel up slightly. After resetting the blade, test the plane again. When you're satisfied with the cut, tap the wedge lightly with a hammer to lock it in place. When you get to know your plane, getting it adjusted will take seconds instead of minutes.

To remove the chisel from the plane, wrap one hand around the plane and push up on the chisel. At the same time, tap on the back of the plane. The chisel will suddenly come loose.

BAND SAW RESAWING GUIDE

Design by Fred Matlack

One way to guide work while resawing on the band saw is to hold it against a high fence. This works fine—if your saw is perfectly tuned, if you have a wide, coarse-cutting resawing blade, if you get the fence perfectly aligned, and if the workpiece has no knots or wild grain.

The resawing guide shown here was designed for an imperfect world. Instead of trying to keep the entire workpiece aligned to the blade, as a fence does, it ·provides a guiding point. This lets you steer the work-piece during the cut to keep it on track.

MAKING THE JIG

Make the resawing guide from a ¾ × 6 × 8-inch scrap of plywood. On the band saw, cut the curve approximately as shown in the *Overall View.* Then use a belt sander to chamfer both sides of the guiding edge as shown in P*hoto* 36-1. No need to be exact here: The goal is to create a narrower pivot point.

USING THE JIG

Put a coarse, wide blade in your band saw. Place the guide on the saw table as shown in P*hoto* 36-2. Position the guiding edge slightly in front of the blade, so that the

workpiece will contact the guide just before the cut starts. Position it so that the distance between the blade and the guide is the desired thickness of the resawed pieces. It is a good idea to resaw ⅛ inch thicker than the desired final thickness, then dress the stock to final thickness on the planer. When the guide is properly positioned, clamp it to the saw table.

Before resawing, joint the edge of the stock that rides on the table and the edge that runs against the guide. If you're slicing several pieces off the same board, joint the freshly cut face before making the next cut.

There is no need to lay out the cutting line. Set a roller stand on the outfeed side of the saw, and you are ready to go. You'll need

OVERALL VIEW

Chamfer both sides of the guiding edge.

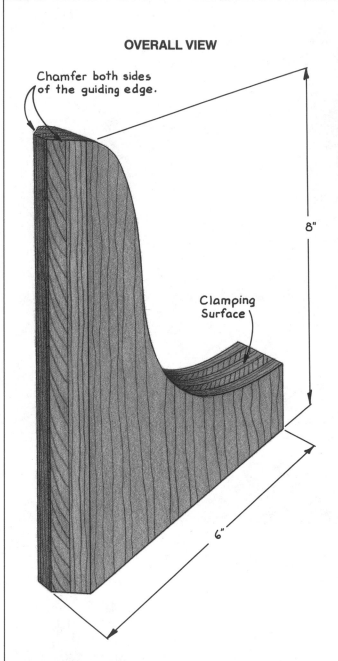

8"

Clamping Surface

6"

Photo 36-1   Use a belt sander to chamfer both sides of the guiding edge.

to the right. If the blade pulls left, steer left. This will take the sideways tension off the blade and allow it to track straight again. When the blade straightens out, do the same with the workpiece. The procedure will take a little practice, because it probably is the reverse of what intuition tells you to do. It may help to realize that the physics are the same as when your car fishtails on a slippery road: You need to steer the front of the car in

the stand for any piece long enough to tip off the end of the table at the end of the cut. You won't be able to exert much downward pressure at the cut's end.

Begin feeding the piece into the blade. Now comes the real secret to this guide: Don't watch the cut. Instead, keep your eye on where the blade passes between the guide blocks as shown in Photo 36-3. Your goal is to keep the blade running between the blocks without drifting to either side. If the blade starts to pull closer to the guide on the right, steer the front of the workpiece slightly

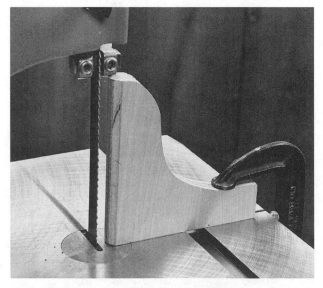

Photo 36-2   Position the guide slightly in front of the band saw blade.

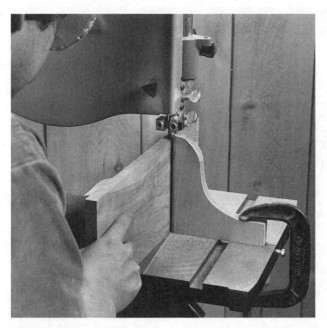

Photo 36-3 **To keep the cut straight, watch that the blade remains centered between the band saw's guide blocks.**

the direction that the rear end slides. This takes the sideways pressure off the tires, so that you can straighten out the car and regain control.

Every band saw blade pulls at least slightly to one side or the other. This is because the set of the teeth is never the same on both sides. So you'll most likely have to steer slightly to one side throughout the cut to compensate. This is like driving a car that needs a front-end alignment. It's a steady pressure that you get used to. To continue the analogy a little further, knots and wild grain in the wood will act like icy patches in the road; you'll need to make sudden, temporary adjustments to get back on track.

All of this takes a little practice. You might want to try resawing a few pieces of scrap wood before you slice into that curly maple. Before long, though, you'll be resawing wood like an Alaskan driving in the snow.

CURVED SANDING BLOCK

Design by Tim Steen

This block is for sanding large concave surfaces, such as the inside of a curved door. It has two parts, a base and a clamp, which are held together with one 2-inch-long drywall screw.

The block shown here will work well for most gradually curved surfaces. However, you can tailor it to the job at hand. For a more severe curve, increase the distance between the top and bottom of the base and draw a tighter radius. Decrease the distance between the top and bottom of the base to draw a gentler curve.

Make the base and the clamp from one piece of wood. For the block shown here, start with a blank that measures 1¼ × 4½ × 8 inches. Set a compass to draw a 4½-inch radius and lay out the curve of the base as shown in the *Overall View.* The curves at the top and bottom of the clamp don't need to be exact, so lay them out freehand to create a clamp that is ¾ inch thick. Lay out the cut that separates the two parts.

Cut the block on the band saw. First cut the perimeter of both parts. Then cut the parts in two. Finally, cut the inside curve on the clamp. Mark the center point on the top of the clamp. Hold the base and clamp together. Predrill through the clamp into the base for a 2-inch drywall screw.

Cut a strip of sandpaper to approximately 1½ inches wide and about 11 inches long. Wrap the ends of the strip around the ends of the base, and tuck them under the clamp. Drive the screw, and you are ready to sand.

OVERALL VIEW

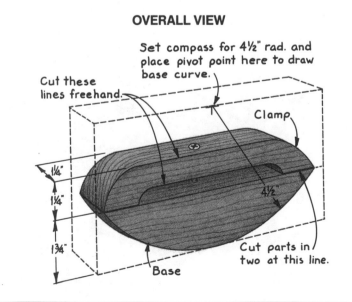

Cut these lines freehand.

Set compass for 4½" rad. and place pivot point here to draw base curve.

Clamp

1¼"

1¼"

1¾"

4½"

Base

Cut parts in two at this line.

SANDPAPER CUTTER

Design by Andy Rae

How much sandpaper have you cut to size in your lifetime?" asks woodworker Andy Rae. "Personally, I don't have a calculator big enough to answer that question."

And so Rae was motivated to design this simple jig to cut sandpaper quickly. The jig shown here cuts standard 9 × 11-inch sheets into thirds to fit a third-sheet sander. Pop the sandpaper into the jig and rip it along a plastic laminate straightedge. The jig cuts a pack of sandpaper—100 sheets—into 300 pieces in about three minutes. You can use the same idea to cut whatever sizes you commonly use in your shop.

MAKING THE JIG

1 Make the base. Cut a piece of hardboard, medium-density fiberboard, or plywood to the dimensions in the Materials List. Drill a 1-inch-diameter hole into one corner for hanging the jig.

2 Make and attach the fences. The fences shown here are made from maple, but any wood will do. Rip a 24-inch piece to the width in the Materials List. If you want your jig to look like the one shown here, square both ends and rout a Roman ogee on one edge and both ends of the piece. The Roman ogee is just for looks. You can rout any edge treatment you like, or just leave the fences square.

Now crosscut the stock into three fence pieces. The dimensions are in the Materials List. Miter one end of the long fence as shown in the *Overall View*. Make a matching miter on one end of the 4⅝-inch-long fence, and bevel the other end. Bevel one end of the 6⅞-inch-long fence.

Attach the fences to the base with glue and brads, positioning them as shown in the *Overall View*. Make sure the fences are flush with the edges of the base.

3 Make the straightedge. Cut a scrap of plastic laminate to the dimensions in the Materials List. Cut the 90-degree angle on one end to make it hang neatly on the wall with the jig. Drill a 1-inch-diameter hanging hole to correspond to the hole in the base.

OVERALL VIEW

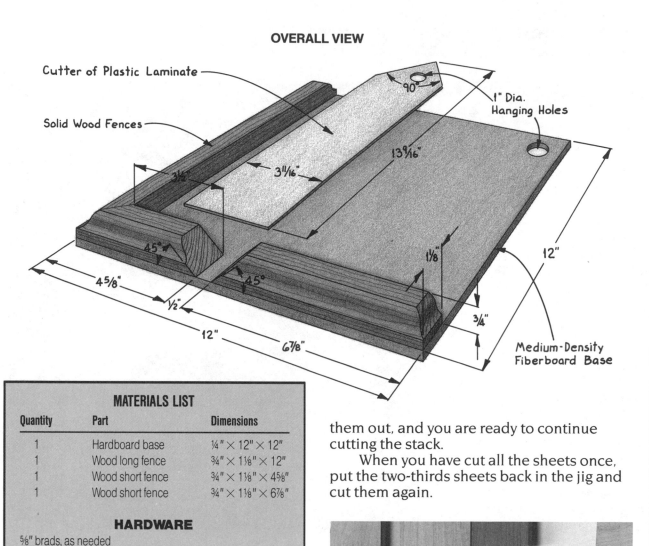

Cutter of Plastic Laminate

Solid Wood Fences

90°

1" Dia. Hanging Holes

13⁹⁄₁₆"

3¹¹⁄₁₆"

3½"

45°

45°

1⅛"

4⅝"

½"

¾"

12"

6⅞"

12"

Medium-Density Fiberboard Base

MATERIALS LIST		
Quantity	Part	Dimensions
1	Hardboard base	¼" × 12" × 12"
1	Wood long fence	¾" × 1⅛" × 12"
1	Wood short fence	¾" × 1⅛" × 4⅝"
1	Wood short fence	¾" × 1⅛" × 6⅞"

HARDWARE

⅝" brads, as needed
¹⁄₁₆" × 3¹¹⁄₁₆" × 13⁹⁄₁₆" plastic laminate, 1

them out, and you are ready to continue cutting the stack.

When you have cut all the sheets once, put the two-thirds sheets back in the jig and cut them again.

USING THE JIG

Lay the jig on a flat surface. Put up to 100 sheets of sandpaper (a full carton) in the jig, with the abrasive sides down. If you stack the paper face up, it will dull the straightedge. Push the sandpaper tightly against the fences. Now lay the straightedge over the paper and push it tightly against the fences as well.

Now lift several sheets at once and tear them out of the jig. You'll find that the finer the grit, the more sheets you can rip at once. The sheets in your hand are still two-thirds size. Put them aside. The pieces underneath the straightedge are sized for the sander. Lift

Photo 38-1   **The two parts of the sandpaper cutter are designed to hang neatly together on the wall.**

SANDING BLOCK

Design by Andy Bukovsky

Why use a sanding block? A sanding block is much like the sole of a plane. It provides a hard, flat surface that guides the sandpaper. Without a sanding block, it's very easy to sand small depressions into a surface. These depressions may not be visible while you're sanding, but once you've applied finish, you'll be able to see them from across the room.

This sanding block is sure to become one of the most-used jigs in your shop. It is designed to use all but a small percentage of the available abrasive.

The block shown here is sized to use a half-sheet of sandpaper. To make a full-sheet block, just double the length to 11 inches and leave all other dimensions the same. If you decide to make two blocks, cut a groove in one long block, and then

crosscut it to make two blocks. You can also make two wedges at the same time, planing one piece to the right taper and then crosscutting it.

Make your block and wedge from a softwood such as pine or basswood, so that you will be less likely to mar your work.

MAKING THE JIG

1 Make the block. If necessary, glue two pieces of stock together to get the thickness you need. Cut the block to the dimensions in the Materials List.

2 Groove the block. With a dado cutter in the table saw, cut a groove down the center of one face as shown in the *Overall View.*

3 Make the wedge. Cut the wedge to the size in the Materials List. Taper the wedge to the profile shown in the *Overall View.*

USING THE JIG

Wrap a piece of sandpaper around the block and fold the edges into the groove. Insert the wedge to hold the paper in place.

OVERALL VIEW

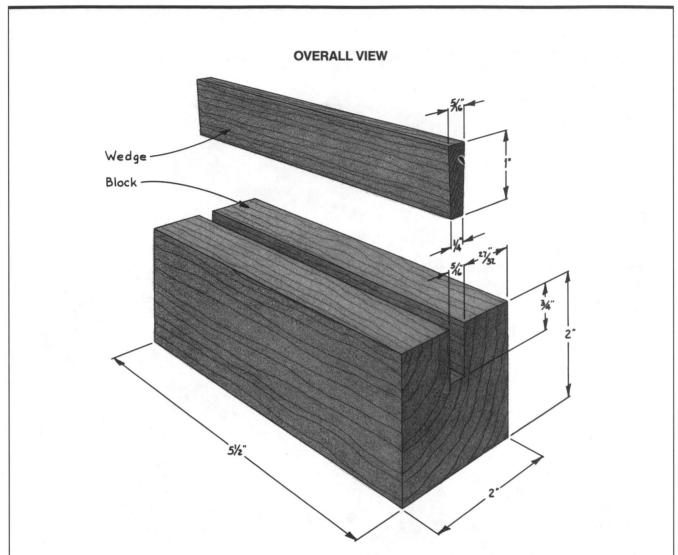

Wedge

Block

5⁄16"

1"

¼"

27⁄32"

5⁄16"

¾"

2"

5½"

2"

You can use all sides of the block. As one face wears out, simply turn the block onto a fresh one. You'll find that the narrow faces on both sides of the wedge are handy for sanding edges that are ¾ inch wide or narrower. The wedge acts as a fence to guide the block.

MATERIALS LIST		
Quantity	Part	Dimensions
1	Softwood block	2" × 2" × 5½"
1	Softwood wedge	5⁄16" × 1" × 5½"

SPLINE MITERS ON THE TABLE SAW

Design by Andy Rae

The miter joint is one of the most elegant joints in woodworking. It exposes no end grain; if you match it right, face grain can seem to flow around corners.

Unfortunately, the miter joint also is one of the weakest joints in woodworking. Because you make it by gluing end grain to end grain, you can't count on glue to hold it together. There are dozens of ways to reinforce this joint—including dowels, biscuits, nails, and screws. But for the best mix of strength, ease of execution, and classy looks, you can't beat a spline. Once you've assembled the joint, you cut a groove in the corner and insert a spline. Often, the spline is made from a contrasting wood to add an accent to the joint.

The jig shown here is designed to cut spline

grooves on the table saw. Once you set it up, cutting a spline takes only seconds. The *Overall View* shows the jig cutting spline grooves in a picture frame. But you could also use the jig on a box with mitered corners.

Make several grooves in each corner, and reinforce them with splines. For a jig that takes this idea one step further to create fake dovetails, see "Mock Dovetails and Spline Miters with the Router," page 80.

MAKING THE JIG

1 Cut the base. The base shown here is made from medium-density fiberboard (MDF), but you could use plywood instead. Cut it to the dimensions in the Materials List.

2 Make the plywood supports. Cut these pieces to the dimensions in the Materials List. Cut one side of each support to a 45-degree angle, as shown in the *Overall View*. Make sure this cut is exactly 45 degrees. On the jig shown here, the top outside corners of the supports are rounded to a radius of about 2 inches. This can be done with a jigsaw or a band saw. It's done just to make the jig more pleasing to the eye and the hand.

OVERALL VIEW

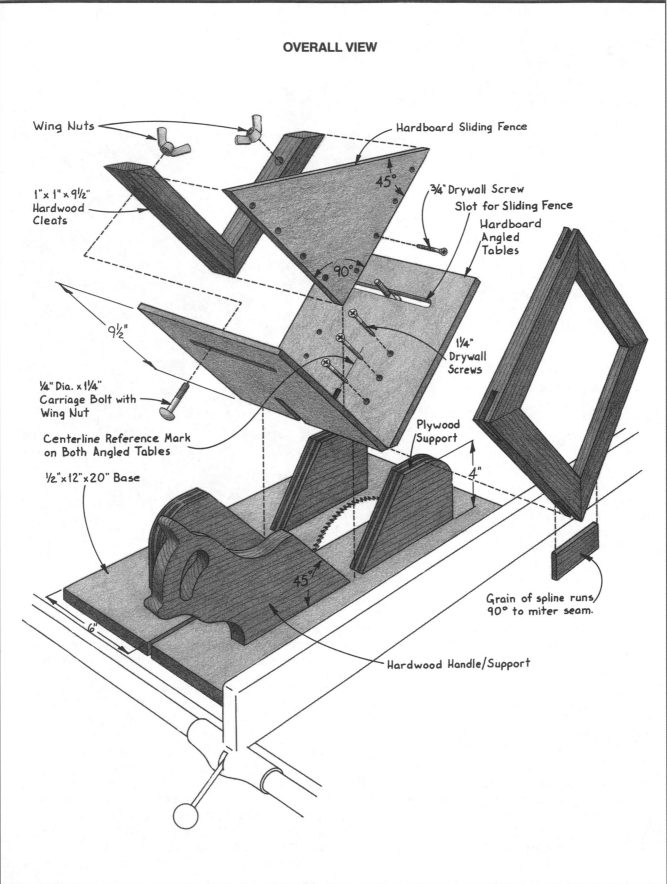

Wing Nuts

Hardboard Sliding Fence

1"x 1" x 9½" Hardwood Cleats

45°

¾" Drywall Screw

Slot for Sliding Fence

Hardboard Angled Tables

90°

9½"

¼" Dia. x 1¼" Carriage Bolt with Wing Nut

1¼" Drywall Screws

Centerline Reference Mark on Both Angled Tables

Plywood Support

4"

½"x12"x20" Base

45°

6"

Grain of spline runs 90° to miter seam.

Hardwood Handle/Support

MATERIALS LIST		
Quantity	**Part**	**Dimensions**
1	MDF* base	½" × 12" × 20"
3	Plywood supports	¾" × 4" × 6½"
1	Hardwood handle/support blank	¾" × 8" × 14"
2	Hardboard angled table blanks	¼" × 8½" × 10"
1	Hardboard sliding fence	¼" × 10" × 10"
2	Hardwood cleat blanks	1" × 1" × 10"

*Medium-density fiberboard

HARDWARE

1¼" drywall screws, as needed
¾" drywall screws, as needed
¼" dia. × 1¼" carriage bolts with wing nuts, 2

LAYING OUT THE HANDLE

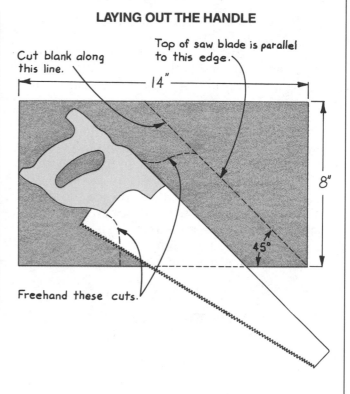

Cut blank along this line.

Top of saw blade is parallel to this edge.

14"

8"

45°

Freehand these cuts.

3 Make the hardwood handle/support. You could get by with a simpler handle than the saw handle design shown here. But if you take a little extra time to make this handle, you'll be glad you did. It's not hard to make, and it really does improve your control over the jig, making it safer and more accurate. A saw handle is designed to provide control while pushing down and away from you in one motion. That's exactly what you need for many table saw jigs—the ability to push the work across the table while resisting the blade's tendency to push the work up.

To make the handle, cut a hardwood blank to the dimensions in the Materials List. Make an accurate 45-degree cut across the width of the blank as shown in *Laying Out the Handle*. Now pick out your favorite handsaw, the one that feels just right in your hand. Lay the handsaw on the blank as shown. The handle should be in the upper left-hand corner and the top edge of the blade should be parallel to the 45-degree cut. Trace the grip. Working freehand, extend the tracing lines to the edges of the blank as shown. The exact layout of these connecting lines is not important.

Cut the outside shape of the handle on the band saw or with a jigsaw or coping saw. Drill a hole in the middle of the grip cutout and cut the shape with a jigsaw or coping

saw. Now rasp, file, and sand the handle until it is pleasing to your hand.

4 Attach the supports to the base. Predrill and countersink the supports, including the handle, for 1¼-inch drywall screws. Glue and screw the supports to the base. Place the handle on the right side of the jig as shown in the *Overall View*, so that the handle will travel between the rip fence and blade. Position the supports in pairs to form two Vs as shown in the *Overall View*. Position the pairs 4 inches apart, equidistant from the four sides of the base. Make sure they are exactly parallel to the long edges of the base.

5 Cut, slot, and attach the angled tables. On this jig, the tables are made from hardboard. Shop-grade plywood would work fine, too. Cut the tables to the dimensions in the Materials List. Then cut a 45-degree bevel along one shorter edge of each piece. Rout a slot in each angled table to accommodate the carriage bolts that will hold the sliding fence, as shown in the *Overall View*. Rout each slot in one pass with a ¼-inch-diameter straight bit in a table-mounted router. Plunge each angled table onto the bit as described in "Making Stopped Cuts on the Router Table," page 24.

Center the tables on the supports. Predrill and countersink the tables for 1¼-inch drywall screws, and screw them to the supports.

6 Attach the sliding fence. Cut the sliding fence to a square of the size given in the Materials List. Cut the stock in half across the diagonal to make the fence.

Two hardwood cleats reinforce the side of the sliding fence farthest from the blade. Make the hardwood cleats from a piece of stock cut to 1 × 1 × 22 inches. Crosscut the stock in half by making a 45-degree cut. Put

the pieces together at right angles, and position them along the sliding fence as shown in the *Overall View.* Cut the cleats so that they are flush with the top of the table.

Predrill and countersink for ¾-inch drywall screws, and glue and screw the sliding fence to the cleats.

Place the sliding fence in the jig and mark where the slots in the angled tables meet the cleats. The fence slides back and forth along these slots, allowing you to position it where needed. Remove the fence and drill through the cleats for the ¼-inch-diameter × 1¼-inch carriage bolts. Put the fence back on the jig, and attach it with carriage bolts and wing nuts.

7 Cut a kerf. Raise the blade to about 1 inch high. Set the rip fence 6 inches from the blade. Rip through the base, cutting it in two and making a cut in the bottom of the angled tables. You might want to write the 6-inch setting on the jig; this will be a standard rip fence setting when you use the jig. Mark the centerline of the kerf on both angled tables as shown in the *Overall View.* Use a square to make this mark perpendicular to the juncture of the tables. Make it a few inches long, so that you won't cut through it at higher blade settings.

USING THE JIG

You can use the jig to cut spline grooves in individual parts. But for most projects, especially picture frames, it is easier to glue up all the miter joints, let the glue cure for at least an hour, and then cut the grooves. This reduces the number of cuts and ensures that the grooves line up across the miters.

Usually, you will want to make the splines as wide as possible. The wider the spline, the stronger the joint. Let's say, for example, you are joining a picture frame that is 1⅝ inches wide and has a ⅜-inch-wide rabbet around the inside back edge, as shown in *Calculating Spline Depth.* To determine the maximum depth of the groove, measure along the seam of the miter joint, from the outside corner to the rabbet. In the example, that distance is 1¾ inches. Make the groove about 1½ inches

CALCULATING SPLINE DEPTH

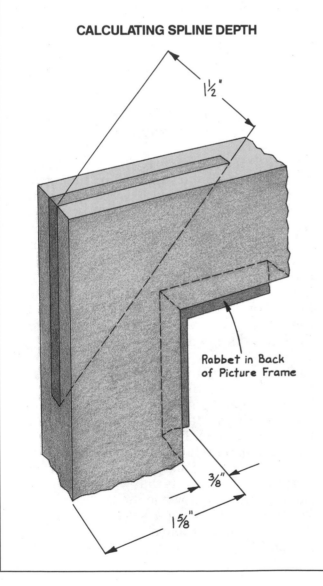

1½"

Rabbet in Back of Picture Frame

⅜"

1⅝"

deep, an easy-to-read measurement that keeps the groove well out of the rabbet.

Cutting ⅛-Inch-Wide Grooves

For small projects such as picture frames, you'll usually want a spline that is about ⅛ inch thick—the width of the saw kerf left by most table saw blades.

Start by setting the rip fence to the standard 6 inches from the blade. Raise the blade to the groove depth plus the thickness of the base. For example, set the blade 2 inches high for a ½-inch-deep groove. If you want to center a groove in the stock, set the sliding fence one-half the stock thickness from the centerline marks—⅜ inch for ¾-inch-thick stock, for example. If you are making multiple grooves, just lay out the centerline of each groove. Adjust the fence to align the layout line with the centerline on the jig.

Check that the sliding fence is square to the edge and surface of both angled tables. Tighten the wing nuts. Secure the workpiece to the fence with C-clamps or spring clamps. Turn on the saw and push the jig over the blade.

Cutting ¼-Inch-Wide Grooves

Let's say you want to cut a ¼-inch-wide groove in a ¾-inch-thick piece. In this case, don't gauge the sliding fence setting by the centerline marks. Instead, set the sliding fence to the left of the saw blade, ¼ inch from the left edge of the saw blade kerf in the angled tables. After making one pass over the blade, turn the work around and make another pass. That is, if the outside face of a picture frame was against the fence, place the inside face against the fence for the second cut.

Making Wider Grooves

Cut grooves wider than ¼ inch with a dado cutter. Since this is done in one pass, set the sliding fence one-half the stock thickness from the centerline.

Making and Inserting Splines

Plane your splines to a thickness that slides in the grooves. This leaves ample room for glue. Make the splines long and wide enough that they extend past the perimeter of the joint. You will cut them flush later. Put glue in the slots and insert the splines with their grain running at 90 degrees to the miter seam, as shown in *Photo* 40-1.

You can make the splines from the same wood as the grooved piece, so that they will only be subtly visible. Or as mentioned, you can use a contrasting wood to accent the project. The splines can become a bold design feature if you leave them proud of the joint and round or otherwise shape them.

If you choose to trim the splines flush, start by cutting them off close to the surface with a fine-cutting handsaw. Most saws have some set to the teeth, so you won't be able to trim flush without scratching the work. Even if you have a special flush trimming saw with no set to the teeth, don't saw the splines flush. Leave the splines about 1/16 inch proud of the surface and then pare them perfectly flush with a sharp chisel. This is because saw blades tear the wood, while chisels slice it, leaving a smooth, crisp-looking finish on the end grain. Don't sand the trimmed end grain of the splines; it will only scratch your nice, clean chisel cut.

Photo 40-1 Insert the splines with their grain at a right angle to the miter seam. Make the splines long and wide enough to trim flush later.

TEMPLATE FOR ROUTING STAIR STRINGERS

*Design by
Douglas Goodale*

In simplest terms, this jig helps rout stringers to hold the steps in a staircase. In a single setup, it helps cut grooves for the stair tread and for the riser, which fits between a tread and the one above it. The grooves are tapered, so you can wedge the tread and riser in place. This is a time-honored and effective method of securing treads and risers in their mortises.

With this jig, there is no need to lay out each tread and riser with a framing square. Instead, you simply slide the jig to a reference point to rout the next riser and tread. What more could you ask from a piece of plywood and a couple of scraps of wood?

This jig works with a flush trimming bit that has a pilot bearing *above* the cutters. (These bits are gener-

ally called pattern cutting bits.) You could also alter the size of the slots slightly and guide the router with a guide bushing.

You can use this jig with whatever bit diameter your router can handle. As a rule of thumb, for a 1- or 1½-horsepower router, use a ½-inch-diameter bit in hardwood. For a softwood stringer, you could use a ⅝-inch-diameter bit.

MAKING THE JIG

1 Cut the parts to size. Cut a piece of plywood for the template to the dimensions in the Materials List. If you will use the jig with a guide bushing, you can make the template from ½-inch-thick plywood, so that it will be a little lighter.

Make sure the blank is perfectly square.

Then draw a diagonal line across the blank and cut it to the right triangle shown in *Laying Out the Template*. The edge isn't a critical part of the jig: Make the cut with either a circular saw or a saber saw.

Cut the cleats to the dimensions in the Materials List.

LAYING OUT THE TEMPLATE

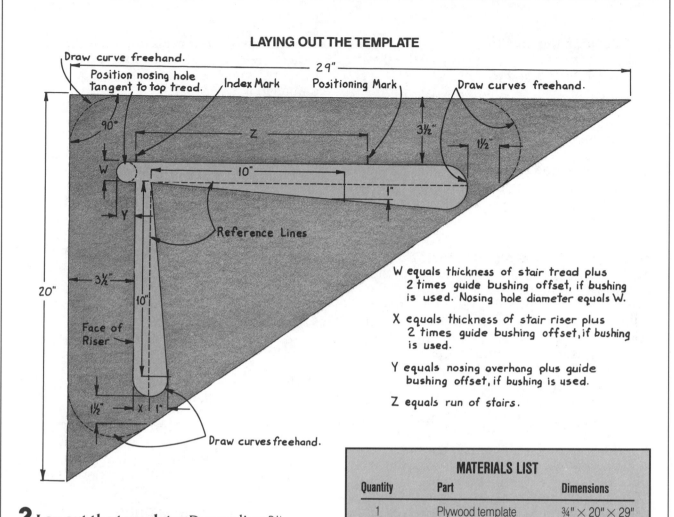

Draw curve freehand.

Position nosing hole tangent to top tread.

Index Mark   Positioning Mark   Draw curves freehand.

29"

3½"

1½"

90°

Z

10"

W

1"

Y

Reference Lines

20"

3½"

10"

Face of Riser

1½"   X   1"

Draw curves freehand.

W equals thickness of stair tread plus 2 times guide bushing offset, if bushing is used. Nosing hole diameter equals W.

X equals thickness of stair riser plus 2 times guide bushing offset, if bushing is used.

Y equals nosing overhang plus guide bushing offset, if bushing is used.

Z equals run of stairs.

MATERIALS LIST

Quantity	Part	Dimensions
1	Plywood template	¾" × 20" × 29"
1	Wood long cleat	¾" × 2" × 30"
1	Wood short cleat	¾" × 2" × 6"

HARDWARE

1" drywall screws, 5

2 Lay out the template. Draw a line 3½ inches from the 29-inch side of the template, as shown in *Laying Out the Template*. Draw a second line 3½ inches from the 20-inch side of the template. These lines mark the top of the tread and the face of the riser. The intersection of the lines is an index mark you'll need later. Make sure you mark it well, as shown in the drawing.

Draw in the bottom of the tread and the back of the riser. If you are routing with a pattern bit, these will be the reference lines shown in the drawing. If you are routing with a guide bushing, the reference lines are offset from the lines you just drew. To determine the offset, subtract the diameter of the bit from the outside diameter of the guide bushing. Divide the remainder by 2. For more information, see "Using Guide Bushings," page 29.

Working from the reference lines, lay out the tapers as shown in *Laying Out the Template*.

The tapers diverge from the reference lines at a rate of 1 inch in 10 inches.

Now lay out the top of the tread and the face of the riser. Add in the offset if you are using a guide bushing. Drawing freehand, lay out the curved ends of the mortises about 1½ inches from the hypotenuse of the jig as shown in the drawing.

The exact profile of the curve isn't critical.

3 Lay out and drill the nosing hole. Conventional stair treads have a fully rounded nosing that overhangs the riser, usually by 1 inch. The best way to create this curve in your template is to drill it.

Position the hole to mimic the tread. The hole must be tangent to the top of the tread and must overhang the front riser by the amount the tread overhangs. On a jig for pattern routing bits, the hole diameter equals the tread thickness. On a guide bushing jig, the diameter of the hole equals the tread thickness plus the offset you calculated previously. When you drill the hole, back up the template with a piece of scrap to prevent splintering the hole on the bottom of the template.

4 Rough-cut the template slots. The cuts for the top of the tread and the face of the rise will show in the finished stringer. This means the corresponding template cuts must be as straight as possible. Do this by making rough saber saw cuts and trimming to the line with a table-mounted router.

First place the saber saw blade in the nose hole and cut the length of the tread, staying about ⅛ inch inside the layout line. The cuts along the tapers don't need to be as perfect as the cuts for the top of the tread and the face of the rise. For this reason, as you cut the round that brings you into the taper under the tread, begin cutting right on the line. Cut on the line for both the tapers and the round at the bottom of the rise. As you come to the cut for the face of the riser, resume cutting about ⅛ inch inside the line.

5 Rout the cuts for the top of the tread and the face of the riser. Chuck a straight bit in a table-mounted router. Set the router table fence 3½ inches from the cutter. Trim the cuts for the top of the tread and the face of the riser.

6 Round the corners of the jig. Drawing freehand, lay out the curved cuts at each corner of the jig as shown in *Laying Out the Template*. These cuts don't need to be a particular shape or radius. They are made to remove excess material, making the jig lighter and handier. Make the cuts with a jigsaw. Ease the outside edges of the jig with sandpaper or a ⅛-inch roundover bit in the router.

7 Make an extra template. While optional, it's a good idea to use this template as a master to make another. If the jig gets damaged in use, you'll have a second one on hand. Make the extra template from the plywood cutoff from the first template.

Place the template over the cutoff. Make sure the square corners are flush, and draw the outline of the mortises onto the cutoff. Cut most of the waste from the mortises with a saber saw, staying about ⅛ inch inside the layout lines. Clamp the finished template over the rough-cut template. Rout the new template to shape with a flush trimming bit or a pattern cutting bit.

USING THE JIG

The top of a finished stringer usually ends with a nosing mortise that houses the nosing on the top landing. It's usually a good idea to cut the stringers 10 or 12 inches longer than finished length, so that you can cut the nosing as if it were a full tread. This provides material to support the jig while routing the last riser and nosing. It also lets you cut the stringer on site for a perfect fit.

Laying Out the Rise Pitch

Let's say, for example, that there's an 8-inch drop from the top of one step to the top of the next on your stairway. The steps are 10½ inches wide, not counting any nosing or overhang. In stair maker's parlance, this stairway has a rise of 8 inches and a run of 10½ inches.

Begin by laying out the rise on the stringer that will be on your left as you walk up the stairs. This is done with a framing square, just as if you were laying out the entire stringer. With this jig, however, you'll only have to lay out the first step.

Mark the bottom of the first riser on the stringer. The exact position will depend on the detail planned for the bottom of the staircase. To lay out the rise and run on the stringer, align the 8-inch mark on the inside of the framing square tongue with the edge of the stringer. Align the 10½-inch mark on the inside of the framing square body with the

LAYING OUT THE RISE AND REVEAL

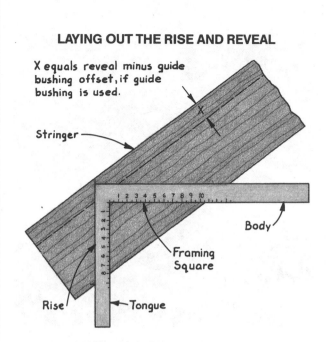

X equals reveal minus guide bushing offset, if guide bushing is used.

Stringer

Body

Framing Square

Rise

Tongue

stringer edge, as shown in *Laying Out the Rise and Reveal*. Slide the square until the outside of the tongue aligns with the mark for the bottom of the first rise, as shown. Draw a line along the outside of the tongue. Extend this line across the width of the stringer.

Laying Out the Reveal

In housed-step construction, the step usually does not run the entire width of the stringer. The space between the nose and stringer edge is called the reveal. Let's say, for example, the reveal will be 2 inches. Lay out the reveal along the entire length of the stringer as shown in *Laying Out the Rise and Reveal*. If you will rout the mortises with a pattern bit, lay out the reveal 2 inches from the top of the stringer. If you will be routing with a guide bushing, subtract the bushing offset you calculated previously from the reveal. Draw a reveal layout this distance from the edge of the stringer. For example, if you will use a ½-inch-diameter bit with a ⅝-inch-diameter bushing, draw the reveal layout line 1¹⁵⁄₁₆ inches from the top of the stringer.

Attaching the Cleats

The cleats keep the jig at the proper angle as you slide it up the stringer. Place the template on the stringer. Align the jig surface

that routs the face of the riser with the riser layout line. Slide the jig along the line until the nosing hole touches the reveal line.

Put the cleats against the stringer. Drive screws through the template to attach the cleats as shown in *Photo 41-1*.

Routing the First Step

Position the jig on the lines you drew to mark the first step. Secure the jig to the stringer with a single drywall screw positioned under the tread and behind the riser, so that the screw hole won't show in the finished stair.

Rout the mortises in two passes. First set the router bit depth to extend beyond the pattern about ¼ inch. Plunge the router into the bottom of the riser mortise so that it cuts into the long cleat as shown in *Routing the Mortises*. Then move the router clockwise around the jig to rout the perimeter of the mortises as shown. When you get back where you started, clean out the waste by moving the router back and forth across the mortises. Don't move the jig yet.

Photo 41-1 Align the jig with the riser layout line and the reveal line. Then screw through the template to attach the cleats.

ROUTING THE MORTISES

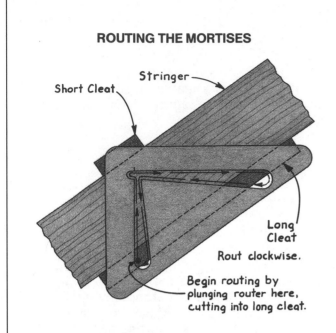

Short Cleat

Stringer

Long Cleat

Rout clockwise.

Begin routing by plunging router here, cutting into long cleat.

Photo 41-2 Starting from the bottom step, glue and wedge the risers and treads into the stringers.

Making the Positioning Mark

Before you remove the jig, make a mark to help position it for the next cut. Start at the jig's index mark. Measuring from the index mark, lay out the run along the top of the tread—10½ inches in the example. Mark the stringer at this point.

Making the Second Cut

Remove the screw and slide the jig upstairs until the face of the rise meets the positioning mark on the stringer. Put the screw back through the jig into the stringer. Rout the second step. Continue this process up the stringer.

Routing the Mating Stringer

Use the other side of the jig to rout the stringer that will be on your right as you walk upstairs. Mark where the cleats meet the edge of the jig. Remove the cleats from the

jig. Position them on the other side of the jig so that they align with the marks you made. Screw the cleats in place.

Lay out the rise, run, and reveal on the right stringer, so you can check that the cleats are correctly positioned. Rout the right stringer.

Assembling the Stair

Usually it is easiest to put the risers and treads in the stringers and then install the assembled stair carriage. Do this on a pair of sawhorses before you attach the stringers to the stairwell.

Start at the bottom step. Put the riser and tread in position. Squirt plenty of glue between the inside of the tread and the taper. Do the same for the riser. Put glue on the wedges and tap them snugly into place as shown in *Photo* 41-2. Repeat this process for each step.

CIRCULAR SAW STRAIGHTEDGE GUIDE

Design by Andy Bukovsky

This straightedge guide is one of the simplest, most common jigs used by woodworkers and carpenters. You'll find it in various sizes and materials, depending on the job at hand. It's designed to cut plywood—although you could use it to guide a router or any other portable power cutting tool.

The jig consists of a base and a fence. The optional cleat shown in the *Overall View* is a refinement that ensures the cut will be square. Make the guide wide enough that when you guide the circular saw against it, you cut one edge off the base. The freshly cut edge marks the exact path of the saw blade. Place this edge of the jig along a layout line, and the saw automatically cuts to the line.

Andy Bukovsky's straightedge guide, shown here, is typical of how jigs often reflect the need and materials of the moment. He was making cabinets from particleboard covered with plastic laminate. He had a table saw for ripping the cabinet sides to width, but the sides were too long for accurate, safe cutting on the table saw. None of the cabinets was more than about 24 inches deep. So Bukovsky made his jig from a 31-inch-long scrap of particleboard. Plywood would have worked equally well. Since he had scraps of plastic laminate around, he took the trouble to laminate the working surface of the guide. It's optional, but it gave him a durable, smooth guiding surface.

If you don't have a table saw with a large outfeed extension table, you might make a version of this jig for cutting plywood to a manageable size with a circular saw. If you do, make the base and guide 96 inches long, so that you can rip full sheets.

The base shown here is ¾ inch thick. This left plenty of depth for Bukovsky's circular saw to cut through ¾-inch-thick cabinet sides. In that case, you could make the jig from ½- or even ¼-inch-thick plywood.

OVERALL VIEW

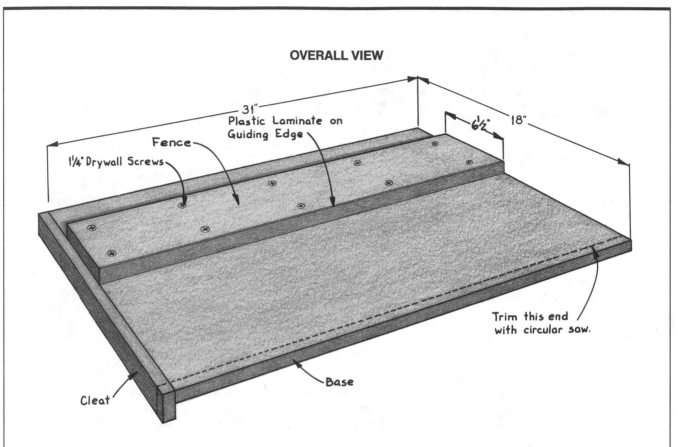

MAKING THE JIG

1 Cut the parts to size. Cut the base, fence, and cleat to the dimensions in the Materials List. Make the cleat as long as the base is wide.

2 Apply the laminate. This strip of laminate is optional, but it's a good idea—especially for particleboard, which is less durable than plywood. Cut a piece of laminate to the width and length in the Materials List. Use contact cement to adhere it to one long edge of the fence. Rout the laminate flush at the edges with a flush trimming bit.

3 Assemble the jig. Position the cleat on the base as shown in the *Overall View.* Screw the cleat to the base. Don't put any screws within 2 inches of the edge you will cut.

Place the fence on the base, with the laminated edge positioned to allow you to trim about 1 inch off the base as shown in the *Overall View.* Make sure that the laminated edge is parallel to the edge you will trim. Screw the fence to the base.

MATERIALS LIST		
Quantity	Part	Dimensions
1	Particleboard base	¾" × to fit × 31"
1	Particleboard fence	¾" × 6" × 31"
1	Particleboard cleat	¾" × 1½" × to fit

HARDWARE

1¼" drywall screws, as needed
1¼" × 31" plastic laminate, 1 (optional)

4 Trim the jig. Place the jig on blocks, across sawhorses, or on a surface you don't mind cutting into. Set the circular saw blade to cut through the base. Hold the saw firmly against the fence and trim the edge of the jig.

USING THE JIG

Place the material to be cut on blocks, sawhorses, or a scrap of plywood you don't mind cutting into. Lay out your cut or cuts.

Place the jig along the layout line. If your jig has a cleat, butt the cleat against one edge and clamp the other end of the jig in place as shown in P*hoto* 42-1. If there is no cleat, clamp both ends of the jig in place.

Add the thickness of the jig base to the blade's cutting depth, so that the saw will cut through the workpiece. Turn on the tool. Place its base firmly against the fence. Make the cut.

Photo 42-1 Position the edge of the jig on the layout line. Clamp the jig in place, making sure the clamp will not get in the way of the saw during the cut.

TAPERING JIG FOR THE PLANER

Design by Nils Falk

This simple jig allows you to use the thickness planer to taper four table legs at once. You can also use it to taper wide workpieces.

The planer jig produces a cleaner cut than table saw tapering jigs such as the "Tapering Jig for the Table Saw" on page 202 or the "Fixed Tapering Jig for the Table Saw" on page 206. The table saw usually leaves circular saw marks and burn marks that require a lot more sanding than the faint ripple left by a planer. The tapering itself probably will take about the same time with both methods. The table saw can do only one leg at a time but does it in one pass. The planer can do four legs at a time but takes four or five passes to get the job done.

The planer jig is fixed; you build it for a specific job. It is designed for legs that

are tapered on one side or on two adjacent sides. It is very quick and easy to assemble. The jig shown here will work on a 12-inch or wider planer. You can make the jig narrower to

accommodate your planer, if necessary.

Before you make the jig, cut the rectangular blanks for your table legs. This way, you can fit the jig's cleats snugly around the legs.

MAKING THE JIG

1 Make the base, table, stops, and cleats. Make the base and table from cabinet-grade plywood. Make the solid wood parts from softwood. Rip the stock to width for the stops and cleats. Cut the cleats to the length of the legs you will taper. Cut the table and the base 2 inches longer than the cleats.

2 Attach the stops and cleats. Predrill the stops and screw them to the table as shown in the *Overall View.* Center four table leg blanks on the jig as shown in *Photo* 43-1. Predrill the cleats and screw them in place as shown. Make sure they are parallel to the long edges of the jig.

3 Attach the table to the base. Drill for two screws that pass through the base into the

OVERALL VIEW

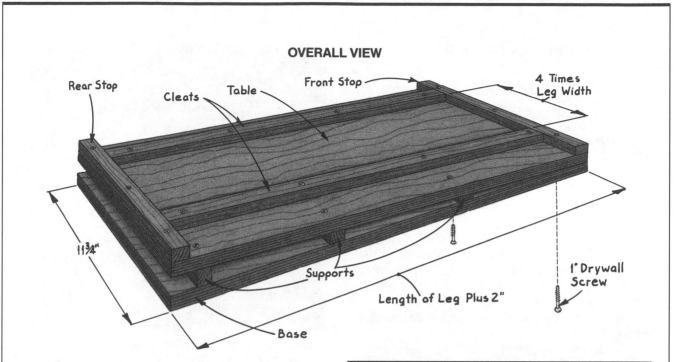

Rear Stop

Cleats

Table

Front Stop

4 Times Leg Width

11¾"

Supports

Base

Length of Leg Plus 2"

1" Drywall Screw

table under the front stop. Drive these screws.

4 Make the supports. The supports prevent the table from sagging from the pressure of the cutters. There is nothing critical about the dimensions of the three supports. To make them, start with a piece of stock that

Photo 43-1   Center four table legs on the jig. Predrill the cleats and screw them in place.

MATERIALS LIST

Quantity	Part	Dimensions
2	Plywood base and table	⅝" × 11¾" × to fit
2	Softwood stops	½" × 1" × 11¾"
2	Softwood cleats	½" × 1" × to fit
1	Softwood support	¾" × ¾" × 11¾"
1	Softwood support	½" × ¾" × 11¾"
1	Softwood support	¼" × ¾" × 11¾"

HARDWARE

1" drywall screws, as needed

measures about ¾ × 2½ × 11¾ inches. Rip the piece into three ¾-inch-wide pieces. Leave one of these rips as it is. Plane another to about ½ inch thick and the third to about ¼ inch thick.

5 Lay out the taper on a blank. Table leg tapers usually begin a few inches from the top of the leg. *Laying Out a Taper* shows a typical example. The point at which the tapers begin has no effect on the jig. Lay out whatever taper you will use on the side of one leg blank as shown in the drawing.

6 Set the taper on the jig. Put the thickest support under the rear stop, between the table and base, as shown in *Setting the Taper.*

LAYING OUT A TAPER

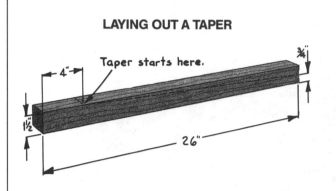

Place the leg along the jig as shown, with the bottom of the leg at the front of the jig. Slide the leg forward until the layout line intersects the top edge of the jig just inside the front cleat. If you run out of leg before the intersection happens, put a ½-inch-thick scrap under the leg.

Slide the support in until the slope of the jig matches the slope of the layout line. Check that the support is square to the side of the jig as shown in P*hoto* 43-2. Make any necessary adjustments, and double-check to make sure the slope of the jig still matches the slope of the layout line. Drive two screws through the table into the support.

Photo 43-2   To set the jig, slide the widest support in until the slope of the jig matches the slope of the layout line on the leg.

Put the thinnest support between the table and base. Slide it forward until it is snug. Secure it with two screws. Do the same for the remaining support.

SETTING THE TAPER

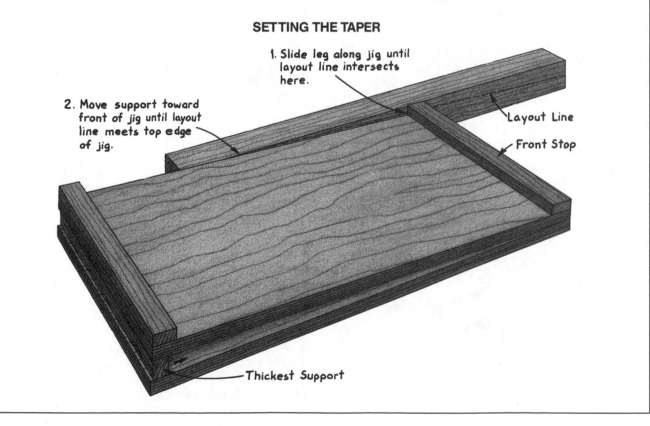

USING THE JIG

Place the four legs in the jig, with the bottom of the legs at the back of the jig. Position the leg with the layout at the outside, so that you can watch the layout line when you run the legs through the planer.

Measure the combined thickness of the jig and the legs at the back of the jig as shown in Photo 43-3. Set the thickness planer to 1/16 inch less than that.

After several passes, make a line along the top of the outside leg. Carry the line down the side of the leg, as shown in Photo 43-4. Lower the planer head one full turn of the crank. Make another pass. Measure how much of the line is planed away. Now you know how much length is tapered with each pass. Use this information to stop the taper at the right location on the leg.

Turn on the planer and feed the front of the jig in first. You are feeding a heavy package into the machine, so be careful to support the jig as it comes out of the planer to avoid snipe. Continue planing in 1/16-inch increments until you have tapered the legs to the layout line.

To taper adjacent sides, turn the legs 90 degrees in the jig. Begin with the same planer setting you used to start the first taper. Continue planing in 1/16-inch increments until you reach the final thickness setting.

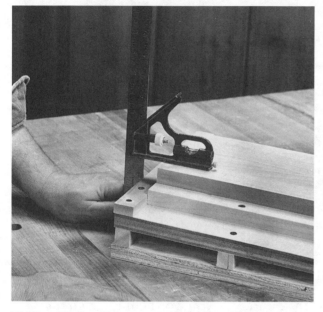

Photo 43-3   Measure the combined thickness of the jig and the legs at the back of the jig.

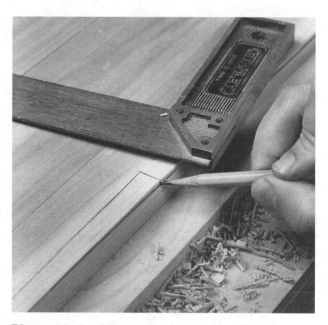

Photo 43-4   After several passes, make a line along the top of the outside leg. Carry the line down the side of the leg. Make another pass and measure how much of the line is planed away.

TAPERING JIG FOR THE TABLE SAW

Design by Mitch Mandel

Tapered legs are very common on Early American table designs, from Hepplewhite to Shaker. Today, legs usually are tapered on either the jointer or the table saw. The jointer requires no jig other than a stop block, and it leaves you with smooth, crisp tapers that are nearly ready for a finish. But tapering on the jointer requires multiple passes and involves lowering the leg over exposed spinning cutter blades. It's one of the most dangerous operations on the shop's most dangerous power tool.

The jig shown here provides a safer way to cut tapers by using the table saw. On the table saw, each taper is made with one cut. The trade-off is that you'll have to spend a little more time cleaning up the cuts with a hand plane or belt sander.

The jig shown here is sized to handle most tapering jobs and still be lightweight and easy to handle. It's most commonly used to taper table legs with square cross sections, but it can be used to rip almost any taper.

If you are planning to taper super-hefty stock—anything over about 1¾ inches thick at its widest point—make the jig from thicker stock, so that you won't cut through the adjusting bar.

MAKING THE JIG

1 Cut the arms. The arms can be made from any construction-grade softwood that doesn't have large knots. Fir is an ideal choice, because it is straight-grained and stable. Rip and crosscut the two arms to the dimensions in the Materials List.

2 Drill the arms. Drill a ⅝-inch-diameter hole about 1 inch deep in one of the arms for the handle, as shown in the *Overall View*. Flip the arm over and drill a ¼-inch-diameter hole for an adjusting bar bolt, as shown in the *Overall View*. Drill a matching ¼-inch-diameter hole into the other arm.

3 Dado for the stop block. Although you could screw the stop block to the end of the arm, you risk hitting the screws with your saw blade. It's better to fit the block into a dado as shown in the *Overall View*.

OVERALL VIEW

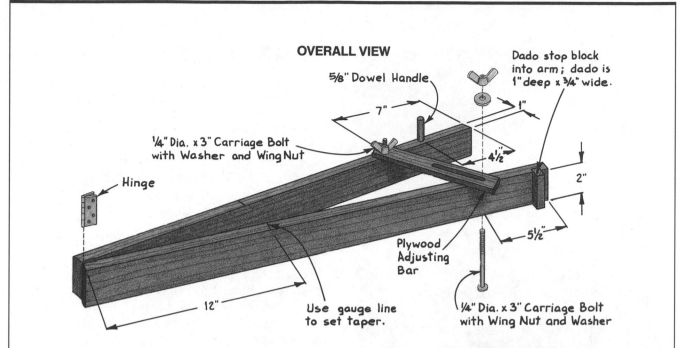

5/8" Dowel Handle

7"

1/4" Dia. x 3" Carriage Bolt with Washer and Wing Nut

Hinge

12"

Use gauge line to set taper.

Dado stop block into arm; dado is 1" deep x 3/4" wide.

1"

4½"

2"

5½"

Plywood Adjusting Bar

1/4" Dia. x 3" Carriage Bolt with Wing Nut and Washer

4 Make the adjusting bar. Begin with an oversize piece of plywood—1½ inches wide and about 18 inches long. Lay out the beginning and end of the slot as shown in the *Adjusting Bar Detail.*

The easiest way to cut the slot is on the table-mounted router, as explained in "Making Stopped Cuts on the Router Table," page 24. Because the exact length of the slot isn't critical, you can simplify the procedure. Put a ¼-inch straight bit in your table-mounted router and set the fence ⅝ inch away from the bit. To help you position the stock, draw an index line on the fence. Draw the line so that it passes through the center of the bit and is perpendicular to the table, as shown in *Photo 44-1.*

Line up the beginning of the slot with the index line on the fence, as shown in *Photo 44-2.* Lower the stock onto the spinning bit

ADJUSTING BAR DETAIL

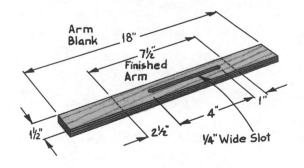

Arm Blank

18"

7½" Finished Arm

1"

4"

2½"

1½"

¼" Wide Slot

MATERIALS LIST		
Quantity	Part	Dimensions
2	Softwood arms	1" × 2" × 24"
1	Dowel handle	⅝" dia. × 6"
1	Hardwood stop	¾" × 1" × 2"
1	Plywood adjusting bar	½" × 1½" × 9"

HARDWARE

¼" dia. × 3" carriage bolts with washers and wing nuts, 2
1½" butt hinge, 1

and move the stock forward. Lift the stock off the bit when the line at the end of the slot crosses the index line, as shown in *Photo 44-3.*

Cut the adjusting bar to length. Drill a ¼-inch-diameter hole ¾ inch from one end of the slot.

5 Assemble the jig. With a chisel, cut hinge mortises on the inside face of both arms as shown in the *Overall View.* Attach the hinge to the arms. Put the carriage bolts into their holes. Put the adjusting bar in place, followed by the washers and the wing nuts. Put glue in the handle hole and tap the handle into place. Put glue in the dado and clamp the stop block in place.

6 Draw the gauge line. This line helps you set the jig to cut the desired taper. Close the

Photo 44-1 Draw an index line on the fence that aligns with the approximate center of the bit.

arms and make a line across them exactly 12 inches from the hinged end. To make this gauge line permanent and accurate, cut it into the wood with a utility knife and then fill it in with a ballpoint pen.

USING THE JIG

To cut a taper on two adjacent sides of a leg, you'll have to calculate the taper of the leg and set the jig accordingly. If you're tapering all four sides, you'll need to taper two adjacent sides, reset the jig, and then taper the remaining sides. Start by ripping a blank to the widest part of the taper. For example, if your taper goes from 1½ inches to ¾ inch, rip the blank to 1½ inches.

Setting the Rip Fence

Set the blade height so that just the teeth will come through the stock. Close the jig so that the arms are against each other. Place the blank in the jig. Put the jig against the rip fence and move the fence until the blade just touches the outside of the stock. (See *Photo* 44-4.) Lock the fence.

Calculating the Taper

The taper is calculated in inches per foot: A 12-inch-long leg that tapers from 2 inches to 1 inch has a taper of 1 inch per foot. Once you know the taper, you set the jig

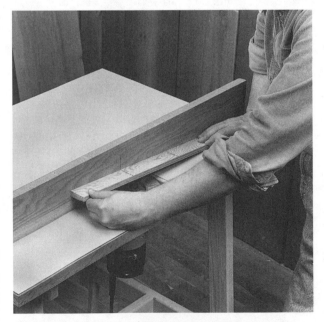

Photo 44-2 Line up the beginning of the slot with the index line on the fence. Lower the adjusting bar blank onto the spinning bit.

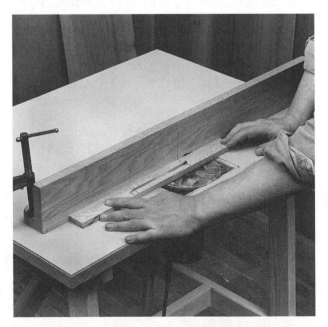

Photo 44-3 Lift the stock off the bit when the line at the end of the slot crosses the index line.

Photo 44-4 Place the jig and the leg blank together against the rip fence. Slide the fence over until the leg touches the blade.

accordingly. To taper a leg like this, you set the arms of the jig 1 inch apart at the gauge line.

Since real life isn't always so tidy, there's a simple formula:

$$\frac{\text{widest width of taper (in inches)} - \text{narrowest width of taper (in inches)}}{\text{length of leg (in feet)}} = \frac{\text{taper}}{\text{(in inches per foot)}}$$

A 24-inch-long leg that tapers from 1½ inches at the top to ¾ inches at the bottom has a taper of ⅜ inch per foot:

$$\frac{1\frac{1}{2}'' - \frac{3}{4}''}{2'} = \frac{3}{8}'' \text{ per foot}$$

Set the arms of the jig ⅜ inch apart at the gauge line.

CALCULATING TABLE LEG TAPERS

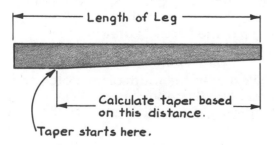

If the taper per foot is a number that isn't easily measured—like ⅓—round it to the nearest sixteenth. One-third, for example, becomes ⁵⁄₁₆.

Some tapers, like those on many table legs, do not run the entire length of the piece. When you calculate the taper, base it on the length of the taper, not the length of the leg, as shown in *Calculating Table Leg Tapers*.

Making the Cuts

Put the jig against the fence, and slide the jig along the fence to cut the taper. Feed the jig steadily to minimize saw marks. Be especially careful at the end of the cut; it's easy to skew the leg and jig, causing the blade to gouge the bottom of the leg.

If you are tapering two adjacent faces, as shown in Photo 44-5, run them both through on the same setting. If you are tapering all four faces, run two adjacent sides through at the same setting and then reset the jig for twice the first setting. If the arms were ⁹⁄₁₆ apart for the first two sides, set them 1⅛ inch apart for the remaining two sides. If the leg has a rectangular cross section, you'll have to reset the fence.

Photo 44-5 To taper two adjacent sides of a leg that is square in section, turn the leg and run it through a second time.

FIXED TAPERING JIG FOR THE TABLE SAW

Design by Andy Rae

Like the adjustable tapering jig, this fixed tapering jig is used mostly for tapering table legs. Since you can't change the taper on this jig, you'll have to make a new one for each taper you want. You'll also find that because it's fixed, this jig is useful only for legs that will be tapered on one or two sides. However, the fixed jig has a few advantages of its own.

The most obvious advantage is that this jig is quicker and easier to make. It is just a piece of plywood with a handle.

The fixed jig is also easier to use. The adjustable jig cuts the wide part of the taper first, so that only the narrow part of the stock is on the table at the end of the cut. As a result, you have to be careful to prevent the stock from twisting at the end of the cut. The fixed jig

eliminates this problem, because you feed the narrow end of the taper into the saw first. Another nice thing about the fixed jig is that it eliminates the math; the taper is laid out on the jig.

Because cabinetmaker Andy Rae uses this jig often, he took the time to carefully shape the handle. You can make a simpler handle from a 2 × 4, as described in "Making the Jig."

MAKING THE JIG

1 Make the base. Cut the plywood base to the dimensions in the Materials List.

Now lay out the notch that holds the piece you'll taper. As an example, let's say we're tapering a 24-inch table leg, as shown in the *Overall View*. The leg is 1½ inches wide at the top and tapers to ¾ inches at the bottom. The taper starts 4 inches from the top of the leg.

The notch begins 3 inches from the bottom of the jig. At this point, the notch is as wide as the bottom of the leg. Lay out the bottom of the notch by drawing a line perpendicular to the edge as shown in the *Overall View*.

Next draw the width of the notch at the point where the taper begins. As shown in the drawing, the width is equal to the top of the leg.

OVERALL VIEW

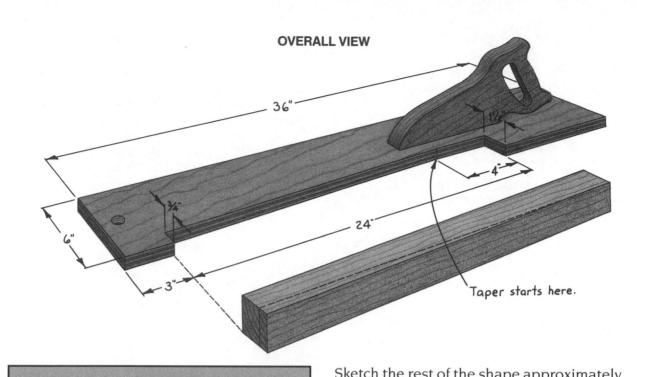

36"

¾"

6"

3"

24"

4"

Taper starts here.

MATERIALS LIST		
Quantity	Part	Dimensions
1	Plywood base	¾" × 6" × 36"
1	Hardwood handle blank	1¼" × to fit × 15"

HARDWARE

1½" drywall screws, 4

Draw a line across the jig marking the top of the leg.

To finish laying out the notch, connect the ends of the lines that mark the bottom of the leg and the beginning of the taper. Continue this line until it meets the line marking the top of the leg.

Cut out the notch with a band saw or jigsaw. Drill a hanging hole at one end of the jig.

2 Make the handle. The handle shown on this jig was made by tracing a handsaw handle. Pick your favorite handsaw, the one that feels just right in your hand. None of the dimensions of the handle is critical. Use *Laying Out the Handle* as a guide. Start with a 1¼-inch-thick hardwood blank. Make the blank about 15 inches long and at least ½ inch wider than the saw handle. Lay the saw on the blank and trace the handle.

Sketch the rest of the shape approximately as illustrated.

Cut the outside shape of the handle on the band saw or with a jigsaw or coping saw. Drill a hole in the middle of the grip cutout and cut the shape with a jigsaw or coping saw. Now rasp, file, and sand the handle until it is pleasing to your hand.

For a simpler handle, use a piece of 2 × 4 about 8 inches long. Round the top edges of the piece with a block plane until it is pleasing to grip. Sand all but the bottom with 80-grit sandpaper to make sure there will be no splinters.

3 Assemble the jig. Glue and clamp the handle in place. Countersink through the bottom of the base into the handle for four

LAYING OUT THE HANDLE

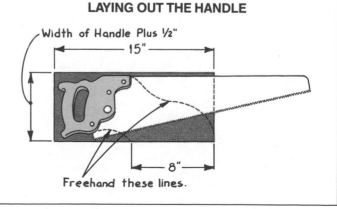

Width of Handle Plus ½"

15"

8"

Freehand these lines.

1½-inch drywall screws. Insert the screws and remove the clamp. Write "Set fence at 6 inches" on the jig. No matter what taper you made the jig for, you will always set the rip fence this far from the saw blade.

USING THE JIG

Cut blanks to the final length and to the final width and thickness of the top of the leg. If you are planning to mortise the legs, do it before you taper them.

No matter what taper you've cut in the jig, the rip fence setting is the same. Set the table saw fence 6 inches from the blade. Place a blank in the jig and rip a taper.

To taper an adjacent side, just turn the leg 90 degrees so that the side you just tapered is facing up. Rip the second taper.

Tip: Keep the cutoffs; they make great shims.

MAKING ROUND TENONS ON THE RADIAL ARM SAW OR TABLE SAW

Design by Ben Erickson

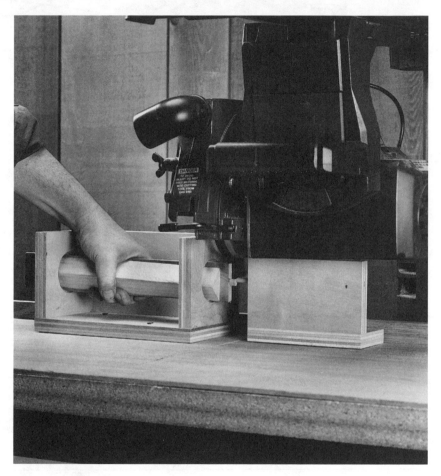

When Ben Erickson was faced with the task of making louvered shutters, he found himself nearly overwhelmed by the number of louvers that had to be tenoned. He experimented with different methods of making the round tenons. He tried plug cutters; he tried filing the square ends round; he tried chiseling them round. Nothing worked.

Finally, Erickson hit upon the method shown here, which uses a dado cutter on the radial arm saw. While the radial arm saw is the best tool for the job, the jig can easily be adapted to the table saw, as described in "Making the Jig."

"It worked great, was extremely accurate and, as a bonus, fast," Erickson said of the jig. "I can turn both ends of about three louvers in a minute. I have since seen a similar version of this idea on a shutter-making machine from the 1800s, so I guess there really is nothing new under the sun."

While this jig was designed with louvered shutters it mind, it can be used to tenon chair legs or any other time you need round tenons. A bigger version could even be used to tenon 4 × 4 porch posts.

The jig is little more than a couple of pieces of plywood with holes drilled into them. The holes are sized to hold the workpiece snugly. To cut a round tenon, you slip the stock into the holes and turn it. A dado blade mounted on the saw arbor trims the exposed stock round.

Square pieces can be inserted into the jig by themselves, but rectangular pieces (such as louvers) need to be supported on each side with triangular blocks that keep them centered in the jig. The jig shown here can handle pieces up to about 3½ inches wide. The guide blocks screw in place, so make different-size blocks for different-size pieces. You can use the same base for all of the blocks.

If you have a choice of machines, pick the radial arm saw. A dado head has a more limited depth of cut on the table saw. This reduces the potential of the jig.

RADIAL ARM SAW OVERALL VIEW

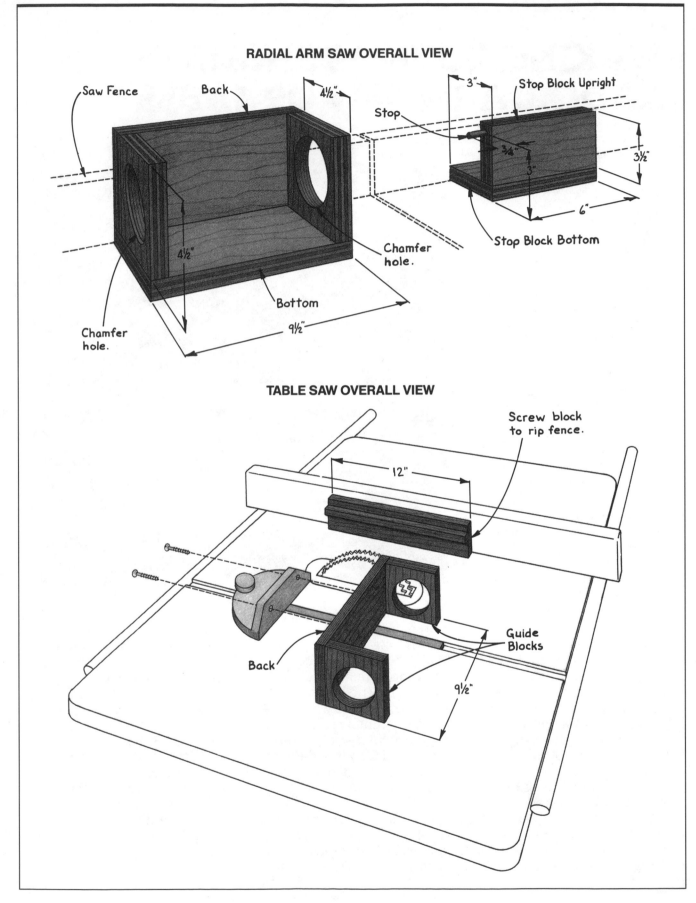

Saw Fence

Back

4½"

3"

Stop Block Upright

Stop

¾"

3"

3½"

6"

Chamfer
hole.

4½"

Bottom

Stop Block Bottom

Chamfer
hole.

9½"

TABLE SAW OVERALL VIEW

Screw block
to rip fence.

12"

Back

Guide
Blocks

9½"

MATERIALS LIST

For the Radial Arm Saw:

Quantity	Part	Dimensions
1	Plywood bottom	¾" × 5¼" × 9½"
1	Plywood back	¾" × 4½" × 9½"
2	Plywood guide blocks	¾" × 4½" × 4½"
2	Wood triangular blocks	To fit
1	Plywood stop block bottom	¾" × 3" × 6"
1	Plywood stop block upright	¾" × 3½" × 6"
1	Stop dowel	¼" dia. × 1½"

For the Table Saw:

Quantity	Part	Dimensions
1	Plywood back	¾" × 4½" × 9½"
2	Plywood guide blocks	¾" × 4½" × 4½"
4	Wood triangular blocks	To fit
1	Hardwood stop block	¾" × 2¼" × 12"

HARDWARE

1⅝" drywall screws, as needed

MAKING THE JIG

1 Make the base. For the radial arm saw, cut the bottom and back to the dimensions in the Materials List. Glue and screw the two pieces together as shown in the *Radial Arm Saw Overall View.* For the table saw, cut just the back as shown in the *Table Saw Overall View.*

2 Make the guide blocks. Cut the guide blocks to the dimensions in the Materials List. While you are cutting the guide blocks, you might want to cut a few extras for future use. In most cases, you will want to make the workpiece first and then drill the hole to fit.

To lay out the holes on the radial arm saw jig, mark diagonals across each block to find the center. At these center points, drill holes for the size of the workpiece you will be tenoning. For the table saw jig, center the holes across the block, but position them so that there's only about ¼ inch between the circle and the bottom of the block, as shown in the *Table Saw Guide Block Detail.* This will allow your dado cutter to cut as deeply as possible.

For louvers or other thin, rectangular pieces, the diameter of the hole will be the width of the piece. On square pieces, the diameter of the hole will be the diagonal of the workpiece. For round stock, the diameter of the hole will equal the diameter of the workpiece. This is illustrated in the *Radial Arm Saw Guide Block Detail.* The jig shown here will accommodate pieces with widths, diameters, or diagonals of 3½ inches.

Drill the holes with a commercially available circle cutter, hole saw, or Forstner bit. Run the drill press at a slow speed when boring large-diameter holes. Make a trial cut on scrap stock to check the hole size. Alternately, you can start with a standard-size hole and make the workpieces to fit.

Once the blocks are drilled, chamfer one side of each hole with a piloted chamfering bit in a table-mounted router. This will help the work slide into the jig easily.

TABLE SAW GUIDE BLOCK DETAIL

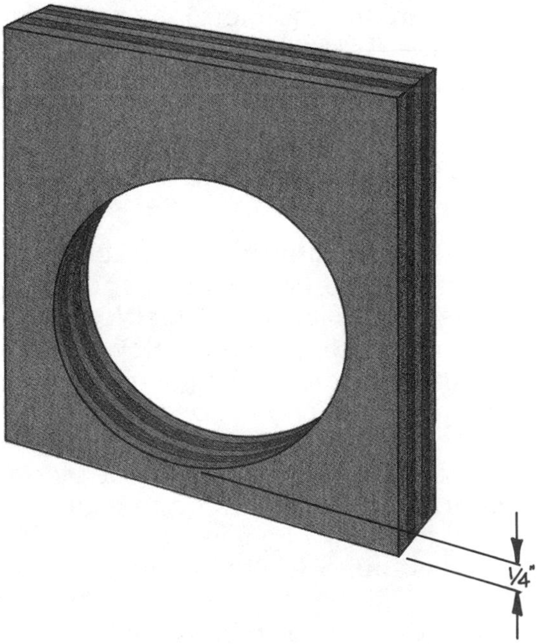

**RADIAL ARM SAW
GUIDE BLOCK DETAIL**

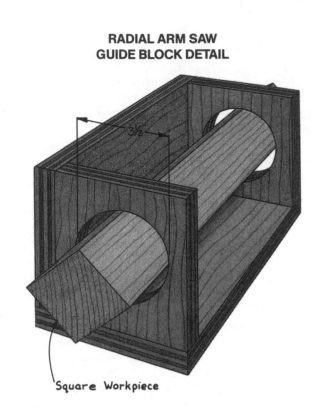

Square Workpiece

TRIANGULAR BLOCK DETAIL

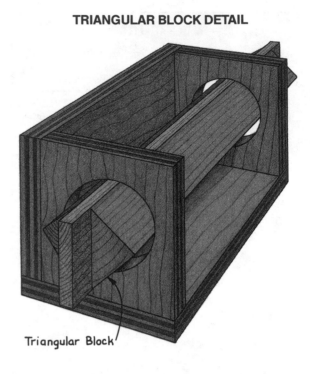

Triangular Block

3 Attach the guide blocks. For the radial arm saw, screw a block to each end of the base and to the back as shown in the *Radial Arm Saw Overall View*. For the table saw, glue and screw the guide blocks to the back as shown in *Table Saw Overall View*. With either saw, make sure the chamfers face away from the saw blade. This will make inserting workpieces safe and easy. If the stock is very short, move the block farthest from the saw blade toward the center of the jig to shorten the distance between the two blocks.

4 Make the triangular blocks. If you are cutting louvers or other wide, thin pieces, you will need to make triangular blocks to stabilize the work in the guide blocks. The size and shape of these triangular blocks depend on the size and shape of the workpiece. Make the blocks long enough to protrude slightly outside each guide block. The important thing is that the triangular blocks cradle the workpiece and fit into the guide blocks snugly. Cut them out on the band saw to the shape required. An example is shown in the *Triangular Block Detail*.

5 Make the stop block. For the radial arm saw, cut the stop block bottom and upright to the dimensions in the Materials List. Glue and screw the two pieces together as shown in the *Radial Arm Saw Overall View*. Drill a ¼-inch-diameter hole about ¾ inches deep. Position the hole as shown in the *Overall View*. Slip the stop dowel into the hole, but do not glue it in place. You might have to replace it if it inadvertently gets cut off.

For the table saw, cut the stop block to the dimensions in the Materials List. Rabbet the stop block as shown in the *Table Saw Overall View*. The exact profile of the stop depends on the size of the workpiece. Make the distance between the saw table and the stop tongue equal to the radius of the tenon plus ¼ inch.

USING THE JIG

When you cut the pieces to be tenoned, make two or three extras to test your setup. On either the radial arm saw or the table saw, you will be able to fine-tune the tenon diameters, if necessary, by raising or lowering the blade slightly. On projects with multiple parts where both ends of each part are to be tenoned, it is important to cut all the stock to exactly the same length before tenoning the ends in the jig. This keeps the distance between the tenons identical on all the parts.

Lay out the tenon length on one of the workpieces. There is no need to lay out the tenon diameter if that diameter equals the thickness of the workpiece. Otherwise, use a compass to lay out the tenon diameter on the end of the workpiece. To find the center point on a rectangular or square piece, draw diagonal lines. The center of the tenon is where the lines cross.

Set a dado cutter to slightly wider than the length of the tenons you will cut. If the tenons are longer than the maximum width of your dado cutter, set the cutter to its maximum width. Put the cutter on the radial arm saw or the table saw.

With a wobble dado cutter, you'll get a slight taper on the tenon. On shutter louvers, this makes it easier to insert the tenons into their mortises. A stacked dado cutter will provide more uniform tenons.

Using the Radial Arm Saw Jig

Screw the jig base to the saw table, with the jig against the fence. Position the right

Photo 46-2 Align the tenon shoulder with the left side of the blade. Slide the stop dowel into place against the end of the workpiece and clamp down the stop block.

side of the jig about 1½ inches to the left of the blade.

Slide a workpiece into the jig. If the tenon diameter is to match the workpiece thickness, position one workpiece face horizontally as shown in *Photo* 46-1. Raise the arm of the saw until the blade just passes over the work. Otherwise, lower the blade until it meets the tenon layout circle.

Slide the workpiece to the right until the left edge of the blade aligns with the tenon shoulder. Place the stop dowel against the workpiece as shown in *Photo* 46-2. Then turn the workpiece vertically to make sure it will remain in contact with the dowel as you rotate it to make the tenon. This may mean you'll have to move the stop toward the front of the saw. When you find the proper position, screw the stop block to the saw table. Lock the saw carriage so that the center of the blade is over the centerline of the workpiece. Slide the workpiece back out of the way.

Start the saw. Advance the workpiece until it meets the stop. Grasp the work between the guide blocks and rotate it in the jig to make the cut. With small stock, you can

Photo 46-1 Slide the workpiece into the jig with one face positioned horizontally.

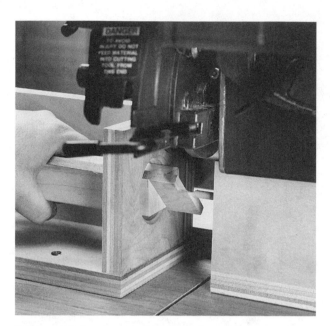

Photo 46-3 Grasp the workpiece between the guide blocks. Rotate small workpieces clockwise (away from you) into the cutter for the best cut. Rotate larger workpieces counterclockwise to prevent kickback.

Photo 46-4 Screw the stop block to the table saw work fence.

rotate the work clockwise (the top edge will go away from you) as shown in *Photo* 46-3. This will provide a better cut. In most machine operations, you would rotate the stock counterclockwise to prevent kickback. But kickback is not a problem with small pieces such as shutter louvers, because they are contained within this jig. Just be sure to keep a good grip on the workpiece, so that it does not spin out of your hand. For cutting larger pieces—for example, chair leg tenons—rotate the piece counterclockwise for safety.

If the tenon you are cutting is longer than the width of your cutter, butt the workpiece against the stop and rotate it once. Then pull the workpiece away from the stop block and make another rotation to complete the tenon.

Using the Table Saw Jig

Screw the jig to the miter gauge as shown in the *Table Saw Overall View*. Then place the miter gauge on the table saw backward. This gives you good access to the work as it is being cut.

Photo 46-5 Clamp a stop to the outfeed side of the saw table to position the jig. The centerline of the workpiece should line up with the center of the blade.

Screw the stop block to the rip fence as shown in *Photo* 46-4. Place a workpiece in the jig. If the tenon diameter is to equal workpiece thickness, then raise the dado cutter until it brushes the bottom of the workpiece.

Otherwise, raise the cutter until it reaches the tenon layout circle on the end of the workpiece. Position the miter gauge so that the center of the workpiece is in line with the center of the blade. Hold the jig in this position. Clamp a stop to the outfeed side of the saw table to keep the miter gauge from sliding any farther as shown in *Photo* 46-5.

Move the workpiece to the right until the shoulder of the tenon lines up with the left side of the blade. Move the rip fence over until the stop touches the workpiece, and lock it in place. Start the saw. Advance the miter gauge until it hits the stop on the table. Be sure to keep a good grip on the workpiece and to hold it against the stop on the fence as you move the jig.

Once the miter gauge hits the stop on the table, rotate the workpiece so that the top comes toward you as you make the cut. If the tenon is longer than the width of your dado cutter, pull the workpiece away from the stop and rotate it again to complete the tenon.

TABLE SAW TENONING JIG

Design by Ben Erickson

This jig lets you safely hold a workpiece when you're cutting tenons or bridle joints on the table saw. The jig straddles the rip fence, which guides the jig. The handle keeps your fingers clear of danger. The removable vertical fence stabilizes the stock. When the fence becomes too worn to support the stock properly, remove the fence and replace it.

The jig shown here was made for a rip saw fence that is 1¼ inches wide × 3 inches high. If your fence dimensions are different, just change the dimensions of the center block and handle to fit, as described in "Making the Jig."

MAKING THE JIG

1 Cut the parts to size. Choose stable, dense hardwood such as cherry or hard maple for the sides and center block. Quarter-sawn stock, if you can find it, is less likely to warp than plain-sawn wood. To further prevent warping, use wood that has had several weeks to adjust to the atmosphere in your shop.

Plane the center block and handle to about ¹⁄₁₆ thicker than your rip fence. Plane the sides to final thickness. Size the center block so that it will clear the rip fence and any adjustment nuts on top of the fence. Cut all parts to their final widths and lengths.

2 Test fit the jig. Clamp the sides to the center block and slip the assembly over the rip fence. Check how much side-to-side play there is. Plane the center block in ¹⁄₃₂-inch increments until the jig slips onto the rip fence with no side-to-side play. If the jig becomes too tight, cut a rabbet on the inside of one side as shown in the *Overall View*.

3 Cut the handle notch. The center block is notched to accept the handle. Lay out the notch as shown in the *Overall View*. Cut the notch with two passes of the dado cutter on the table saw. Set the cutter or blade to 1¾ inches high. Guide the block with a miter gauge.

OVERALL VIEW

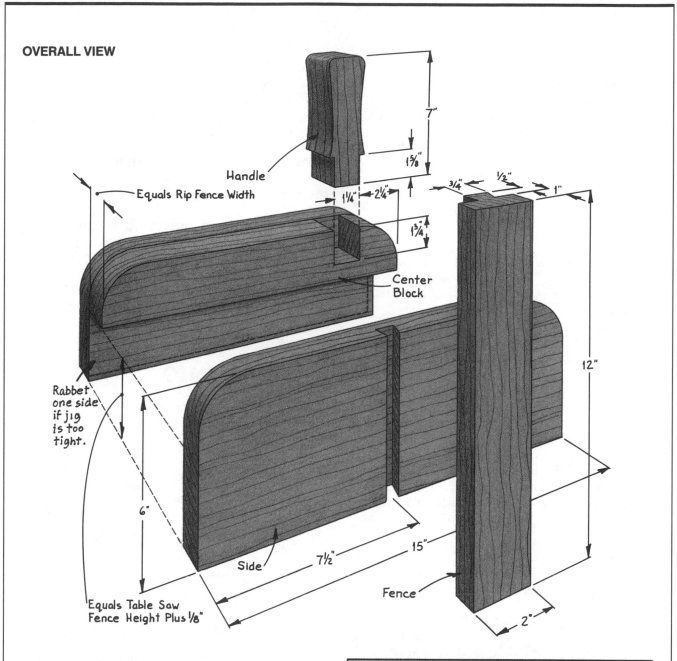

Handle

Equals Rip Fence Width

7"

1⅝"

1¼" ◄─► 2¼"

¾"   ½"   1"

1¾"

Center Block

12"

Rabbet one side if jig is too tight.

6"

Side

15"

7½"

2"

Fence

Equals Table Saw Fence Height Plus ⅛"

4 Glue up the jig body. Glue and clamp the sides to the center block. Avoid getting glue on the inside of the jig and in the handle notch. Be sure the two sides and center block are flush across the top. After the glue dries, remove the clamps, and plane or scrape off the excess glue from the top and ends. If necessary, true the jig's top on the jointer and its ends on the table saw.

5 Cut the dovetail and dovetail slot. The detachable fence is joined to the jig with a sliding dovetail, as shown in the *Overall View*.

MATERIALS LIST		
Quantity	Part	Dimensions
2	Hardwood sides	1" × 6" × 15"
1	Hardwood center block	1¼" × 2⅞" × 15"
1	Hardwood handle	1¼" × 1¾" × 7"
1	Hardwood fence	1½" × 2" × 12"

The dovetail on the fence and the dovetail slot in the side are made with two passes of a ½-inch dovetail bit. While you are set up to cut this joint, make a dozen or so extra fences. This will save you from having to set up to cut sliding dovetails every time you need a new fence.

Cut the dovetail slot across one side of the jig as shown in the *Overall View*. Neither the size nor the exact placement of the slot is critical. Just place the slot about halfway between the front and back of the jig. Cut the slot and the fence dovetail as described in "Routing Sliding Dovetails," page 27. Make the joint snug, so that you have to tap the fence into the side.

6 Cut the jig to shape. On the band saw, round the ends of the jig as shown in the *Overall View*. The exact shape is not important; just find a can or another round object to trace. Sand and scrape to clean up the saw marks. Round-over the edges with a ¼-inch-radius roundover bit on the table-mounted router.

7 Cut the handle to shape. Cut the front and back of the handle to fit into the notch in the center block as shown in the *Overall View*. Make these cuts on the table saw with a dado blade. Shape the handle on the band saw to fit your hand. Scrape and sand away the saw marks. Round-over the edges with a ⅜-inch

roundover bit on the table-mounted router. Glue the handle in the notch.

8 Finish the jig. Finish sanding the jig. Apply two coats of a penetrating oil finish to all surfaces and let dry.

9 Attach the fence. Tap the fence into the dovetail slot with a mallet until it is flush with the bottom of the jig.

10 Wax the fence and jig sides. After the finish has dried, lightly sand and wax the inside surfaces and bottom of the jig. This will help the jig slide more easily. Don't use wax with silicone in it. Silicone can contaminate the surfaces of your work and cause problems with some finishes.

USING THE JIG

As mentioned, you can make bridle joints as well as tenons with this jig. The standard mortise-and-tenon joint, shown at left in P*hoto* 47-1, is the stronger joint. The advantage of the bridle joint, shown at right in P*hoto* 47-1, is that you can make both parts of the joint with the tenoning jig. The bridle joint, also called an open mortise-and-tenon joint, is strong enough for most work, especially with modern woodworking glue. Either joint can be further locked with pegs. As with any machine work, it's always a good idea to lay out and test your cuts on scrap stock. Make sure the scrap is the same dimensions as your workpieces. If you are making mortise-and-tenon joints, make the mortise first, so that you can fine-tune the tenons to fit. For a bridle joint, it doesn't matter which part you make first, as either can be adjusted to fit.

Cutting deep tenons or bridles puts a lot of strain on your table saw. Use a sharp blade, and feed the stock slowly and steadily.

Making Tenons

Lay out the tenon on the end of your test piece. Cut the tenon shoulders first. Use the rip fence as a stop as shown in P*hoto* 47-2. Guide the workpiece with the miter gauge as you cut each shoulder.

Photo 47-1   At left is a mortise-and-tenon joint. At right is a bridle joint, also called an open mortise-and-tenon joint.

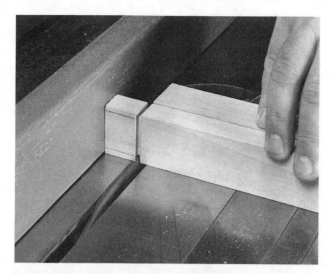

Photo 47-2 Cut the tenon shoulders first, using the rip fence as a stop.

LAYING OUT BRIDLES AND TENONS

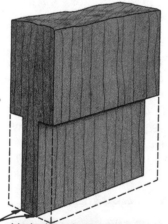

Align saw blade to outside of layout lines to cut tenon cheeks.

Align saw blade to inside of layout lines for bridle.

Place the tenoning jig on the table saw fence. With the saw turned off, hold the work upright against the jig's fence and slide the jig toward the blade. Move the saw fence to align the saw blade with a layout mark on the workpiece as shown in P*hoto* 47-3. Make sure the blade is on the waste side of the layout lines, as shown in *Laying Out Bridles and Tenons*. Then back the jig away. Raise the blade to a height equal to the length of the tenon. Start the saw and make the cut.

If the tenon is to be centered on the piece, simply turn the piece over to cut the other cheek. Test fit the tenon in a mortise. Adjust the fence position until you get a snug joint.

If the tenon is not centered, cut the first cheek on both ends of your test scrap, in case you need to make any adjustments. If you have no practice with the jig, you might want to cut the first cheek in a few pieces of scrap. Then cut the first cheek on all the workpieces. Now adjust the fence for the second cheek. Cut the second cheek on a piece of scrap and test its fit in the mortise. Adjust the saw fence until you get a snug joint. Then cut the second cheek in all the workpieces.

Shim between the workpiece and the jig with tape to make very slight adjustments in the tenon thickness. This is usually easier

Photo 47-3 Move the rip fence to align the saw blade with the layout mark on the workpiece.

than trying to make minute adjustments in the rip fence. Masking tape and plastic packing tape make great shims for this purpose. You can also add tape to the inside surfaces of the jig if it becomes loose from wear or warpage. If the jig becomes too tight, remove some stock from the inside with a cabinet scraper.

You can cut two tenon cheeks simultaneously by using two saw blades with a spacer between. Commercial spacer sets are available, or you can make your own from plywood, Plexiglas, or aluminum. Again, you can fine-tune the spacers with tape.

Regardless of how you cut the tenons, you will want to back up the stock to prevent tearout where the blade exits the piece. If the jig fence is new, it will act as a backup. After you have changed the setup a few times, creating a few cuts, tape a piece of ¼-inch-thick plywood to the front of the fence as a backup, as shown in *Photo* 47-4.

Photo 47-4   Tape a strip of ¼-inch plywood to the fence to prevent tearout.

Making Bridles

Cutting a bridle is much like cutting a tenon. In fact, the bridle layout will be the same as its matching tenon. (See *Laying Out Bridles and Tenons*.) The difference is that on a tenon, you cut away the outside, leaving the middle of the stock. On a bridle, you cut away the middle, leaving the outside.

Lay out the bridle. Align the saw blade to the inside of a layout line as shown in *Laying Out Bridles and Tenons*. Adjust the saw blade height to the bridle depth and make the cut. Then flip the piece around and cut again. Make both of these cuts in all your workpieces. If there is any waste left between the two cuts, reset the rip fence to remove waste. Run all the workpieces through. Reset the fence as many times as you need to remove all the waste.

After making a test bridle in scrap, you may decide that the saw teeth are leaving the bottom of the bridle too ragged. If so, make the bridle about ¹⁄₁₆ inch short of the layout line. Pare this last bit with a narrow chisel.

When you've cut all the bridle joints, cut matching tenons to fit into them.

Replacing Fences

Every time you change your setup, you'll put a new kerf in the jig fence. After four or five setups, the bottom of the jig's fence will be cut beyond use. When this happens, tap the fence out of its slot and turn it over. When the other end is used, you may be able to cut off both ends and use them again, if the kerfs aren't too long.

VENEER EDGE TRIMMER

Design by Glenn Bostock

It's common practice to attach veneer edge banding that is slightly wider than what it covers. Trimming it flush can be trickier than it looks. A utility knife often causes thin veneer to chip along the grain. Commercially available trimmers never seem to have enough bearing surface, so they often tip and cut into the edge of the stock.

The veneer-trimming jig shown here guarantees a perfect cut every time. The long bottom rail rides against the veneer or banding and keeps the thin layer from chipping. The wide base, in conjunction with the bottom rail, prevents tipping and produces a smoother cut. The optional bevel strip

angles the blade slightly, causing the veneer to bevel away from the edge. The Stanley #71 router plane

attaches easily to the base with two screws, and its handles provide firm jig control.

MAKING THE JIG

1 Make the base. Cut the base to the dimensions in the Materials List. Mill a 1/8-inch-deep × 3/8-inch-wide dado along the center of the base as shown in the *Overall View.* The dado runs the length of the base and provides clearance for waste. Cut the dado with three passes of a 1/8-inch-thick table saw blade.

2 Drill the cutter clearance hole. The router plane cutter or iron passes through a hole centered in the base as shown in the *Overall View.* Drill the hole with a 1 3/8-inch-diameter Forstner bit on the drill press.

3 Cut the bottom rail to size. Make the bottom rail from a scrap piece of hardwood such as maple or cherry. Joint, plane, rip, and cut the bottom rail to the dimensions in the Materials List.

4 Attach the bottom rail to the base. Position the base on the bottom rail as shown in the *Overall View.* Center the rail on the dado as shown in the *Overall View.*

Predrill and countersink the bottom rail for 1 1/4-inch drywall screws. Glue and screw the rail to the base.

5 Attach the optional bevel strip to the base. The laminate trimmer will work with or

OVERALL VIEW

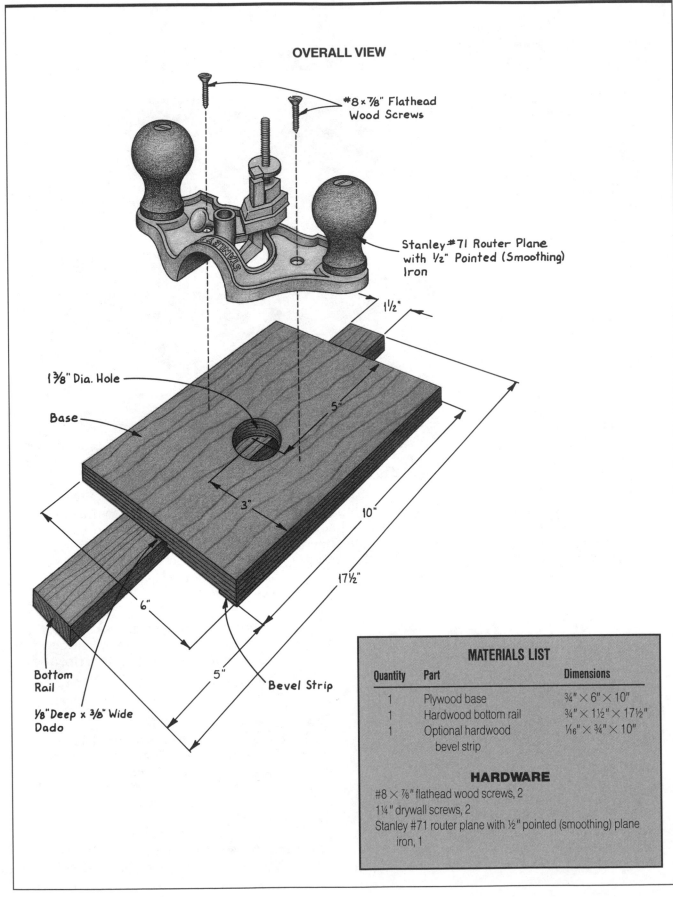

#8 × ⅞" Flathead Wood Screws

Stanley #71 Router Plane with ½" Pointed (Smoothing) Iron

1½"

1⅜" Dia. Hole

Base

5"

3"

10"

17½"

6"

5"

Bottom Rail

⅛" Deep x ⅜" Wide Dado

Bevel Strip

MATERIALS LIST

Quantity	Part	Dimensions
1	Plywood base	¾" × 6" × 10"
1	Hardwood bottom rail	¾" × 1½" × 17½"
1	Optional hardwood bevel strip	¹⁄₁₆" × ¾" × 10"

HARDWARE

#8 × ⅞" flathead wood screws, 2
1¼" drywall screws, 2
Stanley #71 router plane with ½" pointed (smoothing) plane iron, 1

without the bevel strip. By adding the bevel strip, you force the jig to work at a slight angle to the stock, creating a beveled edge. This bevel prevents the veneer from being torn away accidentally while the piece is in use. If you choose to add the strip, rip it from the edge of a ¾-inch-thick piece of hardwood. Glue and clamp the strip to the base in the position shown in the *Overall View.*

6 Attach the router plane to the base. Position the router plane on the base so that the shaft of the cutter just misses the back edge of the clearance hole. Screw the router plane in place with #8 × ⅞-inch flathead wood screws. Lower the cutter until it touches the top of the bottom rail.

USING THE JIG

This jig is very easy to use. First cut your edge banding or veneer so that it overhangs all edges by at least ¹⁄₁₆ inch. Clamp and glue the edge banding or veneer to the workpiece. To trim face veneer, run the jig base along the edge of the workpiece, as shown in *Photo* 48-1. To trim edge banding, run the jig base along the face of the workpiece, as shown in *Photo* 48-2.

As you work, the edge of the bottom rail slides against the veneer or banding, so that the waste is guided into the base dado. As the waste slides past the cutter, it is sliced away, leaving a perfect edge.

Photo 48-1 Trim face veneer by running the trimmer base along the edge of the workpiece.

Photo 48-2 Trim edge veneer by running the trimmer base along the face of the workpiece.

THE
MACHINES

DRILL PRESS
LATHE
PLANER
PLATE JOINER
POWER MITER SAW
RADIAL ARM SAW
ROUTER
TABLE SAW

DRILL PRESS AUXILIARY TABLE

Design by David Schiff

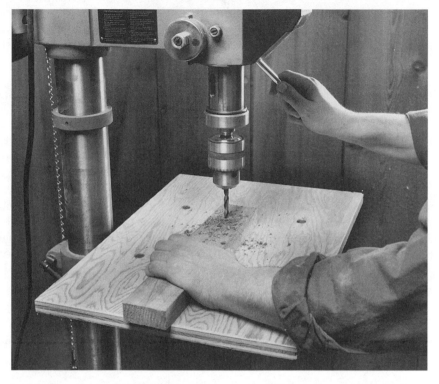

The drill press auxiliary table is just a piece of plywood bolted to the drill press table. Nonetheless, it's so useful that many woodworkers leave one bolted to their drill press at all times. To begin with, the auxiliary table increases the work surface, providing more support to the work and allowing easy clamping around the stops and sides.

The auxiliary table also helps prevent splintering when drilling a hole through a piece. Set the drilling depth about ⅛ inch deeper than the workpiece thickness, and drill through the workpiece and into the auxiliary table. The auxiliary table provides support around the exit hole, helping to eliminate splintering. When the auxiliary table gets too chewed up, dig up another scrap of plywood and use the old

OVERALL VIEW

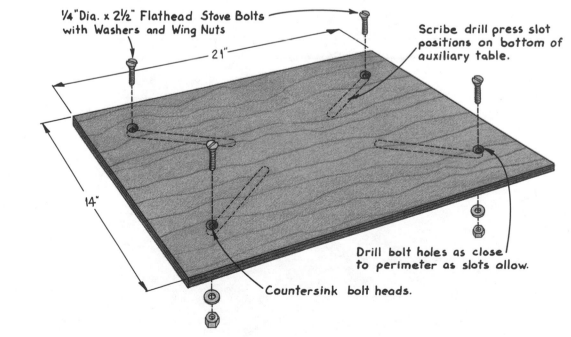

¼" Dia. x 2½" Flathead Stove Bolts with Washers and Wing Nuts

21"

14"

Scribe drill press slot positions on bottom of auxiliary table.

Drill bolt holes as close to perimeter as slots allow.

Countersink bolt heads.

auxiliary table as a template to drill the holes into the new one. It'll probably take about 10 minutes.

You'll find the auxiliary table indispensable if you use a hollow chisel mortiser on your drill press. Chisel mortising requires a lot of pressure. As a result, it's difficult to keep the piece from tilting into the hole in the center of the standard drill press table. The auxiliary table has no hole, eliminating this frustrating problem.

You'll also need an auxiliary table if you plan to build the "Drill Press Extension Table," page 229. The extension table is designed to fit over a ¾ × 14 × 21-inch auxiliary table like the one shown here.

To make the auxiliary table, cut a piece of ¾-inch-thick plywood to 14 × 21 inches. Center the auxiliary table on your drill press table and clamp it in place. Duck under the

table and scribe the position of the slots onto the bottom of the auxiliary table. Remove the auxiliary table.

The flathead stove bolts you use to attach the table must be long enough to go through the auxiliary table and the drill press table, with enough left over for the nut. The bolt diameter isn't crucial, as long as the washers will span the drill press table slots. For most drill presses, ¼-inch-diameter × 2½-inch bolts will do the job.

Drill four holes for the bolts. Drill through the slot layouts as close to the perimeter of the auxiliary table as the slots will allow. (See the *Overall View.*) Counterbore the holes through the top of the table, so that the machine bolts will be flush. Put the bolts through the holes and through the drill press table slots. Put a washer over each bolt and tighten the nuts onto the bolts.

DRILL PRESS EXTENSION TABLE

Design by Andy Rae

It's difficult to drill long boards or sheet goods on the press. You need one hand to operate the press, which leaves only one hand to keep the work from toppling off the machine.

The obvious solution is a long extension table on the drill press. But few shops are cavernous enough to justify dedicating 8 feet of wall space to the drill press. That's why the extension table shown here is designed to store against the wall when it's not being used. Just fold up the legs and pop it off the press.

The key to this table's convenience is lightweight construction. The table shown here is made from ½-inch melamine-coated particleboard. Plain particleboard or plywood would work as well. The table is made rigid by two pieces of 2 × 2-inch aluminum angle that run the length of the front and back edges.

The single leg on each end of the table is there to keep the table from tipping when a long workpiece is hanging off one end. The legs are spindly, because they don't need to support much weight. The legs do need to be adjustable, though, so the bottom part of each leg moves in a sliding dovetail. Pop the table onto your drill press and adjust the height of the drill press table as necessary.

Adjust the legs to match.

The extension table shown here is designed to fit over the plywood "Drill Press Auxiliary Table" described on page 227. That table is 14 inches wide × 21 inches long. If you already have an auxiliary table of a different size on your press, you only need to change the position of the risers and side blocks and, perhaps, the width of the extension table.

MAKING THE JIG

1 Make the table. Rip the particleboard or plywood to the dimensions in the Materials List. The table shown here was made from a sheet of particleboard that was factory-coated with melamine.

It's a good idea to protect the edges, because they'll get banged when you move the table on and off the drill press and stand

OVERALL VIEW

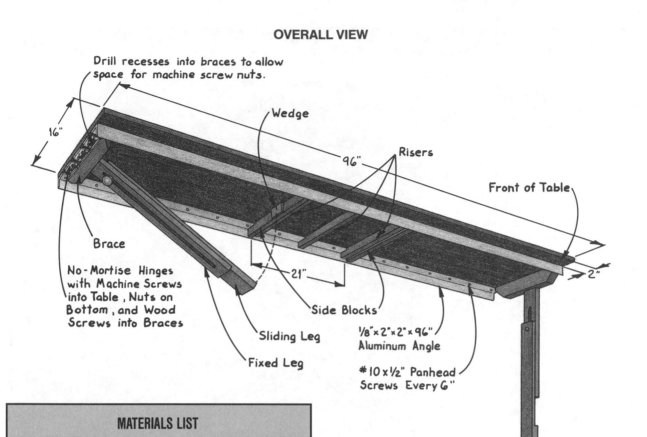

Drill recesses into braces to allow space for machine screw nuts.

16"

Wedge

Risers

96"

Front of Table

Brace

No-Mortise Hinges with Machine Screws into Table, Nuts on Bottom, and Wood Screws into Braces

21"

Side Blocks

2"

Sliding Leg

Fixed Leg

⅛"× 2"× 2"× 96" Aluminum Angle

#10 x ½" Panhead Screws Every 6"

MATERIALS LIST

Quantity	Part	Dimensions
1	Particleboard table	½" × 16" × 96"
2	Wood edgings	¼" × ½" × 96"
2	Wood edgings	¼" × ½" × 16½"
3	Softwood risers	¾" × 1¼" × 14"
2	Softwood side blocks	¾" × 2" × 14"
2	Hardwood braces	1⅛" × 2" × 10"
2	Hardwood fixed legs	¾" × 2" × 28"
2	Hardwood sliding legs	¾" × 2" × 32"
1	Hardwood dowel	½" dia. × 4"
1	Hardwood wedge	¼" × 2" × 2"

HARDWARE

1½" drywall screws, as needed

1" drywall screws, as needed

#10 × ½" panhead screws, as needed

#4 × ⅝" machine screws with nuts, 12

⅜" dia. × 1" machine bolts with washers, 2

1¼" × 3" no-mortise hinges, 6. Available from Woodworker's Supply, 5604 Alameda Place NE, Albuquerque, NM 87113-2100 (800-645-9292). Part #28704.

Plastic knobs with ⅜"-16 through-hole insert, 2. Available from Reid Tool Supply Co., 2265 Black Creek Road, Muskegon, MI 49444 (800-253-0421). Part #DK-57.

⅛" × 2" × 2" × 96" aluminum angles, 2

it against the wall. The edges of the table shown here are covered with melamine edge banding. Melamine edge banding comes in rolls and is backed with a heat-sensitive glue. You apply it with a warm iron and then trim it to width with a chisel or knife. If you prefer, you can protect the edges of your table with scrap wood. Attach the wood edging with glue and brads. Give the wood edging a quick sanding to slightly round the edges and to prevent splinters.

2 Cut and notch the risers and side blocks. Cut the risers and side blocks to the dimensions in the Materials List. Make a ⅛-inch-deep × 2-inch-long notch at both ends of each piece to fit around the aluminum angle as shown in the *Overall View.* Make the notches with a dado cutter in the table saw. Set the cutter to its maximum width and raise it ⅛ inch above the table. Lay out the shoulder of each notch and cut to this line, guiding the piece with the miter gauge. Make several more passes, removing the rest of the waste.

3 Attach the aluminum angles. The aluminum angle is screwed to the bottom of the table with #10 × ½-inch panhead screws. Mark the approximate positions of the blocks and risers on the angle. Then drill ³⁄₁₆-inch-diameter holes about every 6 inches along one face of each piece of angle. Do not drill in the marked areas.

The rear angle must be flush with the back edge, so that the table will clear the drill press post. Place the rear angle as shown in the *Overall View.* Screw it in place.

To position the front angle, remove the plywood auxiliary base from the drill press and use it as a spacer. First butt the auxiliary base against the rear aluminum angle and position the front aluminum angle firmly against the other side. Screw the front angle to the table, sliding the auxiliary base along to keep the angle in position.

4 Attach the risers. The risers and side blocks are glued and screwed to the bottom of the table. Place the table upside down on your workbench. Glue the middle riser in place so that it bisects the length of the table.

To position the side risers, center the auxiliary base over the middle riser. Apply glue and slip the side risers under the auxiliary base so that the risers are flush with the auxiliary base edges. Clamp the risers in place and turn the table over. Drill pilot holes through the top and into each riser, and countersink for three 1-inch drywall screws. Screw the risers in place.

5 Attach the side blocks. Flip the table upside down. Put glue on the side blocks where they will contact the side risers and the bottom of the table. Clamp the side blocks to the table. Countersink and screw the side blocks to the side risers with 1½-inch drywall screws. Let the glue dry overnight and turn your attention to the legs.

6 Make the braces. The legs are tenoned into braces at the top. The braces provide more surface for hinging, making the table more stable. To make the braces, cut two pieces of stock to the dimensions in the Materials List. Shape the braces to the

MORTISE AND TENON DETAIL

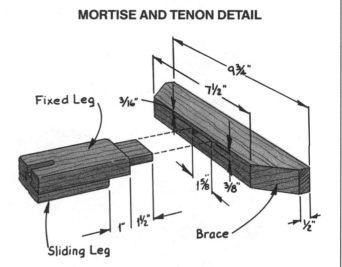

dimensions shown in the *Mortise and Tenon Detail.* Mortise the braces as shown in the *Mortise and Tenon Detail.* For more information on mortising, see "Small Parts Mortising Jig for the Plunge Router," page 132.

7 Cut the fixed legs to size and make the dovetail grooves. The dovetail groove begins at the bottom of the fixed leg and stops about 2 inches from the top. To avoid straining your router and dovetail bit, first remove most of the waste with a dado cutter on the table saw. To do this, cut a stopped dado ⁷⁄₁₆ inch deep × ¼ inch wide down the center of the leg. Stop the dado 2 inches from the end of the board. For more information, see "Cutting Dadoes and Grooves," page 36.

Chuck a ¾-inch dovetail bit in a table-mounted router. Set the bit ⅜ inch high. Rout a groove down the center of each leg. Stop the groove 2 inches from one end of the leg. (See "Routing Sliding Dovetails," page 27.) Rout a groove in each fixed leg that stops 2 inches from one end of the leg. Turn off the router before removing the leg. When the bit stops, pull the leg back toward you until it is free of the bit.

8 Cut the bolt slot in the fixed leg. As shown in the *Sliding Dovetail Detail,* a bolt comes through the dovetail in each sliding leg and through a slot in each fixed leg. A washer and plastic knob thread onto this bolt to loosen and tighten the sliding leg.

Rout this ⅜-inch-wide slot either with a

SLIDING DOVETAIL DETAIL

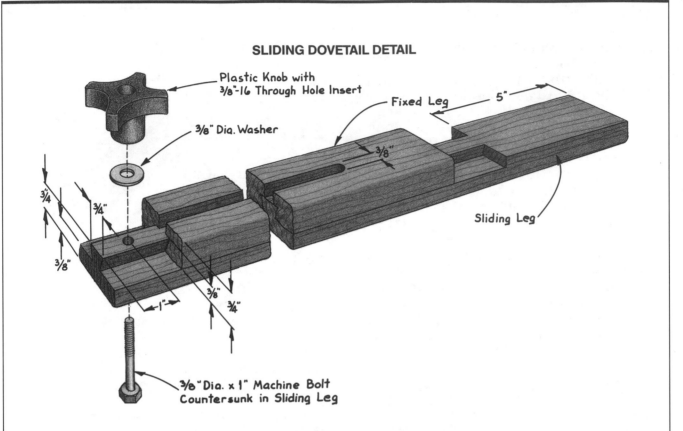

Plastic Knob with 3/8"-16 Through Hole Insert

3/8" Dia. Washer

Fixed Leg

5"

3/8"

Sliding Leg

3/4

3/4"

3/8"

1"

3/8"

3/4"

3/8" Dia. x 1" Machine Bolt Countersunk in Sliding Leg

plunge router and fence or on the router table as described in "Making Stopped Cuts on the Router Table," page 24. Stop the slot 2½ inches from the bottom and 2 inches from the top of the fixed leg.

9 Make tenons on the fixed legs. The dimensions of the tenon at the top of each fixed leg are shown in *Mortise and Tenon Detail.* You can cut these tenons with the "Table Saw Tenoning Jig" described on page 216. Or you can cut the tenons on the table saw without a jig, as discussed in "Making Joints," page 39.

10 Dovetail the sliding leg. "Routing Sliding Dovetails" on page 27 shows how to cut this dovetail on the router table. If you were making this sliding dovetail as a furniture joint, you would want it to be snug. But for the legs, the joint should be loose enough that the weight of the sliding legs causes them to drop when you loosen the knob. This means the dovetail in the sliding leg must be a scant ¾ inch. Test your router table setup on scrap until you get a dovetail that slides easily in the groove.

When you get the setup right, rout each sliding leg, stopping 5 inches from the bottom as shown in the *Sliding Dovetail Detail.* Draw a line square across the bottom of the dovetails. Chop along the line with a chisel to create square shoulders on the dovetail.

11 Round the edges of the legs. Assemble the legs and make sure they work properly. Then round the four long edges with a ⅜-inch roundover bit in the router. (See *Sliding Dovetail Detail.*) If you like, you can skip the routing and just round the edges slightly with sandpaper.

12 Install the bolt. Drill a ⅜-inch-diameter hole through the dovetail in each sliding leg. Locate the hole about 1 inch from the top of each sliding leg. Place the bolt through the bottom of the sliding leg as shown in the *Sliding Dovetail Detail.* Trace the bolt head onto the back of each sliding leg. Remove the bolt and chisel a hex-shaped recess, so that the bolt will be flush to the surface and won't be able to turn when you tighten and loosen the knob. Assemble the legs, machine bolt, washer, and knob. A pair of router handle knobs was used on the legs shown in the photograph. The Materials List provides a source for the handles shown in the drawings.

13 Glue the legs to the braces. Put glue into each mortise and insert the leg tenons into the braces. Make sure that the edges of the legs and braces are flush. If not, remove the leg, flip it over, and reinsert the tenon. Drill a ½-inch-diameter hole through each joint and pin it with a piece of ½-inch-diameter dowel. Cut off the dowel on both ends and pare it flush with a chisel.

14 Hinge the legs to the table. Hinge each leg to the bottom of the table with three no-mortise hinges as shown in the *Overall View*.

Attach the hinges to the braces first, using the wood screws that come with the hinges. Wood screws won't hold in particle-board or plywood, so attach the hinges to the table with #4 × ⅝-inch machine screws and nuts. To do this, position the braces 1⅛ inches from the ends of the table and mark the hinge screw holes on the bottom of the table. Predrill the holes, then turn the table over and countersink for the machine screw heads. Insert the screws, put the hinges over the screws, and install the nuts.

Open the legs. The hinge nuts will prevent the legs from folding all the way out. Mark where the tops of the legs hit the nuts. Close the legs and drill out shallow recesses in the braces, so that the legs can close over the nuts.

15 Make and install the wedges. The wedges are glued to the outside of the side blocks. They keep the legs from swinging open when you move the table around.

There should be ¼ inch between the legs and the side blocks, but measure the difference in case it is different. To make the wedges, start with a piece of ¼-inch-thick × 2-inch-wide scrap of wood that is at least 10 inches long. Clamp it to your bench, and then use a hand plane or belt sander to taper both ends. Cut off 2-inch lengths from both ends. Put glue on the wedges, put them in place, and then close the legs to act as clamps until the glue dries.

DRILL PRESS POSITIONING GUIDE

Design by Fred Matlack

This simple drill press fixture takes minutes to make and will save you hours of layout time.

Let's say, for example, that you want to drill a hole 2 inches from the top of a piece and center it on the piece's width. Unfortunately, you need to make 48 identical holes in 48 identical pieces. Lay out the hole on one piece. Put the piece on the fixture, against the stops. Put the fixture on the press, and move the fixture to align the layout mark with the drill press bit. Clamp the fixture to the drill press table and drill the hole. You don't need to lay out the hole on the remaining pieces. Just put them against the stop and drill the hole.

This jig is unusual in

that it does not have a single crucial dimension. Any bits of scrap will do. Just make

the base wide enough to support the work and long enough that C-clamps can

OVERALL VIEW

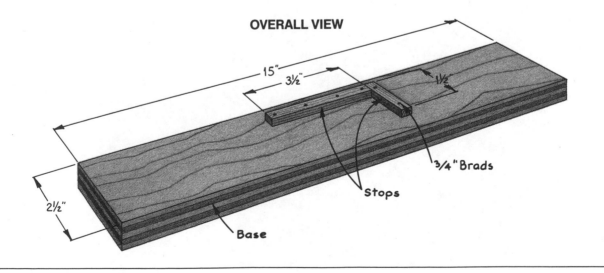

15"

3½"

1½"

3/4" Brads

Stops

2½"

Base

MATERIALS LIST

Quantity	Part	Dimensions
1	Plywood base	¾" × 2½" × 15"
1	Wood stop	¼" × ⅜" × 3½"
1	Wood stop	¼" × ⅜" × 1½"

HARDWARE

¾" brads, as needed

reach it from the ends of the drill press table. The stops can be any size, as long as there is enough wood to drive brads into. The fixture shown here is narrow because it was made to bore dowel holes into small stiles and rails.

Do take the trouble to make the stops square to each other. But the stops don't need to be perfectly square to the base.

If you are working on pieces that are not rectangular, start with a base large enough to support the piece. Lay the work-piece on the base and scribe part of its perimeter on the base. Then tack down as many stops as you'll need to orient the piece.

BOWL FINISHING CHUCK

Design by Ernie Conover

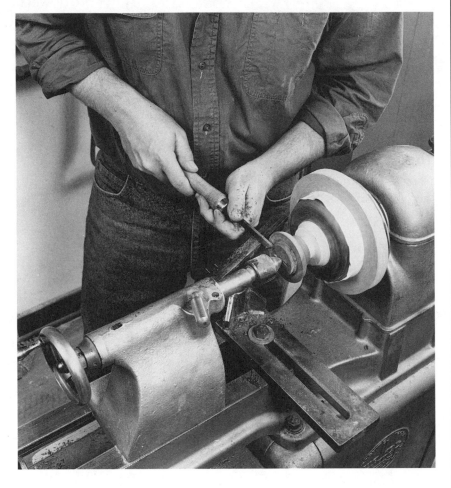

Making the final cuts on the bottom of a bowl always is a problem. The headstock of the lathe gets in the way. And since the bowl is attached from the bottom, you can't get to that surface to polish it. The bowl finishing chuck shown here solves the problem. It lets you mount the bowl on the lathe with the bottom facing out, away from the headstock. This chuck is made from a disc of plywood or medium-density fiberboard (MDF), with a groove cut in it to match the rim of your bowl. The bowl is held in place with tape. Sometimes pressure from the tailstock is used as well.

MAKING THE JIG

1 Cut out the chuck. Draw a circle on a piece of plywood or MDF that is 1 inch larger in diameter than your bowl. Cut this disc on the band saw.

2 Turn the chuck. Screw the chuck to a face plate and mount it on the lathe. Switch on the lathe and turn the chuck round with a scraper. While the lathe is still running, mark the center with a pencil. Shut off the lathe. Lay out the outside and inside diameters of your bowl rim on the chuck with a compass. Make the layout line dark enough that you can see it with the lathe running.

Switch on the lathe again and use a parting tool to turn a ¼-inch-deep groove between the layout lines.

USING THE JIG

Put tape around the rim of the bowl and press the bowl into the groove, as shown in *Photo* 52-1. If the bowl rim is true and the groove is tight enough, the tape alone will hold the bowl in place. However, this is not often the case. Most of the time, it's worthwhile to use the tailstock to help hold the bowl in place, as shown in *Photo* 52-2. Once you have secured the bowl, switch on the lathe and finish the bottom of the bowl.

OVERALL VIEW

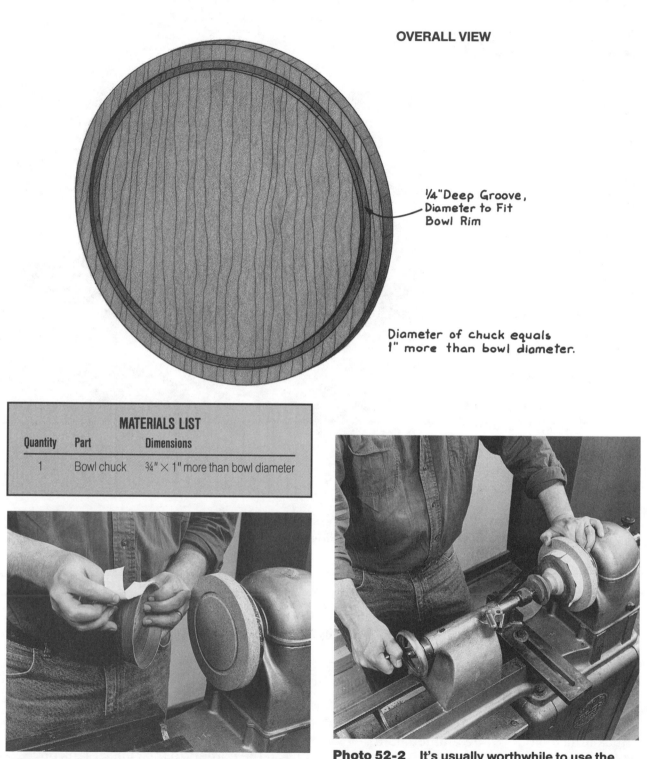

¼"Deep Groove,
Diameter to Fit
Bowl Rim

Diameter of chuck equals
1" more than bowl diameter.

MATERIALS LIST		
Quantity	Part	Dimensions
1	Bowl chuck	¾" × 1" more than bowl diameter

Photo 52-1   Put tape around the rim of the bowl and press the bowl into place on the chuck.

Photo 52-2   It's usually worthwhile to use the tailstock in addition to the tape to hold the bowl in place.

JAM CHUCK

Design by Ernie Conover

There are many ways to hold work on a lathe, ranging from $300 commercial chucks to strips of double-stick tape stuck on a face plate. One inexpensive method is to make and use a jam chuck. A jam chuck uses friction to hold the workpiece in place. It consists of a block of wood screwed to a face plate, with a slightly tapered recess turned in its face. The workpiece is jammed into the recess, and the taper holds it securely. This is the same principle that tools with a Morse taper use.

It is best to start by holding small things with jam chucks until you get used to the limitations. Turner Ernie Conover offers what he calls the first rule of jam chucks: "Thou shalt not jam-chuck anything thou are not prepared to get hit in the head with." Once you get used to the technique,

objects as large as croquet balls can be safely jam-chucked.

Jam chucks have several advantages. They are inexpensive, so you can make one to fit a specific project. Work can always be made to run true. You never waste wood for a spigot or foot, which the metal chucks require. Jam chucks don't leave marks on the work, and they can be set up quickly. For certain applications, a jam chuck is the tool to use.

MAKING THE JIG

1 Rough out the chuck blank. Make the chuck from a block of fine-grained hardwood. The size in the Materials List is approximate. Make the chuck to fit the project you have in mind. It should be at least ¾ inch larger in diameter than your workpiece. This will allow for a minimum wall thickness of ⅜ inch. You may have to glue up the chuck blank from thinner blocks of wood. Square one end of the chuck blank to the sides. This end must be flat, so that it will seat well against the face plate. Cut off the corners of the chuck blank on the band saw, leaving the blank roughly octagonal in shape. This makes it much easier to turn.

2 Mount the face plate on the blank. Center the face plate on the flat end of the

OVERALL VIEW

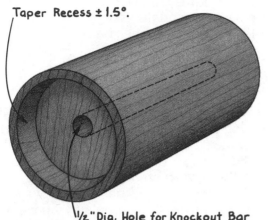

Taper Recess ± 1.5°.

½"Dia. Hole for Knockout Bar

MATERIALS LIST		
Quantity	Part	Dimensions
1	Hardwood chuck	4" × 4" × 6"
HARDWARE		

#12 × 1½" sheet-metal screws, as needed

blank and secure it with screws. Sheet-metal screws hold very well in end grain.

3 Turn the blank. Mount the blank on the lathe and turn it round. Turn a tapered recess in the face of the blank to fit your workpiece as shown in the *Overall View.* Cut the recess with a bowl gouge or a round-nosed scraper as shown in *Photo 53-1.* The sides of the recess should taper in at about 1.5 degrees. Check the taper with your workpiece. If the piece will not stay in the chuck, you have too much

taper. If the piece goes in too far and does not grab, you do not have enough taper. In either instance, you simply have to rework the taper with your chisels. You can keep reworking the chuck until you get to the screws that hold it to the face plate.

4 Drill the chuck. Drill a ½-inch-diameter hole through the chuck as shown in the *Overall View.* This will enable you to slide a bar or dowel through the lathe spindle and into the chuck to loosen the work when you are

Photo 53-1   Cut the recess in the jam chuck with a bowl gouge or a round-nosed scraper.

Photo 53-2   Rap the workpiece once with a mallet to seat it in the jam chuck.

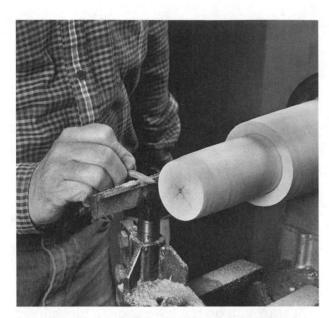

Photo 53-3 To make sure the workpiece is centered in the chuck, turn on the lathe and hold a pencil against the workpiece. Turn off the lathe and tap where the pencil has marked.

finished turning. If your lathe does not have a hollow spindle, you can drill a hole through the chuck at an angle, so that the hole comes out the side of the chuck instead.

USING THE JIG

Mount your work in the chuck by simply pressing it into the recess. Rap it once with a mallet to seat it securely, as shown in Photo 53-2. To make sure the workpiece is centered in the chuck, turn on the lathe and hold a pencil against the workpiece as shown in Photo 53-3. Turn off the lathe and tap where the pencil has marked the workpiece. Once you get the piece centered and well-seated, you are ready to turn.

LATHE CENTER SCRIBE

Design by
Michael Dunbar

A lathe center scribe is used for drawing a horizontal line along a turning's edge. The line lies in the same plane as the lathe's centers. The jig is handy for laying out details that are equally spaced around the turning. It is particularly useful for laying out reeds or flutes that will be carved by hand. The scribe works best on a lathe with a flat bed. It works on a lathe with a double tube bed. It will not, however, work on a lathe with a single tube bed, as it will not ride consistently on the rounded surface.

The dimensions given are for a scribe that will work well on most big lathes. If it doesn't seem right for your machine, you will have to modify the dimensions to suit your needs.

MAKING THE JIG

1 Make the foot. Cut stock for the foot to the dimensions in the Materials List. The coved corners on the foot are not necessary for function; they just dress up the scribe a bit. If you choose to cut the coves, cut them on the band saw as shown in the *Foot Detail*. Drill holes for the upright and the machine bolt as shown in the *Foot Detail*. Use the band saw to cut the saw kerf as shown.

2 Make the upright. For the upright, cut a length of ¾-inch-diameter dowel to the size in the Materials List. Drill a ⁵⁄₁₆-inch-diameter pencil hole through the upright as shown in the *Upright Detail*. Drill a centered hole through the top of the upright for the T-nut. The T-nut

FOOT DETAIL

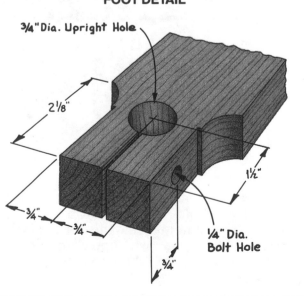

3/4"Dia. Upright Hole

2⅛"

1½"

¾"   ¾"

¾"

¼" Dia. Bolt Hole

OVERALL VIEW

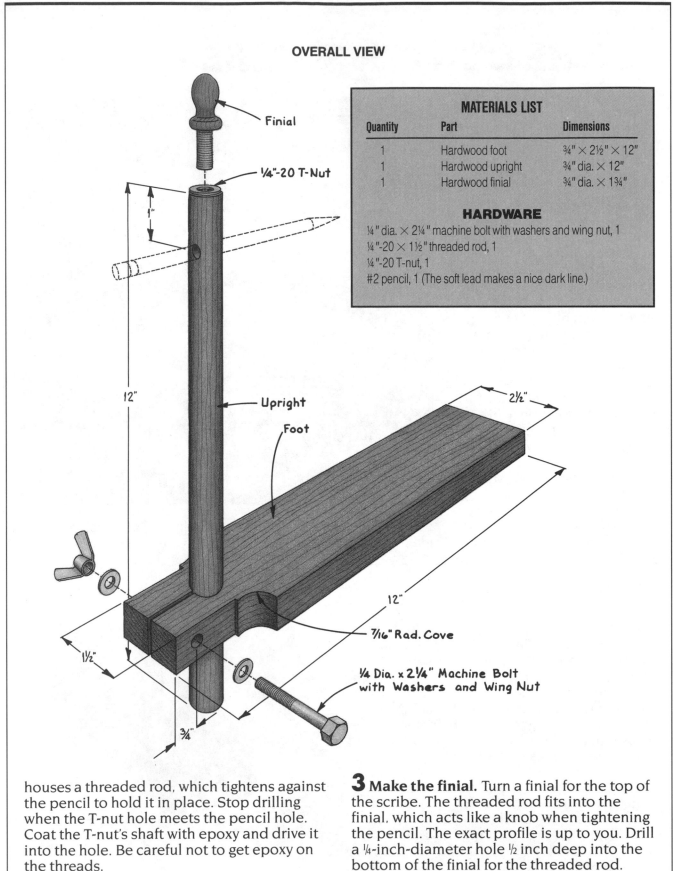

Finial

¼"-20 T-Nut

1"

12"

Upright

Foot

2½"

12"

7/16" Rad. Cove

1½"

¾"

¼ Dia. x 2¼" Machine Bolt
with Washers and Wing Nut

MATERIALS LIST		
Quantity	Part	Dimensions
1	Hardwood foot	¾" × 2½" × 12"
1	Hardwood upright	¾" dia. × 12"
1	Hardwood finial	¾" dia. × 1¾"

HARDWARE

¼" dia. × 2¼" machine bolt with washers and wing nut, 1
¼"-20 × 1½" threaded rod, 1
¼"-20 T-nut, 1
#2 pencil, 1 (The soft lead makes a nice dark line.)

houses a threaded rod, which tightens against the pencil to hold it in place. Stop drilling when the T-nut hole meets the pencil hole. Coat the T-nut's shaft with epoxy and drive it into the hole. Be careful not to get epoxy on the threads.

3 Make the finial. Turn a finial for the top of the scribe. The threaded rod fits into the finial, which acts like a knob when tightening the pencil. The exact profile is up to you. Drill a ¼-inch-diameter hole ½ inch deep into the bottom of the finial for the threaded rod.

UPRIGHT DETAIL

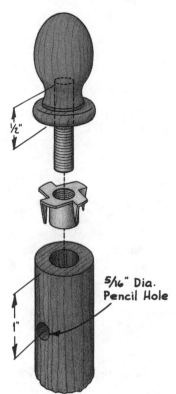

½"

5/16" Dia.
Pencil Hole

1"

Epoxy the threaded rod in place. Be careful not to get epoxy on the exposed threads.

4 Assemble the scribe. Put a washer on the bolt, slide the bolt through the hole in the foot, add another washer, and thread on the wing nut. Put the upright in its hole and tighten the wing nut to hold it in place. Slip the pencil through the pencil hole until the point protrudes 2 or 3 inches. Tighten the finial to hold the pencil in place. There should be just a small gap between the finial

and the upright when the pencil is in place. If the gap is too big, grind a little off the bottom of the threaded rod.

USING THE JIG

Place the foot of the scribe on the lathe bed and adjust the upright until the pencil point aligns with the point in the drive center. Tighten the wing nut to retain this setting. Mount the piece to be scribed on the lathe. Hold the foot flush on the bed and slide it along, allowing the pencil to draw a line on your work as shown in P*hoto* 54-1. The scribe can be used in conjunction with an indexing head if you need to draw lines that are evenly spaced around the turning.

Photo 54-1 Hold the foot of the center scribe on the lathe bed. Slide it along, allowing the pencil to draw a line on your work.

MANDREL CHUCK FOR THE LATHE

Design by Ernie Conover

Mandrel chucks solve the vexing problem of holding hollow work on the lathe. They can be used individually or in pairs to mount rings, tubes, bracelets, and napkin rings quickly and securely for turning. You can make them any size to fit your project needs.

A mandrel chuck is a gently tapered, hardwood cylinder. Slide the workpiece on the chuck until it wedges in place.

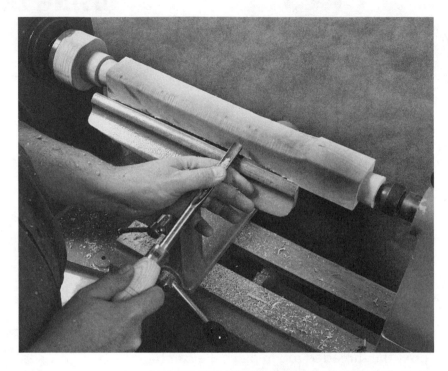

MAKING THE JIG

Turn the cylinders. Screw the mandrel stock to a face plate. Mount the plate on your lathe. Turn the stock until you form a cylinder. From there, taper the chuck to the profile

MATERIALS LIST

Quantity	Part	Dimensions
1	Mandrel	1¾" × 1¾" × 4"
1	Mandrel plug	1¾" × 1¾" × 3"

OVERALL VIEW

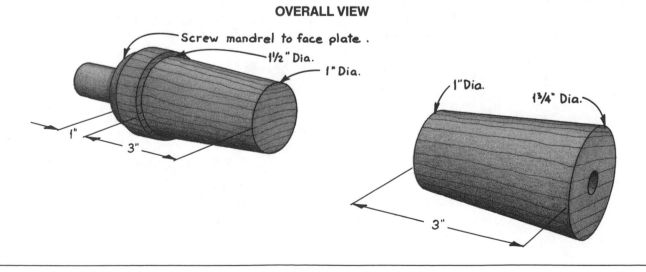

Screw mandrel to face plate.
1½" Dia.
1" Dia.
1"
3"

1" Dia.
1¾" Dia.
3"

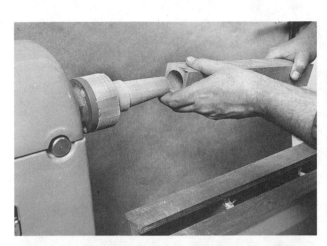

Photo 55-1   Slide the work onto the mandrel chuck until it wedges in place.

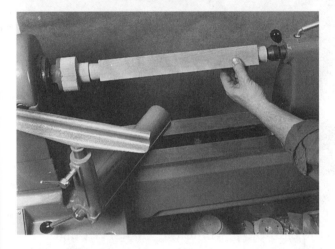

shown in the *Overall View.* This taper will work well in most situations. As you get used to using mandrel chucks, you will sense how much taper you need for a given situation. If you need to support a long, hollow piece, turn a tapered plug as shown.

USING THE JIG

To use a mandrel chuck, slide your work onto the chuck until it wedges in place, as shown in P*hoto* 55-1. Turn the lathe by hand to make sure the work will run true. Tap the piece with a mallet to align it, if necessary. If you are turning a long, hollow tube, support it with a mandrel plug on the lathe's tailstock as shown in P*hoto* 55-2. To fasten the plug, put the cylinder on the mandrel, slide the plug into the cylinder, and advance the tailstock.

Photo 55-2   If you are turning a long, hollow tube, support it with a mandrel plug on the lathe's tailstock.

LATHE PATTERN HOLDER

Design by Phil Gehret

When turning chair legs, spindles, or balusters or duplicating any part, it is very helpful to have a pattern right behind the turning. This provides constant feedback as to how your turning is shaping up.

The pair of pattern holders shown here clamps between the ways of your lathe. Just rest the pattern on a drywall screw driven into each holder.

The holders shown here use two old knobs that woodworker Phil Gehret always knew he'd use someday. The bolts bottomed out inside these knobs, so Gehret added three washers between each knob and base. This allows

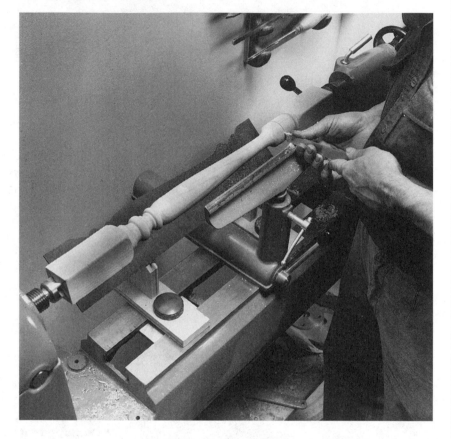

the bolts to pull the clamp pads tight. You could eliminate the washers by using through knobs or wing nuts.

MAKING THE JIG

1 Cut the parts to size. Cut the bases, pattern supports, and clamp pads to the dimensions in the Materials List. Measure 2½ inches along one long side of each pattern support to lay out the angled cuts shown in the *Overall View.* Make the angled cuts.

2 Drill the holes. Lay out ³⁄₁₆-inch-diameter holes in the bases and clamp pads as shown in the *Overall View.* Drill the holes.

3 Assemble the holders. Position a pattern support on a base as shown in the *Overall View.* Counterbore and predrill through the base and into the pattern support for two drywall screws. Insert the screws. Repeat the procedure for the other pattern holder.

Drive a drywall screw into the angled end of each support to hold the pattern. Center the screw from side to side and position it ½ inch from the lower edge of the angled side, as shown in the drawing. Drive the screw until the head protrudes ¾ inch.

Put the bolts through the clamping pads, the bases, and the washers. Screw the knobs in place.

OVERALL VIEW

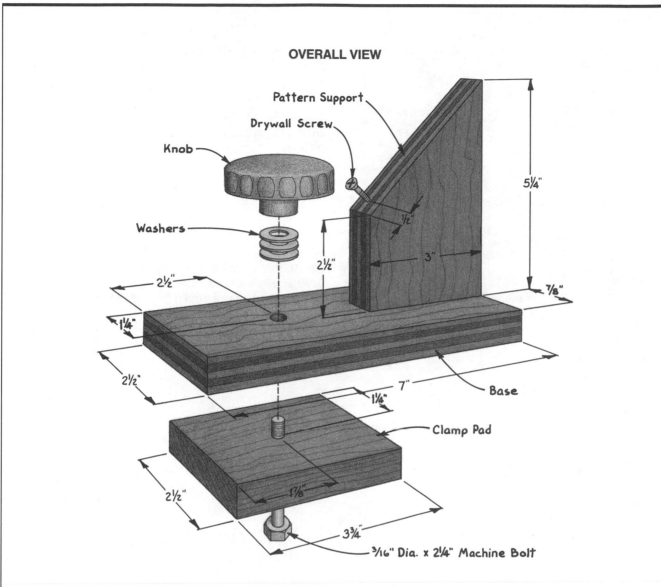

Pattern Support
Drywall Screw
Knob
Washers
5¼"
½"
2½"
3"
7⁄8"
2½"
1¼"
2½"
7"
1¼"
Base
Clamp Pad
1⅞"
2½"
3¾"
³⁄₁₆" Dia. × 2¼" Machine Bolt

MATERIALS LIST		
Quantity	**Part**	**Dimensions**
2	Plywood bases	¾" × 2½" × 7"
2	Plywood pattern supports	¾" × 3" × 5¼"
2	Hardwood clamp pads	⅜" × 2½" × 3¾"

HARDWARE

1¼" drywall screws, 6
³⁄₁₆" dia. × 2¼" machine bolts, 2
Washers, as needed
Knobs or wing nuts to fit bolts, 2

USING THE JIG

To put the holders on the lathe, turn the clamp pads perpendicular to the bases, so that the pads fit between the ways. Then turn the pads parallel to the bases to capture the ways between pad and base. Tighten the knobs.

For exact duplication, make an accurate, full-scale drawing of the shape you will turn. Attach the drawing to a piece of hardboard. Cut the shape carefully on the band saw, cutting inside the layout lines. Keep the cutoff intact, as you'll use it later to check the profile. Rest the pattern on the holders. Use the pattern as a visual aid as you turn the piece roughly to shape. When you get close

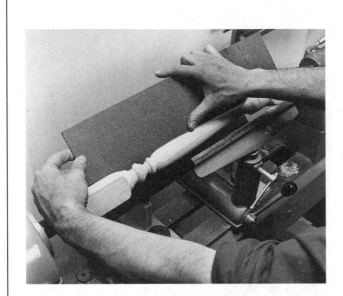

to the final profile, use the cutoff as a gauge, holding it against the turning until it fits into the profile, as shown in Photo 56-1.

For work where exact duplication is not crucial, such as round tapered legs, you can turn one piece and then place it on the holders as a visual guide for subsequent turnings.

Photo 56-1 When you get close to the final profile, use the pattern cutoff as a gauge, holding it against the turning until it fits the profile.

A STEADY REST FOR THE LATHE

Design by Andy Bukovsky

Turning long, slender spindles on a lathe can be a real trial. They flex, vibrate, and generally make a nuisance of themselves as they spin. This steady rest was designed to make delinquent spindles behave. It mounts on the lathe near the center of the turning. Three ball bearings provide extra support and stability to the work as you turn. They stabilize the most unruly spindle without marring the surface. The ball bearings are narrow, so you can turn all but a little bit of the spindle before you have to move the jig.

As shown in the *Overall View*, the ball bearings are mounted on the ends of three adjustable arms. Position the arms to support the spindle and then fix the posi-

tion by tightening the three wing nuts.

This steady rest was designed to fit a full-size

lathe with a flat bed. You may have to alter the dimensions to fit the size and style of your lathe.

MAKING THE JIG

1 Cut the parts to size. Cut all the parts to the dimensions in the Materials List.

2 Make the base. Rout a slot in the base for the ⅜-inch-diameter × 2½-inch carriage bolt. (See "Making Stopped Cuts on the Router Table," page 24.) Position the slot as shown in the *Overall View*.

3 Make the upright. Cut the upright on the band saw to the shape shown in the *Upright Detail*. Rout the dadoes for the arms with a

table-mounted router. Position the dadoes as shown in the *Upright Detail*. Rout the slots in the center of the dadoes for the ⁵⁄₁₆-inch-diameter × 2-inch carriage bolts. Again, refer to the *Upright Detail* for placement.

4 Assemble the base and upright. Using glue and 1⅝-inch drywall screws, attach the upright to the base so that the bottoms of the pieces are flush. Cut a 45-degree angle on one end of the inside brace. Cut the blank for the diagonal brace in half to form a triangle.

OVERALL VIEW

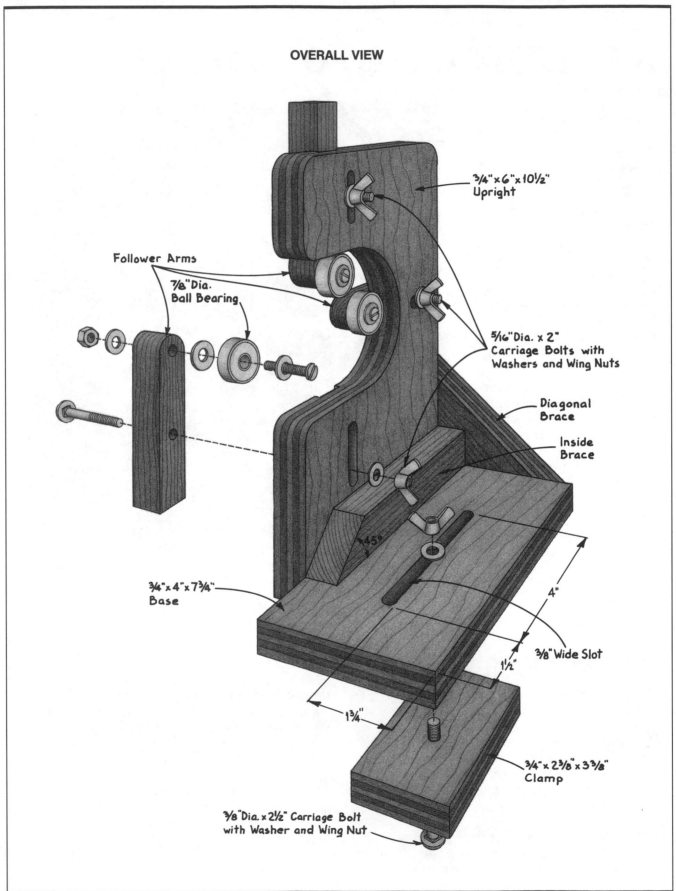

3/4" x 6" x 10½"
Upright

Follower Arms

7/8" Dia.
Ball Bearing

5/16" Dia. x 2"
Carriage Bolts with
Washers and Wing Nuts

Diagonal
Brace

Inside
Brace

45°

4"

3/8" Wide Slot

1½"

3/4" x 4" x 7¾"
Base

1¾"

3/4" x 2⅜" x 3⅜"
Clamp

3/8" Dia. x 2½" Carriage Bolt
with Washer and Wing Nut

MATERIALS LIST

Quantity	Part	Dimensions
1	Plywood base	¾" × 4" × 7¾"
1	Plywood upright	¾" × 6" × 10½"
1	Plywood diagonal brace	¾" × 3½" × 3½"
1	Maple brace	¾" × 1³⁄₁₆" × 6"
1	Plywood clamp	¾" × 2⅜" × 3⅜"
3	Maple arms	¾" × ¾" × 4½"

HARDWARE

1⅝" drywall screws, as needed
1½" machine screws, diameter to fit ball bearings' inside
   diameter, with washers and nuts, 3
⅜" dia. × 2½" carriage bolt with washer and wing nut, 1
⁵⁄₁₆" dia. × 2" carriage bolts with washers and wing nuts, 3
⅞" outside diameter ball bearings, 3

Use glue and 1⅝-inch drywall screws to fasten the braces to the jig, positioning them as shown in the *Overall View*. Drill a hole in the center of the clamp. Slide the ⅜-inch-diameter × 2½-inch carriage bolt through the clamp and up through the slot in the base. Secure the bolt with a washer and a wing nut.

5 **Make the followers.** On the belt sander, round the bearing end of each follower arm to a ⅜-inch radius. Drill two holes through each arm as shown in the *Arm Detail*. Note that the horizontal arm is shorter than the other two. Screw the bearings in place, then attach the arms to the jig with the ⁵⁄₁₆-inch-diameter × 2-inch carriage bolts, washers, and wing nuts, as shown in the *Overall View*.

USING THE JIG

Mount the jig on the bed of your lathe. The clamp will hang below the bed to lock the jig in place. Slide the jig to the center of your turning. Move the jig back and forth until the upper and lower arms are centered

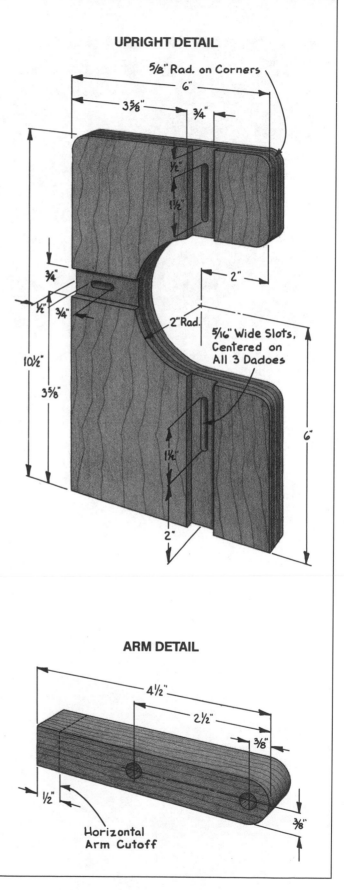

UPRIGHT DETAIL

5/8" Rad. on Corners
6"
3⅝"
¾"
½"
1½"
¾"
½" ¾"
10½"
3⅝"
2"
2" Rad.
5/16" Wide Slots, Centered on All 3 Dadoes
1¼"
6"
2"

ARM DETAIL

4½"
2½"
⅜"
½"
⅜"
Horizontal Arm Cutoff

Photo 57-1   Tighten the clamp to hold the steady rest in position.

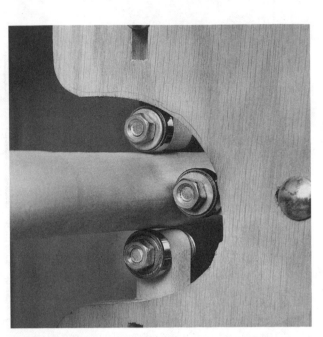

Photo 57-2   Adjust the followers so that they rest lightly on the turning.

on the axis of the turning. Tighten the clamp to hold the jig in position, as shown in Photo 57-1.

Adjust the followers so that they rest lightly on the turning as shown in Photo 57-2. Be careful not to push the turning out of line. Tighten the wing nuts. The steady rest is now ready to stabilize the spindle as you turn.

PLANER BOARD FOR THIN STOCK

Design by Andy Rae

If you've tried to put stock thinner than about ¼ inch through the thickness planer, chances are the results were a ragged, chewed-up mess. Thin stock is pliable, and as a result, the planer's bed rollers bend the piece up into the revolving knives, chewing up the edges and even splintering the stock.

The planer board solves the problem by placing a flat supporting surface between the workpiece and the rollers. The board itself is a piece of sealed medium-density fiberboard (MDF). Cleats attached to the bottom at both ends keep the board in place as the stock moves through the planer. Two more cleats run along the sides, proud of the top, to keep the stock from

skewing off the board.

The dimensions in the Materials List are for an old 12-inch Parks planer. You'll need to size this fixture to fit your own machine.

MAKING THE JIG

1 Make the board. It is important that the board be flat, stable, and smooth. The board shown here is made from sealed MDF. You can buy this material factory-sealed, sometimes called filled MDF. Or you can seal the board yourself with a few coats of lacquer or polyurethane. Another option is to cover the top of the board with plastic laminate.

Most planers have lips on each side of the table, so that stock can't skew off the table during planing. If your planer has these lips, size your board to fit between them. If there are no lips, make the board ½ inch narrower than the table. In either case, make the board 2 inches longer than the table.

2 Make and attach the side rails. These rails perform the same function as the lips on the table and should be at least ¼ inch proud of the planer board. The rails should rest on the lips, as shown in P*hoto* 58-1.

Make the rails the same length as the planer board. Predrill and counterbore the rails, then glue and screw them to the sides of the board.

OVERALL VIEW

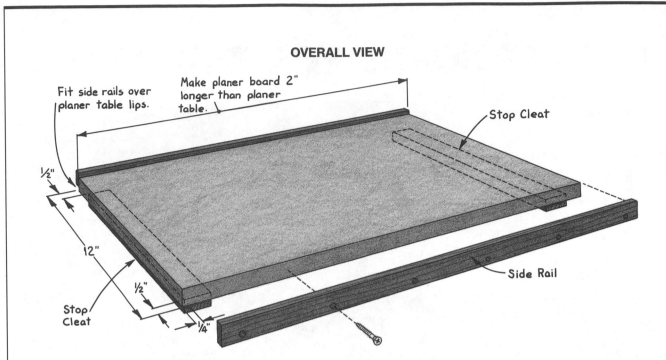

Fit side rails over planer table lips.

Make planer board 2" longer than planer table.

Stop Cleat

½"

12"

½"

¼"

Stop Cleat

Side Rail

If there are no lips on your planer, make the rails 1 inch wide, and attach them so that they rest on the planer table.

3 Attach the stop cleats. Cut these cleats to the thickness and width in the Materials List. Make them about 1 inch shorter than the width of the board. Predrill and countersink

Quantity	Part	Dimensions
1	MDF* board	¾" × 12" × 23"
2	Hardwood side rails	¼" × ¾" × 23"
2	Hardwood table stop cleats	¼" × ¾" × 11"

MATERIALS LIST

*Medium-density fiberboard

HARDWARE
#4 × ¾" flathead wood screws, as needed

Photo 58-1   The rails of the planer board should rest on the lips of the planer bed.

for one cleat, positioned about ¼ inch from the front or back edge of the board. Attach the strip with glue and four or five screws.

Crank the table all the way down (or the cutters all the way up). Place the jig on the planer table. Pull the installed stop cleat tightly against one end of the planer table. Clamp the other stop cleat in position on the opposite end of the table, making sure that it is snug against the edge of the table. Predrill and countersink. Then glue and screw the cleat in place.

4 Wax the jig. Rub paste wax onto the top surface of the planer board. Because the jig covers the bed rollers, the wax is necessary to help the workpiece slide over the planer board easily. Add more wax occasionally.

USING THE JIG

Crank the table and cutters far enough apart to let you slide the planer board between. Snap the jig into position with a rap of your palm.

When setting thickness, remember to allow for the thickness of the jig. If your knives are sharp and your planer is properly adjusted, you'll have no problem planing stock down to ⅛ inch. If your stock is straight-grained and has no knots, you can probably go even thinner. Otherwise, you are better off finding someone with a thickness sander to dimension the stock for you.

When planing thin stock, it is particularly important to stand to one side as the stock goes through the planer. It is possible for the stock to break. If this happens, the pieces probably will continue through the outfeed side, but they could get thrown back through the infeed side.

PORTABLE PLANER EXTENSION BED

Design by Fred Matlack

Portable and affordable, a new generation of thickness planers has been a boon to home woodworkers as well as to pros with limited shop space. These small, lightweight machines do an admirable job of surfacing rough lumber for a fraction of the cost of a stationary planer.

The portables do have an Achilles' heel, though. Their short beds do not support long stock well. This can make the planer awkward to use, and you frequently end up with deep snipes at the end of the stock. Fortunately, it is easy to solve this problem by building the extension bed shown here. In addition to providing more support for the workpiece, the extension bed makes the

planer more stable in use.

The extension bed works with any portable planer that has a stationary table. The

fixture consists of two planks bolted to the bottom of the planer and a feed roller set on each side of the machine.

MAKING THE JIG

1 Cut the planks to size. Cut the planks to the dimensions in the Materials List. Use a durable hardwood such as oak or maple for a long-lasting jig.

2 Make the hub blocks. You want the tops of the rollers to be in the same plane as the surface of your planer's bed. This means the thickness of the hub blocks depends on the height of your planer bed. As shown in *Determining Hub Block Thickness*, subtract the radius of the roller from the height of the

planer bed, then add ½ inch to the result to get the thickness of the hub block. Plane stock for the hub block to this thickness, then cut the blocks to the width and length in the Materials List.

Lay out holes ½ inch from the top of the hub blocks as shown in *Determining Hub Block Thickness*.

3 Mount the hub blocks. Position the hub blocks on the planks as shown in the *Overall View*. Predrill into each hub block for two

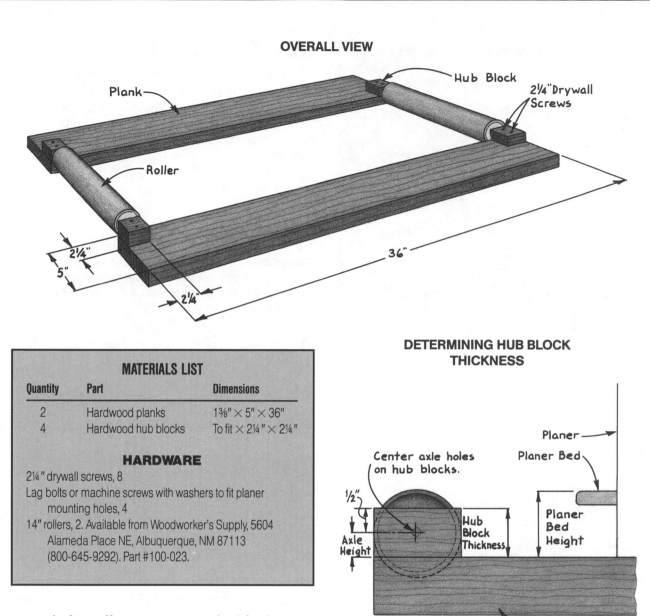

OVERALL VIEW

Plank

Hub Block

2¼"Drywall Screws

Roller

2¼"

5"

2¼"

36"

MATERIALS LIST

Quantity	Part	Dimensions
2	Hardwood planks	1⅜" × 5" × 36"
4	Hardwood hub blocks	To fit × 2¼" × 2¼"

HARDWARE

2¼" drywall screws, 8

Lag bolts or machine screws with washers to fit planer mounting holes, 4

14" rollers, 2. Available from Woodworker's Supply, 5604 Alameda Place NE, Albuquerque, NM 87113 (800-645-9292). Part #100-023.

DETERMINING HUB BLOCK THICKNESS

Center axle holes on hub blocks.

½"

Axle Height

Hub Block Thickness

Planer

Planer Bed

Planer Bed Height

Plank

2¼-inch drywall screws. Screw the blocks to the planks.

4 Mount the rollers and the planer. Set up the planks side by side on your workbench. Slide the rollers into the hub blocks. Make sure that the rollers are perpendicular to the planks. Center the planer on the planks. Mark mounting holes, then set the planer aside. Drill for lag bolts or machine screws. Secure the planer to the planks with washers and lag bolts or machine screws.

5 Fine-tune the roller height. Unplug the planer. Raise the cutter head as high as it will go. Slide an accurate straightedge through

the machine as shown in P*hoto* 59-1. (A 36-inch level works well.) Check that the tops of the rollers are in the same plane as the top of the planer bed. Check both rollers at the right side, left side, and middle. If the blocks are too thick, remove them and sand them a little thinner, using a belt sander. If the blocks are too thin, sandwich a few sheets of paper or cardboard between the planks and blocks and screw the blocks back in place. When you get the height you want, trim the paper or cardboard flush to the sides of the blocks with a utility knife.

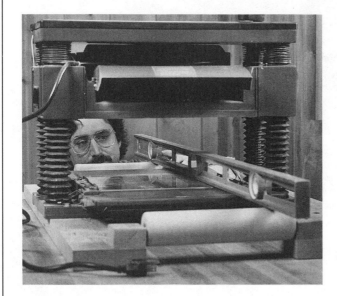

USING THE JIG

Using the jig is simply a matter of running boards over the infeed roller and on through the machine. Be careful not to get your fingers pinched between the outfeed roller and a board as it emerges from the planer.

Photo 59-1 Slide an accurate straightedge through the planer to check that the tops of the rollers are in the same plane as the top of the planer bed.

ADJUSTABLE PLATE JOINER STOP

Design by Ben Erickson and Ken Burton

 plate joiner can make short work of cutting the joints for a face frame. But making end grain cuts in narrow frame parts can be risky. The two anti-kickback points on the joiner do not contact the stock. This can result in a dangerous kickback. The adjustable plate joiner stop provides lateral support and prevents kickback.

This stop makes your work faster and more accurate as well as safer. It is adjustable, so you can set it to center all your cuts on a particular width rail. This eliminates the need to lay out each cut.

Make this jig from a piece of acrylic plastic and a hardwood fence as shown in the *Overall View*. Attach it to

your joiner with roundhead machine screws, threaded into holes drilled into the joiner's movable fence. By

making an alternate fence as described in "Making the Jig," you can make cuts in angled workpiece ends.

MAKING THE JIG

1 Cut the parts to size. Cut the hardwood fence and the acrylic plastic base plate to the dimensions in the Materials List. If you wish to make an alternate fence, the dimensions will depend on the angle of your stock. The *Alternate Fence Detail* shows the dimensions of a fence for pieces that have 45-degree miters.

2 Cut the groove in the acrylic base plate. As mentioned, the jig's base plate is attached to the joiner fence with two ¼-inch-diameter × 1-inch roundhead machine screws. These

screws fit through a slot in the base plate. With a ¼-inch straight bit in your table-mounted router, cut the slot through the base plate as shown in the *Overall View*. Run the base plate along a fence to guide the cut. Replace the ¼-inch bit with a ½-inch bit and counterbore the slot. Make the counterbore so that the heads of the machine screws will be recessed completely beneath the surface of the plate.

The heat generated when routing plastics can cause the chips to melt and fuse

OVERALL VIEW

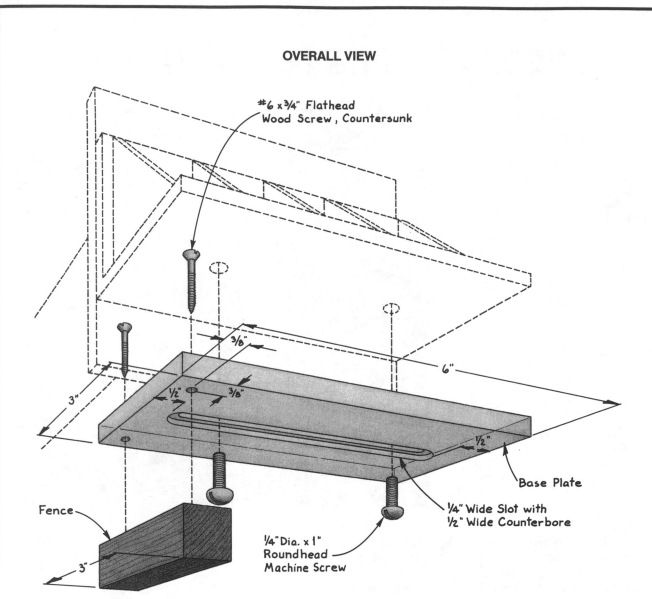

#6 x ¾" Flathead Wood Screw, Countersunk

⅜"

3"

½"   ⅜"

6"

½"

Base Plate

¼" Wide Slot with ½" Wide Counterbore

Fence

3"

¼" Dia. x 1" Roundhead Machine Screw

together in the cut behind the bit. If this happens, make another pass to clear the slot. To help prevent this from happening, use sharp bits, make shallow cuts, and feed the work briskly. For more information, see "Making Stopped Cuts on the Router Table," page 24.

3 Attach the fence. Drill and countersink two holes in one end of the base plate as shown in the *Overall View.* Position the base plate on top of the fence. Make sure the fence and the sides of the base plate are square to each other. Mark the centers of the holes through the plate onto the fence. Drill ⁵⁄₆₄-inch pilot holes into the fence and attach

MATERIALS LIST		
Quantity	Part	Dimensions
1	Hardwood fence	¾" × ¾" × 3"

HARDWARE
#6 × ¾" flathead wood screws, 2
¼" dia. × 1" roundhead machine screws, 2
⅜" × 3" × 6" acrylic plastic base plate, 1

the fence to the plate with two #6 × ¾-inch flathead wood screws. Double-check to be sure the fence is square to the sides of the plate.

ALTERNATE FENCE DETAIL

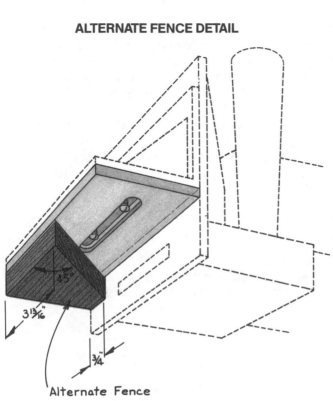

Alternate Fence

4 Attach the jig to the plate joiner. Turn the joiner upside down on your bench, as shown in P*hoto* 60-1. Place the jig on the joiner's fence with one side of the base plate against

Photo 60-1 Hold the jig in place on the biscuit joiner and mark the slot location on the joiner's fence with a sharp pencil or scribe.

the joiner's housing and the jig's fence to the right of the cutter, as shown in the photo. Clamp the jig in place and mark the slot location on the joiner's fence with a sharp pencil or scribe. Remove the jig from the joiner.

Carefully mark the joiner's fence for machine screw holes. First trace around the slot, marking the joiner fence. Lay out the slot centerline as shown in *Positioning the Machine Screws*. Make marks across the center-line, approximately 1 inch from each end of the slot. This 1-inch offset makes the fence adjustable. Make sure that drilling through

POSITIONING THE MACHINE SCREWS

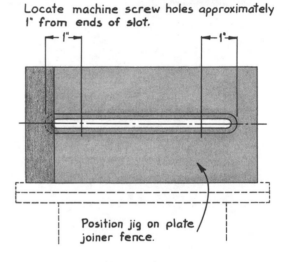

Locate machine screw holes approximately 1" from ends of slot.

Position jig on plate joiner fence.

these points won't interfere with any rein-forcement webs or other holes. Center-punch the hole locations to mark them.

Drill the holes on the drill press with a #7 or $\frac{13}{64}$-inch drill bit. (See "Drilling Metal," page 4.) Tap the holes with a $\frac{1}{4}$"-20 tap. Use a light oil to help lubricate the tap as you cut. For more information, see "Tapping and Threading Metal," page 6. Attach the jig to the fence with the roundhead machine screws.

USING THE JIG

To set up the jig for a job, loosen the machine screws that hold the jig in place. Hold the workpiece against the jig's fence as

shown in Photo 60-2. Slide the jig laterally until the workpiece is correctly aligned with the cutter. Set the workpiece aside and tighten the machine screws to lock the jig in place. Double-check to be sure that tightening the screws did not misalign the jig.

To make the cut, clamp the workpiece down. Even with this jig, it is not safe to hand-hold work you are cutting. Align the joiner on the end of the piece and plunge the cutter forward into the stock.

Photo 60-2   To set up the jig for a job, hold the workpiece against the fence. Slide the jig laterally until the workpiece is correctly aligned with the cutter.

PLATE JOINER BASE EXTENSION

Design by Ben Erickson

When you are cutting plate slots at the end of a piece, a plate joiner's face plate and fence don't provide enough support to make accurate cuts. This most often comes up when cutting slots at the top or bottom of a carcase side to join it with a carcase top or bottom. The fence is over the top of the piece, and only about ¾ inch of the face plate is in contact with it. You have to balance the tool in this precarious position while you make three or four cuts.

The plate joiner base extension is simply a block that bolts to the joiner's face plate, adding plenty of extra support. The block is easily removed when you

don't need it. The only modification you'll have to make

to your joiner is to drill and tap two holes into the base.

MAKING THE JIG

1 Cut the block to size. Cut a block of stable hardwood to the dimensions in the Materials List. Mahogany would be a good choice, because it is very stable and easy to work. Make sure the faces of the block are square.

2 Drill the bolt holes. It is very important that the holes in the extension block line up perfectly with the holes in the biscuit joiner. To ensure this, first drill the holes into the extension block, then clamp the block to the joiner base. Drill the holes into the joiner base using the holes in the extension block as a guide.

Drill two holes into the extension block as shown in the *Overall View*. Use a #7 or ¹³/₆₄-inch drill bit. Remove the movable fence and the blade from the joiner. Clamp the block on the base of the joiner so that it is flush with the face plate, and drill the holes through the joiner base with the same bit.

3 Tap the holes. Draw a line across the joiner and the extension block, so that you can easily align the two again, then remove the block from the joiner. Cut threads in the holes in the base with a ¼"-20 tap. Use a light oil to lubricate the tap, so that it cuts cleaner.

OVERALL VIEW

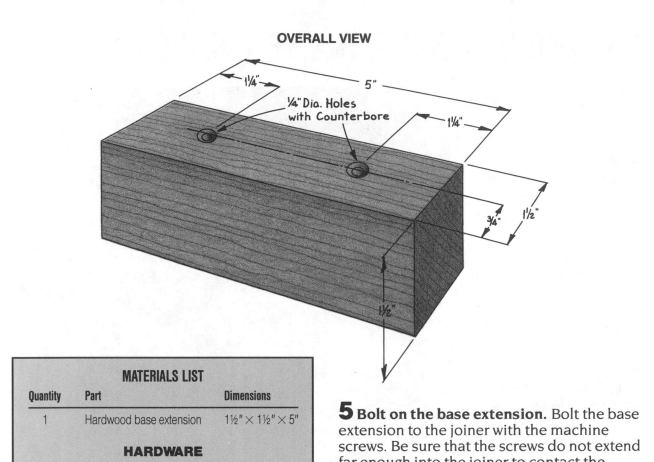

¼" Dia. Holes
with Counterbore

MATERIALS LIST		
Quantity	Part	Dimensions
1	Hardwood base extension	1½" × 1½" × 5"

HARDWARE

¼" dia. × 1¾" flathead machine screws, 2

For more on cutting threads, see "Tapping and Threading Metal," page 6.

4 Enlarge and countersink the holes in the extension block. Now that you have the holes in the joiner and extension block aligned, you need to enlarge the holes in the block, so that the bolts will slide through. Drill out the holes with a ¼-inch bit on the drill press. Then countersink them to fit the heads of the machine screws.

5 Bolt on the base extension. Bolt the base extension to the joiner with the machine screws. Be sure that the screws do not extend far enough into the joiner to contact the blade. If necessary, cut them shorter with a hack saw or grinder.

USING THE JIG

Bolt the jig to your joiner. Check the alignment of the block and the joiner with a straightedge to make sure that the block is flush with the face plate. Gently tap the block with a mallet if you need to adjust it. Lay out the cuts and adjust the fence and cutting depth just as you would without the extension block. Make the cuts.

POWER MITER SAW TABLE

Design by Jim Tolpin

his compact portable table improves the power miter saw in two ways. It brings the tool to a comfortable working height, and it provides plenty of support for long workpieces.

The power miter saw, or chop saw, has become vital to the finish carpenter who wants to bring shop precision to the job site. It also is popular with woodworkers who don't want to invest the money and shop space required for the chop saw's bigger cousin, the radial arm saw. Although the chop saw is less versatile than the radial arm saw, it is more precise and requires less adjustment. However you use your saw, you'll find this table is just what you

need. It's easy to transport and ready to work anywhere there are a couple of sawhorses. Just put the notches over the horses. In the shop,

this fixture can be stored against the wall, while the saw gets stowed under the bench.

MAKING THE JIG

1 Make the table. The table becomes narrower at the ends to make it lighter and a little easier to work around. Begin with a flat piece of hardwood plywood cut to the dimensions in the Materials List.

Draw the curves shown in the *Overall View* freehand. No particular radius is required; you just want to eliminate any sharp corners you might bump into while working. Cut the curves with a saber saw.

2 Make and attach the stock support legs. The distance between the bottom of your saw and the cutting surface is the height of the stock supports. The legs are ¾ inch shorter than that, to allow for the thickness of the stock supports. For example, if the saw's cutting surface is 5 inches high, the legs should be 4¼ inches high. Rip a piece of plywood to 4 inches wide and then crosscut the four legs to height. Predrill and countersink through the bottom of the table into

OVERALL VIEW

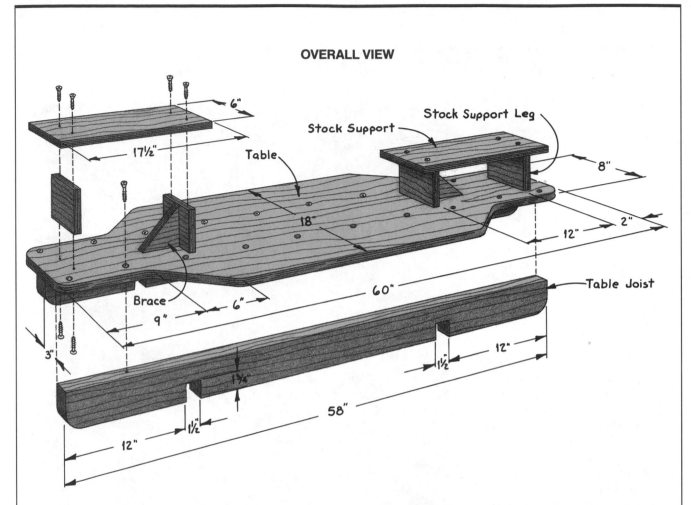

each support leg for two drywall screws. Glue and screw each support leg into place.

3 Make and attach the braces. Cut one piece of plywood to the dimensions in the Materials List. Draw a diagonal line between two corners. Cut the piece in half along this line with a jigsaw or on the table saw. Put glue on perpendicular edges of the braces and position them as shown in the *Overall View.* Attach the braces to the table and the legs by predrilling and countersinking drywall screws.

4 Make and attach the stock supports. Cut the stock supports to the dimensions in the Materials List. Put glue on the top edges of the legs. Postion the stock supports on the legs as shown in the *Overall View.* Predrill the stock supports and attach them to the legs with drywall screws.

MATERIALS LIST		
Quantity	Part	Dimensions
1	Hardwood plywood table	¾" × 18" × 60"
4	Plywood stock support legs	¾" × 4" × to fit
2	Braces	¾" × 4¼" × 4¼"
2	Stock supports	¾" × 6" × 17½"
2	Solid wood table joists	1½" × 3½" × 58"

HARDWARE

1½" drywall screws, as needed

5 Make and attach the table joists. Make the table joists from construction-grade 2 × 4s. Cut them to length and then joint one edge of each. Notch the bottom of each 12 inches from each end as shown in the *Overall View.* Put glue on the jointed edges and attach the joists with drywall screws about every 6 inches. Bolt the saw to the table.

RADIAL ARM SAW TABLE AND FENCE

Design by Ken Burton

T he radial arm saw is a remarkably versatile machine. It can do almost anything a table saw can do and even a few things the table saw can't do. But to really work well, the radial arm saw must be set up accurately. This requires a perfectly flat table because most saw adjustments are referenced from the table surface. The table and fence system shown here is designed to provide a good reference surface. It also will help you make clean, accurate cuts. The fence includes a self-clamping stop block for making repetitive cuts to exactly the same length.

The radial arm saw table actually is two tables with a fence sandwiched between, as shown in the *Overall View*. The front table bolts in place. The back table and fence are then clamped against the front table. The fence is removable, so that when it wears, it can easily be replaced.

This system uses a dou-

ble layer of medium-density fiberboard (MDF) for the tables and a stable hardwood, such as mahogany, for the fence. MDF is a very stable sheet product available from most good lumberyards. The front table is covered with a piece of ¼-inch-thick plywood or hardboard. Since a radial arm saw must cut into the table surface as it is used,

the surface must also be replaceable.

The front table of this system has notches where it meets the fence. These notches provide places for sawdust to fall, so that it doesn't accumulate between the fence and the table, making your cuts inaccurate. The stop is rabbeted for the same reason.

MAKING THE JIG

1 Make the tables. Your radial arm saw may require a table size different than specified. Measure your saw carefully and alter the dimensions in the Materials List if necessary. The front table must be wide enough that the blade cannot run off the front. The back table

OVERALL VIEW

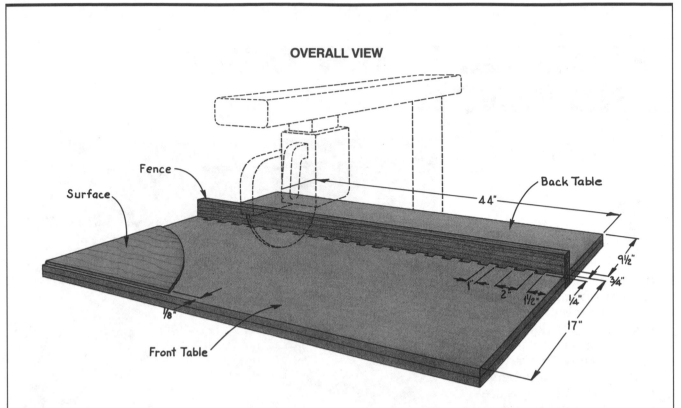

must be wide enough to allow you to retract the blade completely behind the fence. To make ripping convenient, the table should not extend beyond the saw base more than about 2 inches on each side.

The front and back tables are each made from two pieces of MDF laminated together. Cut the pieces an inch or so wider and longer than called for in the Materials List. Glue the pieces together on a flat surface. (The table on a table saw would be ideal.) When the glue dries, cut the tables to size.

2 Cut the notches. The back edge of the front table is notched as shown in the *Overall View.* Lay out the notches on the table as shown.

Cut the notches in several passes with a ¾-inch-diameter straight bit in a table-mounted router. Set a fence on the router table so that about ¼ inch of the bit is exposed. Set the depth of cut at about ½ inch. Mark the bit location on the fence. Rout the notches using the layout marks and the marks on the fence to position the saw table. After you rout all the notches with the bit at the first setting, increase the depth of cut to 1 inch and rout them again. Then increase

MATERIALS LIST		
Quantity	**Part**	**Dimensions**
2	MDF* front table	¾" × 17" × 44"
2	MDF* back table	¾" × 9½" × 44"
1	Hardwood fence	¾" × 3" × 44"
1	Plywood surface	¼" × 16¾" × 44"
1	Hardwood stop block	¾" × 1½" × 3"
1	Hardwood spacer	⅜" × 2½" × 2⅜"
1	Hardwood back	¾" × 1½" × 2½"

*Medium-density fiberboard

HARDWARE

¼" dia. × 1½" eyebolt with T-nut, 1
Bolts or screws to attach table to saw, as needed
¾" brass nails, as needed

the depth of cut to 1½ inches to finish the notches. For more on routing notches, see "Cutting Dadoes and Grooves," page 36.

3 Make the fence. Cut the stock for the fence to the dimensions in the Materials List. While you are cutting, you might want to make an extra fence or two to have on hand.

4 Install the tables and fence. Bolt or screw the front table to your saw. The owner's manual will give instructions on how to do this.

Slide the rear table into position. Slip the fence between the two tables and tighten the clamps on the saw to lock it in place. Then adjust the table so that it is parallel to the saw arm.

Check that the arm and table are parallel by watching the saw as it travels over the table. First remove the blade from the saw. Pivot the motor so that the arbor points straight down. Lower the arm until the tip of the arbor just clears the table surface. Move the motor along the arm until it's over the back of the front table. To help gauge the relationship between the arbor and the table, lay a plastic-coated playing card under the arbor as shown in Photo 63-1. Lower the arm until the arbor brushes the card. Draw the saw toward you. If the arbor pins the card to the table, stop. Lower the front of the table. If the arbor loses contact with the card, stop. Raise the front of the table.

Photo 63-2   Hold a framing square with one leg against the fence. Run the arbor along the other leg to make sure the arm is square to the table.

Adjust the table until the arbor maintains slight contact with the card for the full width of the table. Pivot the arm from side to side and check the table with the card at various places to ensure that the whole assembly is not tilted.

Next adjust the arm so that it is square to the table. Hold a framing square with one leg flush with the back edge of the table and the other leg against the saw arbor as shown in Photo 63-2. Draw the carriage forward. If the arbor moves away from the square or tries to climb on top of it, stop. Loosen the bolts that lock the arm in position and adjust the arm until the arbor follows the square perfectly. Tighten the adjustment bolts.

Pivot the motor so that the arbor is parallel to the table. Replace the blade. Then set the blade square to the table.

Photo 63-1   Use a playing card to check that the arm and table are parallel. Lower the arbor until it brushes the card at the back of the table. Draw the saw toward you. If the arbor pins the card, lower the front of the table. If the arbor loses contact with the card, raise the front of the table.

5 Add the plywood surface. Cut the plywood surface to the dimensions in the Materials List. Position the plywood on the front table, leaving about a ⅛-inch-wide gap between the plywood and the fence. There should also be about ⅛ inch of table showing at the front edge. This is left clear so that the front of the table can be used as reference.

Tack the plywood down with brass nails. Keep the nails away from the normal cutting paths.

6 Make the stop. Cut the stop block, spacer, and back to the dimensions in the Materials List. Rabbet one end of the stop block as shown in the *Stop Block Detail.* Drill a hole into the back piece for the T-nut as shown. Drive the T-nut into the hole. Glue the stop block and the back to the spacer. Make sure the grain of the spacer runs perpendicular to the block and back. This will make the stop stronger. Also, make sure the block and back are flush along both edges of the spacer. When the glue dries, thread the eyebolt through the T-nut and place the stop on the fence. The eye provides a good grip for tightening the bolt.

USING THE JIG

This table and fence system is not so much a jig as an upgrade to your radial arm saw. For more information on using the radial arm saw, see "Radial Arm Saw," page 12.

To use the stop, position it along the

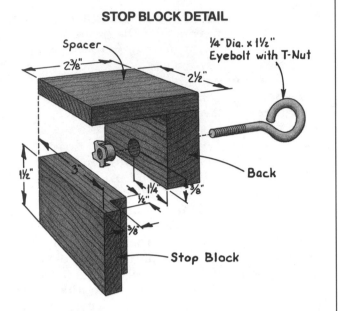

STOP BLOCK DETAIL

Spacer

2⅜"

2½"

¼" Dia. x 1½" Eyebolt with T-Nut

Back

1½"

3

1¼"

½"

⅜"

⅜"

Stop Block

fence at the needed distance from the blade. Then butt your stock against it as you cut. This will ensure that all the pieces you cut are the same length. Be sure to hold on to the part of the stock that is against the stop; otherwise, the saw may kick it back at you. This means that the stop will always be to the left of the blade, so that you do not have to reach across the saw to hold the work.

ROUTER TABLE

Design by Phil Gehret

In essence, a router table is a flat surface with a hole in it, so that you can mount your router underneath with the bit sticking up. Once you mount your router this way, you've turned it into a shaper, vastly increasing its versatility.

You'll appreciate a router table the first time you use your router to make moldings. A hand-held router tips if you try to run it over a molding that's only a couple of inches wide. And even if the molding is 5 or 6 inches wide, you can't clamp it to your bench without the clamps blocking the router.

You'll find yourself using the router table even when a hand-held router would do the job. Because the bit sticks up, it's easier to watch your work. And it's easier to slide a workpiece over a table than it is to keep control of a heavy router with a bit spinning at 20,000 rpm. A router table also makes it easier to use a fence and stops.

A router table can be as simple as a piece of plywood with a hole in it. At the other extreme, you can mount your table on a cabinet complete with drawers for bits and other accessories.

The router table you see here strikes a balance. Its top provides plenty of support for any routing work. It

has a simple and convenient 3-inch-high fence that should handle most work you'll encounter. The oak base is heavy and rigid. The splayed legs provide as much stability as possible while keeping out of your way as you work and clamp around the top of the table.

Because you might not want to dedicate that much floor space to the router table, the base is assembled with machine screws and threaded inserts. It takes only a few minutes to disassemble the base. It stores easily and will even fit in a car trunk, making this a great router table to

take to the job site.

The table itself is a 1-inch-thick piece of plywood edged with solid oak. It's covered, top and bottom, with a plastic laminate, such as Formica. On top, the laminate provides a smooth, durable work surface. The bottom is laminated to prevent uneven moisture movement from warping the table. It is essential that a router table be perfectly flat.

The router table plan includes a square piece of polycarbonate that replaces the base on your router. This polycarbonate base fits into a rabbeted hole in the table. The base makes it easy to

OVERALL VIEW

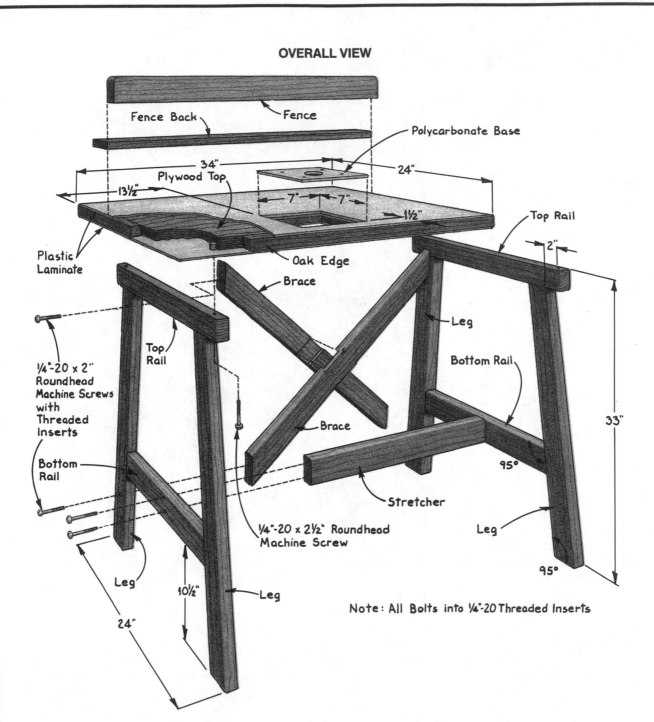

Fence Back

Fence

Polycarbonate Base

34"

Plywood Top

24"

13½"

7" 7"

1½"

Top Rail

Plastic
Laminate

Oak Edge

2"

Brace

Leg

¼"-20 x 2"
Roundhead
Machine Screws
with
Threaded
Inserts

Top
Rail

Bottom Rail

Brace

33"

Bottom
Rail

95°

¼"-20 x 2½" Roundhead
Machine Screw

Stretcher

Leg

Leg

10½"

Leg

Note: All Bolts into ¼"-20 Threaded Inserts

95°

24"

pop the router out of the table to change bits. And it's only ¼ inch thick, so you don't lose the cutting depth you would by mounting the router directly to the bottom of the table.

The table shown here was assembled with a biscuit joiner. If you don't have a biscuit joiner, you can easily do the job with

dowels. You won't need a doweling jig with the method described in "Making the Jig."

MAKING THE JIG

1 **Make the tabletop.** Cut the plywood for the top to the dimensions in the Materials

MATERIALS LIST

Quantity	Part	Dimensions
1	Plywood top	1" × 22½" × 32½"
2	Oak long edges	¾" × 1" × 34"
2	Oak short edges	¾" × 1" × 24"
4	Oak legs	1⅛" × 2½" × 31"
2	Oak bottom rails	1⅛" × 2½" × 16⅜"
2	Oak braces	1⅛" × 2½" × to fit
2	Oak top rails	1⅛" × 2" × 22"
1	Oak stretcher	1⅛" × 2½" × 23½"
1	Oak fence	1" × 3" × 34"
1	Oak fence back	1" × 3" × 34"

HARDWARE

¼"-20 × 2½" roundhead machine screws, 4
¼"-20 × 2" roundhead machine screws, 8
25" × 35" plastic laminate, 2
¼" × 7" × 7" polycarbonate base, 1
¼"-20 threaded inserts, 12

List. Joint, rip, and plane stock for the oak edges, but leave it 1 inch longer than needed.

Miter one end of each edge piece. Put a piece in place along the table edge and align the miter with the corner. Mark for the other miter and cut it. Glue and clamp the piece to the table. Fit an adjoining edge piece to the table. Mark for the next miter. Continue around the table, marking, cutting, and clamping as you go.

2 Laminate and trim the tabletop. Cut two pieces of plastic laminate to the dimensions in the Materials List. The pieces are purposely larger than the finished size. Attach one piece of laminate to the top of the table with contact cement, allowing the laminate to overhang all the edges. Attach the other piece to the bottom.

Rout the laminate flush with the edges with a 45-degree piloted bit set to cut ⅛ inch deep. Mounting and trimming the laminate this way allows you to position it on the plywood without worrying about exact alignment.

3 Make the base parts. Rip, plane, and joint stock for the base parts to the dimen-

sions in the Materials List. The end of each leg is cut at a 95-degree angle, as shown in the *Overall View*. First cut one edge to 95 degrees. Lay out and make another 95-degree cut 31 inches from the first. Note that the miters are parallel to each other. Cut all four legs, making them exactly the same length.

Make a 95-degree miter on both ends of each bottom rail, cutting the rails to length in the process. Note that these miters are not parallel to each other. Cut the braces to 1⅛ × 2½ × 37 inches. You will cut them to fit later.

4 Join the legs to the rails. Attach the bottom rails first. Put the legs and bottom rails flat on the bench, with the rails positioned against the legs. Make a mark across the joint for positioning joinery biscuits. Make each joint with two biscuits as shown in *Photo 64-1*. Put glue in the biscuit slots and on the joints. Put the biscuits in place and clamp the joints together.

Because the legs slope, the clamps will slip when you tighten them. To prevent this, cut clamping cauls on the band saw that have a 95-degree taper on one face. Clamp as shown in *Photo 64-2*.

If you don't have a biscuit joiner, put a leg in position against a rail and clamp both

Photo 64-1 Use two biscuits for each joint between the legs and rails.

Photo 64-2 Because the legs meet the rails at an angle, the clamps will slip as you tighten them. To prevent this, use tapered clamping cauls, so that the clamp jaws will contact parallel surfaces.

parts to the bench. Drill two ⅜-inch-diameter holes through the rail and about 1 inch into the leg. Put glue on the joint and in the holes. Tap two ⅜-inch spiral hardwood dow-

Photo 64-3 As an alternative to biscuit joining, you can drill holes through the legs into the rails and join the parts with dowels.

els through each rail and into the leg as shown in *Photo* 64-3. Cut the dowels off flush with the top of the rail. Repeat this process for each leg.

When the glue dries, position the top rail on the legs, and either dowel or biscuit in place.

5 Attach the stretcher to the bottom rails. The stretcher is bolted to the two leg assemblies. Lay out two holes at each end of the stretcher as shown in the *Stretcher Detail*. Drill ½-inch-diameter holes about ¼ inch deep. Put a ²³⁄₆₄-inch-diameter bit in the drill. Place it in the center of each ½-inch-diameter hole and drill a hole at least ¾ inch deeper. The ¼-inch-deep holes are counterbores that will help you drive the threaded inserts below the surface.

Lay out corresponding holes in the rails with dowel centers, as shown in *Photo* 64-4. The dowel center will leave small marks on the rail. Drill ⁵⁄₁₆-inch-diameter holes through the rail at these points.

Drive the threaded insert into the stretcher with the help of a ¼"-20 × ¾-inch hex head bolt, as shown in *Photo* 64-5. Thread a nut onto the bolt and screw the threaded insert up against the nut. Drive the insert into the hole with a wrench as shown. Stop when

STRETCHER DETAIL

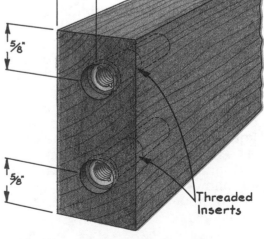

Drill ²³⁄₆₄" dia. x 1" deep holes for ¼"-20 threaded inserts.

Photo 64-4 Drill holes into the stretcher for threaded inserts. Place dowel centers in the holes and use them to mark corresponding holes in the rails.

the nut hits the bottom of the counterbore. Repeat this process for the other holes.

Attach the stretcher to the leg assemblies with four ¼"-20 × 2-inch roundhead machine screws.

6 Make the braces. Cut one end of each brace at 45 degrees. Lay out the second cut

Photo 64-5 Thread a nut onto a bolt. Thread the insert onto the bolt until it hits the nut. Use a wrench to drive the insert into the hole.

by making a simple full-scale drawing. Lay out two parallel lines, 23½ inches apart and about 36 inches long, on a flat surface, as shown in *Laying Out the Braces.* Draw a perpendicular line at the base of the first two lines as shown. Position one brace on the layout with the miter aligned as shown in the drawing. Mark for the 45-degree miter on the other end of the brace. Repeat this process for the other brace. Make the two miter cuts.

As shown in the *Overall View,* the braces are half-lapped so that they cross each other in the same plane. To mark the braces for the half-laps, place the braces on the full-scale drawing so that they cross each other. Align all four ends to the parallel lines. Use a square to check that the braces cross at a 90-degree angle. Mark where the braces cross each other. Cut half-lap dadoes ⁹⁄₁₆ inch deep with a dado cutter on the radial arm saw or table saw.

The braces are attached to the legs with ¼"-20 × 2-inch roundhead machine screws as shown in the *Overall View.* Position the braces between the legs as shown. Lay out holes

LAYING OUT THE BRACES

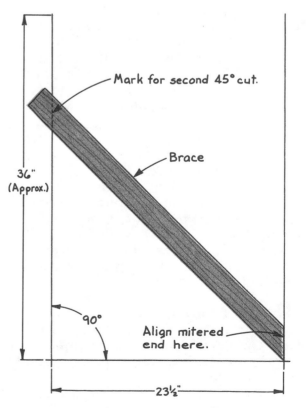

that will pass through the legs and into a point centered in the end of the leg. Drill, counterbore, and insert a threaded insert as before. Assemble the braces across the legs.

Mark the legs and braces so that you can realign the holes easily if you remove the braces.

7 Round the edges of the base. Rout a ¼-inch roundover on all edges of the base except those that are part of the joinery. Remove the braces to rout them, but leave them attached to each other. Reattach the braces when you're done routing.

8 Attach the top to the base. Center the top on the base and clamp it in place. Drill ⁵⁄₁₆-inch-diameter holes through the top rails into the top. Position the holes as shown in the *Overall View*. Remove the top and enlarge the holes with a ²³⁄₆₄-inch-diameter drill bit. Make the holes about ¾ inch deep. Be careful not to drill through the top of the top. Counterbore just ⅛ inch or so. Screw threaded inserts into the holes in the top. Attach the top and the base with ¼"-20 × 2½-inch roundhead machine screws.

9 Make the insert. The polycarbonate insert in the Materials List is sized for a 6-inch-diameter router base. If your router base is a different size, make the base and hole 1 inch longer and wider than your base.

Cut the polycarbonate to size with a combination blade on the table saw. Lay out the rounded corners with a ⅜-inch-diameter radius on a circle template. Round the corners on a belt sander.

Remove the plastic subbase from your router. Center the subbase on the insert and use it as a template to lay out screw holes and the hole for bits to pass through. Drill these holes to the same diameter as the holes in your subbase. Counterbore the screw holes.

10 Rabbet and cut the insert hole. Position the insert on the router table as shown in the *Overall View*. Make sure the insert is not over the braces. Trace around the insert with a sharp pencil.

As mentioned, the insert sits in a

⅜-inch-wide rabbet. The following procedure ensures that the insert will fit cleanly in the rabbet, even if the hole for the rabbet is cut imperfectly.

Put a ⅜-inch straight bit in the router and set the depth to the thickness of the insert. Use a straightedge clamped to the table to guide the router as you cut a groove around the inside perimeter of the insert layout as shown in *Photo 64-6*. You will have to position the straightedge four times to do this. Now use a saber saw to make the hole by following the inside edge of the groove as shown in *Photo 64-7*.

Attach the router to the insert and place the insert in the hole.

11 Make the router fence. Joint and plane stock for the fence and fence back to the dimensions in the Materials List. The exact width and thickness of these pieces is not important. It is important that they be jointed and planed perfectly square and straight. Cut the fence and fence back to the lengths in the Materials List. On the band saw, round the top corners of the fence to a radius of about ¾ inch as shown in the *Overall View*.

With a ¼-inch-radius roundover bit in the

Photo 64-6   Use a straightedge clamped across the table to guide the router as you cut a groove around the inside perimeter of the insert layout.

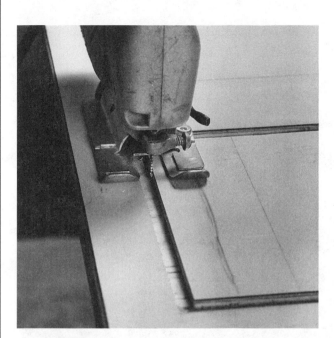

Photo 64-7 Make the insert hole by cutting along the inside of the groove with a saber saw.

router, round the top edges of one side and both ends of the fence back. Glue and clamp the fence back to the fence. Before the glue dries, make sure the fence and back are perfectly flush along the bottom. Rout a ¼-inch-radius roundover on all top edges of the fence.

USING THE JIG

When you mount your router under a table, you create a stationary power tool with its own realm of setups. You'll find a detailed discussion under "Table-Mounted Routing," page 22.

Many edge treatment setups require you to bury a router bit in the fence. For example, you can make a ⅜-inch-wide rabbet with a ¾-inch-diameter bit by exposing only one-half of the diameter of the bit. The rest of the bit is hidden by the fence. (See "Rabbets," page 26.) These setups require you to make a notch in the fence as shown in *Photo* 64-8. Make this notch the first time you need to bury a bit. To do this, set the router bit for the height you need for the job at hand. Turn on the router. Clamp one end of the fence to the router table. Pull the fence over the bit until the bit disappears under the fence. Turn off the router. Now adjust the fence until the required amount of bit protrudes. Clamp the other end of the fence to the router table.

Few router bits will create a notch bigger than about 1 inch. A notch of this size won't affect how the fence works for other operations.

Photo 64-8 To notch the fence, clamp one end of the fence to the table, turn on the router, and pivot the fence into the spinning bit.

CROSSCUT FENCE

Design by Andy Rae

ike the crosscut box on page 283, the crosscut fence replaces the miter gauge when crosscutting long or wide pieces. It greatly increases the guiding surface, making crosscutting safer and more accurate. You can attach stops and cut several pieces to exactly the same length.

The crosscut fence has an advantage over the crosscut box, however. It's perfect for pieces that require dadoes and rabbets that are exactly the same depth. First cut the dadoes with the crosscut fence. Then cut the rabbets by guiding the piece along the rip fence with the saw's standard miter gauge. Because the crosscut fence is bottomless, you can cut the

rabbets without resetting the blade height. As a result, the rabbets and dadoes are the same depth, and the cabinet is more likely to go together square.

The crosscut fence shown here will let you cut stock up to about 2¼ inches thick. You can cut thicker stock if you increase the thickness of the brace.

MAKING THE JIG

1 **Prepare the bar stock for the runners.** Most commonly, table saw miter gauge slots are ⅜ inch deep × ¾ inch wide. If these are the dimensions of your slots, you probably can purchase the stock off the shelf at your local metal yard. Be sure to pick the straightest stock you can find. If your miter gauge slots are an unusual size, have a machinist mill the stock for you. Let him know the stock must be flat and straight.

Each bar has three holes in it. One hole is for the flathead wood screw that holds the fence, and two holes are threaded for the machine bolts that hold the brace. Drill and countersink 7¼ inch from one end of each

bar for the screw as shown in the *Overall View.* Flip the bars over and drill holes for the machine bolts as shown in the *Overall View.* Tap threaded holes into each bar. See "Drilling Metal," page 4, and "Tapping and Threading Metal," page 6.

2 **Make the brace.** Cut the three pieces of plywood that make the brace. Glue, stack, and clamp these together. Let the glue cure overnight. Remove the clamps. With a jigsaw or band saw, cut a 2-inch radius on two corners of the brace as shown in the *Overall View.* The brace shown here was constructed a little differently because Andy Rae discov-

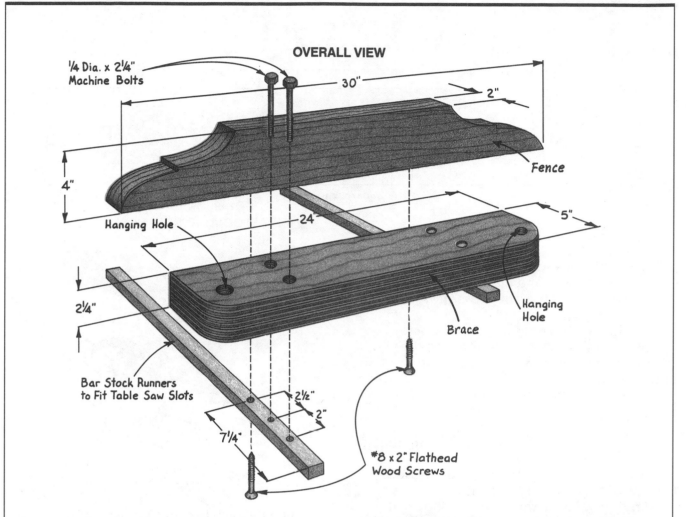

OVERALL VIEW

¼ Dia. x 2¼" Machine Bolts

30"

2"

Fence

4"

Hanging Hole

24"

5"

2¼"

Bar Stock Runners to Fit Table Saw Slots

Hanging Hole

Brace

2½"

2"

7¼"

#8 x 2" Flathead Wood Screws

ered the brace needed a third layer of plywood after he had bolted the jig together.

3 Make the fence. Joint, plane, and cut a piece of hardwood to the dimensions in the Materials List. It is essential that the fence be straight and flat and that it remain that way. Select a straight-grained piece of stock. Hard maple, used for the fence shown here, is an excellent choice, because it is stable and durable. Other good choices would be cherry or birch.

Lay out the fence as shown in the F*ence Pattern*. The shaped sides reduce the weight of the fence, making it easier to handle. You can substitute a simple curve for the ogee shape, if you like.

4 Attach the fence to the runners. The fence must be perpendicular to the runners and centered over the screws that hold it in place. To locate the screw holes in the

MATERIALS LIST		
Quantity	Part	Dimensions
3	Plywood brace	¾" × 5" × 24"
1	Hard maple fence	2" × 4" × 30"

HARDWARE

#8 × 2" flathead wood screws, 2
¼" dia. × 2¼" machine bolts, 4
Steel bar stock, thickness and width to fit × 24", 2

bottom of the fence, place the runners in the saw's miter gauge slots with the countersinks down. Use a framing square or other large square to align the screw holes as shown in *Marking for F*ence *Alignment*. Align the short arm of the square with a miter gauge slot. (The side of the saw may not be perfectly parallel to the slots.)

Put the jig's fence against the long arm of

FENCE PATTERN

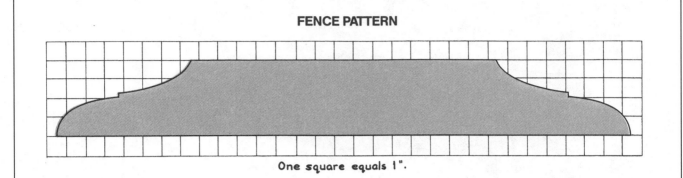

One square equals 1".

the square so that the center of the fence is aligned with the saw blade. Transfer the screw hole locations to the front of the fence. Move the square and mark where the front of the fence meets the runner, as shown in the drawing.

Transfer the lines marking the screw holes from the front of the fence to the bottom of the fence. Mark a point midway along each line. Predrill the fence and attach it with screws at these points.

5 Attach the brace. Place the jig in the miter gauge slots. Check to make sure that it is square with the slots, and make any necessary adjustments. Measure the locations of the bolt holes, and lay out corresponding holes on the brace, as shown in *Locating Bolt Holes*. Counterbore the top of the brace deep enough that the machine bolts will firmly grab the runners but will not

LOCATING BOLT HOLES

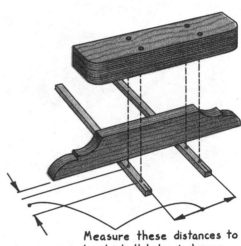

Measure these distances to locate bolt holes in brace.

protrude through the bottom. Then drill ⁵⁄₁₆-inch-diameter holes into the brace.

Temporarily attach the brace to the runners. Make sure that the fence is square and that the jig runs smoothly.

Unbolt the brace and put glue on the edge that meets the fence. Reassemble the jig, leaving the bolts slightly loose. Clamp the brace to the fence. Place the jig in the miter gauge slots. Check very carefully that the crosscut fence is square to the slots. Tighten the bolts and check again that the jig runs smoothly in the slots.

6 Drill hanging holes and apply wax. Let the glue cure overnight, then remove the clamps. Wax the runners and the underside of the fence and brace. If you like, drill hanging holes in the brace as shown in the *Overall View.* You can hang the fence on nails in the wall. Even more convenient is to tap a couple of screws into the side of your saw and hang this jig there.

MARKING FOR FENCE ALIGNMENT

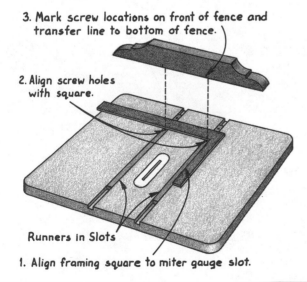

3. Mark screw locations on front of fence and transfer line to bottom of fence.

2. Align screw holes with square.

Runners In Slots

1. Align framing square to miter gauge slot.

ANGLE GUIDE FOR CROSSCUT FENCE

Design by Andy Rae

This very simple jig lets you skip the tedious adjusting and test cutting involved in setting the miter gauge when mitering on the table saw. The jig is little more than an angled spacer clamped to a shop-made crosscut box that rides in the miter gauge slots. Once you've clamped it in place, the jig holds the stock at the proper angle. No muss, no fuss, no measuring. It's jig making at its most basic: You create a setup once, very carefully. Then you have the setup on hand whenever you need it.

The angle guide can be used with the bottomless "Crosscut Fence," page 278, or the "Crosscut Box," page

283. The jig described here is for 45-degree cuts. You can make this jig to any angle you need.

MAKING THE JIG

1 Make the cleat. Cut the plywood for the cleat to the dimensions in the Materials List. Tilt the table saw blade to the angle you want the jig to cut—45 degrees for the jig shown. Use this setup to miter one end of the cleat as shown in the *Overall View.*

2 Make the gauge. Cut the plywood for the gauge to the dimensions in the Materials List, making sure the piece is perfectly square. For a 45-degree angle guide, draw a diagonal line from opposite corners. If you want a different angle, lay it out with a protractor. Cut just to the waste side of the layout line. To trim the edge smooth, clamp a wooden straightedge along your layout line. Rout the edge smooth by guiding a flush trimming bit against the straightedge. For more information, see "Pattern Routing" on page 28.

3 Assemble the jig. Put glue on the cleat and line up its mitered edge with the guiding edge of the gauge as shown in the *Overall View.* Screw the cleat to the gauge with six 1¼-inch drywall screws.

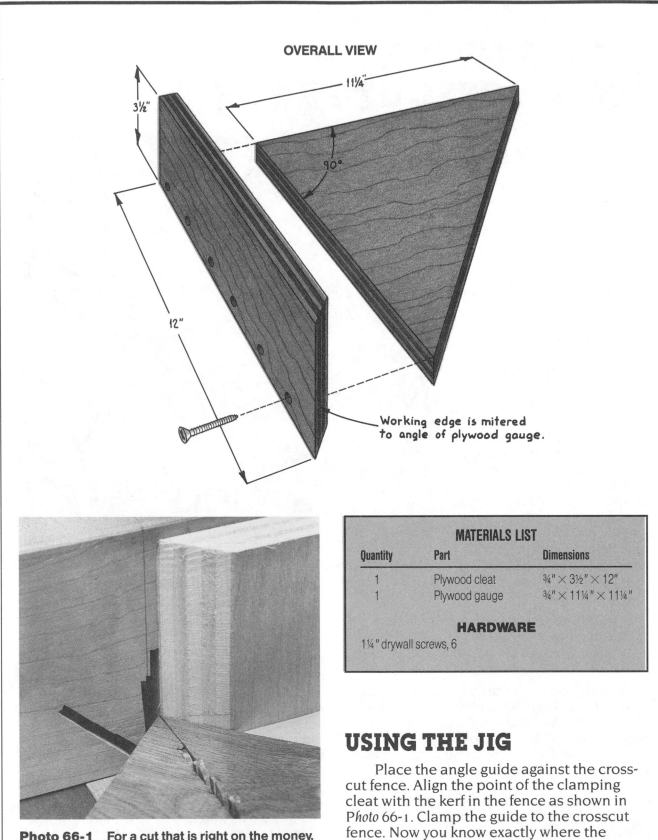

OVERALL VIEW

3½"

11¼"

90°

12"

Working edge is mitered to angle of plywood gauge.

Photo 66-1 For a cut that is right on the money, align the point of the clamping cleat with the kerf in the fence.

MATERIALS LIST		
Quantity	Part	Dimensions
1	Plywood cleat	¾" × 3½" × 12"
1	Plywood gauge	¾" × 11¼" × 11¼"

HARDWARE

1¼" drywall screws, 6

USING THE JIG

Place the angle guide against the crosscut fence. Align the point of the clamping cleat with the kerf in the fence as shown in Photo 66-1. Clamp the guide to the crosscut fence. Now you know exactly where the outside of the miter cut will be. Put the stock against the guide and make the cut.

CROSSCUT BOX

Design by Fred Matlack

This simple crosscut box will greatly increase the crosscutting accuracy of your table saw. The miter gauge is fine for crosscutting small stock. But when the stock gets more than about 20 inches long, it becomes more difficult to get an accurate cut with only the miter gauge behind the work. The crosscut box provides a 24-inch-long fence behind the workpiece. Also, the workpiece rides in the box, so you don't have to overcome the friction of sliding a long piece along the saw table while trying to hold it firmly against a few inches of miter gauge. As a result, the workpiece won't tip away from the fence, ruining the accuracy of your cut.

The long fences on the crosscut box give you a place to clamp stop blocks, as described in "Using the Jig." This makes the crosscut box perfect for cutting several pieces to exactly the same length.

By adding the "Angle Guide for Crosscut Fence" described on page 281, you can use the crosscut box to make angled cuts.

The crosscut box consists of a square plywood base with solid wood fences on opposite sides. The box slides along the saw table on two solid wood runners attached to the bottom of the base. Fence extensions increase the fence height where the crosscut box passes over the table saw blade. This prevents the blade from severing the box, even with the blade set at maximum height. Even if you don't anticipate cutting thick stock, add the extensions anyway. It would be tragic to accidently cut through the box while your hand is resting on the part of the fence that goes over the blade. The extensions provide an important visual and tactile clue: Make it a strict habit to keep your hands away from the extensions during a cut. Doing this will make the crosscut box a very safe accessory for your table saw.

OVERALL VIEW

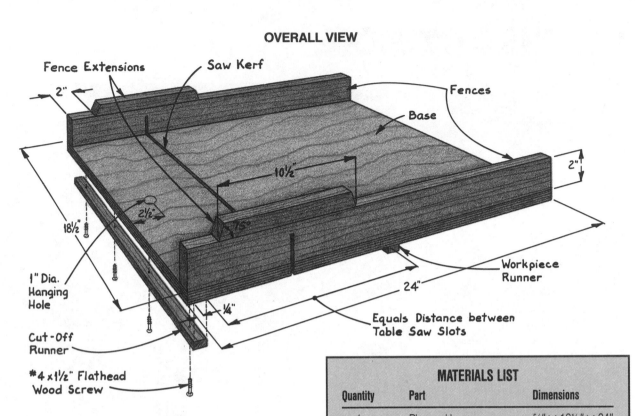

Fence Extensions

Saw Kerf

Fences

2"

Base

10½"

2"

2½"

75"

18½"

1" Dia.
Hanging
Hole

¼"

24"

Workpiece
Runner

Equals Distance between
Table Saw Slots

Cut-Off
Runner

#4 x1½" Flathead
Wood Screw

MAKING THE JIG

1 Cut the parts to size. Make the base from plywood. Make the other parts from a stable, durable hardwood such as maple or cherry. Make the runners the same width as your slots and ¼ inch thinner than the slot depth. Cut the rest of the parts to the dimensions in the Materials List. Cut the base so that the plywood face veneer grain runs in the same direction as the long sides, as shown in the *Overall View.* Joint and plane the fences perfectly straight.

Cut an angle of about 75 degrees on both ends of both fence extensions. There is nothing critical about this angle; the cuts just give the jig a more finished look.

2 Attach the cut-off runner. Predrill and counterbore each runner for four screws. The runners run parallel to the short sides of the base, as shown in the *Overall View.* With a square, draw a line ¼ inch in from one short side. Put glue on one runner and screw it along the inside of the layout line. Clean up glue squeeze-out with a wet rag or sponge.

MATERIALS LIST

Quantity	Part	Dimensions
1	Plywood base	⅝" × 18½" × 24"
2	Hardwood runners	Cut to fit your saw.
2	Hardwood fence extensions	¾" × 1" × 10½"
2	Hardwood fences	¾" × 2" × 24"

HARDWARE

#4 × ½" flathead wood screws, 8

3 Attach the workpiece runner. Lower the blade below the saw table. Place the first runner in one of the miter gauge slots. Mark for the position of the second runner as shown in P*hoto* 67-1. Extend a layout line across the bottom of the jig. Glue and screw the runner along the line. Clean up any glue squeeze-out.

4 Fine-tune the runners. Slide the runners back and forth in the slots a few times. If you find that the jig sticks at certain points, it means that at least one of the runners is slightly bowed. When you take the base off the saw, you may see dark spots where the runners were binding. Sand the runners at these points. When the runners operate smoothly, round their edges slightly with sandpaper.

Photo 67-1   With one runner already attached, place the jig on the saw and use a knife to mark the position of the second runner.

Photo 67-2   Lower the blade below the table. Place the runners in the miter gauge slots, turn on the saw, and crank the blade up through the base.

5 Make the kerf. By cutting a saw kerf through the base, you can position the fences so that they are perfectly square to the base. This ensures square cuts. Before you cut the kerf, consider how you will most often use the crosscut box. On many table saws, the miter gauge slots are not equidistant from the saw blade. If this is the case with your saw, decide whether you want the cutoff to be on your right or your left. If you want the cutoff to be on the right, put most of the box to the left of the blade. If you want the cutoff on your left, put most of the box to the right of the blade.

Crank the table saw blade below the table. Put the runners in the miter gauge slots and center the base roughly over the blade. Turn on the saw and raise the blade as far as it will go through the base as shown in *Photo 67-2.* Don't cut through either edge of the base.

6 Glue up the fences. Glue and clamp a fence extension to each fence. Position the extensions 2 inches from one end of the fences as shown in the *Overall View.*

7 Glue the fences to the base. When the glue on the fences has set, remove the clamps. Apply glue and position the fences on the base so that they are perfectly square to the saw kerf. Clamp, and double-check for square. Remove all glue squeeze-out with a damp sponge or rag.

8 Finish the jig. If you like, drill a hole for hanging the crosscut box on the wall or the base of your saw. Position the hole as shown in the *Overall View.* Round the edges of the fences with sandpaper to make them more pleasing to the hand. Wax the bottom of the base and the runners to make the jig work more smoothly.

USING THE JIG

Put the box on the saw with the kerf over the blade. Raise the blade to about 1 inch. Run the box over the blade, completing the cut through the base and making kerfs in the fences.

Mark the cut on the edge of the workpiece.

Photo 67-3 Align the cut mark on the workpiece with the kerf in the base.

Photo 67-4 Clamp a stop block to the fence to cut multiple pieces to the same length.

Align the mark with the workpiece side of the kerf as shown in P*hoto* 67-3. If you want to cut other pieces to this same length, place a stop block against the other end of the workpiece. Clamp the stop block to the fence as shown in P*hoto* 67-4.

Turn on the saw. Keep your hands away from the fence extensions as you run the box over the blade. For additional cuts to the same length, just butt the workpiece against the stop and make the cut.

SLIDING STOP

Design by Andy Rae

This stop, designed to work with the "Crosscut Fence" on page 278, makes quick work of cutting multiple parts to the same length. The jig is simply a length of solid wood with a plywood stop screwed to one end. It clamps to the back of the sliding crosscut fence. The stop can be adjusted for lengths as short as 12 inches or as long as about 40 inches. If you crosscut longer stock, make the bar longer. For shorter stock, a stop block can be clamped directly to the sliding crosscut fence.

MAKING THE JIG

1 Cut the bar. Select a flat, straight piece of hardwood and cut it to the dimensions in the Materials List. The bar for the jig in the photograph is beaded along both sides. That's only because it was left over from a job that called for beaded stock.

2 Cut the stop. Cut a piece of ¾-inch-thick plywood to size, and cut a notch in it as shown in the *Stop Dimensions*.

3 Assemble the jig. There's nothing exact about how the stop is positioned on the bar. You have just two requirements: The notch in the stop must clear the little step between the two curves on the end of the crosscut fence; and the stop should ride about ¹⁄₁₆ inch above the surface of the table. To find the right position, place the crosscut fence on the saw as shown in *Aligning the Stop to the Bar*. Place the bar on the crosscut fence braces, with the 1½-inch face against the back of the fence. Align one end of the bar with the step between the curves. Clamp the

STOP DIMENSIONS

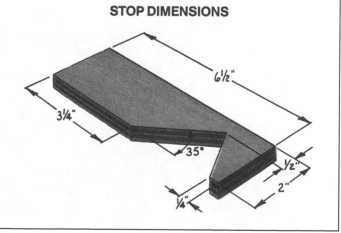

OVERALL VIEW

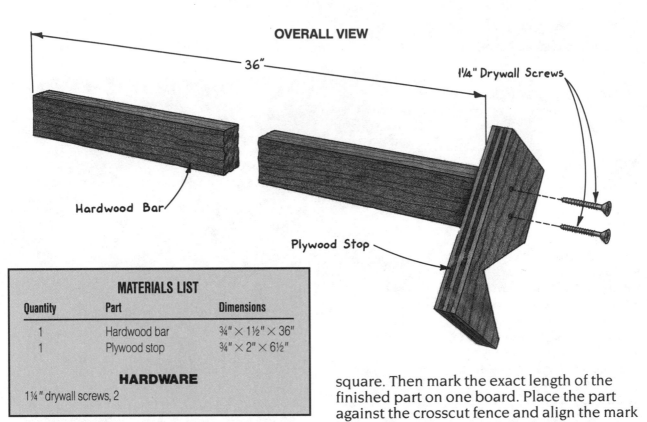

36"

1¼" Drywall Screws

Hardwood Bar

Plywood Stop

MATERIALS LIST		
Quantity	Part	Dimensions
1	Hardwood bar	¾" × 1½" × 36"
1	Plywood stop	¾" × 2" × 6½"

HARDWARE

1¼" drywall screws, 2

bar in place. Now place the stop in the right position against the bar. Predrill two holes through the stop and into the bar. Attach the stop with drywall screws.

USING THE JIG

A stop is the quickest, most accurate way to ensure that multiple parts are cut to the same length. First cut one end of each part square. Then mark the exact length of the finished part on one board. Place the part against the crosscut fence and align the mark with the saw blade. Position the stop against the other end of the board, and clamp it to the crosscut fence. Check that the mark is still aligned to the blade. If necessary, loosen the clamp and adjust the position of the stock. Make the cut. (If the length must be absolutely exact, you might crosscut a piece of scrap first.) Measure the piece to make sure the length is right. No further measuring or marking is necessary. Just butt each piece against the stop and crosscut it.

ALIGNING THE STOP TO THE BAR

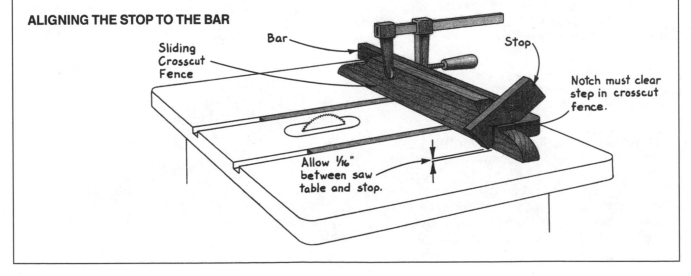

Sliding Crosscut Fence

Bar

Stop

Notch must clear step in crosscut fence.

Allow 1/16" between saw table and stop.

TABLE SAW TURNOFF

Design by Andy Rae

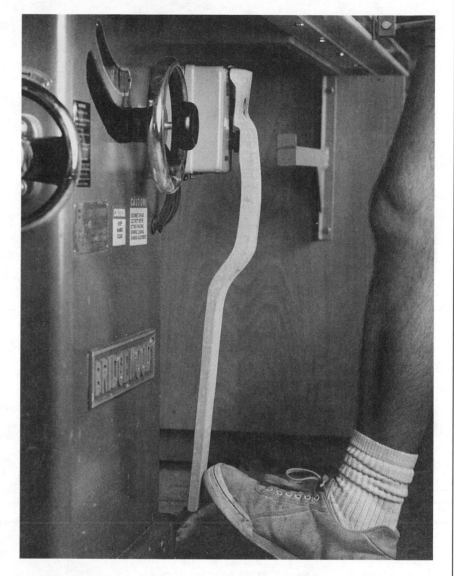

In case of an emergency, this jig lets you turn off your table saw with a quick tap of the foot. Like most safety jigs, it's easy to build but sometimes difficult to get around to building. After all, you can always get the job done without it. Or can you? Here, in his own words, is what finally compelled Andy Rae to design and build this jig:

"I was crosscutting a 4 × 8-foot sheet of ¼-inch plywood one day, and being in a hurry, I was working without a helper or any sliding table setup. Needless to say, the plywood started to bind in the blade halfway through the cut. Then it jumped up onto the blade, where it proceeded to swing in a wild arc—right into my left wrist.

"After the swelling subsided and the color of my arm changed from purple to a more acceptable greenish yellow, I sat down and designed and built this jig. I consider it a must in any shop where you find yourself alone, trying to do things that are really two- or even three-man operations."

Rae considers himself lucky: He only got smacked by the wood. He could have cut himself badly. But in any event, the ability to shut off the saw with a tap of the foot would have prevented the accident.

There's another advantage to this fixture. If small children visit your shop, it camouflages those pretty red and green buttons behind an uninteresting chunk of wood. It also recesses the "on" button behind a hole, making it tougher for little fingers to press.

The jig is built from oak for its strength, although other hardwoods would do the job. The directions explain how to adapt the dimensions in the Materials List to fit your saw.

OVERALL VIEW

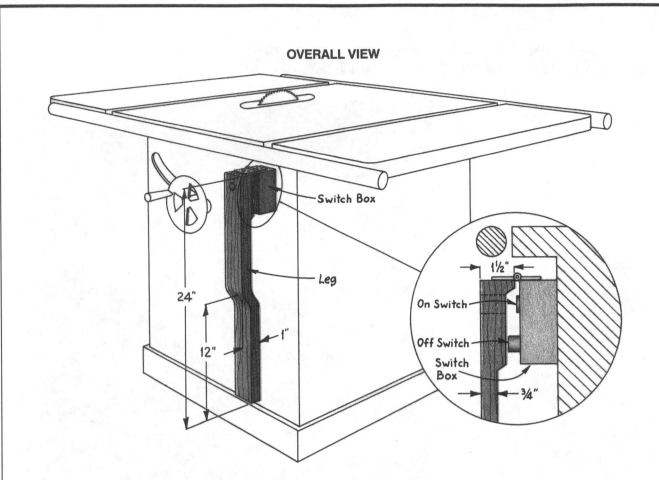

Switch Box

Leg

24"

12"

1"

1½"

On Switch

Off Switch

Switch Box

¾"

MAKING THE JIG

1 Prepare the stock. The turnoff fixture is made from a piece of 2 × 2½-inch stock. To determine the length of the stock, measure from the top of your switch box to the floor and subtract 5 inches. (This space will let you sweep around the saw.) Mill a piece of stock to size. If you don't have a 2-inch-thick piece, glue up two or three pieces. You might want to glue it up in any event: It will make the piece a little stronger.

2 Lay out the cuts. This fixture takes advantage of a safety feature built into the magnetic start switches used on machines: The "on" switch is recessed, while the "off" switch protrudes. Hold the stock beside the buttons, and draw a cut that will leave enough stock at the top for hinging while letting the fixture hang about ⅛ inch from the "off" switch, as shown in *Overall View.* Then lay out the rest of the shape as shown. The bottom part of the fixture is cut in about 1 inch, so that it doesn't

get kicked by accident. The exact shape of the leg isn't critical. You'll probably vary it to fit yourself and your saw. A couple of tips: Leave the top of the leg about 1½ inches wide to hold the hinge; and shape the leg so that when it's hanging straight down, one face hangs about ⅛ inch from the "off" switch.

About 12 inches from the bottom of the leg, cut the curve shown to keep the bottom end of the leg out of your way when working. For strength, no part of the leg should be thinner than ¾ inch.

MATERIALS LIST		
Quantity	**Part**	**Dimensions**
1	Oak leg	2" × 2½" × 24" *
	*Cut to fit.	

HARDWARE

¼" dia. × ⅜" machine bolts with nuts, 2
1½" × 2" butt hinge with screws, 1

3 Make the cuts. Cut along the layout lines with a band saw. If you don't have a band saw, make the cuts by working slowly with a long jigsaw blade.

4 Attach the hinge. Attach the hinge to the switch box with ¼-inch-diameter × ⅜-inch machine bolts and nuts. You'll have to drill holes into the switch box for the bolts. Open the switch box and make sure you won't hit any wires when drilling. If necessary, redrill the holes on the hinge to match those in the box.

Put the cover back on the box. Hold the leg in position while you mark it on the top for the hinge holes. Drill the holes and attach the leg. Test that the fixture will turn the machine off. If it doesn't work, you'll be able to see where the leg needs to be repositioned or reshaped.

5 Drill an access hole. When you are satisfied with how the fixture works, mark it to show the location of the "on" switch. The switch shown here has round buttons, while many newer machines have rectangular buttons. Either way, a round hole will work. Drill the hole slightly larger than the diameter or width of the button. Then bevel the outer face of the hole either with a gouge or with a beveling bit in the router. Sand the fixture to prevent splinters.

EXTRA
HANDS

ASSEMBLY

FEATHERBOARD

PLYWOOD HANDLING

PUSH STICKS

ROLLER STAND

WORK SUPPORT

CABINET ASSEMBLY STAND

Design by Nils Falk

If you make cabinets, especially if you work alone, you owe it to yourself to take 30 minutes to assemble four of these simple stands. Never again will you wince as a cabinet side topples off the bench during a glue-up. Just slip the sides into these stands, and apply glue to the cabinet joints. Clamp and square up the cabinet at your leisure.

Each stand consists of a ¾ × 6 × 12-inch plywood base and two ¾ × 4 × 12-inch plywood supports. Start by cutting plywood to these dimensions. Put a scrap from the cabinet you're building between the plywood supports. Put the scrap and supports on the plywood base. Mark the location of the supports with a pencil line. Glue and screw the supports to the base. Drill and countersink for six 1¼-inch drywall screws, and drive them through the base into the supports.

OVERALL VIEW

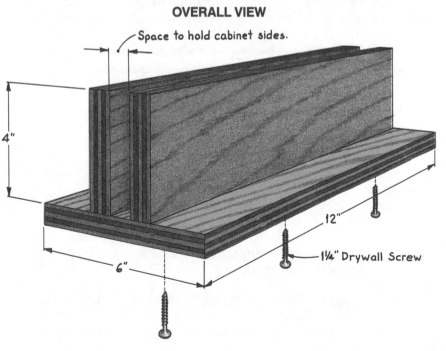

Space to hold cabinet sides.

4"

12"

6"

1¼" Drywall Screw

FEATHERBOARD

Design by Fred Matlack

Featherboards are essential safety equipment in any woodworking shop. You'll find frequent use for the featherboard when running stock through a table saw, router table, or shaper.

A featherboard is a piece of wood cut at an angle at one end. The angled end is then cut repeatedly to form fingers. Usually you clamp a featherboard in place so that the fingers flex, pushing the work against the fence. The finger flex allows you to push a piece forward but not back. The featherboard not only holds a piece firmly against the fence but also helps eliminate kickback.

Featherboards can be made any size to serve the purpose at hand. Simply cut a piece of scrap at an angle and cut a series of slots. You can clamp or screw featherboards in place. You can also shape one end and use it as a hand-held featherboard for shorter workpieces. The jig shown here is a good size for general work on the table saw or router table. The eyescrew in the end keeps it hanging in a convenient spot near the tool. This is important: If you can't lay your hands on it right away, you might be tempted not to use the featherboard.

MAKING THE JIG

1 Cut the stock to size. Cut the stock for the featherboard to the dimensions in the Materials List. Springy wood such as ash or oak works best, but any wood will do in a pinch.

2 Cut the angle. Cut the end of the board at an angle of about 45 degrees.

3 Cut the fingers. Draw a line across the board to indicate the length of the fingers as shown in the *Overall View.* Cut the fingers on the table saw using the rip fence as a guide.

For the featherboard shown, start by setting the fence 5¼ inches from the blade. This allows for a ¼-inch-wide finger plus a ⅛-inch saw kerf. Cut in to the line, then stop the saw. After the blade stops, pull the board out of the cut. Move the fence over ⅜ inch and repeat. Continue this process across the board. Sand and finish the featherboard with a penetrating oil if you wish. Screw the eyescrew into the solid end.

OVERALL VIEW

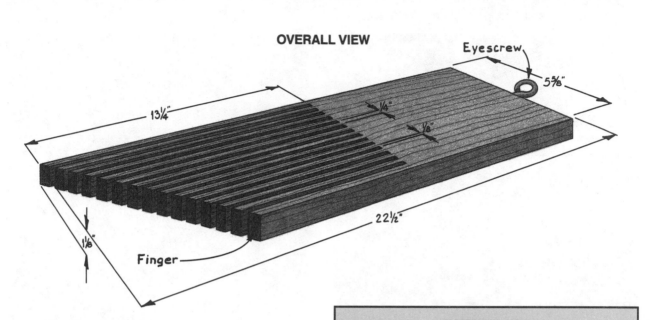

Eyescrew

5⅝"

13¼"

¼"

⅛"

22½"

1⅛"

Finger

USING THE JIG

Clamp the featherboard to the machine in a position where it can push the stock against the fence. This position will vary from machine to machine. Sometimes two or more featherboards can be used, as shown in *Photo* 71-1. One featherboard holds a piece tight to the fence; the other holds the piece firmly against the saw table.

MATERIALS LIST		
Quantity	Part	Dimensions
1	Hardwood featherboard	1⅛" × 5⅝" × 22½"

HARDWARE

⅜" dia. eyescrew, 1

Using the Featherboard on the Table Saw

On the table saw, position the featherboard on the infeed side of the blade as shown in *Photo* 71-2. Never use it on the outfeed side of the blade, because it would pinch the cut closed on the blade.

Use the stock you will be cutting to help position the board. Hold the stock against the fence and push the featherboard up against it. Push the board against the workpiece until the fingers flex slightly, as shown in *Photo* 71-3. Clamp the featherboard in place. The slight flex in the fingers should be enough to hold the work snugly against the fence but not so tight that pushing the stock is difficult.

On a router table or shaper, the placement is not as critical, because there is usually not a kerf to worry about pinching. Again, use the stock you will be cutting to position the featherboard and clamp it in place.

Photo 71-1 Sometimes two featherboards can be used. One holds the work against the table, while the other holds the work against the fence.

Photo 71-2 On the table saw, always position the featherboard on the infeed side of the blade. Never use it on the outfeed side because it would pinch the cut closed on the blade.

Photo 71-3 To adjust the position of the featherboard, push it against the workpiece until the fingers flex slightly.

PLYWOOD CADDY

Design by Glenn Bostock

Dragging 4 × 8 sheet goods around the shop is no fun. They're heavy, unwieldy, and just plain big. Here's a nifty little cart that takes some of the pain out of working with sheet materials. It uses a couple of wheels and three pieces of scrap wood. You can purloin the wheels from an old lawn mower or break down and buy them new at the hardware store.

When you're finished, you'll have a high-performance shop vehicle with great cornering ability. Be careful, however, if you have youngsters about. You may find that they like your new toy as much as you do.

MAKING THE JIG

1 Cut the parts to size. Cut the parts to the dimensions in the Materials List. The dimensions aren't critical. Just make the spacer about ⅛ inch thicker than the thickest sheet goods it will carry. The cart shown here has a ⅞-inch-thick spacer so that ¾-inch-thick plywood slips easily into the cart.

2 Bevel the sides. These bevels act as a funnel to make it easier to slip the sheet goods into the cart. Cut the bevels along the inside of the sides as shown in the *Overall View.* Raise your table saw blade to about 1½ inches. Tilt the blade a few degrees and run the sides past it.

3 Assemble the cart. Glue and screw the sides to the spacer. Make sure they are flush along the bottom and at the ends. Don't put screws near the point where the axle will go through.

4 Drill the axle hole. Locate the axle hole as shown in the *Overall View.* Drill the hole on the drill press, all the way through the cart. If you have to use a hand drill, drill from both sides to help keep the hole perpendicular.

OVERALL VIEW

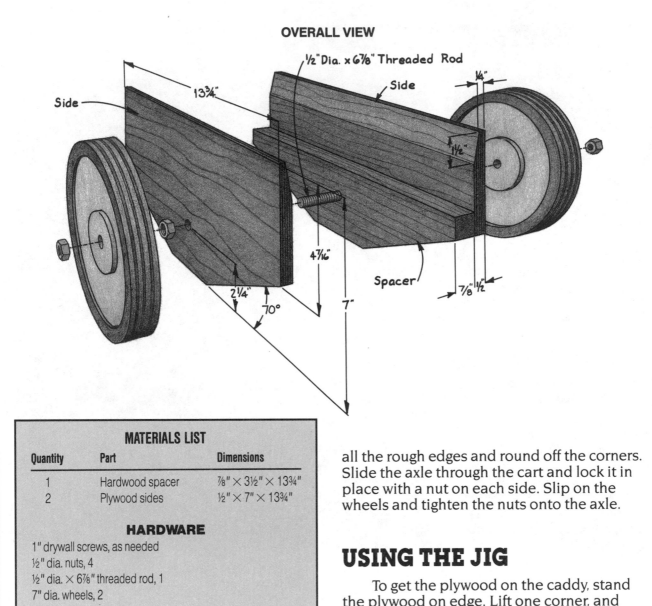

MATERIALS LIST

Quantity	Part	Dimensions
1	Hardwood spacer	⅞" × 3½" × 13¾"
2	Plywood sides	½" × 7" × 13¾"

HARDWARE

1" drywall screws, as needed
½" dia. nuts, 4
½" dia. × 6⅞" threaded rod, 1
7" dia. wheels, 2

The hole specified is ½ inch in diameter, because the wheels on the cart shown required a ½-inch-diameter axle. Drill the hole to match your wheels.

5 Finish the cart. Cut the bottom corners off the cart as shown in the *Overall View.* Sand all the rough edges and round off the corners. Slide the axle through the cart and lock it in place with a nut on each side. Slip on the wheels and tighten the nuts onto the axle.

USING THE JIG

To get the plywood on the caddy, stand the plywood on edge. Lift one corner, and slip the caddy in place so that it's roughly in the middle of the sheet.

The caddy is easiest to use if you tip the sheet into it so that the caddy is about in the middle of a long side. If you've tight turns to make and enough ceiling clearance, you can tip the sheet so that the caddy is in the middle of a short side. In this case, maneuvering will be more of a balancing act.

JOINTER PUSH STICK

Design by Fred Matlack

Jointing the face of a board without a push stick is one of the most foolish things a woodworker can do. Without a push stick, there is no good way to get a grip on the board. Without steady downward and forward pressure, a board can kick back or even break. If that happens, you can easily find yourself minus a few fingers. The most important function of a push stick is to keep your hands away from those hungry cutters.

Safety is enough reason to make a push stick for your jointer, but it is not the only reason. When you use a push stick, the pressure you apply is spread evenly along the length of the board. This helps ensure a flat board.

The push stick consists of a board with a heel on one end and a handle on top. The heel hooks over the trailing edge of the board, pushing the board forward. Any kind of handle you might make or have around will work, as long as you can get a firm grip and it is securely fastened to the push stick. The handle shown here is easy to make, and it is specifically designed for its purpose. Notice that the handle leans forward. This transfers more of the downward and forward pressure of your hand to the front of the board you are jointing. As a result, the front of the board will be firmly on the infeed table as it enters the jointer knives. The pressure will be transferred smoothly to the outfeed table as the majority of the board moves over the knives.

The push stick shown here has a mahogany sole, a pine handle, and an oak heel only because those were the scraps on hand. Make yours from whatever scrap you have handy.

MAKING THE JIG

1 Make the base. Cut the sole and the heel to the dimensions in the Materials List. Lay out and drill the ¾-inch hole in the sole as shown in the *Overall View*. This hole is for hanging the jig when it is not in use.

OVERALL VIEW

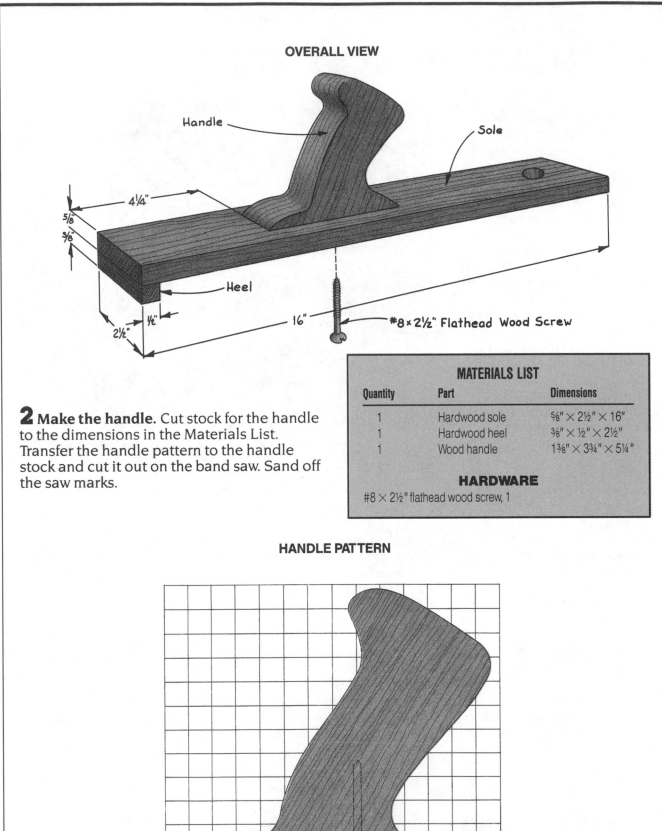

Handle

Sole

4¼"

5/8"

3/8"

Heel

½"

2½"

16"

#8 × 2½" Flathead Wood Screw

2 Make the handle. Cut stock for the handle to the dimensions in the Materials List. Transfer the handle pattern to the handle stock and cut it out on the band saw. Sand off the saw marks.

MATERIALS LIST		
Quantity	Part	Dimensions
1	Hardwood sole	5/8" × 2½" × 16"
1	Hardwood heel	3/8" × ½" × 2½"
1	Wood handle	1⅜" × 3¾" × 5¼"

HARDWARE

#8 × 2½" flathead wood screw, 1

HANDLE PATTERN

One square equals ½".

3 **Shape the parts.** Round-over the edges of the handle with a ⅜-inch-radius roundover bit in a table-mounted router. Switch to a ¼-inch-radius roundover bit, and round-over the top edges of the sole and the circumference of the hole.

4 **Assemble the jig.** Predrill the handle, and glue and screw it to the sole in the position shown in the *Overall View*. Glue the heel in place. Finish the push stick with a coat of penetrating oil.

USING THE JIG

Set the jointer tables for a shallow cut, usually no more than ¹⁄₁₆ inch, when surfacing boards. If you can hear the motor slowing during the cut, you are cutting too deeply.

To create a smooth surface with the jointer, you must use a slow, steady feed rate. The jointer will always leave little ripples, but the cut will be smoother with a slow feed rate. If the pressure isn't constant, you'll find gouges in the jointed surface.

To use the push stick, turn on the jointer and place the board on the infeed table. Use your left hand to press the board against the table. Hook the push stick over the back of the board, grasp the handle with your right hand, and begin pushing the board into the cut.

For safety, remove your left hand from the board well before it reaches the cutters. Never put your hand directly over the cutters. The stock can break, exposing your hand to the blades. Once the first part of the board has crossed the cutter head, move your left hand to the part of the board over the outfeed table. Apply downward pressure with your left hand and forward pressure with the push stick. Continue pressing on the board and the push stick until the entire board has passed over the cutters.

TABLE SAW PUSH STICK

Design by Fred Matlack

Keep this push stick by your table saw and reach for it any time that ripping a board requires passing your hands over the throat plate that surrounds the blade. Make the push stick from any ¾-inch-wide scrap of solid stock.

Use the pattern shown in the *Overall View* to lay out the push stick on the stock. The exact shape is not important, as long as the hook forms a 90-degree angle. Cut the push stick on the band saw. Drill the ¾-inch-diameter hanging hole as shown. Smooth the push stick and round its edges with sandpaper.

When making narrow rips, place the push stick within easy reach and begin the cut without the push stick. Reach for the push stick when the end of the board is 2 or 3 inches outside the throat plate, as shown in the photo. Hold the stick firmly on the board as shown until the cut is completed.

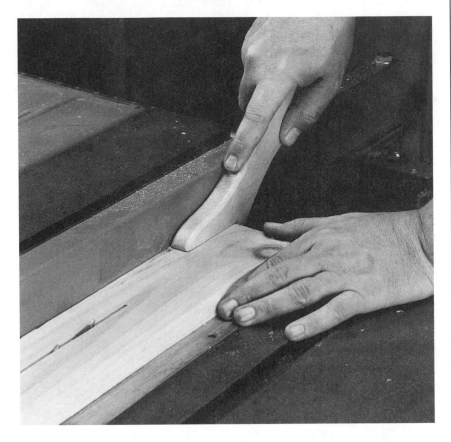

OVERALL VIEW

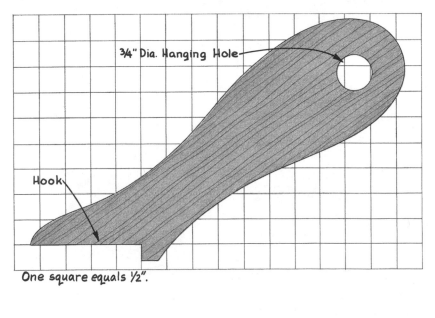

¾" Dia. Hanging Hole

Hook

One square equals ½".

ADJUSTABLE ROLLER STAND

Design by Ben Erickson

Working alone in the shop has its advantages. You never have to wait in line for a machine. You get to choose which radio station gets drowned out by the router. The miter gauge doesn't miraculously get set to some goofy angle. The chuck key for the drill press is right where you left it, wherever that was.

There are some draw-backs, of course. There is no one to blame for putting away the chisels without sharpening them, no one to clean up the spilled glue on the workbench, and no one to remember to buy more screws because they got used up on the last job.

These are small hassles. Working alone really be-comes a problem when it comes time to cut up that stack of plywood for those bookcases you've been mean-ing to build. In fact, that's probably why the bookcases haven't been built yet. You might ask someone to give you a hand, but good help is hard to find. Besides, who-ever you find will probably want to borrow your new paring chisels to scrape the old finish off some flea mar-ket find.

The solution is to build yourself a helper in the form of one of these roller stands. Better yet, build two. That way, you'll have more support for very long work. Or you can put one to the side of the saw when the work is wide as well as long. These adjustable stands have qualities that are rare in human assistants. They won't question your tech-nique, they work for free, and they're incredibly loyal. Just don't expect scintillating conversation.

The stand consists of a lap-jointed base attached to a hollow, square column. A 2 × 2-inch square post slides in the column and is held in place by a big wing nut. A U-shaped bracket, mortised to the top of the post, sup-ports the roller.

The stand can be made from scrap lumber. You can use softwood construction lumber, except for the center support post. Make this post from hardwood to ensure that the bolt head doesn't strip out its mortise. You can use a rolling pin for the roller, or buy a steel roller from a woodworking supply company.

OVERALL VIEW

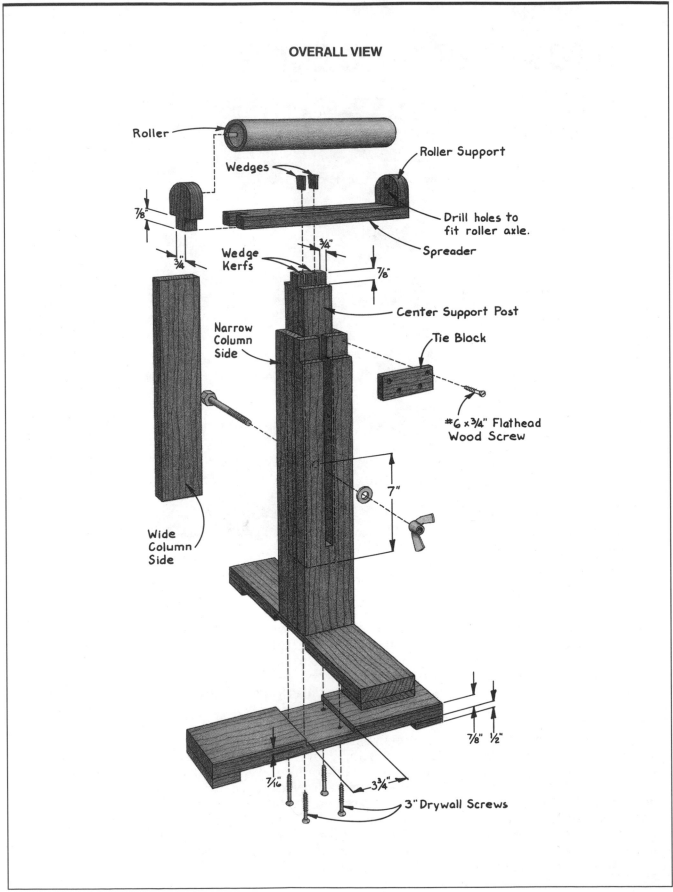

Roller

Wedges

Roller Support

7/8"

3/4"

Wedge Kerfs

3/4"

Drill holes to fit roller axle.

Spreader

7/8"

Center Support Post

Narrow Column Side

Tie Block

#6 x 3/4" Flathead Wood Screw

Wide Column Side

7"

7/8" 1/2"

7/16"

3 3/4"

3" Drywall Screws

MATERIALS LIST

Quantity	Part	Dimensions
1	Spreader	$\frac{7}{8}" \times 2" \times 12\frac{3}{8}"$
2	Base cross members	$\frac{7}{8}" \times 3\frac{3}{4}" \times 18"$
4	Foot blocks	$\frac{1}{2}" \times 3\frac{3}{4}" \times 2"$
2	Wide column sides	$\frac{7}{8}" \times 3\frac{3}{4}" \times 22\frac{1}{2}"$
2	Narrow column sides	$\frac{7}{8}" \times 2" \times 22\frac{1}{2}"$
1	Tie block	$\frac{1}{4}" \times 1\frac{1}{4}" \times 3\frac{3}{4}"$
1	Center support post	$2" \times 2" \times 23\frac{3}{8}"$
2	Roller supports	$\frac{7}{8}" \times 2" \times 3"$

HARDWARE

#6 $\times$ ¾" flathead wood screws, 4

3" drywall screws, 4

½" dia. $\times$ 3½" machine bolt with washer and wing nut, 1

2" dia. $\times$ 10½" rolling pin with ball bearings, 1*

*You can replace the rolling pin with a steel roller, available from Woodworker's Supply, 5604 Alameda Place NE, Albuquerque, NM 87113 (800-645-9292). 14" roller: part #100-023. 22" roller: part #801-127.

MAKING THE JIG

1 Cut the parts to size. Cut all parts except the roller supports to the dimensions in the Materials List. Cut a piece of stock to ⅞ $\times$ 2 $\times$ 8 inches (it must be at least this long). This piece will be used later to make both roller supports. Make the spreader 1⅞ inches longer than the rollers.

2 Make the base. Cut the lap joint in the base cross members as shown in the *Overall View*. Make the joint with a dado cutter on the table saw or radial arm saw. Glue and clamp the base together and let dry.

3 Attach the foot blocks. Glue a foot block to each end of the base cross members. For a secure glue joint, be sure to orient the grain on the blocks parallel to the grain on the base cross members. These ½-inch-thick feet keep the stand from rocking on an uneven floor.

4 Glue up the column. Glue and clamp the four column sides together. Make sure the hole in the middle measures 2 inches square. Avoid getting glue inside the column. It has to remain clean inside, so that the post can run up and down freely.

5 Cut the adjustment slot and attach the tie block. Set up a ½-inch-wide dado cutter on the table saw. Cut a centered kerf down the length of one of the wide column sides. Stop the cut about 6 inches from the end of the column. Clean up the end of the cut with a chisel.

You can simply screw the tie block to the column at the top with #6 $\times$ ¾-inch flathead wood screws. However, the stand will look neater if you recess the tie block so that it is flush to the face of the column, as shown in the *Overall View*. To do this, put your widest straight bit in the router and set the cutting depth to ¼ inch. Guiding the router with a straightedge clamped across the column, rout a dado 1¼ inches from the top of the column. Move the straightedge closer to the top of the column and make additional passes until you have created a rabbet for the tie block.

6 Attach the base. Screw the base to the column with four 3-inch drywall screws as shown in the *Overall View*.

7 Make the roller bracket and the post tenon. The spreader will be attached to the post with a mortise-and-tenon joint, as shown in the *Overall View*. The roller supports will be attached to the spreader with open mortise-and-tenon joints, as shown. Lay out a ¾-inch-wide $\times$ 2-inch-long mortise centered on the spreader. Also lay out ⅞-inch-deep $\times$ ¾-inch-wide open mortises centered on each end of the spreader. Put a ¾-inch-diameter straight bit in a plunge router. Put an edge guide on the router and set the guide ⅝ inch from the cutting edge of the bit. Rout each of the three mortises in four passes, going about ¼ inch deeper each time. Square the corners of the mortises with a chisel.

Make a tenon on each end of the stock that you prepared in Step 1 for the roller supports. (See "Making Joints," page 39.)

The tenon dimensions are shown in the *Overall View.* Use the same table saw setup to make the tenon on the end of the post. Cut the roller support stock into two 3-inch-long pieces. Round the tops of the supports on the band saw or with a saber saw. (The exact curves aren't important.) Smooth these cuts with a belt sander.

Drill the holes for the roller's axle in the supports. Make these holes the same diameter as the axle.

Glue up the bracket. Some commercially available rollers come with spring-loaded axles, so you can build the bracket before inserting the roller. If you are using a rolling pin, assemble the bracket around the pin. Use a rolling pin with ball bearings for longer life.

ALIGNING THE STAND

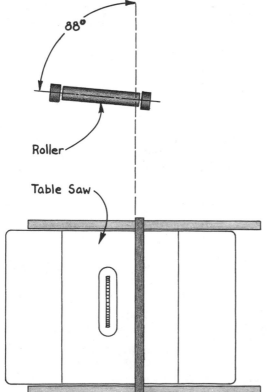

8 Finish the post. Test fit the post in the column. Plane or scrape it, if necessary, until it slides up and down smoothly. Drill the ½-inch-diameter hole for the lock bolt as shown in the *Overall View.* Slide the bolt through the hole and carefully trace around the bolt's hex head. Remove the bolt and chisel a mortise in the post to accept the bolt head. It should fit snugly, so that the mortise will keep the bolt from turning as you tighten the wing nut to lock the post in place.

The post tenon is wedged into the spreader mortise, so cut slots for the tenon wedges with a dovetail saw. Glue the bracket to the post. Drive the wedges into the slots in the tenon to reinforce the joint.

9 Apply finish. Finish sanding the jig and gently round-over all edges. Finish the jig with your favorite wood finish. Penetrating oils are fast and easy to apply. When the finish has dried, remove the tie block. Slip the bolt through the post and slide the post into the column. Lock it in place with the washer and wing nut. Install the roller, and your new helper is ready to serve.

USING THE JIG

Place the roller stand in the desired location. If the floor is uneven, slide a wedge under one of the feet until the roller stand is stable. Adjust the roller to the right height. Find the height by extending a straight board, on its edge, across the machine table and over the jig. Or you can sight across the machine table to the roller. Once you've set the roller to the right height, draw a line on the post flush with the column top. Write the name of the machine on the post for future reference.

If you use the roller on the outfeed side of the table saw, angle the jig slightly to help keep the work against the fence, as shown in *Aligning the Stand.*

SHOP HORSES

*Design by
Frederic L. Hanisch*

Shop horses increase the versatility of your shop space. This is important for any shop, especially a small one.

Toss an old door on top of a couple of horses, and you have an instant work surface. Put the horses behind your table saw, and you have outfeed support for ripping. Horses serve as a temporary base for a router table. Put them by the lumber rack, and you can lay out stock as you select it.

The horses shown here are designed so that the crosspieces are flush with the sides of the legs. Combined with the "Clamp Racks" on page 59, the horses become a clamping station that works better than your bench.

These horses are made from oak because it's strong and readily available. Any hardwood will work well, however. The horse shown in the *Overall View* is at a good

general working height for most people. Change the height to suit your needs. If you plan to use the sawhorses as a table saw outfeed, make them about ½ inch lower than the table saw surface. To build horses to support hand sawing, bend your knee and measure from the floor to under your knee. Make the horses 2 inches shorter

than this measurement. These shorter horses are also great for supporting project tables for kids.

Whatever size you choose, the stock and joinery dimensions shown here will work. As a rule of thumb, to keep the horses stable, don't make them taller than they are wide.

MAKING THE JIG

1 Prepare the stock. Mill wood to the thickness given in the Materials List, and cut the parts to size.

2 Mortise the crosspiece and legs. For extra gluing surface and strength, the legs are joined to the crosspiece with twin tenons. Lay out the mortises as shown in *Crosspiece*

OVERALL VIEW

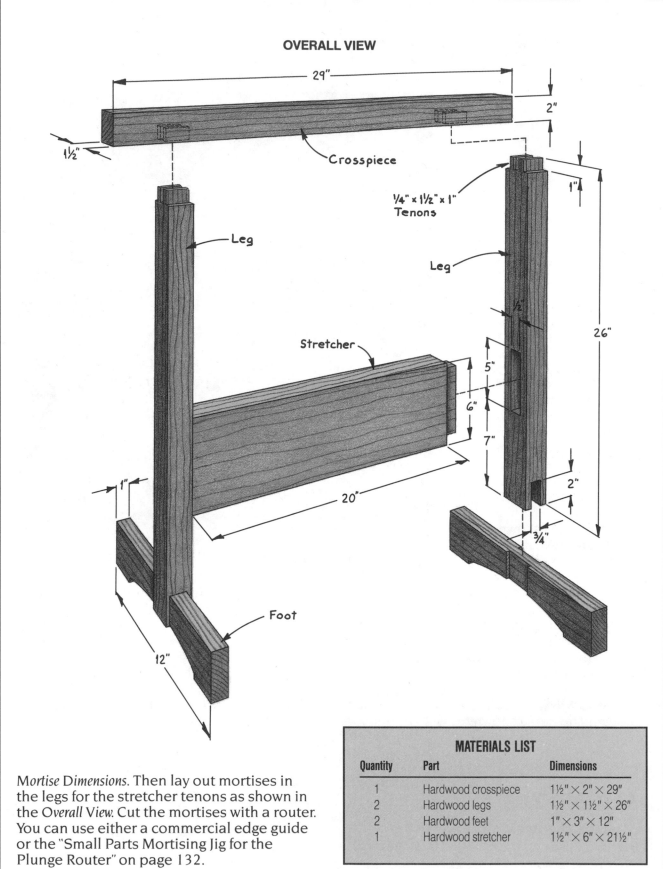

29"

2"

1½"

Crosspiece

¼" × 1½" × 1"
Tenons

Leg

Leg

1"

½"

26"

Stretcher

5"

6"

7"

Leg

1"

20"

2"

¾"

Foot

12"

Mortise Dimensions. Then lay out mortises in the legs for the stretcher tenons as shown in the *Overall View.* Cut the mortises with a router. You can use either a commercial edge guide or the "Small Parts Mortising Jig for the Plunge Router" on page 132.

MATERIALS LIST		
Quantity	**Part**	**Dimensions**
1	Hardwood crosspiece	1½" × 2" × 29"
2	Hardwood legs	1½" × 1½" × 26"
2	Hardwood feet	1" × 3" × 12"
1	Hardwood stretcher	1½" × 6" × 21½"

CROSSPIECE MORTISE DIMENSIONS

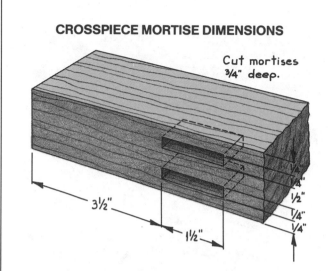

Cut mortises 3/4" deep.

3½"   1½"   ¾"   ½"   ¼"   ¼"

table saw. Before cutting the dadoes, test the blade height by dadoing both sides of a piece of scrap that is as thick as the feet. Adjust the blade height for a snug joint.

The slight arcs in the bottom of the feet help the horses remain stable on a bumpy surface. Lay out the arcs as shown in the *Foot Layout* and cut them on the band saw or with a jigsaw.

3 Cut the tenons and open mortises in the legs. The upper end of each leg has two tenons; the lower end is a slip joint that fits over the foot. Lay out both the tenons and the slip joint as shown in the *Overall View*. First cut kerfs to define the shoulders of the twin tenons. Then finish the tenons and cut the slip joints with the dado cutter on the table saw. For more information, see the "Table Saw Tenoning Jig," page 216. Leave the dado cutter on the saw for the next step.

4 Cut the dadoes and arcs in the feet. The legs fit over the feet as shown in the *Overall View*. Lay out the dadoes shown in the *Foot Layout* and cut them with a dado cutter on the

5 Cut the tenons in the stretcher. Cut the stretcher tenons to the dimensions shown in *Stretcher Tenon Dimensions*. This can be done either with the "Table Saw Tenoning Jig," page 216, or as described in "Making Joints," page 39.

STRETCHER TENON DIMENSIONS

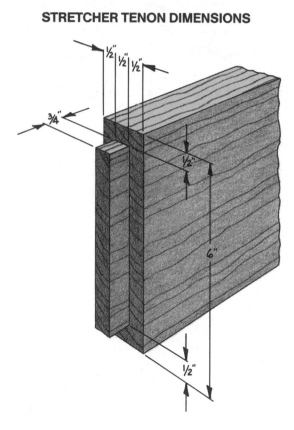

½" ½" ½"   ¾"   ½"   6"   ½"

FOOT LAYOUT

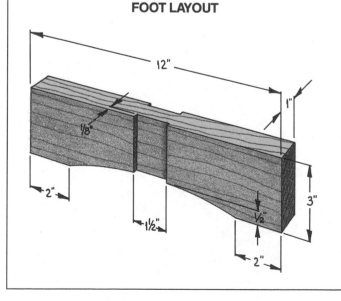

12"   1"   ⅛"   2"   1½"   ½"   3"   2"

6 Assemble the horse. Assemble the saw-horse in a series of glue-ups. First put glue in the leg mortises. Insert the stretcher tenons and clamp the joint together. Check that the assembly is square. After at least 30 minutes, remove the clamps. Put glue in the cross-piece mortises and clamp them to the legs as shown in P*hoto* 76-1. When the glue sets, remove the clamps. Apply glue to the dadoes in the feet and put the legs in place. Clamp the joint with a C-clamp as shown in P*hoto* 76-2.

7 Chamfer the edges. With a piloted bit in the router, chamfer all the edges.

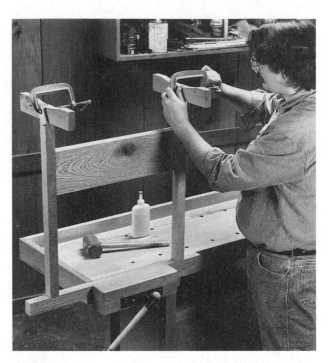

Photo 76-2 Use C-clamps to clamp the joints between the feet and legs.

Photo 76-1 Put glue in the crosspiece mortises and clamp the crosspiece to the legs.

INDEX